Tonkin Gulf and the Escalation of the Vietnam War

Edwin E. Moïse

TONKIN GULF

and the Escalation of the

VIETNAM WAR

The University of North Carolina Press
Chapel Hill and London

The paper in this book meets the guidelines for permanence and durability
of the Committee on Production Guidelines for Book Longevity of the
Council on Library Resources.

Library of Congress Cataloging-in-Publication Data
Moïse, Edwin E., 1946–
    Tonkin Gulf and the escalation of the Vietnam War / Edwin E. Moïse.
        p.   cm.
    Includes bibliographical references and index.
    ISBN 0-8078-2300-7 (cloth: alk. paper)
        1. Tonkin Gulf Incidents, 1964. 2. Vietnamese Conflict, 1961–1975.
I. Title.
DS557.8.T6M65   1996
959.704'3—dc20   96-12159
                                                    CIP

00 99 98 97 96   5 4 3 2 1

To my wife, Rebecca

Contents

Table, Maps, and Figures

Table

Maps

Figures

Preface

On the night of August 4, 1964, two U.S. Navy destroyers, cruising in the Gulf of Tonkin off the coast of North Vietnam, reported that they were being attacked by torpedo boats. The report was an error. The night was very dark, and the radar was playing tricks and showing ghost images that the men on the destroyers mistakenly interpreted as hostile vessels. The United States, however, reacted strongly to this supposed attack on the American flag. On August 5, American aircraft carriers launched airstrikes against North Vietnam. On August 7, both houses of Congress, in a rush of patriotism, passed the "Tonkin Gulf Resolution," giving President Johnson the authority to take "all necessary measures" to "prevent further aggression." When the Johnson administration was sending large American military forces to Vietnam in later years, it sometimes cited this resolution as giving it the authority to do so.

The incorrect report of August 4 did not really "cause" the outbreak of large-scale war in Vietnam. By August 1964, Washington and Hanoi were already on a collision course. The level of combat in South Vietnam, and the level of outside support on both sides, were increasing; meanwhile the United States was sponsoring a program of covert operations against North Vietnam, which had so aroused the navy of the Democratic Republic of Vietnam (DRV) that three torpedo boats had made a genuine attack on a U.S. destroyer two days earlier, on the afternoon of August 2. (The August 2 incident had left some Americans expecting the North Vietnamese to attack U.S. ships, and thus set the stage psychologically for the mistaken report of a North Vietnamese attack on the night of August 4.)

If reports from the Gulf of Tonkin had not caused President Johnson to order airstrikes against North Vietnam in August 1964, something else would have done so within a few months. Some other excuse could have been found to persuade the Congress to pass a resolution giving the president the authority to take the actions he felt necessary; the administration had already been working on preliminary drafts of such a resolution for several months.

Despite this, the Tonkin Gulf incidents—the real one of August 2 for which the United States did not retaliate, and the imaginary one of August 4 that provoked the airstrikes and the Tonkin Gulf Resolution—deserve careful attention, for at least four reasons:

1. If we wish to understand the broad pattern of forces that made a collision between Washington and Hanoi inevitable, we can at least derive valuable clues from a look at the incident that actually did lead to the first direct collision.
2. To say that a collision was inevitable is not to say that its results were inevitable. If the first U.S. airstrikes against North Vietnam had happened a few

months later in retaliation for some other incident, the circumstances would have been different and the long-term consequences might have been very different. In this sense it is possible to argue that the mistaken report of August 4 did change the course of history.

3. Those who argue that it makes little difference whether there was really an attack on the two destroyers August 4 are thinking only of evaluating U.S. behavior. The pattern of U.S. policy indeed looks about the same, whether one believes that the United States bombed North Vietnam August 5 as a result of an actual attack on U.S. destroyers or only as a result of a mistaken belief that there had been such an attack. The same does not apply, however, to Vietnamese policy. In one version, the DRV was so eager to get in a fight with the Americans that it sent naval vessels sixty miles out from its coast to attack two U.S. ships. In the other, the DRV, having had more sense than to do such a thing, was falsely accused of having done so, and was bombed in retaliation for the imaginary attack, under circumstances that would have left the DRV convinced that the United States had decided to escalate the war and had concocted the imaginary incident deliberately in order to provide an excuse for the escalation; DRV moves during the following months would in part have been based on this belief. The difference between these two pictures of DRV policy is not trivial.

4. Finally, I am profoundly disturbed by the extent to which the appearance of this incident differed from its reality. When the U.S. government reported that the North Vietnamese had attacked two U.S. destroyers on August 4, 1964, everyone believed this report. The evidence presented to the public seemed to leave no room for reasonable or even unreasonable doubt. Some of the real facts began to surface in 1967, and soon, most people who were interested in the question began to doubt that there had actually been an attack against U.S. warships on the night of August 4. In 1986, however, the U.S. Navy published a history of the early years of the Vietnam War; the chapters devoted to the Tonkin Gulf incidents, and the American response to those incidents, totaled seventy pages.[1] This heavily documented account contained much detail that had not been available to the public before, and once again the evidence of an attack seemed overwhelming. If I had not already been far enough along with my research to be able to spot the errors and omissions, I would probably have been convinced. An American officer who was actually present on the night of August 4 told me he was afraid that the navy's history would be so generally accepted that in the future, when he said on the basis of his own experience that no hostile vessels came anywhere near the American warships on that night, people would not believe him.

When the U.S. government presented its story of how North Vietnamese torpedo boats had attacked the two destroyers on August 4, I was fooled; I accepted it without question. This is not too disturbing; there are more important things I believed at the age of eighteen that also turned out not to be true. What worries me is that if a similar story were to be presented to the public tomorrow, I would probably believe it again; it was that convincing. I think that all of us, in sheer self-defense, need to get a better understanding of how so powerful an illusion was generated: the appearance of a battle where no battle had taken place.

This book is based primarily on American sources, the most important of which have been declassified government documents and interviews with retired U.S. Navy personnel. The three chapters analyzing the supposed battle of August 4 are based almost entirely on American sources. There are no Vietnamese witnesses because no Vietnamese were anywhere in the area.

In the remainder of this book, in piecing together the overall pattern of actions, plans, and mutual misunderstanding that was leading the United States and the DRV toward war with one another, I have tried to gather information from both sides. Without Vietnamese sources, one can get a very incomplete picture. I wish I had been able to make much more use of Vietnamese sources; the amount I was able to learn during one rather brief trip to Vietnam was not comparable to what I have been able to get in research conducted sporadically for over ten years in the United States.

The conditions under which I conducted interviews in the United States and Vietnam were very different. When I spoke with Americans, whether face-to-face or by telephone, it was on a one-to-one basis, and it was with the understanding that they would have the right to see on paper what it was that I thought they had said, correct any errors, and then decide whether they would permit me to cite them as sources. (A few footnotes in this book cite "officer interview," without giving the name of the American officer in question. In most cases this means that the source accepted the accuracy of what I showed him in any written notes of the interview, but said he did not want to be cited by name as the source. In a few cases it means that I was unable to obtain any comment from a source, either confirming or denying the accuracy of my notes of the interview. I assure the reader that when I cite an anonymous "interview" for an incident, the source is a person having direct knowledge of the incident—either he was a participant, or he was in a position where reading reports on the incident was part of his job. I do not give footnotes citing "officer interview" to give the impression I have a good source when I am in fact relying on mere rumor.)

I could not use the same ground rules when I was conducting interviews in Vietnam, in May of 1989. When I cite statements from these interviews, I am working simply from my tape recordings and/or written notes of these interviews; there was no practical way for me to allow the subjects to check this record for accuracy. Also, in most cases I was not alone with my subjects.

Though I can use written materials in Vietnamese, I do not speak the language at all. I was able to talk with Colonel Bui Tin directly in French; for much of the time we were talking we were alone in the room. All my other interviews were conducted through interpreters supplied by the Committee for Social Sciences of the Socialist Republic of Vietnam, and occurred in group situations—either I was interviewing a group of three or more people, or else I was interviewing a single individual but with several onlookers aside from the interpreter.

The delays involved in translation broke up the flow of communication, and in some cases made it difficult to cover in the available time all the subjects I wanted to cover. I do not believe that the interpreters ever deliberately altered or censored the statements of the people I was interviewing. My interviews were conducted mainly with people whose rank was much higher than that of the interpreters; I cannot seriously believe my interpreters would have dared to second-guess such people about what should or should not be revealed to a foreigner.

The Vietnamese certainly made no effort to ensure that everyone gave me the same story. On the contrary, over and over again I found one person contradicting what I had been told by another, on matters both trivial and vital. Twice, people of slightly higher rank listened without protest while statements they had made to me were contradicted by people of slightly lower rank.

Overall, I got the same impression from my interviews both with Vietnamese and with Americans: that the people with whom I was talking were trying to remember a very complicated and confusing series of events more than twenty years in the past, and were doing their best to tell me the truth about those events. When different people provided conflicting information, some of them had to be wrong, but I did not take this to imply that they were being dishonest.

Only once did I conclude after an interview that what I have been told had been seriously dishonest, and this was not a case of national loyalties; the man in question was an American who was fabricating stories discreditable to the U.S. government. When I have found my sources in conflict, I have usually found Americans contradicting other Americans, or Vietnamese contradicting other Vietnamese. There are hardly any issues on which my sources have lined up neatly by nationality, all the Vietnamese saying one thing and all the Americans saying something different.

There was one point on which all of the Vietnamese advocated a viewpoint I could not accept. All said they believed that the United States had planned, ahead of time, the sequence of events that culminated with the airstrikes of August 5, carried out in retaliation for the supposed incident of the previous night. This had been the view in Hanoi right from the start; an article in the November 1964 issue of the DRV Navy journal *Hai Quan* (Navy) said: "After fabricating the 'second Tonkin Gulf incident,' the Americans used it as a pretext to retaliate. But actually, all their plots were arranged beforehand."[2]

This was precisely what I would have believed had I been in the place of the Vietnamese. I am convinced, on the basis of my own research on the way Washington handled the affair, that these events had not been planned, and that the report of the second incident had not been a deliberate fabrication. The first time I tried to explain this to historians in Hanoi, however, I felt embarrassed. I was quite sure that President Johnson had been making an honest mistake when he bombed the DRV in "retaliation" for an action the DRV had not committed, but I was acutely aware of how preposterous this tale must have sounded to my audience. The fact that the people with whom I was dealing in Hanoi not only remained polite, but continued to give me a very impressive degree of cooperation, including access to military information that had not previously been in the public domain, reflected a degree of open-mindedness on their part for which I am grateful.

I owe thanks to a great many people who have helped me in my research, through interviews or otherwise. I would like to express my gratitude to Sam Adams, George Allen, Richard Asche, Richard Bacino, George Ball, John J. Barry III, James Bartholomew, Phil Bucklew, Bui Duc Tung, Bui Tin, Bui Tong Cau, William Bundy, Clark M. Clifford, Ray Cline, Richard Corsette, George Edmondson, David Elliott, Daniel Ellsberg, Joe Fanelli, Cathal L. Flynn, Jr., Alvin Friedman, Ilya Gaiduk, William Gibbons, Robert Gillespie, Regina Greenwell, Samuel Halpern, Maureen Harris, Donald Hegrat, John Herrick, Thomas L. Hughes, David Humphrey, Bryce D. Inman, Chad James, Roy L. Johnson, J. Norvill Jones, Burton L. Knight, Judith Ladinsky, Robert Laske, Lawrence E. Levinson, Luu Doan Huynh, Wesley McDonald, Patrick McGarvey, Robert S. McNamara, David Mallow, Edward Marolda, Gerrell Moore, Nguyen Khanh, Nguyen Nam Phong, Nguyen Ngoc Chinh, Nguyen Sang, Herbert Ogier, Sven Öste, Bruce Palmer, Jr., Patrick Park, Pham Hong Thuy, Pham Van Chuyet, Ed Pirie, Charles Schamel, Joseph Schaperjahn, John H. Shattuck, Jr., Douglas Smith, Ronald Stalsberg, Jack Stempler, James B. Stockdale, James Thomson, Jr., Sedgwick Tourison, Henry L. Trewhitt, Trinh Tuan, Bill Wells, David Wise, and Randall Woods.

I offer my apologies to anyone whose name has inadvertently been omitted from the list. The omissions surely include many librarians and archivists at the libraries of Clemson University, Harvard University, the University of South Carolina, and the University of Texas; the Library of Congress; the Naval Historical Center; the National Archives (both in Washington and at the Suitland Reference Branch); the Lyndon B. Johnson Presidential Library; the libraries of the People's Army of Vietnam, and of the State Committee for Social Sciences of the Socialist Republic of Vietnam; and the National Library of Vietnam.

I am grateful to the State Committee for Social Sciences of the Socialist Republic of Vietnam for its assistance in my research, which included arranging my access to many of the institutions and individuals listed above.

I am grateful to Clemson University for its support, and in particular to my department head, David Nicholas, for his tolerance of the way I kept telling him, year after year in conferences on goals and accomplishments for each year, that I was about to finish my study of Tonkin Gulf.

Abbreviations Used in the Text

Abbreviations for sources are listed before the notes.

AA	Anti-aircraft
AAC	Anti-Aircraft Common (shell that can be set to detonate either by proximity or on impact)
ARVN	Army of the Republic of Vietnam
Chicom	Chinese Communist
CIA	Central Intelligence Agency
CIC	Combat Information Center
CINCPAC	Commander in Chief, Pacific [Admiral Harry Felt to June 1964, then Admiral Ulysses S.G. Sharp]
CINCPACFLT	Commander in Chief, Pacific Fleet [Admiral Ulysses S.G. Sharp to June 1964, then Admiral Thomas Moorer]
CNO	Chief of Naval Operations [Admiral David L. McDonald]
COMSEVENTHFLT	Commander, Seventh Fleet [Admiral Roy L. Johnson]
COMUSMACV	Commander, U.S. Military Assistance Command, Vietnam [General Paul Harkins to June 1964, then General William Westmoreland]
comvan	communications van
CSS	Coastal Security Service
DRV	Democratic Republic of Vietnam
ECM	Electronic Counter Measures (detection of enemy radar)
FY	Fiscal Year
HF	High Frequency
INR	Bureau of Intelligence and Research (State Department)
JCS	Joint Chiefs of Staff
LDNN	*Lien Doi Nguoi Nhai* (frogman unit)
Ltjg.	Lieutenant Junior Grade
MACSOG	(see SOG)
MACV	Military Assistance Command, Vietnam
MAROPS	Maritime Operations
NSA	National Security Agency
NSAM	National Security Action Memorandum
NSC	National Security Council
NVN	North Vietnam

OPLAN	Operations Plan
PAVN	People's Army of Vietnam
PFIAB	President's Foreign Intelligence Advisory Board
PGM	patrol gunboat
PT	patrol torpedo (torpedo boat)
PTF	fast patrol boat (acronym used for certain vessels the size of a PT boat but not equipped with torpedoes)
RVN	Republic of Vietnam
SACSA	Special Assistant for Counterinsurgency and Special Activities
SEAL	Sea, Air, Land (U.S. Navy special operations forces)
SOG	Special Operations Group (later Studies and Observations Group)
SVN	South Vietnam
T	*Tau* (Vietnamese for vessel)
USAF	United States Air Force
VHF	very high frequency
VN	Vietnam
VNAF	[Republic of] Vietnam Air Force
VNN	[Republic of] Vietnam Navy
VT-frag	shell designed to detonate on proximity to the target

Tonkin Gulf and the Escalation of the Vietnam War

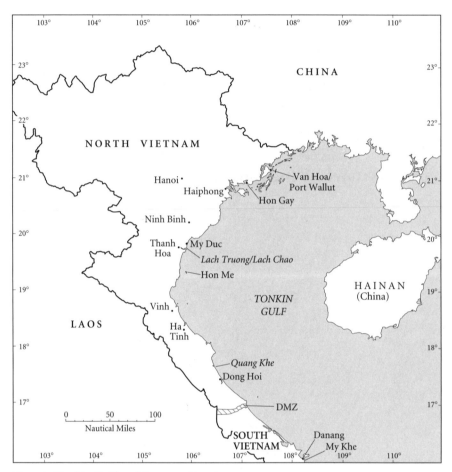

Map 1. Tonkin Gulf and Surrounding Areas

Covert Operations

1 The Vietnam War began in 1959 and 1960. For the first few years the fighting in South Vietnam was carried out, on both sides, mainly by native South Vietnamese. The government forces known as the ARVN (Army of the Republic of Vietnam) had a great advantage in firepower, but the Communist-led guerrillas generally called the Viet Cong had the edge in stealth, conceal-ment, and political skills.

By 1963, the situation had become so bad that the United States connived at a military coup that overthrew Ngo Dinh Diem, president of the Republic of Vietnam (RVN) since the mid-1950s. American officials had for a while managed to ignore Diem's gross mismanagement of the war in the countryside, but they could not ignore the religious crisis that pitted the Catholic Diem against Buddhist leaders in an overwhelmingly Buddhist country, beginning in May 1963. Some senior Ameri-cans pointed out that there was no reason to suppose the ARVN generals would do a better job of running South Vietnam, but Diem had become such a disaster that the final decision was that the United States should gamble on a change. As U.S. Ambassador Henry Cabot Lodge put it a week before the coup, "It seems at least an even bet that the next government would not bungle and stumble as much as the present one has."[1]

This gamble did not work out very well. Having overthrown Ngo Dinh Diem in November 1963, ARVN officers spent the next several years busily plotting to overthrow one another in further coups. General Nguyen Khanh, premier at the time of the Tonkin Gulf incidents, had come to power in a coup in January 1964. The ARVN's conduct of the struggle in the countryside did not improve follow-ing Diem's overthrow, and during 1964 it became apparent that the guerrillas were winning the war. Viet Cong units were growing larger, their armament was improving, and they were increasingly able to face ARVN units in open battle. Government control in the countryside was eroding.

American policymakers were aware that the Viet Cong were almost all native South Vietnamese—indeed the proportion of South Vietnamese was higher among the guerrillas than among the forces fighting on the side of the government—but they assumed that North Vietnam (formally the Democratic Republic of Vietnam, or DRV) was the real cause of the problem in the South. They were of course tempted to retaliate through attacks on the North. There had been various types of covert action directed against the North for some time; by mid-1964 Washington was seriously thinking about going to overt military action.

This chapter describes what the United States had actually been doing to North Vietnam in the months before Tonkin Gulf, a program of very minor covert raids. Chapter 2 describes the discussions that had been going on among U.S. officials about the possibility of doing something on a considerably larger scale. The overall trend was toward a greater use of military force, but it is important not to see this trend as the implementation of any coherent long-term plan. Long-term plans—many of them—were indeed drawn up, but what actually happened, each month, was whatever looked like a good idea at the time. The policymakers never committed themselves to any of the long-term plans, and they did surprisingly little actual preparation to get their forces ready to carry out the plans that were being drawn up.

Making the decisions month by month and step by step, each step too small for anyone to expect it to have a decisive long-term result, discouraged long-term thinking. Robert McNamara, secretary of defense through most of the 1960s, commented recently in his memoirs: "We tilted gradually—almost imperceptibly—toward approving the direct application of U.S. military force. . . . But we never carefully debated what U.S. force would ultimately be required, what our chances of success would be, or what the political, military, financial, and human costs would be if we provided it. Indeed, these basic questions went unexamined."[2]

Covert Pressures on the North

In the late 1950s, the American-supported government in South Vietnam had been doing very little by way of covert action directed against the North. It sent agents there, but these were for the most part simply spies. They did not need to carry conspicuous equipment and could come and go on wooden junks, which looked just like the fishing boats that were so numerous along the North Vietnamese coast, and could pass unnoticed. U.S. involvement in these operations was peripheral.

Around 1960, the United States shifted from merely providing assistance for what were essentially RVN operations against the North to functioning as a full partner. William Colby, the CIA station chief in Saigon, was assigned to strengthen RVN capabilities for infiltration of the North. He brought in specialists in various aspects of clandestine operations to train both the Vietnamese agents destined for missions to the North and the people who would transport them there. On May 11, 1961, President Kennedy approved National Security Action Memorandum (NSAM) 52, directing an increase in covert paramilitary operations against North Vietnam, and an expansion in the forces available for such operations. The United States wanted to send not just lone spies but heavily armed teams, many of which were to be airdropped into the mountainous interior of the DRV. South Vietnamese air force personnel under Colonel (later General and Prime Minister) Nguyen Cao Ky flew the planes for the first such missions;[3] Chinese pilots brought in from Taiwan flew some later ones.

Like many covert operations of the period, this program was supposed to remain concealed from the American people even if it could not be concealed from Hanoi. Colby later commented: "In order to provide a 'plausible denial' that the Vietnamese or the American government was involved in these operations, I set up an alleged Vietnamese private air-transport corporation—VIAT— and arranged that it contract with some experienced pilots from the Agency's old friends on Taiwan."[4]

"Plausible denial" was compromised when one of the planes was shot down in Ninh Binh Province of North Vietnam on July 1, 1961, and the Hanoi press published confessions by men who had been aboard stating that they had been trained by Americans and sent by the RVN.[5]

The airdropping of teams into North Vietnam began in the first half of 1961, and occurred sporadically thereafter. An incomplete U.S. government listing shows three drops totaling eleven men in May and June 1961, and then little activity for eight months; three drops totaling nineteen men from April to June of 1962, and then none for nine months; sixteen drops totaling ninety-five men from April to early December 1963, then none for four and a half months; and ten drops totaling sixty-seven men from late April through July of 1964. From 1961 onward, almost all the men involved were captured promptly after they landed.[6]

The United States was not the only government providing training and assistance. The RVN sent eighteen men to Taiwan for training in underwater operations in August 1960, and then in February 1961, Ngo Dinh Can (brother of President Ngo Dinh Diem) went to Taiwan and arranged for Chiang Kai-shek's government to send twenty instructors to Vietnam to conduct training at Danang and Vung Tau. The *Lien Doi Nguoi Nhai* (LDNN, literally "frogman unit") was formally established in July 1961; the successful students from among the group sent to Taiwan for training in 1960 formed the nucleus for the LDNN.[7] By mid-1964, the CIA reported that there were "several hundred military and paramilitary personnel" from Taiwan in South Vietnam, and that there were plans to increase the number still further.[8] Many of them worked as flight crew on the transport planes that dropped agent teams into North Vietnam; others worked in intelligence, listening in on Communist radio communications and training Vietnamese to do the same.[9]

Some other results of the relationship with Taiwan were more surprising. One cooperative project ended with the capture of twenty-six men described by the DRV as "US–Chiang Kai-shek spy commandos," after landing on the coast of Quang Ninh province (in the northern section of North Vietnam) on the night of July 28–29, 1963. The personnel were all from Taiwan, and indeed the operation was really mounted from there, but the raiding party had stopped for three days at Dao Long, an island twelve miles off the South Vietnamese coast near Danang, where they switched to three smaller vessels from the two trawlers that had brought them from Taiwan. They had been planning to operate against both the DRV and China, in the border area between the two countries. This was not the first such incident; a similar group had been caught in the same area on July 16, 1961, and a third was caught on October 23, 1963. It is said that in at least the second and third incidents, the local security forces had had advance warning that the "spy commandos" were coming, and were ready for them. Cooperative action broke down temporarily after the November 1963 coup that overthrew Ngo Dinh Diem, but in March 1964 the new government of Nguyen Khanh signed an agreement with Taipei to resume cooperative action on raids against North Vietnam and China.[10]

OPLAN 34A

By 1963, William Colby, who by this time had been promoted from Saigon to Washington, where he was in charge of CIA covert operations for the whole Far East, was becoming disenchanted with the CIA's operations against North Vietnam. The Communist leaders' control over the population was simply too strong; teams of agents sent in from the South, whether by sea or air, were being killed or captured with dismaying regularity, and Colby felt that the CIA should stop sending them.[11] The U.S. military, however, was ready to step in as the CIA's enthusiasm faded. In January 1963, the Joint Chiefs of Staff sent a team of high-ranking officers, headed by Army Chief of Staff Earle Wheeler, to South Vietnam to evaluate the progress of the war. Among the recommendations of the team was "that we should do something to make the North Vietnamese bleed."[12]

In May, the Joint Chiefs of Staff directed Admiral Harry G. Felt—who as Commander-in-Chief, Pacific (CINCPAC) commanded all U.S. military forces in the Pacific area including Vietnam—to produce a plan for "hit and run" operations against the North, to be carried out by the RVN with U.S. assistance.

These raids were to be "non-attributable" (the United States had to be able to pretend it was not responsible for them).[13] CINCPAC produced a preliminary draft known as Operations Plan (OPLAN) 34-63, which was endorsed by the Joint Chiefs on August 14 and again, perhaps after some modifications, on September 9. It was further discussed at a conference on Vietnam strategy held in Honolulu on November 20, 1963. Colby attended the conference and "told McNamara that putting teams into the North did not and would not work," but his advice was rejected. "The CIA's lack of success was dismissed as the result of the small scale of effort that a civilian agency could undertake"; the agency was directed to assist the military in a larger program.[14]

By December 15, MACV and CIA together had worked out a modified version of OPLAN 34-63, which was designated OPLAN 34A. The proposed actions against the North were in four categories of increasing severity, ranging from rather minor harrassment up to "aerial attacks conducted against critical DRV installations or facilities, industrial and/or military, such as POL storage areas, thermal power and steel plants, the loss of which would result in crippling effect on the DRV potential to maintain a stable economy and progress in industrial development."[15] These attacks were supposed to be carried out without the direct involvement of U.S. forces. Given the capabilities of the South Vietnamese Air Force at this time, this description of the damage that could be inflicted by air attacks on North Vietnamese industry looks rather optimistic.

On December 12, Secretary McNamara had told Ambassador Lodge that President Johnson wanted plans and recommendations as follows: "Covert operations by South Vietnamese forces, utilizing such support of US forces as is necessary, against North Vietnam. Plans for such operations should include varying levels of pressure all designed to make clear to the North Vietnamese that the US will not accept a Communist victory in South Vietnam and that we will escalate the conflict to whatever level is required to insure their defeat."[16] This was, to put it bluntly, silly. No level of *covert* operations could have proved to the North Vietnamese that the United States would escalate the conflict to whatever level was required.

When OPLAN 34A was completed shortly afterward, its supposed aim was "in concert with other military and diplomatic actions in the Southeast Asia area, to convince the DRV leadership that its current support and direction of war in the Republic of Vietnam and its aggression in Laos should be reexamined and stopped." Those who drew up the plan, however, offered no promises that it would actually accomplish such a goal. On the contrary, they said they expected that the DRV would retaliate for attacks at the second and third of the four levels defined by the plan by escalating the level of Communist violence in South Vietnam and Laos. They said the DRV might respond even to the very punishing air attacks in the strongest of the four categories not by reducing its support for the war in South Vietnam but by escalating that support, and they warned that the United States should be "prepared to follow up with supporting operations in offsetting DRV reactions."[17]

An interdepartmental committee in Washington, chaired by Marine Corps Major General Victor Krulak, Special Assistant for Counterinsurgency and Special Activities (SACSA) to the Joint Chiefs of Staff, selected some of the less risky options from the MACV/CIA draft and drew up a twelve-month plan in three phases of increasing intensity. On January 16, 1964, President Johnson approved this modified version of OPLAN 34A and ordered that Phase I, consisting of quite modest actions, be implemented during the four months from February through May.[18]

The maritime operations actually conducted during that four-month initial phase were a disappointment; of the thirty-three actions on the schedule, only a third had actually been completed by June 1.[19] The ones successfully accomplished included the landing of commandos for raids or sabotage missions, and the seizure of at least one fishing boat off the coast of North Vietnam (see below).

On May 19, when the Joint Chiefs sent a list of operations for the second phase (June through September) of OPLAN 34A to the secretary of defense, they based it on current evaluations of the situation and the capabilities of the available forces, not on the second-phase plan General Krulak had drawn up in January.[20] The operations that actually were approved for the second phase were less ambitious than those contemplated in either the plan drawn up in January or the May 19 proposals from the Joint Chiefs.

The Special Operations Group (SOG) was established under MACV on January 24, 1964, and given responsibility for the covert raids against the North. (SOG's formal name was changed late in 1964 to the less revealing "Studies and Observations Group.") SOG was often referred to as MACV-SOG or MACSOG to indicate its affiliation with MACV. This establishment of a military organization to handle covert operations against the North was part of a broader shift in responsibility for paramilitary operations in Vietnam; what had formerly been CIA programs carried out with support and cooperation from the military became military programs carried out with support and cooperation from the CIA. Operation Switchback had transferred large paramilitary operations within South Vietnam, much more important than the covert raids against the North, from CIA to military control in 1963.

The United States, the RVN, and OPLAN 34A

The published record on OPLAN 34A has been confused not only by the secrecy surrounding the program, and the deliberate dishonesty implied by "plausible denial," but also by the fact that it was an umbrella embracing a tremendous variety of operations, some of which had already been in progress for some time before they were absorbed into OPLAN 34A. Confusion is especially easy over the relative roles of Washington and Saigon in OPLAN 34A. The most important activity for which the Americans and their Vietnamese allies operated small boats off the coast, for example, was a program to interdict the movement of Communist men and supplies into or within South Vietnam. This involved stopping and searching many fishing boats, among other things. The vessels carrying out such searches in 1964 were South Vietnamese. When Secretary McNamara was questioned by Senate committees about the OPLAN 34A raids against the North Vietnamese coast, he described them as an extension of the anti-infiltration program into North Vietnamese waters, carried out by the same vessels, again an essentially South Vietnamese operation (see Chapter 4).

This was misleading in two ways. First, while anger over infiltration was indeed a major motive for the United States wanting to arrange attacks on North Vietnam, there was no effort to focus those attacks on facilities having a direct connection with infiltration. Suggestions that OPLAN 34A was targeted against infiltration have appeared as recently as 1991 in statements by former Secretary of State Dean Rusk and former Assistant Secretary of State for Far Eastern Affairs William Bundy; these suggestions find no support in the actual OPLAN 34A target lists.[21]

Second, the raids against North Vietnam were carried out by a quite separate force, much less under the control of the RVN than the anti-infiltration forces. The raids against the North Vietnamese coast were not really an RVN program carried out with American assistance; they could better be described as an American program carried out with RVN assistance. In the early 1960s, when the maritime raids were controlled by the CIA, General Nguyen Khanh, Chief of Staff of the General Staff, Republic of Vietnam Armed Forces, decided that he wanted to inspect the base outside Danang from which these raids were mounted. He had to go to President Ngo Dinh Diem to arrange permission to do so. By 1964, General Khanh was prime minister in Saigon, and the demands on his time were such that he did not ask the Americans for details of the maritime raids against North Vietnam. He says that if he had asked the Americans for detailed information, he is not sure whether they would have given it to him or not.[22]

Although the RVN supplied many of the personnel for OPLAN 34A, the RVN was not consulted while it was being written. Only on January 21, 1964, after President Johnson had already given the order to carry out the first four-month phase of attacks on the North, did Ambassador Lodge brief RVN President Duong Van Minh on OPLAN 34A.[23]

The Vietnamese counterpart organization to MACSOG was the Strategic Technical Service (STS), formally established February 12, 1964. It was derived from what under Ngo Dinh Diem had been called the Topographic Exploitation

Service. Later in the war the STS would be renamed the Strategic Technical Directorate (STD).[24]

A SOG history summarized the relationships between U.S. and Vietnamese organizations: "Planning and operational control were retained by the United States Government. . . . Overall planning concepts were coordinated between STD [STS] and MACSOG; however, there was little or no coordination on proposed operations, their authorization and scheduling."[25]

A subordinate group, the Coastal Security Service (CSS), was the Vietnamese counterpart organization to the U.S. Naval Advisory Detachment (NAD) in Danang; the CSS and NAD both had their headquarters in a building in Danang called the "White Elephant." Unlike their superiors in the STS, "CSS officers participated jointly with counterpart NAD personnel in the planning, briefing and debriefing of mission personnel."[26] There is no way to tell how much information the CSS officers in Danang may have passed on to higher Vietnamese authorities in Saigon, but if the Americans did not themselves give details of OPLAN 34A raids to the STS, and the passage quoted above indicates they did not, it seems very unlikely that they gave such details to any Vietnamese organization in Saigon, or that they encouraged the CSS to do so.

Relations between SOG and its Vietnamese counterpart organizations were not always close. Coordination in regard to air operations against North Vietnam was impeded during 1964 by the fact that "US security regulations render[ed] it impossible for STS personnel to visit SOG working areas."[27] A SOG official history commented:

> Periodically, during the development and expansion phases of the MAROPS program, the motivation and capabilities of VN-assigned personnel were frequently challenged; discipline was neither in accord with US standards nor remedied by CSS officers. Desertion rates were at critical levels; there was indifference to material damage and loss; attainment of military goals was distantly second to mercenary gain; and black marketing of US-provided resources was accepted. The lack of VN leadership during the early period was a much lamented US concern and joint relationships were degraded at times to letter writing protest exchanges vice coordinated efforts.[28]

Maritime Forces Based at Danang

In November 1962, a base for maritime raids against North Vietnam was established at My Khe, just outside Danang. U.S. Navy SEALs trained the raiding parties. The SEALs normally rotated in and out on six-month tours. The CIA had overall responsibility for the program until 1964, but CIA personnel did not participate directly in the training program; they left that to the SEALs.

In 1962 or 1963, there was an incident in which one of the Vietnamese the

SEALs were training was captured on a raid into North Vietnam. When his captors examined the lifejacket the man was wearing, they saw that something had been painted over. Removing the paint, they discovered the name of the American officer whose jacket it had been before it was passed to the Vietnamese. Photos of this lifejacket were used in North Vietnamese propaganda.[29] The embarrassment of this incident may help to explain the effort that was being made by 1964 to avoid even giving American-made equipment to the raiding parties.

Just east of Danang lay the Tien Sha Peninsula, with Monkey Mountain at its northern tip. My Khe Beach formed the east coast of the peninsula, from Monkey Mountain southward to Marble Mountain. By early 1964, facilities for raids against North Vietnam spread for a considerable distance along this beach. The docks for the vessels that carried the raiding parties north were right at the foot of Monkey Mountain. The raiding parties they carried lived and trained in a series of relatively small camps, none accommodating more than twenty or thirty men, strung out along the beach. One camp was for South Vietnamese Marines. One was for the LDNN, a scuba-trained group (see above) that Lieutenant Cathal L. Flynn, commander of the SEAL detachment, thought of as the Vietnamese equivalent of an American underwater demolition team. One camp was for Nung. (The Nung, an ethnic group possessing a formidable military reputation, come from the highlands of North Vietnam. About 15,000 of them, mostly soldiers who had fought on the French side in the First Indochina War, came south in 1954–55 following the Geneva Accords.) Another camp was for a group called "Ching" of whose exact identity Lieutenant Flynn was not certain. All of the men were military, including the Nung. Some were "very, very experienced fighters." There was one Nung who had commanded a machine-gun team in the bloody fighting of the first half of 1951, defending one of the fortified positions with which the French Army blocked the Viet Minh thrust into the Red River Delta.[30]

The way the different groups were kept separate from one another represented CIA practice. The compartmentalization was not completely effective— the different groups could see one another's training exercises—but "it wasn't a bad way to run things."[31]

The American SEALs trained the men at all these camps. They taught rubber-boat techniques, scuba techniques, cross-beach operations, and explosive demolition techniques. At first, they also taught the use of 3.5-inch time-delay rockets, provided by the CIA. A team could land quietly, set up the plastic launch tubes so the rockets were aimed at the target, start the time pencils, and be on their way home before the rockets went off. These rockets, however, were "pretty hopeless," for at least three reasons. They were not very accurate, the time pencils were not reliable, and worst of all, the rockets were dangerously prone to going off accidentally while being handled. Lieutenant Flynn was once helping a man with a triple pack of the rockets on his back get off a truck. The impact of the man's feet hitting the ground was enough to set off all three rockets, just past Flynn's face. On another occasion, some of the SEALs were removing rockets from a magazine. One rocket took off, hit the wall of the magazine, detonated, and set the magazine on fire. Lieutenant Flynn's second-in-command suffered white phosphorus burns, not too severe, but bad enough that the man had to return to the United States for treatment.

The rockets were used a few times on operations against the North, but they proved so unsatisfactory that 57-mm recoilless rifles were substituted. These were light infantry cannon, in which much of the exhaust gas was directed to the rear instead of forward out the muzzle, so that recoil was almost eliminated and the weapon could be operated without needing the heavy mount that allows a normal cannon to absorb recoil.

Carrying out effective raids on the North was not at all easy. Quang Khe, for example, a base for patrol vessels of the North Vietnamese navy located inside the mouth of the Gianh River in Quang Binh province of North Vietnam, was a high priority; it had first been attacked, unsuccessfully, in May or June of 1962. At this time the LDNN "frogmen" were carried north in a comparatively slow motorized junk, which took more than twenty-four hours to get them to the Gianh river. The low speed was an even worse problem if the objective were more distant; one of these vessels that set out on a raid on the afternoon of August 13, 1963, did not reach its target area in Hong Quang (northeast of Haiphong) until the evening of August 15.[32]

Three new attempts to attack patrol vessels in Quang Khe were made in February and March 1964; by this time American-made Swift boats, much faster than the junks, were being used. On each occasion the plan was to have men in scuba gear—the standard team seems to have been four men, though there may have been only two men involved in the third attempt—blow up patrol vessels moored at the base.

In the raid that occurred during the night of either February 13 or February 16 (sources give different dates), the engine noise of the boat delivering the raiders was heard, and some local people who were fishing saw and reported some sign—probably bubbles rising to the surface of the water—of the passage of the four "frogmen" swimming up the river toward their target. Security forces quickly went after them. Three were captured; the fourth exhausted his strength in the water, trying to evade pursuit, and drowned.[33]

The U.S. Navy SEAL detachment advising and training the raiding parties was rotated around the end of February 1964. Lieutenant Flynn headed the new detachment. At the time it arrived, there were a dozen men in the detachment, including Flynn. Three additional SEALs were later added, and four U.S. Marines also worked with them at My Khe. They had been given some Vietnamese language instruction but were not fluent; they communicated with their Vietnamese trainees mainly through interpreters.

The next attempt against Quang Khe was made on the night of March 12. Before this, an exercise was staged at Cua Viet, a river mouth in South Vietnam that resembled the mouth of the Gianh River closely enough for all the elements of the attack plan to be rehearsed there. A Swift boat was to deliver the men to a point offshore. They were then to go by inflatable rubber boat to a sandbar near the mouth of the river, and from that point they were to swim upriver to where the target vessel was docked. In the exercise, they were to attach one limpet mine—a time-delayed explosive device—to the vessel that had been moored in the river as their target. In the real raid, they would carry several limpet mines and try to attack several North Vietnamese vessels.

The rehearsal seemed to go perfectly; the American observers on the target vessel reported that the limpet mine had indeed been successfully attached, though of course it was not actually detonated. The Americans were impressed; the complexity of the operation, and the length of the swim from the sandbar to the target vessel, had made it a pretty difficult exercise.

The arrangements for transporting the observers back to the base at My Khe broke down, and they remained at Cua Viet for several days longer than had been planned. During this interval, they noticed distinctive footprints on the bank of the river, and realized that the frogmen had not actually swum underwater from the sandbar to the target vessel; they had walked up the bank of the river for most of the distance. By the time the observers got back to My Khe and reported this, the four frogmen had already departed for the actual raid against the North Vietnamese base at Quang Khe.[34] All four men were lost. A DRV account says they were caught in the water swimming upriver, but one member of the team recently told Sedgwick Tourison that they were on land; the boats they had been sent to attack had not been in the expected location, and they had gone on shore looking for some "target of opportunity" to attack. There was another attempt against Quang Khe, also unsuccessful, three nights later.[35]

A new Vietnamese LDNN officer arrived to take charge of the LDNN group at My Khe soon after this, probably before the end of March. Under this man's leadership, the LDNN group improved, and indeed became the best of the various groups that the SEALs were training at My Khe. All the groups were good; there were no "real losers" after the problems in the LDNN group were cured. Many of the skills of these men soon lost their relevance, however, when improvements in North Vietnamese coastal defenses made it too dangerous to send landing parties ashore.[36]

The first successful attack using 57-mm weapons was on what was supposed to be a militia post. When the team returned, they said it had turned out to be a factory for the manufacture of *nuoc mam* (Vietnamese fish sauce); Flynn was not sure whether they were joking or not. In any case, the success of the operation was good for morale. This is probably the operation that shows in the records as having occurred on the night of June 12, 1964, targeted at Hai Khau, just west of Cape Mui Ron. The twenty-six men in the team that carried out this operation suffered no losses.[37]

A raid of this size would not have been practical using Swift boats, which typically carried only four to six commandos per mission. But in the first half of 1964, the U.S. had strengthened the force available for such raids by sending eight larger vessels called PTFs to Vietnam. Six were new Nasty-class boats with diesel engines, recently purchased from Norway. The other two were old American-made PT boats whose torpedo tubes had been removed; these had gasoline engines.

U.S. officers both in Danang and Saigon expressed doubts about the old PT boats even before they arrived. Higher authorities argued that they should at least be tried. They were indeed tried, and found unsafe for a whole series of reasons. First, the high-octane gasoline they used as fuel posed unacceptable risks of explosion if they came under enemy fire. Second, When the engines were stopped, vapor lock sometimes made them difficult to restart. This could have posed great danger when one of these boats had landed a party on a hostile coast and then had to wait, engines off, for that party to complete its mission and reembark. Third, the engines were very noisy. Fourth, it was hard to get the engines into reverse. This caused minor bumps in the harbor; it could have been more serious when the boats were dropping off or picking up landing parties in hostile waters.[38] In addition to the safety problems, the fact that the PTs were of American manufacture put them in violation of the general policy that the weapons and other equipment used in raids in the North were not to be of American origin.

The Nasty was a better boat for such operations than the PT, but still not perfect. The Nasty had been designed as a fast vessel to be used for short-range defense of national waters. It lost a significant part of its speed when loaded with the men and weapons of a landing party, plus the extra fuel tanks needed for long-range raids against North Vietnam.[39]

The raids of July 30 and August 3, 1964, are probably the only ones in which the American-built PTs participated, and they had serious engine trouble on both of these operations. They were soon retired from combat operations, which were performed by the Norwegian-built Nasty boats, supplemented eventually (after escalation of the war had reduced the importance of disguising the American role in such operations) by new American-built boats similar to the Nasty.

These boats were under the direct control of a U.S. Navy Mobile Support Team at the My Khe base, commanded from March 1964 onward by Lieutenant Burton L. Knight. Above Knight (and presumably also above Flynn) were two chains of command. In regard to actual combat operations, the boats and the men who ran them were under SOG in Saigon. (While CIA had handed over responsibility for such operations to SOG, it still retained a considerable role in their conduct; most of the Americans with whom Knight dealt locally in Danang were CIA.)[40] From SOG the operational chain of command went up through SACSA (the Special Assistant for Counterinsurgency and Special Activities in the Pentagon) to the 303 Committee of the National Security Council.[41]

The permanent affiliation of the U.S. Naval personnel in Danang, however, was with the Naval Operations Support Group, headed by Captain Phil H. Bucklew and based in Coronado, California. This organization was responsible for those U.S. Navy forces involved in special operations in the Pacific area, and it retained a supervisory role over the men it supplied to SOG for various operations in Vietnam.

When the fact that such raids were occurring became known, the public position of the U.S. government was that the raids were South Vietnamese government operations, and that the only people aboard the boats, when they went on raids against the North, were RVN military personnel. At the other extreme, most of the published literature on the subject suggests that men of a great many nationalities, including Americans, participated.

As has been noted above, the United States had begun hiring Chinese personnel (from Taiwan) for aerial operations against the North some time before, and when OPLAN 34A was being drawn up, the use of some "third-nation" (neither Vietnamese nor American) personnel was assumed.[42] A great variety of people seem to have been involved, at one time or another, in the covert operations force based at Danang. The personnel involved changed from one month to another. Not all of the people who were trained for missions to the North were actually sent on such missions. The people aboard the Swifts were sometimes different from the people aboard the PTFs. Finally, on each vessel, there was a distinction between the landing party (the people with guns who actually tried to blow up bridges, for instance) and the people who were responsible for running the vessel, getting the landing party to and from its objective. The captains of the vessels were often of nationalities that never appeared among the landing parties.

The boat crews were trained and supervised by Knight's Mobile Support Team, at a single facility. The landing parties were based at various small camps strung out along My Khe Beach. Knight had hardly any contact with them; they were trained and supervised mainly by Cathal Flynn's SEALs. The best available information indicates that:

—Each of the three Swift boats had a Norwegian captain who also served as navigator, with three Vietnamese crewmen under him—helmsman, gunner, and interpreter. The three Norwegians were sometimes referred to by other personnel in Danang as "the Vikings." They had been recruited in Norway (probably with prior approval from the Norwegian government) in July 1963, but did not arrive in South Vietnam until August. Their last operation was probably on May 27, 1964; they left Vietnam on June 16. They might technically have been considered mercenaries, but it is unlikely that they were truly motivated by money; their pay was not that generous. Knight recalls that their performance was excellent, and they were much missed when their contracts expired and they departed. Flynn did not have so high an opinion of the Norwegians.[43]

By June, Chinese were being trained as captains for the Swifts to replace the departing Norwegians,[44] but there is doubt that these Chinese ever went on missions to the North; the Swift boats seem to have stopped such missions by the time the training of the Chinese was completed.

—According to Knight, the landing parties operating from the Swifts were nominally Montagnard (ethnic minority groups living in the highlands of Vietnam), but in fact included people from parts of Asia other than Vietnam. In the only specific Swift operations for which the makeup of the landing parties is known, however, in February and March of 1964, Vietnamese members of the LDNN were involved.

—The original plan had been to have the key positions on the PTFs filled by Germans, with Vietnamese (or Montagnards) working under them. The Germans proved unsatisfactory—excessive consumption of beer during working hours seems to have been involved—and they were fired. They tried to hang onto their jobs, claiming they had contracts, but a CIA representative "made them offers they could not refuse."[45] It is not clear whether the Germans ever actually went on any operations; they may have been fired before training of PTF crews was completed and PTF combat operations began. Their replacements, the men actually commanding the PTFs on missions in July and August, were Vietnamese.

—The landing parties operating from the PTFs were predominantly made up of ethnic Vietnamese.

This diversity helps to explain the wild conflicts between different published accounts of the raids against North Vietnam. A great many statements have been published about who was aboard the raiding vessels, but these statements seldom distinguish between captains, crews, and landing parties, or specify a date.

Knight's impression was that the most effective operations carried out from Danang were conducted by the Swifts. This was due partly to the professional skill and daring of the "Vikings," perhaps also to the fact that the Swifts set out on operations in a reasonably unobtrusive manner. The Swift boats loaded weapons and landing parties at night, and set out on operations late at night or early in the morning. The loading and departure of the PTFs was much more conspicuous. Flynn, on the other hand, feels that the landing parties working from the Swifts were not very successful.

Anthony Austin has said that, to the extent to which there were Vietnamese included in the crews of these boats, they did not wear RVN naval uniform and none of them belonged to the South Vietnamese navy; they were mercenaries.[46] This is an exaggeration, though there is some truth behind it. SOG personnel demands were met partly by the Vietnamese military and partly through the hiring of "volunteers." The SOG command history refers to difficulties obtaining adequate personnel from the South Vietnamese navy, and a "dependence on civilian mercenaries" that was presumably a result of this, early in 1964.[47] U.S. officers repeatedly expressed a wish that personnel be found who would be motivated by patriotism rather than by financial incentives, but such personnel simply could not be found in sufficient numbers.[48] It seems likely, however, that Vietnamese mercenaries were found more among the landing parties than the boat crews in 1964. There is good evidence that the Nasty boat crews belonged to the South Vietnamese navy and wore its uniform while on operations.[49]

Lieutenant Knight did not find the Vietnamese crews supplied for the PTFs very satisfactory, but this may have been at least partly because the RVN Navy did not have any personnel really qualified for the work; none of its men had ever operated such high-tech vessels before. A later SOG history commented that the Nasty was so sophisticated a craft that it would have posed difficulties even for experienced U.S. Navy personnel. "Damage attributable to VNN crew negligence, indifference or ignorance was commonplace."[50]

The RVN Navy had said it was assigning the cream of its men to this program, and the officers in particular were convinced they were the cream. Indeed, their sense that they were entitled to be treated as an elite caused problems. There was a mini-revolt soon after they arrived; they were demanding more pay, better food, and better living conditions. Lieutenant Knight was not in a position to suppress this revolt, but an agency (which he cannot identify precisely) that he considered a South Vietnamese equivalent of the CIA was and did so. Judging by the bruises, the suppression had involved physical beating of the officers involved.[51]

One of the murkiest questions is whether U.S. military (mostly navy) officers and men, who trained Vietnamese and third-nation personnel for 34A operations, ever went along on combat operations against the North. This seems clearly to have been forbidden by U.S. policy, but was the prohibition actually respected? Captain Phil H. Bucklew, who as head of the Naval Operations Support Group was responsible for the U.S. Navy personnel in question, believes that they habitually violated the prohibition. Indeed, he is not aware of any cases in which the PTFs from Danang went on combat operations without American personnel aboard. His recollection is that the Americans were running the boats, with Vietnamese along in what was essentially an apprenticeship role. He states that there were suggestions during 1964 that Vietnamese officers and men be given actual responsibility for handling the boats on combat missions, but that these suggestions had been opposed on the grounds that the Vietnamese did not have the skills.[52]

Vice Admiral Roy L. Johnson, commander of the U.S. Seventh Fleet starting in June 1964, recalls that the Vietnamese crews had proved unreliable. When sent out for an operation against the North, they sometimes just cruised around in circles for a few hours off shore, and then filed a false report claiming that they had conducted the assigned operation. American crews had to be substituted for the Vietnamese. Admiral Johnson is "pretty sure" that American crews were being used on raids against the North Vietnamese coast by August 1964; if the change had not come by this time, it came soon after.[53]

Officers of lower rank, however, closer to the actual situation than Admiral Johnson and Captain Bucklew, deny that this was true.[54] Lieutenant Knight says that the personnel under him who trained the captains and crews of the vessels did not go along on operations. The only occasion on which any of Knight's men went north of the seventeenth parallel was when one of the Nasty boats had fouled its engine during an operation; Knight and some other Americans had to take another boat and go to the rescue. This barely took them north of the seventeenth parallel, however, and it did not take them into combat.[55]

The Americans who trained the landing parties might have had more reason to go along on missions than the Americans under Knight who trained the captains and crews. The captains and crews were not in great danger, and this author has not in fact seen any record of casualties among them in 1964. The landing parties, however, faced the likelihood of combat against greatly superior numbers and suffered losses on several operations. At the beginning of April, CINCPAC reported to the JCS that since the implementation of OPLAN 34A had formally begun,

> all air resupply missions and the five attempts to infiltrate teams by sea on sabotage missions have failed. . . .
>
> It is obvious that any person with the requisite degree of intelligence to be recruited for such operations who knew the history of repeated failures and loss of personnel in operations against NVN, and who knew the relative difference in the intelligence collection capabilities on both sides would think twice about offering his services.[56]

If the U.S. Navy SEALs in Danang wanted to maintain morale among the Vietnamese teams they were training as landing parties, they would have been very strongly inclined at least to go along on the boats on raids against the North, if not actually land with their trainees. If any U.S. Navy personnel went along on raids against the North, this is probably how it occurred. The preponderance of evidence, however, is that this did not happen. The firm statements of two of the Norwegian Swift-boat captains that no Americans ever went along on missions to the North[57] seem particularly convincing. Those U.S. Naval officers who say otherwise, while their opinions must be taken seriously, were not as close to the situation.

Author Douglas Valentine recently published a very specific account of SEAL participation in an OPLAN 34A raid. He had placed an advertisement asking to talk with anyone who had served in the Phoenix Program in Vietnam. One man who answered the advertisement said that he had served in Vietnam as a SEAL in 1964 on operations similar to those that would later be carried out under the Phoenix Program. He also described how he and one other SEAL had personally led a South Vietnamese landing party in an OPLAN 34A raid against the North Vietnamese island of Hon Me, on the night of July 30, 1964.[58]

This story, however, is not credible. The fact that this man has no documentation for his story—his navy service records do not even show that he served in Vietnam—is far from conclusive. The secrecy of SEAL operations was such that it was not terribly unusual during the war for a man's records to be doctored to eliminate references to service in the war zone as a SEAL. In this case, however, the story simply does not fit the known facts. The man says, for example, that he arrived in Vietnam aboard the U.S. guided missile destroyer *Lawrence* in early January 1964. At that time, the *Lawrence* was actually moored in the U.S. naval base at Norfolk, Virginia. The physical shape of Hon Me plays a key role in his story of the operation; he describes it as a long narrow island, all flat except at its northwest end. It is in fact approximately circular, and equally hilly on all sides. Other aspects of his story, while not provably false, are wildly implausible. He says, for example, that he never met the men of the raiding party he led against Hon Me until he was aboard the boat taking them north for the raid. Admittedly the U.S. government did some bizarre things in Vietnam, but if it had wanted a SEAL to lead these men on a mission, it surely would have assigned one of the SEALs who had been training them at My Khe for months, not some total stranger. It seems safe to discard the whole story as a fabrication.[59]

It is easier to determine who controlled the raids than who actually carried them out. The chain of command was not simple (see above), but it was entirely American. For many years, public statements by U.S. officials referred only to "South Vietnamese" raids against North Vietnam. Even in secret communications at the time, recently declassified, the same phrase appears. But those of the recently declassified communications that discuss specific decisions about the raids—which targets are to be hit, and when—never mention that the RVN has been or needs to be consulted about the decisions; the U.S. government was in control.

It was explicitly U.S. policy to exclude the headquarters staff of the RVN Navy from involvement in the direction of OPLAN 34A operations; the only RVN agencies the United States allowed to be involved were those specifically dedicated to covert operations. One possible reason is that there were times during 1964 when the Saigon government not only wanted a more rapid escalation of conflict with the North than the United States thought prudent, but was willing to defy the wishes of the U.S. government in its pursuit of rapid escalation (see below). Control of the maritime operations would have given Saigon far too great a capability for provoking violent incidents.

There may also have been concerns over the issue of competence. Captain Joseph Drachnik, upon finishing his tour as chief U.S. advisor to the RVN Navy early in 1964, reported (in general, not in a specific comment on OPLAN 34A): "Vietnamese Navy officers and men . . . seem almost incapable of doing valid planning by themselves. It is as if they did all things by rote rather than by the use of intelligent judgment. . . . U.S. advisors must be placed at all levels, high and low, where ingenuity of any type is needed. . . . These advisors must be maintained in place as long as we want each element to be productive. It will disintegrate upon their removal."[60]

What is surprising, however, is that so little effort was made to establish a pretense that the raids on the North were South Vietnamese operations. Admiral Sharp recommended long before the PTFs arrived in Vietnam that in order to avoid possible embarrassment they be "stricken . . . at least for record purposes from the US Navy records," but the United States did not even begin going through the motions of transferring them (by a nominal "lease" in which no monetary payment was involved) from the U.S. Navy to the RVN until November 1964, several months after they began to conduct raids against North Vietnam.[61] MACV resisted leasing the PTFs to the RVN Navy, on the grounds that this might encourage the RVN Naval Staff to demand a role in directing the operations on which the vessels were used, and also that in the event of another coup in Saigon, the vessels might be used to support one faction of the RVN Armed Forces against another. MACV suggested that leasing the PTFs to the RVN Joint General Staff, instead of to the RVN Navy, would minimize these risks. The problem that blocked leasing of the vessels to any Vietnamese body for a long time, however, was that the Chief of Naval Operations wanted to ensure that the United States would retain the ability to get them back if an "urgent need" for them arose elsewhere in the Pacific area. MACV, arguing that no leasing arrangement could be worked out under which it would be practical for the United States to reclaim the boats in an emergency, decided not even to discuss the matter with the RVN. The individual Vietnamese PTF captains in Danang signed documents accepting custody of the boats, but there was no transfer (nominal or real) of the PTFs to the RVN Navy as an institution until later.[62]

Top officials in Washington probably did not realize that the involvement of the U.S. Navy in the 34A raids was as direct as it actually was. Ray Cline, Deputy

Director for Intelligence at the CIA, has commented: "I assumed that an effective cover arrangement had been made to transfer the boats and other military equipment to formal Vietnamese ownership while retaining essential elements of operational command and control. If this transfer was not made by appropriate paperwork correspondence, the U.S. authorities involved were sloppy and in bureaucratic error."[63] Cline's opinion is that no civilian member of the government at his level or above would have been likely to check this kind of detail. Indeed, a July 24 memo to President Johnson written by Special Assistant for National Security Affairs McGeorge Bundy (brother of Assistant Secretary of State for Far Eastern Affairs William Bundy), dealing with a conversation he and McNamara had had with the president about OPLAN 34A, makes it very clear that Bundy had not been paying much attention to OPLAN 34A, and strongly suggests that McNamara and Johnson had not been doing so either.[64]

Increasing the Tempo of Attacks

The frequency with which small parties of men were infiltrated into North Vietnam, both by sea and by air, increased substantially as 1964 progressed. The shift was especially dramatic in regard to airdropped teams; no teams had been dropped from January through mid-April, but there were nine men dropped in late April, thirteen in May, twenty-three in June, and twenty-two in July.[65]

Losses were heavy. The attacks of February 13 and March 12 and 15 aimed at North Vietnamese naval vessels at Quang Khe have already been mentioned; all participants in these raids were killed or captured. Seven men were landed from a Swift boat on the coast of Ha Tinh province March 16, and nine on the coast of Quang Binh province March 17, in order to attack bridges on Highway 1, the main main road running along the coast. Both operations failed; two men were lost each time. The six men of Team Attila were all captured after having been airdropped into mountainous Thanh Chuong district of Nghe An province on the night of April 25–26. The six men of Team Lotus were captured after being airdropped onto a mountainous section of Quy Chau district, Nghe An province, on the night of May 19. When they were tried early in August, the DRV announced that this was the ninth such group brought to trial since the beginning of the year.[66]

Team Scorpion had very bad luck when dropped into Yen Bai province on the night of June 17–18. Members of the local militia, attending a meeting on defense against raids such as theirs, heard an aircraft passing over, ran out of the room where they were meeting, and actually saw the six parachutists coming down from the plane. The leader of the team was captured before he could disentangle himself from his parachute; the rest were rounded up the following day.[67]

The raiding groups that had the greatest impact, of course, were the more fortunate or more competent ones that avoided capture and completed their missions; these came by sea rather than by air. Two groups that conducted raids on the night of June 12—the one already mentioned that attacked the militia post/fish sauce factory, and one that landed on the coast and blew up the Hang bridge in Thanh Hoa province, escaped without casualties. There is one source who claims that the DRV deliberately "allowed" the destruction of the bridge to succeed.[68] In the absence of details or a plausible motive for such an action, however, this claim must be considered suspect—"no way" was Cathal Flynn's comment. He added that the landing party in fact exchanged fire with local defense forces.

On the night of June 26–27, a seven-man demolition team supported by twenty-four Marines destroyed a bridge along Route 1, also in Thanh Hoa province. They killed two bridge guards and four other DRV personnel, without losing any of their own men.[69]

The group of either twenty-three or thirty-one men that used 57-mm recoilless rifles to attack a reservoir pump house near the mouth of the Kien River (part of the water supply system for the town of Dong Hoi), on the night of June 30–July 1, accomplished its mission but suffered some casualties. PTF-5 and PTF-6 landed the attack team by rubber boat shortly after midnight. The team destroyed the target but came into heavy combat with DRV forces. The PTFs closed and shelled the attacking troops with 20-mm and 40-mm guns, which helped the landing force to escape and apparently to bring out two local militiamen as prisoners, but the landing force lost two of its own men. The Americans assumed that the two lost men had been killed in action.[70] In fact, at least one of the missing men had been captured alive. Under interrogation, he told his North Vietnamese captors that he had also been a member of the team that had destroyed the Hang Bridge. He said that the commandos had developed a good deal of confidence in their ability to attack targets from the sea and get out safely, but that they were all afraid of dropping into North Vietnam from the air.[71]

The man's attitude was reasonable, given the record of operations over the preceding months, but OPLAN 34A was pushing the DRV to upgrade its coastal defenses. The days when Swifts or PTFs could put men ashore in reasonable safety were coming to an end as increasing numbers of machine gun positions, very hard to spot in the aerial photographs available to the men planning the raids, were established in the trees along the beaches. The SEALs spent considerable effort training members of the landing parties to fire 57-mm recoilless rifles accurately from rubber boats—the man firing the weapon would have it resting on his shoulder—and some of them indeed became very accurate.[72] There is no definite indication, however, that this startling technique was actually used on a raid against the North.

On July 15, another commando group landed on the coast north of Ron and suffered casualties in an encounter with local defense forces.[73] By the end of July and the beginning of August, what had formerly been landing parties were simply firing at their targets directly from the PTFs that carried them north.

If targets were to be shelled directly from the PTFs, a weapon more powerful than the 57-mm seemed desirable. Thus 81-mm mortars, and large recoilless rifles (either 90 mm or 106 mm), were brought in. Cathal Flynn is not certain, however, that these larger weapons were actually used in any raids against the North during the period he was at My Khe.

The first of a new series of operations directed against North Vietnamese fishing boats was carried out May 27. At least one PTF and at least one Swift boat captured a fishing vessel twenty to thirty miles north of the DMZ. The fishing boat and its crew of six were taken back to Lao Cham Island, off Danang. The crew was interrogated and indoctrinated for a few days, then released to the North, with their boat, on June 2.[74] Three fishing boats were seized on July 7, and two more on July 20.[75] At approximately this time, the Americans planning these operations decided on an unpleasant modification of the procedure. Instead of returning fishing boats to the fishermen intact when they were released, as American records say was done with the fishermen seized in late May, or even sinking them when the seizure was made, as fishermen in Nhat Le (near Dong Hoi) said had been done in June 1964 (though there is some doubt as to whether they were remembering the date accurately),[76] the Americans decided that fishing boats should be left drifting, with booby traps aboard, in the areas where the seizures had been made.[77]

As the tempo of the maritime operations increased, so did the need for intelligence information about the area of the operations. U-2 aircraft photographed North Vietnam regularly from very high altitude. The U-2s operated from Bien Hoa Air Base, a few miles from Saigon, often flying back and forth between there and a base in the Philippines. The simultaneous presence at Bien Hoa of two U-2s in early July 1964[78] suggests that flights over North Vietnam were probably quite frequent. U-2 photography was the main source of target intelligence for OPLAN 34A raids during the first half of 1964. On the mornings after 34A raids, a U-2 flying from the Philippines to Bien Hoa would photograph the targets, and the pictures would be at SOG headquarters in Saigon around noon.[79] At some point during the year (the exact date was probably in August, just after the Tonkin Gulf incidents), a program of aerial photography by unmanned drones operating at much lower altitudes was added. The possibility of having U.S. aircraft do nighttime radarscope photography of the Gulf of Tonkin was also under discussion by June 1964.[80]

Thoughts of Escalation

Proposals for Overt Attacks on the North

Robert McNamara, just back from a trip to South Vietnam in March 1964, described OPLAN 34A as "a program so limited that it is unlikely to have any significant effect."[1] More recently, he said that the raids "were so unimportant, they were pinpricks, they were accomplishing *nothing*."[2] William Bundy similarly called the raids "pinpricks . . . pretty small potatoes."[3]

As long as the United States limited itself to clandestine, pinprick raids against North Vietnam, there would be little risk but also little gain beyond the fact that senior officials would be able to say (to one another and to themselves) that they were doing *something*. When the JCS asked CINCPAC—Admiral Felt—to evaluate the OPLAN 34A raids against the North, he replied that these raids had not accomplished much and were not likely to, and that aerial bombing and mining would be much more effective ways to attack the North.[4] Henry Cabot Lodge, U.S. ambassador in Saigon, grumbled that OPLAN 34A did not even bother the North Vietnamese enough to make them protest very loudly. He wanted at least "to make them scream. Could rocket carrying planes, flying along the North Vietnam–Laos border, let something go on the pretext that they had been fired on and were firing back?"[5] In fact Ambassador Lodge, and others both in Washington and in Saigon, wanted to go much farther than this. U.S. officials had occasionally mentioned the possibility of major military pressures against North Vietnam as early as 1961, but it was in early 1964 that this possibility began to receive serious and widespread consideration. On February 20, President Johnson ordered: "Contingency planning for pressures against North Vietnam should be speeded up. Particular attention should be given to shaping such pressures so as to produce the maximum credible deterrent effect on Hanoi."[6] Contingency planning for bombing the North occurred more or less continuously for the next year.

Some of the plans called for having the RVN Air Force do the bombing, or having U.S. pilots do it "under Vietnamese cover," pretending that the RVN Air Force had done it. The latter possibility reflected a system that had already been in use within South Vietnam for about two years under the code name "Farmgate." When Farmgate aircraft with U.S. military pilots bombed guerrilla forces in South Vietnam, the rule was that there must always be a Vietnamese aboard every plane. This allowed the United States to pretend that the missions were South Vietnamese, with the Americans just going along for training purposes. Many senior officials felt that if North Vietnam had to be bombed, the job should be handled (at least at first) either by the South Vietnamese Air Force or by Farmgate aircraft, rather than by the regular squadrons of the U.S. Air Force and Navy. Until early 1964 Farmgate had been using relatively old propeller-driven planes not too different from those flown by the genuine Vietamese pilots of the South Vietnamese Air Force, but the Joint Chiefs of Staff were recommending that B-57 jet bombers be added to the Farmgate force.[7]

It is doubtful, however, that the Joint Chiefs had much faith in such half-measures. On March 2, they told McNamara that "US intentions and resolve to extend the war as necessary should be made clear immediately by overt military actions against the DRV."[8] William Sullivan, the Secretary of State's Special Assistant for Vietnamese Affairs, attended a meeting of the Joint Chiefs, along with Secretary McNamara, at some date probably in the first half of March. Afterward he told Michael Forrestal of the National Security Council Staff "that he was impressed by the vehemence of opinion in the JCS for strong overt U.S. action against the North."[9] Sullivan remembered Chief of Naval Operations David McDonald as having been particularly outspoken, but Air Force Chief of Staff Curtis LeMay probably felt at least as strongly about the matter.[10]

Toward the middle of March, Secretary McNamara and General Taylor went to Saigon to confer with Ambassador Lodge and others there. McNamara later recalled:

The risk of Chinese escalation and the possibility that air attacks would neither break the will nor decisively reduce the ability of the North Vietnamese to continue supporting the insurgency in the South were recognized. But, because no better alternative appeared to exist, the majority of the group meeting in Saigon favored such attacks! This was the sort of desperate energy that would drive much of our Vietnam policy in the years ahead. Data and analysis showed that air attacks would not work, but there was such determination to do something, anything, to stop the Communists that discouraging reports were often ignored.[11]

McNamara was more cautious than the Joint Chiefs and the people with whom he had conferred in Saigon, but not much more cautious. The report he presented March 16 on his return to Washington advised against immediate bombing of the North, but proposed that the United States immediately begin preparatory work, to be able to begin such bombing if necessary.[12] The president and the National Security Council discussed McNamara's report March 17 and approved the recommendations in it as National Security Action Memorandum 288. The Joint Chiefs of Staff immediately directed CINCPAC to draw up a more detailed contingency plan; the result was CINCPAC Operations Plan 37-64, approved in April. Like NSAM 288, it covered possible U.S. actions in Laos, Cambodia, and South Vietnam as well as in North Vietnam. Still more detailed planning followed the initial approval of OPLAN 37-64, with analysis of various targets in North Vietnam, and the type of attack and scale of attack that would be needed to inflict specified degrees of damage on particular targets. The result eventually became known as the "94 Target List," though the number of targets had not quite reached ninety-four when the Joint Chiefs approved preliminary drafts of this list on May 27 and May 30.[13]

Some of the attacks on North Vietnam contemplated under OPLAN 37-64 could be carried out by the genuinely Vietnamese units of the VNAF; the largest would require the Farmgate force already in South Vietnam, augmented by some B-57 bombers. There were few illusions about the ability of such limited operations to achieve the plan's ostensible goal of ending North Vietnamese support for the guerrillas in South Vietnam. On the contrary, it was made clear that the United States, before initiating OPLAN 37-64, would have to move to Southeast Asia not just the modest forces necessary to carry out the plan but also the much larger forces that would be needed if the enemy reacted to OPLAN 37-64 by escalation. This was realistic; the bombing contemplated in this plan was far weaker than that actually conducted between 1965 and 1967. Even the initiation of that much heavier bombing was followed not by any decline in infiltration, but by a massive increase.

At about the time OPLAN 37-64 was being written, the Defense Department was also drawing up scenarios for the implementation of NSAM 288, which Secretary McNamara sent to the Joint Chiefs on April 23. The outline was the same as in OPLAN 37-64: very small forces would be used to make covert attacks on the North, but much larger forces would be held available in case the DRV or China responded to the covert attacks with some major escalation. The Joint Chiefs pointed out, correctly, that the details of the scenario did not match this broad outline. The section of the scenario describing what might actually be done with the larger forces quite clearly described not any response to enemy escalation, but simply an effort to achieve the original goals of the covert attacks, using large forces operating overtly. The Joint Chiefs recommended that the fig leaf be removed, and that the plan openly acknowledge that the reason the large forces were being gathered was to carry out large attacks on the North, if the small covert attacks proved futile.[14] The true thinking behind CINCPAC's OPLAN 37-64 presumably followed the same logic.

Another difficulty with NSAM 288 and OPLAN 37-64 was that they called for preparations to be made for the VNAF to conduct airstrikes against North Vietnam. No practical preparations could be made, however, without involving the VNAF, and it would be more than four months before the Johnson administration was willing to tell the Saigon government about the U.S. plans for attacks on the North.

A plan for escalation of the war leaked to the press in late February or early March. It called first for a blockade of Haiphong harbor, then raids against the North Vietnamese coast, and finally for bombing of strategic targets in North Vietnam, carried out by U.S. pilots under either the American or the South Vietnamese flag. *Newsweek* called this the "Rostow Plan," but Walt Rostow, chairman of the State Department's Policy Planning Council, probably had not had much to do with it. Rostow had begun talking about direct attacks against North Vietnam all the way back in 1961, when he worked in the White House. Some U.S. officials began calling the idea of attacking the North the Rostow plan. By the time this phrase spread to the American press and finally even to Hanoi, however, Rostow's move to the State Department had removed him from involvement in detailed planning for Vietnam.[15]

It is not surprising that there were charges from Hanoi that the United States had decided on a coherent plan of escalation and was carrying out that plan. In a statement issued probably before the end of March, the high command of the People's Army of Vietnam (PAVN, the North Vietnamese army) described the OPLAN 34A raids as being intended to prepare the way for the attacks on a much larger scale called for by the Rostow plan. According to this statement, "spy commandos" were being sent north to learn more about the situation there, military, political, and economic; to learn more about the attitude of the Communist Party, the government, and the people of North Vietnam toward the liberation of the South; to carry out acts of sabotage; and to encourage counterrevolutionaries in North Vietnam.[16]

This was a logical reading of American behavior, but it was not correct. OPLAN 34A was not intended to clear the way for a more important program that the Americans had decided to carry out; it was something done simply because the Americans felt they had to do something, while President Johnson and his advisors tried to decide whether to carry out more important programs.

In May, the Johnson administration began thinking in serious and immediate terms about the possibility of hitting North Vietnam. This new attitude was prompted not only by the gradual evolution of the situation in South Vietnam, but also by sudden gains that Communist forces had made in central Laos. The National Security Council Executive Committee discussed the issue on May 24.

Secretary McNamara said . . . We must concentrate on the most crucial points and acknowledge that the measures to support South Vietnam are restricted. They will not substitute for the use of force against North Vietnam. We do not have a solution and these proposals will not save us. . . .

Secretary McNamara said that where our proposals are being carried out now, the situation is still going to hell. We are continuing to lose. Nothing we are now doing will win. . . .

Secretary McNamara said the probability is that further weakening will occur in South Vietnam. The question is whether we should hit North Vietnam now or whether we can wait. South Vietnam is weaker now than it was in January, but we can ride through for a few additional weeks, even with further weakening.[17]

None of the others at the meeting endorsed McNamara's view of the extent of the emergency, but none argued forcefully against it either. General Taylor said it was too soon to conclude that the relatively new government of Nguyen Khanh would be unable to cope with its problems. Dean Rusk seemed to believe, for reasons he did not specify, that the situation in South Vietnam must really be better than all the reports said it was. Nobody at the meeting seemed clearly opposed to the idea of attacks on North Vietnam, though Taylor "said the military would prefer to wait until fall before military action was taken."[18] The meeting apparently was continued on May 25. It ended by recommending that the president reach a firm decision that the United States would attack North Vietnam at some unspecified point in the future unless the military situation in South Vietnam and Laos improved enough, in the interim, "to make military action against North Vietnam unnecessary." It was hoped that American preparations for these attacks would constitute the final threat that would persuade Hanoi to rein in the Communist forces in South Vietnam and Laos, and thus avoid being attacked by the United States.[19]

On May 23, a Draft Presidential Memorandum had been completed laying out a thirty-day schedule for initiating open military action.[20] On D−30 (thirty days before D-Day, the day open bombing of North Vietnam was to begin), President Johnson would make a speech in general terms, asking the Senate and House of Representatives to pass a joint resolution approving past actions and authorizing the administration to do whatever was necessary in the future. This resolution would be passed about D−20. From there, crucial items on the schedule included:

(D−15) Get [RVN Premier] Khanh's agreement to start overt South Vietnamese air attacks against targets in the North . . . and inform him of U.S. guarantee to protect South Vietnam in the event of North Vietnamese and/or Chinese retaliation. . . .

(D—3) President informs U.S. public (and thereby North Vietnam) that action may come. . . .

(D—1) Khanh announces that all efforts have failed and that attacks are imminent. (Again he refers to limited goal and possibly to "carrot"). . . .

(D-Day) Launch first strikes. . . . Initially, these strikes would be by South Vietnamese aircraft; they could then be expanded by adding FARMGATE, or U.S. aircraft, or any combination of them.

(D-Day) Call for conference on Vietnam (and go to UN). State the limited objective: Not to overthrow the North Vietnam regime nor to destroy the country, but to stop DRV-directed Viet Cong terrorism and resistance to pacification efforts in the South.[21]

Symptomatic of the U.S. attitude toward the Saigon government at this time was the fact that Premier Khanh was not to be asked to consent to this plan until the thirty-day countdown was half-over.

The U.S. Congress was to pass, by D—20, a resolution "authorizing whatever is necessary with respect to Vietnam." The U.S. public was not to be informed until D—3 "that action may come." In context, it is plain that the Congress was not to be told, when the resolution was presented, that the executive branch intended to use it almost immediately as authority for overt attacks on North Vietnam. Since the question would certainly be asked, the apparent implication was that the Congress would be told, falsely, that attacks on the North were not planned for the near future. This is relevant, since such a resolution was in fact presented to the Congress with just such assurances in August 1964, and then used to provide a legal foundation for bombing of the North starting in 1965. There were, however, people in the administration who realized that to give such assurances and then reveal them less than a month later to have been false would not be wise. The day after the schedule quoted above was drawn up, a revised version was drafted in the Defense Department, in which the president was to explain his plans "probably in specific terms" to at least the key leaders of Congress before the passage of the resolution; this would have precluded any serious deception of the Congress as a whole.[22]

Abram Chayes, legal advisor in the State Department, produced a preliminary draft of the resolution in May, which was then worked over by others at State, Defense, and the White House. Only a few phrases of the draft of May 25 match those in the version actually presented to Congress in August.[23] The May draft was longer and went into more detail about what the Congress was authorizing the president to do, though not so much detail as to mention explicitly the idea of attacks on North Vietnam. A revised version dated June 11 was shorter than the May 25 draft, and closer to the version actually presented to the Congress in August.[24]

A Special National Intelligence Estimate of May 25, representing the consensus of the intelligence community, said that the Communist leaders might
respond to the proposed bombing campaign with temporary restraint of the
insurgencies in South Vietnam and Laos, while intending to resume the insurgencies at a later date. But the SNIE made no promises; it said that even if the
United States went to large-scale overt bombing, threatening the leaders of the
DRV with "destruction of their country," those leaders would not necessarily
pull back even temporarily. "There would . . . be a significant danger that they
would fight."[25]

The people who actually drew up the scenarios for attacks on the North were
even more pessimistic than the intelligence community. Like the authors of
OPLAN 34A and OPLAN 37-64, they did not predict that their proposed operations would result in even temporary restraint from Hanoi. Both the thirty-day
scenario dated May 23 (quoted above) and the revised version dated May 24
indicated that the air attacks on North Vietnam being proposed were more
likely to lead to an intensification of Communist military pressure in South
Vietnam and Laos than to any reduction of that pressure.[26]

Fear of retaliation was one of the main restraints on overt U.S. action against
the DRV in this period. General Westmoreland later said the reason he did not
favor any action against the North going beyond minor covert operations was
that he considered the most likely result of serious attacks on the North would
be the direct intrusion of the North Vietnamese army in the fighting in South
Vietnam. Direct involvement of the North Vietnamese army would increase the
total strength of the Communist forces in the South to a level with which the
Saigon government would be utterly unable to cope.[27]

Four of the five members of the Joint Chiefs of Staff (General Taylor was the
dissenter) believed that the United States should attack North Vietnam in a
much more destructive fashion than that contemplated in the Draft Memorandum that had been presented at the May 24–25 NSC meetings. In a paper dated
June 2, the majority of the Joint Chiefs in fact considered the goal for U.S. action
contemplated by many policymakers—inflicting enough pain on North Vietnam to "cause the North Vietnamese to decide to terminate their subversive
support of activity in Laos and South Vietnam"—and rejected it as "inadequate."
The damage inflicted should be great enough not merely to halt DRV support of
the Viet Cong and Pathet Lao, but to ensure that such support would not be
resumed at some later date.[28]

On June 2, 1964, at a conference in Honolulu, major American policymakers
decided not to recommend the sort of escalation contemplated in the Draft
Presidential Memorandum. Before this decision, however, they had come close,
"very close indeed" according to William Bundy, to recommending to President
Johnson that overt bombing raids be begun against North Vietnam.[29] The
reason, again, was worry about the results if such raids were answered by Com-

munist escalation—increased action by the Viet Cong guerrillas already in South Vietnam, intervention by North Vietnamese forces in South Vietnam, or even intervention by Chinese forces. There was no clear agreement on how likely such Communist escalation was, and very strong disagreement on how danger-ous it would be. General Taylor believed that if the Chinese intervened on a large scale, a force of five to seven divisions, partly American but also including troops from some allied nations, should be able to deal with the problem. Admiral Harry Felt, who as CINCPAC was in a sense the host of the conference, believed that the only possible counter to a major Communist escalation would be the use of nuclear weapons; the number of ground troops that would be required to handle such a problem without using nuclear weapons was so large as to be completely out of reach. The section of the record describing his views does not even specify that it would be *Chinese* intervention that would necessitate the use of nuclear weapons, and it appears very possible that he was saying even a fight against the PAVN would have to go nuclear. As to the question of possible escalation by the Viet Cong, General Westmoreland did not believe that they had the capability to do significantly more than they already were doing, while Ambassador Lodge believed that they "could make Saigon uninhabitable."[30]

General Taylor said at this meeting that the government should not reason itself into inaction; he seems to have felt that doing *something* was inherently desirable. Ambassador Lodge and General Westmoreland pushed the same atti-tude considerably farther. They said "that the situation in South Vietnam would 'jog along' at the current stalemated pace unless some dramatic 'victory' could be introduced to put new steel and confidence into Vietnamese leadership. General Westmoreland defined 'victory' as a determination to take some new vigorous military commitment, such as air strikes against Viet Cong installa-tions in the Laos corridor. Ambassador Lodge defined 'victory' as a willingness to make punitive air strikes against North Vietnam."[31] In other words, U.S. airstrikes in Laos or North Vietnam would constitute, in and of themselves, a "victory"; they did not have to lead to any reduction in the flow of men and weapons into South Vietnam in order to be considered to represent a "victory."

Senior officials had decided at the beginning of June not to recommend a quick initiation of airstrikes against North Vietnam. They continued for an-other week or so to consider the possibility of presenting quickly to Congress the resolution authorizing the president to take such military action as he felt necessary. They did not wish to bring such a resolution before Congress unless it could be passed quickly, overwhelmingly, and without too much discussion of its implications. In the absence of any sudden crisis, such an outcome would be hard to guarantee—hard even to hope for if Congress were seriously distracted. The chances would be best if the administration caught the Congress after the end of debate over the landmark Civil Rights Act of 1964, but before the distrac-tion of the Republican and Democratic Parties' national conventions. A meeting of senior officials on June 10 made what seems to have been a fairly firm decision not to plan on trying to obtain passage of such a resolution within the next few weeks (though William Bundy was still trying to revive the idea two days later).

Robert McNamara later described this decision as if it had simply been a matter of putting off the resolution to a little later in the year, probably September.[32] This is supported by suggestions that the administration was actually feeling out key senators in June and July, trying to build a base of support for the passage of such a resolution,[33] but this author doubts that the administration would have been willing to risk the questions that would have been asked if the resolution had been presented to the Congress "cold," as a response to the overall situation in Vietnam. McNamara reflected the consensus of the top officials, however, when he suggested at the June 10 meeting "that in the event of a dramatic event in Southeast Asia we would go promptly for a Congressional resolution."[34] The "dramatic event" occurred early in August.

The Defense Budget

Before he became president Lyndon Johnson had not given much attention to Vietnam, or to foreign affairs in general. He had made extravagant statements about how vital it was to defend South Vietnam against Communist aggression, because that was what an American politician was supposed to say. As president, however, he found himself thinking through the implications. He told Bill Moyers in November 1963: "We'll stand by our word, but I have misgivings. I feel like a fish that just grabbed a worm with a big hook in the middle of it." In late August 1964, just before making his formal acceptance of the Democratic nomination for president, he told George Reedy, "Whichever way Vietnam turns out, it is going to be my destruction."[35]

Aside from being pessimistic about the way the Vietnam War might go, Johnson hated it simply because it would force him to spend more on the military than he wanted to. One of the first things he had done as president had been to make deep cuts in the military budget, to allow first for a tax cut and then for the package of domestic programs he called the "Great Society." Different sources use slightly different definitions of what constituted "national defense" spending and thus give slightly different figures, but they all show a substantial drop in defense spending early in Johnson's presidency.

Under John Kennedy, defense spending had been rising consistently. In November 1963, when Kennedy was assassinated, fiscal year 1964 (July 1963 through June 1964) was not quite half over. Kennedy's budget for FY 1964 had called as usual for a substantial rise in defense spending—about $2.6 billion above the FY 1963 level. Actual spending as long as Kennedy lived had followed that projection pretty closely. When Johnson became president he immediately

Table 1. U.S. National Defense Spending, by Fiscal Years (current dollars)

	Contemporary Figures	Retrospective Figures
FY 1961 actual	$47.5 billion	$47.4 billion
FY 1962 actual	$51.1 billion	$51.1 billion
FY 1963 Kennedy budget projection	$52.7 billion	
FY 1963 actual	$52.8 billion	$52.3 billion
FY 1964 Kennedy budget projection	$55.4 billion	
FY 1964 actual	$54.2 billion	$53.6 billion
FY 1965 Johnson budget projection	$54.0 billion	
FY 1965 actual	$50.2 billion	$49.6 billion

Note: Contemporary figures are from the annual budget messages of the presidents to the Congress, in *Public Papers of the Presidents.* The same figures (both projected and actual) appeared in contemporary editions of *Statistical Abstract of the United States.* The projections were made about six months before the beginning of each fiscal year. Retrospective figures are from the 1970 edition of *Statistical Abstract of the United States.* The difference represents retroactive changes in how the category "defense spending" was defined; it is not a matter of adjustment for inflation.

began looking for things to cut, and he managed to cut more than a billion dollars from defense spending for what remained of FY 1964.[36]

Only two months after he became president, Johnson had to send to the Congress his budget for fiscal year 1965 (July 1964 through June 1965). This had not given him much time to look for things he could cut, and the defense budget he sent was only $1.4 billion below Kennedy's for FY 1964. During the following months, however, Johnson continued carving away, and the amount he actually spent on defense in FY 1965 was $3.8 billion below the amount in his budget message to Congress; it was $5.2 billion, or 9 percent, less than Kennedy's defense budget for FY 1964. In actual purchasing power—discounting for inflation—Johnson's FY 1965 defense expenditures were about 11 percent below Kennedy's FY 1964 defense budget. The cuts fell primarily on procurement—purchase of weapons and equipment—and secondarily on research and development.[37]

There is a sense of unreality about these figures. The Johnson administration was thinking very seriously even before the beginning of fiscal year 1965 about the possibility of escalating the Vietnam War, and during the third quarter of the fiscal year President Johnson began the systematic bombing of North Vietnam (Rolling Thunder), and sent U.S. Marine combat units ashore at Danang. For this to have been a year of massive cuts in defense spending seems odd to say the least.

Just as surprising was President Johnson's ability to handle this quietly, without the kind of debate that would get the story into all the histories of the period. Little has ever been said in print about the deep cuts in the defense budget for fiscal year 1965. Maxwell Taylor, for example, Chairman of the Joint Chiefs at the time the FY 1965 budget was being written, has several comments on the budget process in the chapter of his memoirs covering this period; he does not mention that the outcome of the process, that year, was a sharp reduction in the military budget.[38]

Even after escalating the war in 1965, Johnson was tenacious in his efforts to keep the federal budget focused on domestic rather than military spending, and he was far more successful in this effort than most people now remember. He was spending a lot on Vietnam, but he was spending less than Kennedy had on military forces elsewhere in the world; this held down the net increase in military spending. Kennedy had always allocated over 46 percent of the federal budget to defense. Johnson managed to ram this figure down to less than 42 percent in fiscal year 1965. The war then forced it back up, which is what led to Johnson's famous wartime budget deficit, but the highest it went was 45 percent in fiscal year 1968—still less than the lowest level attained under Kennedy.[39]

By late 1964 and early 1965, all of President Johnson's senior advisors except for Undersecretary of State George Ball would be pushing for drastic action in Vietnam. Joseph Califano, Special Assistant to Secretary of Defense McNamara, recalls that by about the end of 1964, "We were poised to increase military activities there and bomb North Vietnam. But Johnson just kept asking more and more questions. In the eyes of the Pentagon he was a querulous wallflower, disappointingly reluctant to join the war dance in Southeast Asia."[40] The priorities revealed by President Johnson's budgets show why he was so reluctant.

The Cost of a Real War

When U.S. policymakers talked about bombing the North, they seldom said how big a war they thought they were risking. They did not, as a group, discuss the subject enough to reach a real consensus. Many comments suggest they were assuming that rather modest U.S. forces would be able to handle anything the enemy could put up.

With hindsight, we can observe what the demands on U.S. forces actually became. Early in 1968, the United States was fighting in South Vietnam against the Viet Cong plus a portion of the PAVN; other elements of the PAVN remained in North Vietnam and Laos. The U.S. commander in South Vietnam, who had at his disposal nine U.S. divisions, several brigades and other U.S. combat units not part of these divisions, two strong South Korean divisions, and some other troops contributed by American allies, was finding the going very heavy; he told his superiors that he "desperately" needed reinforcements.[41]

Few Americans, however, dreamed in 1964 and 1965 that the enemy could be powerful enough for such a force to be needed. OPLAN 32-59, a basis for U.S. contingency planning in the early 1960s, had assumed that six U.S. divisions could handle the whole North Vietnamese Army.[42] McNamara had said in 1961 that he and the Joint Chiefs of Staff believed that even if the worst happened—if not only the DRV but also China became openly involved in the war—the United States would not need to put more than six divisions on the ground in Southeast Asia, not counting troops furnished by U.S. allies.[43] Maxwell Taylor's estimate in June 1964 was even more optimistic; he suggested that if the Chinese sent in major ground forces, then to handle the situation the United States would need only five to seven divisions *including* any troops furnished by allied nations.

Americans outside the top levels of government were for the most part even more optimistic than their leaders. When U.S. troops began landing in Vietnam in 1965, junior officers not in the initial force worried that the war would be won and ended before they got their chance at combat. A Gallup Poll taken in the autumn of 1965 asked Americans how they believed the war would end. The percentage of the public who said they believed the war would end with "Communist victory" or "We will pull out" was zero.[44]

As the ARVN slid toward defeat in 1964, the choice that senior U.S. policy-makers faced was between (1) doing nothing, allowing the Communists to win, and then facing the wrath of a public most of whom would believe that a fairly small U.S. force could have saved South Vietnam without much trouble; or (2) escalating, being careful not to provoke China, and hoping that a war fought only against Vietnamese enemies could be won at a not-too-unreasonable cost. When they managed to forget for a moment the possibility that American escalation might be matched by the other side, the cost could seem very low indeed. Thus McGeorge Bundy proposed at the end of August that the United States consider the "grim" possibility of using ground troops in Vietnam "before we let this country go," and added "I do not at all think that it is a repetition of Korea. It seems to me at least possible that a couple of brigade-size units put in to do specific jobs about six weeks from now might be good medicine everywhere."[45]

Given the political temper of the American people, and the awareness that the United States was by a wide margin the strongest nation the world had ever seen (according to U.S. government figures, the gross national product of the United States was more than four hundred times that of North Vietnam), it is not surprising that doing something looked more attractive than doing nothing.

Instead of a Real War: The Psychology of Escalation

American leaders did sometimes discuss the question of what forces they would need if the conflict grew into a full-scale war. This was, however, a remote contingency. They did not actually prepare for a major war because they never intended to get into one.

Early in 1965, one of America's leading strategic thinkers, Herman Kahn, published a book entitled *On Escalation*. PAVN Colonel Bui Tin saw a copy of Kahn's book not long after it was published. He says that when he started reading it, he quickly decided that Kahn's ideas were in fact the ideas that had been shaping American policy.[46]

Colonel Bui Tin was correct. This is not to say that American policymakers were reading Kahn and borrowing ideas from him. But Kahn did not claim that he was inventing new ideas. What he said, rather, was that he was formalizing, systematizing, and analyzing ideas that were already widespread inside the U. S. government, and already being used to shape policy. This was certainly the case for U.S. policy toward Vietnam during 1964.

Kahn was writing about the ways a nation can handle a conflict with another nation when the issue at stake is not of fundamental importance—not worth a full-scale war. His analysis is phrased in terms of a ladder of escalation—a series of levels of hostilities, from minor threats to all-out war. In any particular crisis—any particular conflict over some rather minor issue—each side knows that it would be better off conceding defeat than climbing the ladder all the way to the top. It is also confident, however, that the other side would also rather concede defeat than climb all the way to the top, so it will be tempted to climb a few rungs in the hope that the other side will chicken out. The danger is that both sides will keep climbing, reacting to one another's moves with counter-moves of their own, until the hostilities escalate to a level disastrous for both sides.

Each side knows that its chances of getting the other to concede will be much improved if it can deprive the other side of hope. Each may be tempted to make public statements describing the stakes in the crisis as being much more impor-tant than they really are, and committing its prestige. The hope is that by deliberately setting up a situation in which it could not back down without humiliation, it can ensure that the other side will give up hope of inducing it to back down. The other side, left to choose between fighting a real war and conceding defeat over an issue that is not really very important, will probably be rational and back down.

This model is a splendidly accurate description of American policy in Viet-nam. South Vietnam was not truly important to the United States. If the war had escalated to the point that it became an all-out conflict between the United States and the major Communist powers, it would probably result in the anni-hilation of both sides. On a somewhat more modest scale, the precedent of Korea seemed obviously relevant. The United States had gone into South Korea in 1950, in order to block an attempted conquest by North Korea. The war quickly spread with a retaliatory attack by the United States against North Korea. This in turn drew in the Chinese, who had not joined the original North

Korean attack on the South, but were willing to fight to defend North Korea. The result was a war much longer and bloodier than the United States had expected or wanted.

If the Vietnam War escalated to the point that the full military forces of the Vietnamese Communists were committed against the United States, even without direct Chinese or Soviet involvement, an American victory would only be attainable at great cost, perhaps more than it was worth. From the viewpoint of the Johnson administration, the *only* scenario that could be considered even remotely acceptable was for the threat of American action to deter Hanoi from ever committing its full forces to the conflict.

The problem was that the logic did not look the same from the other side. While Hanoi was at least as eager as Washington to achieve victory without a major war—a real war between the DRV and the United States obviously being much more dangerous for the DRV than for the United States—South Vietnam was, from the perspective of Hanoi, of absolutely vital significance, a place that really was worth fighting a major war. The Americans, mistakenly believing that Hanoi cared no more about South Vietnam than Washington did, expected that Hanoi would back down in the face of superior force. The leaders of North Vietnam, mistakenly believing that nobody would risk a major war over an area for which it did not have an important use, asked themselves what the Americans were planning to do with South Vietnam. Two of the obvious possibilities were that they were planning to rule it and exploit it economically (which had been the goal of France, the only country with a democratic form of government that had previously waged a serious struggle for control of Vietnam), or that they wanted it as a military base for an attack on the North (an idea the Americans were in fact discussing).

A gun is, in many people's minds, like a magic wand. If you point it at people, they are supposed to do your bidding. The foundation of much of the Johnson administration's policy was an effort to bring to Hanoi's attention, more and more emphatically, the fact that the United States had weapons of overwhelming power aimed at North Vietnam. There was hope at first that mere words could get the message across, that "the strongest possible deterrent to Hanoi's pressing its local advantages in Laos and South Vietnam would surely be a Congressional expression of US steadiness and willingness to go further if need be."[47] Even when the United States passed from threatening large-scale attacks on the North to actually carrying them out, the goal was not to obliterate the DRV, or even really to cripple the DRV, but to persuade the leaders in Hanoi that the weapons arrayed against them were so overwhelming that victory was hopeless, so they would abandon the struggle.

The U.S. government's failure to accept that it might have to back up its words with a serious commitment of American forces is shown by its manpower policies; the total size of the U.S. armed forces declined steadily as a real war grew nearer. The number of Americans in uniform in mid-1964, with a serious war on the horizon, was 122,000 smaller than it had been in mid-1962. By mid-1965, three months after the first overt dispatch of Marine combat units to Vietnam, *the figure had dropped by another 32,000.* This shrinkage in the size of U.S. armed forces was occurring at a time when, thanks to the "baby boom" that began in the late 1940s, the number of men in the prime age group for military service was expanding rapidly.

The number of draftees being inducted into the U.S. armed forces had been at a comparatively high level for peacetime, averaging 14,500 per month, during the period bridging the Kennedy and Johnson presidencies (August 1963 to April 1964). In May 1964 the number dropped to 8,000 and remained at a low peacetime level, averaging 6,400, from May 1964 through March of 1965. In April 1965 the number jumped, but only to a high peacetime level; the average from April to August was 16,400. Only in *September 1965* did the number of draftees inducted go above the highest levels attained in peacetime under Kennedy.[48]

Another crucial aspect of Herman Kahn's escalation model was that it was primarily a model of crisis management. The assumption was that one side would make some minor move, to which the other would react, and then the two sides would keep reacting to one another's moves until the crisis either escalated into war or was settled by a compromise or by one side's backing down. The escalatory moves were discussed almost entirely as reactions to previous escalatory moves.

U.S. policy in Vietnam was indeed very much a matter of short-term moves, reacting to short-term changes in the situation. American policymakers often assumed that their opponents would behave similarly. In fact, Hanoi's policies were shaped much more by long-term goals. During 1964, American actions against North Vietnam were primarily gestures—they were made not in order to accomplish concrete changes in the military situation, but to prove to Hanoi, Saigon, the American public, and the world at large that the United States was not allowing Hanoi's actions to pass without reply. American policymakers tended to assume that when they made a gesture, the response by Hanoi would also be in the realm of gesture; that if the United States did something to which Hanoi needed to reply, the reply would be prompt, conspicuous, and have no lasting effect on the military situation. This assumption would prove very seriously mistaken.

One reason American policymakers assumed that their gestures would be met primarily with gestures from Hanoi was their assumption that Hanoi would recognize American gestures as such. This likewise was mistaken. When the United States sent OPLAN 34A raids against the North Vietnamese coast, and then on August 5 launched airstrikes in retaliation for a supposed attack on U.S.

destroyers, the leaders of the DRV did not ask themselves what signal the Americans were trying to send; they asked what military goals the Americans intended to accomplish.

Public Threats

American officials occasionally made public statements, usually quite vague, suggesting that they might be thinking of taking the war to North Vietnam. In a speech on February 21, President Johnson said that those who directed and supplied "terror and violence" against the people of South Vietnam should "remember that this type of aggression is a deeply dangerous game." His press secretary, Pierre Salinger, explained to reporters afterward that this had been intended as a warning that the United States might have to expand the war to North Vietnam or even to China. When a public furor ensued, the White House backed away from this interpretation of the president's remarks.[49] But then on May 4, William Bundy, in testimony before a House subcommittee, similarly said that the United States was definitely going to "drive the Communists out of South Vietnam," and that if this required "attacking the countries to the north" (the plural implying both North Vietnam and China), "we will have to face that choice." The text was released to the public on June 18.[50]

The top leaders of the Republican Party, including both Richard Nixon and Barry Goldwater (the party's nominees for president in 1960 and 1964, respectively) were less cautious in their statements. On April 16, Nixon strongly urged bombing North Vietnam.[51] On April 18, he told the American Society of Newspaper Editors that the actual liberation of North Vietnam from Communism should be made a goal of the war. Nixon even seemed to be hinting at attacks on China when he said "We cannot have a Yalu River concept in South Vietnam. . . . the rules of the game must be changed." The *Washington Post* interpreted him as meaning only that North Vietnam should not be immune to retaliation, and the parts of his talk suggesting that he thought RVN armed forces could handle the fighting support this interpretation.[52] Nixon was drawing an analogy, however, to the Korean War, in which the United States had made massive attacks on North Korea in retaliation for the North Korean invasion of South Korea. The Yalu River "concept" to which Nixon referred had been the U.S. decision not to spread these attacks beyond North Korea to Chinese territory. For the Vietnamese situation, the Yalu River would appear analogous not to the DMZ dividing North from South Vietnam, but to the border between North Vietnam and China. This interpretation can be supported both by Nixon's statement in this speech that Vietnam was "the right time and the right place to take effective action against Chinese Communist aggression,"[53] and by his statement soon afterward, in an article advocating a more forceful U.S. policy in Vietnam, that the United States had made a mistake in the Korean War by not launching attacks across the Yalu River against enemy sanctuaries in China. Nixon downplayed the risks involved in a confrontation with China over Vietnam, calling China "a fourth-rate military power."[54]

Saigon Calls for Attacks on the North

Proposals for attacks on the North were based not only on a desire to reduce or eliminate northern support for the Viet Cong, but also on hopes that attacks on the North would raise morale in South Vietnam. The March 16 report by Robert McNamara, the recommendations of which the president approved March 17 as NSAM 288, said that if the North were to be bombed, the objective, "while being cast in terms of eliminating North Vietnamese control and direction of the insurgency, would in practical terms be directed toward collapsing the morale and the self-assurance of the Viet Cong cadres now operating in South Vietnam and bolstering the morale of the Khanh regime."[55]

When Secretary McNamara reported back from a trip to Saigon in May 1964, he said that Prime Minister Nguyen Khanh was not urging attacks on the North. "He does not feel that he should strike north before his security situation in the south is improved, possibly by this Fall. No strike to the north is required now, but there may be a psychological requirement to hit North Vietnam at a later time. He feels that because the reaction of the Communists to an attack on North Vietnam is unknown, he must have a U.S. guarantee of protection, i.e., the introduction of U.S. forces, before such an attack is initiated."[56]

If this is in fact the way Khanh was talking in May, he soon changed his mind, and began telling the U.S. that attacks on North Vietnam were crucial to the morale of his government. He pressed first privately and then publicly for what he called *Bac Tien*. This is usually translated "March to the North," but it was sometimes used in ways not actually implying a "march" using ground troops. At some times, Khanh made it clear that he was advocating the total elimination of the Communist government in North Vietnam, but at other times he discussed *Bac Tien* in less ambitious terms.

Khanh told Secretary of State Rusk on May 31 that an extension of the war to North Vietnam would strengthen national unity in the South, would tend to eliminate or postpone internal political quarrels, and would give a morale boost to the Vietnamese people.[57] Khanh told Rusk these attacks should be kept small, so as not to trigger North Vietnamese retaliation in the form of sabotage or even air attacks on Saigon. Rusk gave Khanh what Bundy has described as a "stern lecture" about the risks that widening the war in such a fashion could lead to Chinese involvement or even the danger of nuclear war.[58]

Maxwell Taylor arrived in Saigon on July 7 to replace Lodge as U.S. ambassador. In his first meeting with Khanh after his arrival, Khanh said he wanted attacks on North Vietnam.[59] Taylor soon concluded that what Khanh wanted in the short run was to get the United States committed to "reprisal bombing" of the North, but that this might constitute a first step toward further escalation.[60]

Khanh made his desire for more pressure on the North especially conspicuous as the tenth anniversary of the signing of the Geneva Accords approached. This anniversary was declared a "day of national shame" on the grounds that the Geneva Accords had led to the separation of North from South Vietnam. On July 19, before a huge crowd in Saigon, Premier Khanh carried out a ceremony in which two small containers of earth, representing the soil of North and South Vietnam, were mixed together in a larger container as a symbol that Vietnam was one nation and all the Vietnamese, North and South, were one people.[61] In the speech that followed, he said:

> We have often heard that the people have called for the war to be carried to the North. That is not only a urgent appeal of a million refugees from the North, nourishing their dream of liberating their native land. . . .
>
> This is also the fervent wish of the religious sects, of the Buddhist and Christian communities, who have always thought of the silent church suffering under Communist tyranny.
>
> This still is the enthusiastic demand of the students. . . .
>
> The government cannot remain indifferent before the firm determination of all the people who are considering the push northward as an appropriate means to fulfill our national history.[62]

(Khanh's failure to endorse the American theory that North and South Vietnam were two separate nations might have been a serious embarrassment if the American public had cared about such nuances. Right to the end of the war, the official theory of the government of the Republic of Vietnam was that the two halves of Vietnam should never have been divided, and should one day be reunited.)

Three days later the commander of the air force, General Nguyen Cao Ky, gave a press conference at Bien Hoa Air Base. Ky said that the RVN had recently been airdropping increasing numbers of commandos into North Vietnam. He said that North Vietnam should be bombed, that Hanoi should be destroyed, and that the bombing should also be extended to China. He said his pilots were ready to begin bombing the North immediately; different accounts disagree as to whether he said that the order to begin should indeed be given immediately, or whether he said the timing should be left up to Premier Khanh.[63] MACV believed that Ky in fact wanted such attacks to be carried out immediately.[64]

Rusk asked Taylor to try to restrain Khanh, both because talk about going north distracted attention from the more important task of pacification in the South, and because if the United States did bomb the North, Rusk wanted this to look like an impromptu response to particular acts of Communist aggression, not like the execution of a long-prepared U.S. or South Vietnamese plan.[65]

By the beginning of August, Khanh was moderating his public stance.[66] This helped Secretary of Defense McNamara to get away with giving two Senate committees the impression, on August 6, that Khanh did not feel any strong desire to spread the war to the North.[67]

The real reason for the moderation of Khanh's public stance, however, may have had less to do with American pressure on him than with the fact that the Americans had finally confided to him that they were actually drawing up plans for attacks on the North. Khanh and his government had of course known something about OPLAN 34A, but this was a matter of pinprick raids. They probably heard rumors that the Americans were thinking of something more, but they received no official word until late July.

During the weekend of July 25–26, Khanh met with his cabinet in the town of Dalat. According to a CIA report of the cabinet meeting, "the cabinet members, in particular Prime Minister Khanh, inclined to the view that the Government of Vietnam could never win the war against the Viet Cong as long as North Vietnam remained immune from retaliation."[68] On July 25, Ambassador Taylor reported to the Department of State about Khanh's desire for attacks on the North.[69] The National Security Council directed that Taylor draw Khanh out further on his position and his state of mind:

> If this part of conversation confirms analysis your 213 and 214 that major pressures and frustrations do exist and that it essential to Khanh's position and our relationship with him to go forward, you are authorized to make following points:
>   a. USG has of course made careful study of problems involved in action against DRV and believes it would be useful pursue this subject in more concrete manner in small and select joint group.
>   b. Vital that such discussions be conducted so that they do not leak in any way. Military security alone dictates this, but you should also emphasize to Khanh that leaks can only lead to same problems of clarifying statements and apparent disunity that we have already had in last week, and that these will if anything make it more difficult USG pursue additional courses of action if and when these become necessary. . . .
>   d. . . . you should make these points orally and particularly underscore that USG assuming no commitment to carry out such plans.

FYI: We concur completely that resulting discussions should highlight need for completing preliminary actions, which may take some time to accomplish. You should be prepared to stress particularly such concrete items as the need for additional A1H aircraft and trained pilots, and Khanh himself may suggest importance air defense measures. However, arguments of under-strength ARVN units and need for greater degree of control over VC may encounter response that these aspects are not going to get any better. Hence importance of stress on military essentials for attack itself.[70]

Despite the careful phrasing by which American officials said that they were only discussing contingency plans, and were not committing themselves to final approval for any plan for attacks on the North, it would have been very hard to back down once Khanh had been told about these plans. American policy-makers were deeply worried about the effect on Khanh if they simply rejected the idea of attacks on the North. The effect would have been much worse if they had first dangled the possibility before him, and then taken it away again. Also, Khanh would have been very likely to spill the story to the public in a way politically damaging to the U.S. government.

Ambassador Taylor spoke to Khanh on July 27. He found, as expected, that Khanh very much wanted some sort of attacks on the North. As Rusk had authorized him to do, Taylor told Khanh that the United States was drawing up plans for such attacks and that joint planning between the United States and Khanh's government might begin soon. Khanh said that his morale "had received a lift" from the discussion.[71]

When Ambassador Taylor spoke with Khanh on August 1, Khanh did not seem to be in a big hurry to begin concrete planning for airstrikes against the North.[72] During the following months, however, he says he spent a fair amount of time discussing with the Americans the choice of targets for such airstrikes.[73]

There is no evidence that Hanoi learned quickly what Taylor had said to Khanh on July 27, but given the number of Communist agents in Saigon, the knowledge may have traveled very fast. In particular, Colonel Pham Ngoc Thao might have been told within hours, both because he was a genuinely influential man in crucial sections of the ARVN officer corps, a man whose goodwill Khanh might have wanted to win by keeping him current on his negotiations with Taylor, and because he was Khanh's official press attaché and would have had a need to know why Khanh was moderating his campaign of public pressure for attacks on the North. Colonel Thao was a Communist agent.

Washington was still trying to find some very small escalation that would satisfy Khanh without involving serious risks. The same National Security Council meeting that decided to allow Taylor to discuss with Khanh the possibility of bombing the North directed the Joint Chiefs of Staff to consider military actions to accomplish the following:

a. Contribute directly to the success of the counterinsurgency effort in the Republic of Vietnam (RVN);
b. Reduce the frustration and defeatism of the RVN leaders by undertaking punitive measures against the enemy outside the borders of the RVN;
c. Entail minimum risk of escalatory measures by the enemy; and
d. Require minimum US participation in a combat role.[74]

In response, the Joint Chiefs suggested possible action either in Laos or in North Vietnam. In regard to action against North Vietnam:

> Air missions by unmarked aircraft to mine selected harbors and rivers and to strike prime military targets in DRV could punish the enemy and signal sharply Hanoi and Peking. Non-US air crews would perform these missions. . . .
>
> The actions set forth above are not likely to trigger a communist response escalating the conflict in Southeast Asia beyond present levels; therefore, the Joint Chiefs of Staff do not recommend moving US combat units into or contiguous to the RVN at this time.[75]

As examples of the sorts of attacks that might be made, the Joint Chiefs suggested bombing petroleum storage tanks at Vinh (a key point in the transportation system that moved military supplies from North Vietnam to the Communist forces in Laos and South Vietnam), and mining North Vietnamese navy bases along the coast. They made it plain, however, that the requirements of minimal risk and minimal U.S. combat participation had kept the contemplated operations so small that "these actions would not significantly affect communist support of Viet Cong operations in South Vietnam."[76] It is hard to tell how big a boost to Saigon morale anyone expected to get from such small operations.

The CIA also estimated that the DRV would be unlikely to make any major military response to such bombings, though the CIA estimate listed a number of probable or possible DRV responses "short of major change in the character of the conflict," including perhaps "the more or less covert introduction into South Vietnam of some additional personnel from North Vietnam."[77] William Bundy and Michael Forrestal, however, told the White House on July 31 that bombing of North Vietnam would almost inevitably lead to some form of North Vietnamese retaliation sufficient to require a substantial increase in the number of U.S. military personnel in the area, and that such escalation might perhaps lead to Chinese involvement in the war.[78]

CINCPAC had decided by August 2 that the planning for an expansion of the war would need to be completed by November 1.[79] The date implies that CINCPAC wanted to be ready to carry out such plans promptly after the presidential election, if this turned out to be necessary.

In Saigon, planning for the possibility of attacks on the North proceeded at a moderate pace. Ambassador Taylor got a briefing at MACV, probably on August 1, on the availability of aircraft for missions against North Vietnam, and the availability of Vietnamese qualified either to fly them without assistance or to share the task of flying them with American pilots.[80] The joint planning for airstrikes on North Vietnam, which Taylor had offered Khanh on July 27, seems to have started August 5.[81]

The Laotian Alternative

A few hours after authorizing Ambassador Taylor to discuss the idea of attacks on North Vietnam with Khanh, the State Department (with approval of the Defense Department and the Joint Chiefs) decided to explore another possible means of getting Khanh to stop talking publicly about the subject: "Primarily for reasons of morale in South Viet-Nam and to divert GVN [Government of Vietnam] attention from proposal to strike North Viet-Nam, we are considering proposing to Ambassador Taylor that he discuss with Khanh air attacks on VC supply lines in the Laotian panhandle. . . . Estimate that attacks could begin in early August."[82]

U.S. Ambassador Leonard Unger, in Vientiane, objected strongly to this proposal; he felt it might weaken the already shaky authority of Laotian Prime Minister Souvanna Phouma to a dangerous degree. Communist activities along the Ho Chi Minh Trail, in the southern panhandle of Laos, caused few problems for Souvanna Phouma; they were primarily a problem for South Vietnam. American bombing of the panhandle, on the other hand, might well provoke Communist escalation in central Laos. Souvanna Phouma did not have the resources to cope with such escalation; he would be forced to ask for direct military aid from the United States of a sort that the United States had been, up to that time, reluctant to commit to Laos. Unger believed that the exercise of sufficient pressure on Souvanna Phouma to make him consent to the U.S. proposal might lead to the fall of Souvanna's government. Unger suggested, however, that airstrikes in Laos might be less objectionable if they took the form of "attacks of opportunity on convoys (if related to RECCE flights) and responsive strikes to ground fire."[83]

Ambassador Taylor, in Saigon, found Unger's objections to the original plan convincing, but seized upon Unger's suggestion that airstrikes be justified as responses to ground fire at U.S. reconnaissance flights.[84] Taylor's proposal apparently met a sympathetic reception in Washington. On August 2, MACV proposed an operation to be carried out August 4, in which U.S. aircraft would cut a road in Laos, used for transporting military supplies from North Vietnam to Laos, with a reconnaissance "cover" story. The plan appeared to be a response to suggestions and/or orders from CINCPAC and the Joint Chiefs of Staff,[85] but those suggestions and/or orders were presumably derived from Taylor's proposal. The plan made it clear that the cover story was to be spurious; the targets chosen did not threaten U.S. reconnaissance aircraft.

A few weeks before, there had been a lot of doubt in the Johnson administration about the wisdom of such cover stories. After U.S. aircraft had hit some targets in Laos June 9, the National Security Council had discussed the question of what should be said to the press about the action. The record of the meeting includes the following:

Secretary McNamara said we should say that a U.S. reconnaissance mission was flown in Laos, that it was fired upon, and that the U.S. planes fired back.

Mr. McGeorge Bundy said this statement was not true and strongly cautioned that nothing be said now which later could be used to prove that the U.S. Government had told a lie. He said the U.S. must not risk being exposed as making false statements.[86]

Talking to Different Audiences

The Johnson administration was putting off serious decisions about Vietnam. As William Bundy later described the situation of July 1964,

Those working on policy toward Indochina now accepted it as firm policy that President Johnson would not make any new major decision, or again seriously consider expanding the war, at least until after the election. With the campaign of 1964 just getting under way, many of us saw that there would be a problem of presenting the Administration position so that bombing the North—which we supposed Goldwater would continue to advocate— appeared clearly less attractive than the Administration's approach, "but at the same time not so unattractive that we are tying our hands if we should ever decide we had to do it."[87]

McGeorge Bundy later recalled trying to persuade Johnson not to get carried away, when making campaign speeches extemporaneously, with statements about not getting the United States into a direct combat role in Vietnam: "you didn't want to say something that you'd be sorry about if you did decide to do these things."[88]

In the second half of 1964, the Johnson administration was hoping to convey three conflicting messages to three different audiences.[89] First, it wanted to convince the American public that no war between the United States and the DRV was going to occur; that the crisis in Vietnam could and would be managed without the need for serious attacks on the North. Second, it wanted to convince Hanoi that the United States would attack the North if the tide of battle in the South swung too far to the Communist side. There was hope that such threats could to some extent function as a deterrent. The threat was conveyed in many ways: by OPLAN 34A raids, by public threats, and by private messages carried to Hanoi by Canadian diplomat J. Blair Seaborn, appointed by the Canadian government in 1964 to the International Control Commission created for Vietnam under the Geneva Accords of 1954.[90]

Finally, the Johnson administration wanted to motivate the Saigon government to greater efforts by saying to Saigon what senior American officials often told one another—that the United States was waiting for the tide of battle to shift *against* the Communists in the South, for the position of the anti-Communist forces in the South to become strong enough to provide a firm base from which attacks could be launched against the North. On August 3, for example, Secretary of State Rusk authorized Ambassador Taylor to "reiterate" to Khanh the concern of the United States "that actions against the North be limited for the present to the OPLAN 34A type. We do not believe that SVN is yet in a position to mount larger actions so long as the security situation in the near vicinity of Saigon remains precarious."[91] Khanh had said the same himself in March and again in May, but since then he had grown impatient.

The administration, unfortunately, could not always control who would actually receive which message. The American public was to some extent aware of the threats of escalation aimed at Hanoi. Khanh's government was aware of, and disturbed by, the administration's declarations to the American public that there would be no escalation. Even more serious, however, is the likelihood that Hanoi was aware of what was being said privately both in Washington and in Saigon: that if the Communist forces in the South weakened, the United States would then find the South a more suitable springboard for attacks on the North. This would have given Hanoi a powerful incentive to escalate support for the Communist forces in the South.

It seemed very likely that the administration would have to escalate the war soon after the election; indeed President Johnson had McGeorge Bundy ask Ray Cline, the CIA's Deputy Director for Intelligence, whether the United States could afford to wait that long. Would Vietnam already be irretrievably lost? Cline's evaluation was that it would just barely be possible to put off a major increase in the U.S. effort until after the election; "you're going to have your back to the wall."[92]

President Johnson did not really have an alternative to escalation, but he was able to put it off for a surprising length of time. The war was being lost in slow motion. The situation was bad and was getting worse, and without a major shift in U.S. policy it was going to go on getting worse until the Communists won; but each month it was only a little worse than the month before, so the president's advisors could not tell him that he had to escalate immediately because in another month it would be too late. Many of them said that there was no way the situation could be turned around without a major change in U.S. policy, but this author has seen no indication that any of them understood Vietnam well enough to have been capable of explaining why the current policy could not be made to succeed. So President Johnson was able to tell them, month after month, not just until the election but until early in 1965, to keep trying a little longer.

The Question of PAVN Infiltration

At the end of 1963, the Third Plenum of the Lao Dong Party Central Committee, in Hanoi, decided that the scale of warfare in South Vietnam should be considerably escalated. The Third Plenum also decided upon an increase in the level of North Vietnamese support for the guerrillas in the South, though probably not a direct commitment of PAVN units to the combat in the South.

About seven months later, in July 1964, the government of Nguyen Khanh, in Saigon, began to charge that an overt invasion of South Vietnam by the PAVN had begun. U.S. intelligence officers disagreed. They admitted that the infiltrators from the North had recently begun to include natives of North Vietnam, but they said this was a matter of individuals.[93] Robert McNamara said flatly, "I know of no North Vietnamese military units in South Vietnam," and the United States applied pressure for Khanh's government to retract statements about such units being present.[94]

A CIA report on the interrogation of a prisoner captured in Thua Thien province July 7, who said that he was a native of North Vietnam and had come down the Ho Chi Minh Trail in a group of about 180 such men shortly before his capture, says that there had been other hints that North Vietnamese were being infiltrated into Thua Thien and parceled out among Viet Cong units there, but the capture of this prisoner seems to have represented the first hard evidence of North Vietnamese infiltrators.[95]

U.S. intelligence later concluded that the first PAVN regiment to arrive in South Vietnam did so in December 1964.[96] There appears some possibility that some smaller units had come South as early as July 1964 (the evidence is fragmentary and inconsistent), but even if this was the case, it is not certain that the Khanh government's accusations were based on knowledge of such genuine occurrences. There is one incident that suggests Khanh and his officials may have been talking about the presence of PAVN units in the South simply because they found it politically convenient to do so, without any belief that their statements were true. On July 28, the RVN filed a formal protest to the International Control Commission charging that the 261st and 514th Battalions of the PAVN had recently attacked a place called Cai Be on July 20. Officials at the U.S. Embassy, who were aware that the 261st and 514th were NLF units and had been known as such to both the United States and the RVN since 1962, queried the officer who had written the protest. He said that he was aware that there was "no evidence that these were regular PAVN battalions which had entered SVN as units," but that he had had to call them PAVN battalions because if he had not done so, the ICC would not have taken any action on his protest.[97]

The DRV was substantially escalating its support for the Communist forces fighting in South Vietnam, though not to levels remotely comparable to the level of U.S. support for Saigon. At the same time the DRV was trying, apparently with considerable success, to conceal its actions from the United States. To judge by the documents that have been declassified to date, Washington did not know the extent to which weapons and munitions were being shipped, especially by sea, from the North to the South.

The state of American intelligence was in most respects extremely poor, and there is no evidence that South Vietnamese intelligence was much better. Captain Joseph Drachnik commented: "I believe that intelligence collection is our weakest area in Vietnam. Although hundreds of intelligence officers are in-country, their energies are spent in finding out not more than three-fourths of what their counterparts know. The latter is vague and frequently naive."[98] The fact that Drachnik said he had never seen any evidence that Hanoi was sending weapons into South Vietnam by sea, and said he did not believe that any such shipments were occurring, is striking (if unintended) proof that his criticisms of U.S. and RVN intelligence were justified.

The DRV, China, and the Soviet Union

The Chinese government and press were saying more and more loudly that "the Chinese people will by no means sit idly by while the United States extends its war of aggression in Viet Nam and Indochina." A government statement July 19 said, "Despite the fact that the US has introduced tens of thousands of its military personnel into Southern Viet Nam and Laos, China has not sent a single soldier to Indo-China. However, there is a limit to everything."[99] In private, the Chinese were more specific; Colonel Bui Tin, interviewed in 1989, recalled that the Chinese had promised that in the event of U.S. air attack on the DRV, the Chinese air force would intervene to defend the DRV.[100] China, however, was providing very little concrete military aid—the CIA later estimated Chinese military aid for the year 1964 had been only the equivalent of about U.S. $10 million, and said there had been no known economic aid.[101] This was partly due to China's economic problems in the aftermath of the Great Leap Forward, and partly because China thought the war in South Vietnam should continue to be as it had been— a guerrilla war in which the guerrillas did not operate in large units or use a lot of heavy weaponry.

The American people were unaware even of China's public statements, but it seems likely that U.S. leaders were paying some attention. Indeed, Washington may have exaggerated the willingness of the Chinese to involve themselves in the Vietnam situation. At some point during 1964, someone in the CIA became worried about the possibility that the Chinese might allow the DRV to use Hainan as a base for long-range missiles. This possibility was taken seriously enough that once a month a U.S. nuclear submarine was sent, at some risk, close to the island of Hainan for visual observation of the site where the missiles supposedly were to be based.[102]

The judgment of the State Department's intelligence bureau was that both the DRV and the People's Republic of China wanted to avoid any provocation likely to cause open U.S. bombing of North Vietnam.[103] The DRV, however, was strengthening its air defenses. A Politburo directive initiated a major effort to increase readiness in both anti-aircraft units and the Navy in March 1964; another Politburo directive in June led to further increases in readiness.[104]

There was one report that the DRV had sent at least a thousand men to the Soviet Union for aviation training starting in 1962; some of these were said to have been trained as pilots for MIG jet fighters. When an unusually large number of Vietnamese left the Soviet Union to return to Vietnam in July 1964, the CIA conjectured that the group might include enough of the aviation trainees to form "a nucleus for a PAVN air force."[105] If there were pilots among those returning to Vietnam, they brought no aircraft with them. In 1962, the Soviet Union had been willing to support the DRV to the extent of offering pilot training, and providing weapons such as torpedo boats and torpedoes for them, but things were very different by 1964. Soviet leader Nikita Khrushchev had, in the words of Hungarian diplomat János Radványi, "abandoned" Vietnam "as a place where the Soviet Union should not waste money and energy."[106] Khrushchev may particularly have been alarmed by the escalatory decisions of the Third Plenum at the end of 1963.

The Soviet Union had not cut off all aid to the DRV, but the level was tiny; a retrospective CIA evaluation written in late 1966 indicated that in 1964 the Soviet Union had provided military aid to the DRV worth about U.S. $15 million, and was not known to have provided any economic aid.[107]

Lieutenant General Song Hao published a remarkable article in the August 1964 issue of the People's Army monthly journal *Tap chi Quan doi nhan dan*. It was the lead article, starting on page one; it must have represented the official line at the time. It was, in essence, an effort to persuade doubtful elements in the army to whip up their courage and prepare for the possibility they might have to fight the United States. Song Hao assured them that they could beat the United States, even though the Americans had nuclear weapons (a fact he mentioned repeatedly). He warned against a variety of errors, including overestimating the Americans and thinking they were too strong to fight; underestimating the extent to which the Americans were plotting against North Vietnam, and thinking that the Americans were a problem only in the South (he said in fact that the Americans wanted to conquer the North and reduce it to a colony); and thinking only of the need to continue peaceful construction in the North, neglecting the need to liberate the South. "The American imperialists and their lackeys are using war to invade and dominate our people; our people must use revolutionary war to oppose the invasion."[108]

It was quite clear from the article that no Soviet assistance could be expected. The Soviets could not be regarded as allies or even as friendly neutrals; the "revisionists" (the standard derogatory code word for the leaders of the Soviet Union in writings of the Chinese and their supporters in the Sino-Soviet dispute) were afraid of the Americans, and were sabotaging the international Communist movement, to such an extent that Song Hao said that "our revolutionary armed forces . . . resolutely struggle to the end against imperialism and modern revisionism."[109] If the DRV were indeed to have to fight the Americans, it would need Soviet aid desperately; the implication of the insults directed against the Soviets in this article is that General Song Hao, and presumably the PAVN high command as a whole, had given up hope of obtaining such aid.

A few weeks before, the Communist Party theoretical journal *Hoc Tap* had denounced the revisionists for taking "such base measures as discontinuing assistance, withdrawing experts, tearing up contracts and agreements, practicing economic blockade."[110]

The relationship may actually have been even more tense than these articles suggest. According to PAVN Col. Bui Tin, two senior PAVN officers who disapproved of the decisions of the Third Plenum had requested political asylum in the Soviet Union at the beginning of 1964. As the year proceeded, security personnel were interrogating and in some cases arresting other senior PAVN officers suspected of being "revisionists."[111]

Polish diplomat Mieczyslaw Maneli was able to observe at close range the hostility between the Vietnamese and Soviets, in Hanoi in 1963 and 1964. Soviet Ambassador Suren A. Tovmasyan[112] "was like a caged tiger. He was helpless because he could not 'teach these goddamned Vietnamese' the way his colleagues in the 1940's and 1950's did in Warsaw, Prague, Budapest, and Sofia." Premier Pham Van Dong habitually ignored Tovmasyan at formal occasions, even if they were seated next to one another for an extended period.[113] Finally the Soviets called Tovmasyan back to Moscow, without naming a replacement for him. This left no Soviet ambassador in Hanoi at the time of the Tonkin Gulf incidents. There were still some Soviet military advisors, but their position cannot have been a comfortable one.

The DeSoto Patrol

The U.S. Navy had been conducting occasional patrols since 1962, under the code name DeSoto, along the coasts of several countries in the western Pacific. Two DeSoto patrols had been in the Gulf of Tonkin, off the coast of North Vietnam—one in December 1962, and one in April 1963.

In January 1964, the JCS ordered a new series of DeSoto patrols in the Gulf of Tonkin. The first of these was carried out by the destroyer *Craig*. The base for the DeSoto patrols was Keelung, on Taiwan; the *Craig* set out from Keelung on February 25. The actual work of the patrol began February 28, when the destroyer had not yet entered the Gulf of Tonkin, but was off the south coast of the Chinese island of Hainan.

Various sources disagree as to whether the *Craig*'s orders allowed the ship to approach within four nautical miles of the North Vietnamese coast, or whether the orders were to stay at least four miles from offshore islands and at least eight miles from the coast. One of the main purposes of the mission, and probably the most important, was to gather information on North Vietnamese coastal defenses that would be useful to the OPLAN 34A raids against that coast.[1]

When DeSoto patrols were first started in this part of the world, among their explicit purposes had been to cause annoyance to the People's Republic of China. By 1964, however, the United States was much less eager for trouble with the Chinese, and while the *Craig* was allowed to come within four miles of North Vietnamese islands, the limit for Chinese islands was set at twelve miles.

The cruise passed without incident. Most published accounts suggest that it accomplished very little because bad weather interfered with visibility. The logic is questionable; while visual observation along the North Vietnamese coast had some utility, the most valuable methods of information gathering on such a patrol were electronic. The *Craig* carried a "communications van," containing radio receivers for monitoring local radio communications and analysts to interpret them (see below), and also an "ECM [Electronic Counter Measures] van" containing more equipment for detecting radar signals than a destroyer would normally have carried, and specialists to operate the equipment and interpret the data it gathered.[2] Bad weather would not have interfered at all with electronic data gathering, and indeed might have helped by giving radar stations along the coast a reason to turn their equipment on.

The problem was that the DRV had enough suspicions of what the *Craig* might be doing that emission control was imposed all along the coast; the personnel in the communications van and the ECM van had a boring and frustrating cruise, with essentially no local signals to intercept and interpret.[3]

On July 3, MACV requested that intelligence be gathered about the DRV coastal defenses in the areas where OPLAN 34A raids were to be carried out in the immediate future. It was apparently in response to this request that on July 10, Admiral Ulysses S. G. Sharp (who had just replaced Admiral Felt as CINCPAC) proposed another DeSoto patrol along the North Vietnamese coast, to start at the end of July. The patrol was assigned to the destroyer *Maddox*.

Commander Herbert Ogier was captain of the *Maddox*, but for this voyage Captain John Herrick, commander of the Seventh Fleet's Destroyer Division 192, was on board in charge of the mission. The destroyer was ordered to go no closer than eight miles from the coast, four miles from offshore islands. (U.S. officials were not sure what territorial waters the DRV claimed, but suspected the claim might be twelve miles. The formal U.S. position was that in the absence of a public declaration by the DRV of a greater figure, the United States was entitled to assume that the DRV claimed only three miles.)

The U.S. attitude toward China was much more cautious; the *Maddox* was instructed not to approach the Chinese mainland closer than fifteen miles, or Chinese islands closer than twelve miles.[4] The destroyer was not, however, to avoid China altogether. On the contrary, after traversing the whole length of the North Vietnamese coast, from the DMZ to the Chinese border, the *Maddox* was go to on a little farther. U.S. officials wanted to know about relations between China and North Vietnam; they hoped that the *Maddox* would be able to observe the degree to which coastal defense personnel on opposite sides of the border were coordinating their reactions to the presence of an American destroyer, and passing information to one another about the destroyer's movements.[5]

It has sometimes been said that the purpose of the patrol was to collect information about seaborne infiltration from North Vietnam to South Vietnam, but this was simply a cover story. As Lieutenant Gerrell Moore (the officer in charge of the comvan—see below) put it, "We had no capability to learn anything significant in that area."[6] Admiral Sharp variously described its purpose as "determining DRV coastal patrol activity" and "to update our overall intelligence picture in case we had to operate against North Vietnam."[7] An officer on his staff explained that recent events, including the stationing of a U.S. aircraft carrier battle group at the mouth of the Gulf of Tonkin, articles in the U.S. news media about the possibility of attacking North Vietnam, and increases in 34A raids, might have caused the DRV to increase coastal patrol activities; planning both for the 34A raids and for possible actions by regular units of the U.S. Navy required "more up to date intelligence."[8]

Some accounts state that there was an uneventful DeSoto patrol off North Vietnam in early or mid-July, just before the July-August patrol of the *Maddox*.[9] This is an error, apparently resulting from confusion about a DeSoto patrol carried out by the destroyer *MacKenzie*, which did occur in July but took place in the Sea of Japan off the coast of the Soviet Union. When the *Maddox* arrived on July 26 at the base from which DeSoto patrols operated, the port of Keelung on Taiwan, it moored against the *MacKenzie* to take aboard the "comvan" that the *MacKenzie* had just offloaded. Officers of the *MacKenzie* helped to brief Captain Herrick and the officers of the *Maddox* on DeSoto patrol procedures. Some people have drawn from these events mistaken impressions that the officers of the *MacKenzie* were briefing those of the *Maddox* not just on the general nature of the work done on a DeSoto patrol but on the particular conditions to be expected off North Vietnam, and that the cruise of the *MacKenzie* had been off North Vietnam.

The Comvan

American efforts to eavesdrop on North Vietnamese communications were carried out mainly from fixed installations on land. In regard to the interception of North Vietnamese naval communications, at least, the most important intercept facility was the Naval Communications Station at San Miguel in the Philippines. A smaller facility had recently been established at Phu Bai, just south of Hue in South Vietnam.[10]

In July 1964, a detachment of C-130 aircraft based in Thailand began "flying communications intercept missions off the North Vietnamese coast."[11] There was also a mobile facility, much less frequently used, known as the "communications van" or "comvan." This could be placed aboard a destroyer to give a limited communications intercept capability to a DeSoto patrol. It was a large steel box—originally a shipping container of some sort—containing radio equipment and rather cramped working space for several men.[12]

The comvan that was loaded onto the *Maddox* in Keelung, after being taken off the *MacKenzie*, was the only comvan in the Pacific area. The people who had operated it aboard the *MacKenzie*, however, did not come with it. Instead an entirely new group was put together under Lieutenant Gerrell Moore, the Assistant Operations Officer of the Naval Security Group Activity, based at Shu Lin Kou Air Station on Taiwan. Some of the fifteen men who worked under Moore on the DeSoto patrol came from the same organization; others came from the Naval Communications Station at San Miguel, and from units at Kamiseya, Japan, and at Kaneohe Bay, Hawaii.[13]

Moore's men operated the comvan in two shifts, working twelve hours on and twelve off. There were three work stations at which North Vietnamese communications were monitored. At any given time, there was one man listening to one radio on the VHF wavelengths that the North Vietnamese used for short-range voice communications, especially between vessels. (At this time, the PTs used for this purpose the Soviet P-609 transceiver, operating on frequencies from 100 to 150 megacycles, with an effective range of only about three miles. The greatly superior P-108 did not become available to them until the following year.)[14] The VHF radio had a tape recorder attached. The men monitoring VHF wavelengths of course knew Vietnamese, but in Moore's opinion they did not seem really fluent.

There were also two men listening to radios on the HF frequencies that the DRV used for communication at longer ranges, in Morse code. The HF radios did not have tape recorders attached. There were two analysts, one of whom would be on duty at any given time to interpret any messages picked up by the three listening stations. The total time necessary to decrypt and translate an intercepted message would depend on its length. A long, complex message might take as long as thirty minutes or even an hour. On the *Maddox*, there were only four men outside Moore's team who were cleared to see the texts of intercepted messages. These were Captain Herrick, Commander Ogier, Herrick's flag lieutenant, and Ogier's executive officer.[15]

It is important not to overestimate the capabilities of the comvan. As Moore commented long afterward, it "had been built on a shoestring budget—primarily using equipment discarded by other operating facilities." Its radio listening gear "was standard radio equipment used on Navy ships all over the world on a day-to-day basis. (The old reliable R-390 radio receiver, in fact, was our primary intercept equipment)."[16]

The overall ability of the comvan to monitor North Vietnamese communications did not exceed or even equal that of the permanent facilities at San Miguel and Phu Bai. The fact that the *Maddox* was closer to North Vietnam might in theory have given the comvan an advantage in intercepting VHF transmissions, but in fact the comvan hardly intercepted any VHF messages. Almost all the messages picked up were on HF wavelengths, for which distance was not an important factor. What mattered was that San Miguel and Phu Bai had far more work stations than the comvan did, so they could monitor far more wavelengths at any given time. Between them, they could expect to intercept most of the North Vietnamese navy's message traffic. The comvan, which at any given time could monitor only three wavelengths—two HF and one VHF—could intercept only a fraction of the traffic.[17]

The only piece of really modern, high-tech equipment in the comvan was the on-line teleprinter used to receive messages from San Miguel. If the listening stations at San Miguel or Phu Bai picked up a North Vietnamese message containing information that might be of concern to Captain Herrick, it would be sent to the *Maddox* very highly encrypted. The teleprinter in the comvan would decrypt it immediately and automatically, and print out a copy that would be shown to Captain Herrick, Commander Ogier, and perhaps the other two officers cleared for such information. There was no such rapid and convenient means by which a message intercepted on board the *Maddox* could be passed up the chain of command. If the comvan intercepted a North Vietnamese message about which a report needed to be sent to San Miguel, it would have to be encrypted by hand and then sent out by the destroyer's regular radio transmitter.[18]

Two of the fifteen men Moore brought aboard the *Maddox* were ECM specialists. They did not work in the comvan, which had no ECM gear; instead they worked alongside the destroyer's regular radarmen, providing a greater sophistication in the analysis of North Vietnamese radar signals picked up by the ship's radar than ordinary radarmen.[19]

There is some question as to whether the *Maddox* also carried electronic equipment designed to "stimulate" coastal defenses, creating the impression of a possible threat. Joseph Goulden quotes the orders for the mission as directing the destroyer to "stimulate Chicom–North Vietnamese electronic reaction."[20] Secretary McNamara, queried about this in 1968, said that the destroyer did indeed have equipment for stimulating coastal radar,[21] but he is said later to have retracted this statement, and it now seems clear that his retraction was accurate. If it had been put aboard, its operators would presumably have been included in the team under Lieutenant Moore. Moore not only denies that any such equipment was aboard the *Maddox*, he says he doubts that any such equipment was available to U.S. forces in the Pacific area as early as 1964.[22] Captain Herrick has also denied that the *Maddox* used any such equipment. It is likely that the orders about stimulation of the coastal defenses referred to things the *Maddox* could do without special equipment. The mere presence of the destroyer would have been likely to stimulate the coastal defenses. When that did not seem to be working on July 31, the destroyer at one point simply turned off its ordinary radar, hoping that this would make the coastal defense forces curious and cause them to turn their own radar on. The tactic did not succeed.

It has often been said that the essential purpose for which the *Maddox* was sent into the Gulf of Tonkin was to carry the comvan there. It is easy to succumb to the mystique of communications intelligence, and assume that because intercepting North Vietnamese communications was by far the most highly classified activity carried out aboard the *Maddox*, this must also have been the most important activity. Gerrell Moore, however, strongly and convincingly denies that this was the case. Moore later served on a real intelligence vessel, the sort that actually was sent on missions to eavesdrop on enemy radio communications. He has a strong sense of the extent to which the capabilities of such a vessel exceeded those that the comvan gave the *Maddox*. He says the main mission of the Naval Security Group detachment put aboard the *Maddox* to operate the comvan was not to gather intelligence for future use by other forces, but simply to give Captain Herrick the intelligence he needed, coming from San Miguel via the on-line teleprinter at least as much as from the intercept capabilities of the comvan itself, to reduce the risks involved in a patrol so close to hostile shores. On a real electronics intelligence vessel, the captain's job is to serve the needs of the intercept operators. The Naval Security Group detachment on the *Maddox*, like those routinely placed aboard U.S. aircraft carriers in the western Pacific, was in the opposite situation; its main function was to serve the needs of the captain and provide warning of possible threats.[23]

Certainly the U.S. government wanted whatever information the comvan would be able to acquire via radio interception, but most of the information the destroyer was expected to gather would be obtained by more prosaic means, such as visual observation and photography of the North Vietnamese coast, the use of ship's radar both to locate coastal radar stations and to obtain photographs of the radar profile of the coast for the benefit of vessels that might have to use radar for navigation off the coast at night in future operations, and measurements of the water temperature at various depths with a bathythermograph.

After August 2, the mission of the patrol was substantially altered; "showing the flag," demonstrating that the U.S. Navy had the ability and the will to patrol in the Gulf of Tonkin, came to take precedence over intelligence-gathering of all sorts.

Commander Robert Laske, an officer of the maritime section of SOG, states that from the viewpoint of his organization the DeSoto patrol was simply a nuisance. It did not seem likely to produce information useful for OPLAN 34A raids, and it was sure to bring the coastal defense forces to a high state of alertness.[24] There may, however, have been some confusion within MACV on this issue. It is possible that senior officers in MACV initiated the suggestion that led to the DeSoto patrol under the mistaken impression that their subordinates would find this useful.

The Immediate Background to the August Incidents

When officers of the *Maddox* had their final briefings on Taiwan July 27, they received the impression that no hostile action was likely in the Gulf of Tonkin.[25] Gerrell Moore recalls getting the impression that it was going to be a "leisure cruise," a good opportunity for Commander Ogier to catch up on the paperwork involved in his impending transfer of command of the *Maddox* to another officer.[26] Senior officers of the Seventh Fleet were aware that the OPLAN 34A operations had raised tension in the area, however. A directive from Admiral Johnson that should have been reflected in the briefings on Taiwan indicated that if North Vietnamese patrol craft, aircraft, or radar installations seemed to be paying particular attention to the destroyer, this should not be passed off as routine, as it might have been during past patrols; it should be treated as "a significant event" justifying a special situation report.[27]

There is disagreement as to the level of tension on the destroyer at the beginning of the patrol. Sonarman 2d Class Patrick Park recalls that personal cameras belonging to the crew were confiscated. Shortly after the ship left Keelung, officers began wearing sidearms, which was very unusual. The officers and chief petty officers became increasingly tense and quiet as the patrol went on. Ronald Stalsberg, who was at that time a Gunner's Mate 2d Class, says that there was a general feeling on the destroyer, going into the gulf on July 31, that the U.S. government was sending in the *Maddox* as a sort of experiment, to see if the North Vietnamese would shoot at it. Stalsberg, however, felt fairly secure.[28] Richard Corsette, at that time an ensign, disagrees with Park and Stalsberg; he says that sidearms were not issued until after August 2, that to his knowledge cameras were never confiscated, and that Stalsberg's recollection of "a general feeling the ship was being used for an experiment" is "hogwash!"[29] Gerrell Moore also firmly rejects Park's account; he says the atmosphere was "very relaxed" up until August 2. He says the wearing of firearms by officers definitely did not become common before August 2, and his recollection is that this did not occur until after the incident of August 4.[30]

The level of tension in the gulf had in fact escalated sharply just before the *Maddox* arrived there. On the night of July 30–31, an OPLAN 34A force made up of PTFs 2, 3, 5, and 6 (not Swift boats, as Joseph Goulden mistakenly says)[31] attacked radar and military installations on the islands of Hon Ngu (a.k.a. Hon Nieu, less than four kilometers from the coast of Nghe An province, near the city of Vinh) and Hon Me (twelve kilometers from the coast of Thanh Hoa province). They used 57-mm recoilless rifles—light infantry cannon, less accurate than their normal armament but firing larger shells. On their way back to base on the morning of July 31, the four boats passed within sight of the *Maddox*, which was just entering the Gulf of Tonkin.

Despite the use of 57-mm guns, which was something new—on the only previous occasion that the PTFs had fired at land targets, providing covering fire for the retreat of a landing party that had run into trouble on shore on the night of June 30–July 1, they had used the 40-mm and 20-mm guns that were normal for their type—the DRV seems at least at first to have assumed (correctly) that the raiders on the night of July 30 were the usual South Vietnamese commandos. To judge by this author's interviews in Hanoi, the DRV did not care and may not have known about the legalistic details, the fact that the U.S. Navy

Map 2. The DeSoto Patrol Begins

had retained formal ownership of the vessels instead of going through the motions of transferring them to South Vietnamese control. But the DRV understood the fundamental nature of the raids: they were carried out by Vietnamese personnel working as instruments of American policy.

It is hard to tell how much detailed information Hanoi was able to obtain, and how quickly, about the raiding force. The DRV had a very extensive intelligence network in South Vietnam, and there are even some indications that defense forces along the coast may have had some advance warning about OPLAN 34A raids.[32] A CIA officer who worked in this general area of South Vietnam in 1964 has commented that the ARVN in Danang was comparatively passive; Communist agents would not have found transmitting radio reports to the North from the immediate vicinity of Danang too dangerous to risk, so there should not have been a serious delay from the time Communist agents in

Danang learned something to the time the information was available in Hanoi.[33] Historian John Prados, on the other hand, says (in regard to South Vietnam in general, not Danang in particular) that the Communist espionage network very seldom sent reports to the North by radio; almost always the greater security that could be attained by using couriers was more important than the speed that could be attained by using radio.[34]

The base at My Khe was comparatively accessible, and it would not have been too hard for Communist agents to get jobs on the base. There were U.S. counter-intelligence specialists in Danang, whose job presumably included checking for the possibility that there were Communist agents in the landing teams. Cathal Flynn knows of no evidence of such Communist infiltration having been found, and he did not get the impression, when operations failed, that this was a result of betrayal. The landing parties were normally told about each operation the day before they set out on it. Sometimes, if an operation were simple enough that little time would be required for planning and preparation, the landing party would not be told until the morning of the operation, and then would be kept in isolation until "launch" time in the evening.

The departure of Swift boats on an operation had not been too conspicuous, but Swift boats had stopped going on operations to the North by late July. The departure of PTFs was very conspicuous—they were larger and noisier than the Swifts, and their propellers made large "rooster tails" in the water behind them. They conspicuously set out from the base at My Khe, however, far more often than they actually went on operations to the North. The question is whether hypothetical Communist agents would have been able to tell which departures were for combat missions and which were not.

The process of loading the boats for a real mission was different enough from the process of loading for a practice exercise that an observer looking down at the base from Monkey Mountain might have been able to tell the difference; an observer actually on the base, watching at close range, would definitely have been able to tell the difference. Cathal Flynn believes, though he is not sure, that fake loadouts were sometimes carried out, designed to give hypothetical ob-servers the impression that the boats were going out on a real mission when this was not the case. If this happened, the fakery did not extend to deception of the landing parties; they would not be told that they were going on a mission unless there really was a mission.[35]

After several Vietnamese who had worked on the base disappeared, Lieuten-ant Knight was told they had been Viet Cong sympathizers.[36] CINCPAC com-mented in April 1964 that the DRV intelligence network had "the capability to observe and report on activities at Danang including arrival and departure of boats and observation of personnel in training. With the large number of VC supporters in the RVN the possibility that RVN personnel assigned to SEAL teams and boat crews may be reporting details of operations to Hanoi cannot be overlooked. In addition deposed officials of the Minh government may have passed information on planned NVN operations to DRV sympathizers."[37]

It is a good assumption that Communist agents knew that PTFs with 57-mm recoilless rifles aboard had left My Khe on July 30, but there is no way to be sure how much else they knew about the operation, or how fast their knowledge was transmitted to the North. Some of the early reports published in Hanoi do not even give correct figures for the number of vessels that had participated in the raids (see below).

It was not intended that the *Maddox* participate directly in the OPLAN 34A raids against the North Vietnamese coast, but Admiral Johnson reported that officers of the Seventh Fleet and of MACV had "discussed in detail" the communications links that could be used to get a message from MACV to the *Maddox* "if 'quick reaction' tie-in with special ops required."[38] This suggests that a contingency plan existed for the *Maddox* to intervene if any of the PTFs got in serious trouble off the North Vietnamese coast.

In the absence of such an unfortunate event, it was preferred that the DeSoto patrol and the 34A raids be kept away from one another. There was a certain amount of worry that the *Maddox* might accidentally come too close to one of the raids.[39] Admiral Johnson tried to get MACV to give him the schedule for the raids against the North Vietnamese coast, to make sure that there was no interference between those raids and the *Maddox*'s operations. He was unable to get such a schedule.[40]

The *Maddox* had authority to deviate from its assigned schedule if information turned out to be available in some particular location, valuable enough to justify remaining there longer than scheduled. Admiral Johnson considered such an opportunity a "remote" possibility; he directed that decisions in this regard be made with an "eye on the clock."[41]

The worries that had been expressed in this regard turned out not to have been groundless; a slip in communications on August 3 put the *Maddox* closer to an OPLAN 34A raid than had been intended. The question then arises of why the men involved chose to schedule the DeSoto patrol and the 34A raids so close to one another that they regarded keeping them from conflict as a difficult matter. In January, when the *Craig*'s DeSoto patrol had been planned, CINCPAC had thought that the best way to avoid interference between 34A and DeSoto was to postpone the DeSoto patrol until a time when no 34A raids were occurring.[42] A different approach, however, was taken when plans were made for the *Maddox*'s DeSoto patrol.

It had been noticed that the North Vietnamese tried to prevent the United States from learning too much about their coastal defenses, by turning their coastal radars off during the *Craig*'s DeSoto patrol. Admiral Sharp (CINCPACFLT) and Admiral Felt (CINCPAC) had proposed in May 1964 that the United States take advantage of this by sending a destroyer along with an

OPLAN 34A raid. The plan was for two raiding boats from Danang to travel north along the coast along with a destroyer, with the three vessels so close together that only a single blip would show on the screens of coastal radars. If the North Vietnamese turned off coastal radar sets, and limited themselves to tracking the destroyer by picking up its own radar emissions, the raiding vessels would be able to dash in toward the coast unobserved to attack a target.[43] This proposal was not implemented, but CIA Deputy Director Ray S. Cline states there is "no doubt" in his mind that the people planning these operations consciously decided to take advantage of the other obvious possibility: sending in a DeSoto patrol so soon after a coastal raid that they could be confident of finding an unusually high level of electronic activity.[44]

At any rate, MACV, which had been given the schedule the *Maddox* intended to follow and instructed to take this schedule into account when planning OPLAN 34A raids, chose to intensify its attacks at just this time. The PTFs based in Danang had never before attempted to destroy a DRV target by shelling it directly. The first such operation was the one on the night of July 30–31, a few hours before the *Maddox* entered the Gulf of Tonkin. The second occurred on the night of August 3–4, while the *Maddox* was in the gulf.

It is not clear that the men responsible for the DeSoto patrol understood that MACV intended to be quite so vigorous in arousing coastal defenses during the cruise of the *Maddox*. MACV was given very detailed information about the DeSoto patrol's plans, and instructed to take account of this in formulating its own plans. The officers planning the DeSoto patrol were given far less detail about OPLAN 34A raids; James Bartholomew, one of these officers, comments that he was told neither the locations nor the dates of the 34A raids that were to occur around the time of the DeSoto patrol.[45] Still less seems to have been passed on to Herrick and Ogier during the briefings in Keelung.

There were other incidents occurring inland from the section of coast between Hon Me and Hon Ngu that may have influenced the DRV reaction to the cruise of the *Maddox*. These occurred along Road 7, which started near the coast in Nghe An province and ran northwest into Laos; it was a major supply route for Communist forces in the Plain of Jars, a much-contested area in northern Laos. The first was (like the coastal raids) a planned SOG operation against the DRV: Team Boone was dropped near Road 7, in Nghe An about ten kilometers from the Laotian border, on July 29. One man became separated from the team at the time of the drop, and was apparently captured July 30; seven other members of the team surrendered to local authorities on August 2.[46]

The others appear to have been accidental side-effects of U.S. programs in Laos. On August 1, 1964, eight aircraft were sent on a mission of "armed reconnaissance" (which meant bombing anything that looked like a good target), covering about 100 kilometers of Road 7, from the Plain of Jars eastward to the Vietnamese border. The planes were old T-28s lacking sophisticated navigation gear. The pilots may well have been unfamiliar with the terrain—the United States, which wanted to avoid using American pilots for such missions, had just within the previous month brought into Laos a new contingent of Thai pilots—and for that matter may not have regarded the distinction between Communist territory in Laos and Communist territory in Vietnam as a tremendously important matter. The eight planes on this mission attacked a variety of targets with 500 and 260 pound bombs, and with rockets and .50 caliber machine guns. When U.S. Ambassador Leonard Unger reported to Washington on military operations for the day, he said these planes had destroyed some buildings only about two kilometers from the Vietnamese border.[47]

DRV sources report that on August 1, American-made T-28 aircraft coming from the direction of Laos attacked the border post of Nam Can, on Road 7 just inside the border of North Vietnam, and also the village of Noong De, which also lay on Road 7, and was part of a second line of border posts, set some distance back from the border to give defense in depth. Nam Can was hit again on August 2. One person was wounded on August 1, and four more on August 2. Vietnamese military personnel in 1989 estimated the distance of Noong De from the border variously as eleven or fourteen kilometers; the estimate of almost twenty kilometers, given in some reports dating from 1964, may reflect the travel distance along the twisting course of Road 7.[48]

Deputy Assistant Secretary of State Marshall Green, evaluating U.S. actions in the area soon afterward, decided that the charges of T-28 attacks on North Vietnam were "probably accurate" both for August 1 and for August 2.[49]

Two months before, Ambassador Lodge had cabled from Saigon, "literally eyes only for Rusk and McNamara," a proposal that something be done to inflict sufficient pain on the North Vietnamese to make them "scream." OPLAN 34A did not bother Hanoi enough to elicit much reaction. "We want a scream from them that they had been hit by something coming from our side. I would not object if they blamed us. They could prove nothing. We could either be totally silent, or challenge them to provide proof, or say we are looking into it." Air attacks along the border between North Vietnam and Laos were among the methods Lodge mentioned by which the desired screams could be elicited.[50] Given the existence of such attitudes within the U.S. government, it is not impossible that the attacks on Nam Can and Noong De could have been set up deliberately. There is no direct evidence, however, and given Ambassador Unger's attitudes—it seems most unlikely that he would have consented to deliberate attacks on the DRV carried out by nominally Laotian aircraft, and it is almost as unlikely that any American authority could have authorized such an operation without Unger's consent—the likeliest explanations of the attacks are either that the pilots were genuinely confused in their navigation, or that they decided on their own to extend their mission a little into Vietnamese territory, without having been ordered by the U.S. government to do so.

To sum up events for the two adjoining provinces of Nghe An and Thanh Hoa: an air-dropped agent had been captured on July 30, and seven more on August 2; two locations had been shelled from the sea on the night of July 30–31; two locations had been bombed from the air on August 1, and one had been bombed again on August 2. The people directly carrying out the operations had not been Americans, but in every case the United States had been deeply involved, not just providing advice and funds for operations of the South Vietnamese or Laotian governments. *Nhan Dan* asserted that the presence of the *Maddox* near the Vietnamese coast at the time Nam Can and Noong De were being bombed was a matter of deliberate coordination by the Americans, not coincidence.[51] The DRV surely must also have interpreted the bombing of Nam Can and Noong De as related to the presence of Team Boone in the area; Boone was probably within ten kilometers of Noong De at the time, and patrols searching for the team were probably using Noong De as a base of operations.

Captain Herrick tried to make the patrol of the *Maddox* nonprovocative. His attitude is illustrated by his directive that the ship's guns not be trained on any air or surface target without specific orders. Indeed, he ordered: "Do not permit the guns to be trained or elevated at all while under visual observation of an air or surface contact unless specifically authorized by the commanding officer."[52] But given everything that was happening in late July and early August, it is hard to imagine anything Herrick could have done that would have persuaded the coastal defense forces of Nghe An and Thanh Hoa provinces not to regard the *Maddox* as a dangerous threat.

An added irritant in the situation was reflected in later DRV protests that the *Maddox* had repeatedly "intimidated" fishing boats.[53] The destroyer had intended no such thing, but the protests were apparently sincere; fishing activity in the *Maddox*'s patrol area virtually ceased before the patrol was over.[54] Fishermen and/or officials in coastal areas might reasonably have worried either that the destroyer might be involved in the sort of kidnapping operations that had begun to occur under OPLAN 34A in May, or that it might mistake fishing boats for military vessels and fire on them.

If the *Maddox* were to get in any trouble, there would be help not far away. On July 8, the Joint Chiefs of Staff had ordered CINCPAC to ensure that there always be an American aircraft carrier off the coast of South Vietnam, "to accomplish recon and weather missions and to be prepared to conduct strikes if required." When CINCPAC passed this directive down the chain of command, he strengthened it to require that there always be a large-deck carrier there.[55] At the time of the DeSoto patrol, the carrier at what the Americans called Yankee Station, roughly at the latitude of Danang, was the *Ticonderoga*.

A Note on Course and Time Information

The main source of information on the path followed by the *Maddox* during its patrol is its navigation log.[56] For large portions of the voyage, this log gives the position of the ship, always to the nearest nautical mile and often to a fraction of a mile, at fifteen-minute intervals. As time went on, however, and the crew became fatigued by the pressures of cruising in hostile waters, the intervals between navigation fixes became longer and the frequency of careless errors may have increased. There are a few points at which the sequence of ship's positions recorded in the navigation log is inconsistent with the ship's course as recorded in the deck log, the CIC log, and other records. In these cases the author has generally chosen to rely on the records of the ship's course, which are mutually supporting and seem more reliable. Fortunately, the discrepancies are minor; no important issue would have had to be handled differently if the author had chosen to treat the navigation log as authoritative in places where it disagreed with the other sources.

Some caution also is necessary in regard to the positions recorded in the ship's Surface Search Radar Contact Sheets.[57] These sheets usually give the time an object first appeared on the radar, the location of the *Maddox*, and the range, bearing, course, and speed of the object. The correct time should not have presented any problem. For the range, bearing, course, and speed of the object, the men making the entries would have had no alternative but to work from what appeared on their screens, and one can only hope that they made their computations accurately. They did, however, have an alternative to computing the current position of the ship: simply use the most recent position recorded in the navigation log. In cases where a noticeable time passed between a position being entered in the navigation log and the identical position being entered in the surface search radar contact sheets, it seems best to adjust the position, taking account of the known course and speed of the ship.

All time references in this book for events in the Gulf of Tonkin are given military style, on a twenty-four-hour clock, with a capital letter added to indicate the time zone. Thus when a time is given as 1325H, this means 1:25 P.M., in the H ("Hotel") time zone. Great opportunities for confusion arise in connection with time zone changes during the patrol of the *Maddox*.

While in Keelung, the destroyer had used the local time, known in the navy as Hotel Time or −8. The −8 means that in order to convert Hotel to Zulu Time (Greenwich Mean Time), one subtracts eight hours. Twelve hours are subtracted to convert to Eastern Daylight Time, used in Washington. Thus 1325H corresponds to 0525Z, and to 1:25 A.M. EDT in Washington. (Times of events in Washington are given civilian style in this book, on a twelve-hour clock with A.M. or P.M. added.)

Shortly after leaving Keelung, the destroyer set its clocks ahead one hour to what is misleadingly called India Time (in fact the local time for Japan, not India), or −9. Late in the afternoon of August 2, it set its clocks back one hour to Hotel Time, probably because it was the local time used in South Vietnam. Then, early in the morning of August 3, it set its clocks back another hour to Golf Time or −7, the local time for North Vietnam.

The aircraft carrier *Ticonderoga* was on Golf Time until the night of August 4. It advanced its clocks one hour to Hotel Time at 0001G (which became 0101H) on August 5.

The aircraft carrier *Constellation* was on India Time until the evening of August 4; it set its clocks back one hour to Hotel Time at 1900I (which became 1800H) on August 4.

The greatest care is needed in handling time references, if one is comparing accounts in different sources. The time when the *Maddox* fired its first warning shots at North Vietnamese vessels on August 2 was listed as 1708I in the records of the *Maddox*, but it is 1608H in the U.S. Navy's history of the incident, and it would have been 1508G to the North Vietnamese.

It should not be surprising that time zone errors have crept into various records dealing both with the DeSoto patrol and with the U.S. airstrikes against North Vietnam on August 5. Some personnel on the *Maddox* either never heard or forgot that the ship's clocks no longer showed India Time after August 2, so some of the ship's records for August 3 and 4 that are in fact based on Golf Time are mistakenly labeled as being based on India Time. Chronologies drawn up by Pentagon officials, both military and civilian, for the supposed torpedo boat attack against U.S. destroyers on the night of August 4, contain numerous one-hour errors in timing.

On August 5, a number of crucial messages about the scheduling of the U.S. airstrikes against North Vietnam failed to specify a time zone. When senior officers in the Pentagon asked Pacific Command in Hawaii what time reference the aircraft carriers were using, the CINCPAC War Room reported that the carriers were using Golf Time. The carriers were in fact using Hotel Time. The Pentagon may never have figured out that there had been a mistake on this point; a major report written months afterward still stated that the carriers had been using Golf Time. The same report also contains a map showing an incorrect time zone—Hotel—for North Vietnam.[58]

The chapters in this book describing the DeSoto patrol use Golf Time, since it gives realistic times for local sunrise and sunset and was the time used in North Vietnam and by the *Maddox* during the most crucial portion of the DeSoto patrol. Chapter 9, devoted to the U.S. airstrikes against North Vietnam on August 5, will use Hotel Time. This was the time used by the aircraft carriers conducting the strikes, and since it was exactly twelve hours ahead of Washington time, it makes much easier the task of relating events in Washington to those in the Gulf of Tonkin.

The DeSoto Patrol Begins

The *Maddox* left Keelung on July 28 and approached the Vietnamese coast on the morning of July 31. This was a few hours after the PTFs from Danang had shelled the islands of Hon Me and Hon Ngu.

While heading toward Vietnam, the destroyer had been under emission control, avoiding any use of radar or radio, so as to avoid giving away its presence. The destroyer began partial and selective breaking of this silence at 0629G on the morning of July 31. It was then almost exactly on the seventeenth parallel (the latitude of the division between North and South Vietnam), and approximately in the path of the PTFs then returning from their raid. The *Maddox* remained in that area until the four PTFs had gone by, the first two passing within four miles of the destroyer at 0741G, the second pair passing perhaps even a little closer a few minutes later. The destroyer then moved about fifteen miles toward the coast before resuming full normal radar use at 0835G.[59]

If the DRV had succeeded in tracking the destroyer from the first partial lifting of emission control, and also had managed to track the PTFs this far south, the impression conveyed would have been that a planned rendezvous had occurred. The most plausible interpretation the DRV could have put on it would have been that the U.S. Navy, as part of its plan for the raids, had posted the destroyer at the seventeenth parallel to block any effort at hot pursuit of the PTFs by North Vietnamese patrol boats.

The radar network along the North Vietnamese coast was not very extensive in 1964. If it had been, the OPLAN 34A raiding vessels would not have been able to operate the way they did in the first half of the year, often remaining quite close to the coast for a long time—in some cases almost until dawn—waiting for a landing party to return from the shore. The radar may have improved a bit by the time the *Maddox* arrived at the end of July, but coverage was still far from complete. The *Maddox* was within twelve miles of North Vietnamese territory—Tiger Island—before noon on July 31, but accounts published in Hanoi do not mention the *Maddox* having arrived in the area before the late afternoon of July 31, or even the night of July 31–August 1.[60] The impression conveyed is that observers on shore either were not able to track the destroyer at all during the first few hours of the patrol, or were able to track it only sporadically and were not certain that whatever they may have observed on the morning of July 31 was the same vessel as the one they later identified, considerably further north, as the *Maddox*.

Admittedly, the evidence on this point is not unanimous. In Hanoi and Ho

Chi Minh City in May 1989, this author asked a number of Vietnamese officers about the ability of the coastal radar to track the destroyer, and obtained contradictory answers. All information from sources other than interviews in Vietnam, however, indicates that radar coverage along the North Vietnamese coast was far from complete. The relevant DeSoto patrol records have not all been declassified, but in the portions that are available, there is no indication of coastal radar having been detected until almost midnight on July 31, and the destroyer would have been able to detect such radar at a much longer range than the radar would have been able to track the destroyer.

At 1633G on July 31, the officers on the *Maddox* turned off all their ship's radar, in the hope that this would stimulate the interest of the North Vietnamese and cause coastal radars to be turned on.[61] The use of such a trick implies that the *Maddox* had detected little if any tracking by coastal radars up to that time. Gerrell Moore cannot recall whether the coastal defense forces were tracking the *Maddox* by radar on July 31, but he says that if they were, they were not doing as much radar tracking as they did on August 1. This clearly indicates that they were not tracking the destroyer by radar continuously on July 31.[62]

U.S. government spokesmen, in claiming that there was no connection between the cruise of the *Maddox* and any raids that may have been occurring against North Vietnam, sometimes tried to claim that the lack of a connection was or should have been obvious to Hanoi. Thus Assistant Secretary of State William Bundy, while dodging a clear admission that Hanoi was correct in saying that there had been attacks on Hon Me and Hon Ngu, said publicly not long afterward: "We believe that Hanoi knew, should have known perfectly well where that destroyer was, and that it would have no connection with these attacks on those islands if they took place."[63] Bundy's argument is twice wrong. First, the DRV had no way of knowing where the destroyer had been at the time of the raids. The reason that the DRV did not specifically accuse the *Maddox* of having participated in the raid of July 30–31 was simply that the DRV, having no idea where the destroyer had been, saw no reason to suppose that it, more than any other American vessel, might have had a connection with the attacks on Hon Me and Hon Ngu. Second, if Hanoi *could* somehow have obtained full information on the movements of the destroyer, this information would not have provided proof that the destroyer was innocent; it would strongly have suggested coordination between the *Maddox* and the raiding vessels (see above).

It is hard to tell how much the DRV knew or had guessed about the *Maddox*'s reconnaissance mission. The Americans had gone to a good deal of trouble to make sure that this would not be understood; sailors on the *Maddox* had even repainted the comvan, to make it look more like a part of their ship, shortly after they left Keelung. The imposition of emission control along the coast during the DeSoto patrol carried out by the *Craig* in February and March suggests that the North Vietnamese had had some idea what they were dealing with on that occasion. There is no evidence, however, of a similar awareness during the July-August cruise of the *Maddox*. The available DRV accounts suggest that the North Vietnamese, not realizing that the destroyer was carrying special electronic listening gear, assumed that it was what it appeared to be: a warship whose main working tools were five-inch guns. The most plausible missions for such a ship in the gulf were intimidation, support of the vessels making raids against the coast, or actual shelling of the coast. The *Maddox* would have been an appropriate vessel for the Americans to send if they wanted to do more serious shelling of the North Vietnamese coast than the PTFs from Danang could manage, and the *Maddox* would indeed be sent on just this mission in later years.

Discussing the U.S. decision to have the 34A raids and the DeSoto patrol taking place at the same time, William Bundy has said, "Rational minds could not readily have foreseen that Hanoi might confuse them."[64] This and other suggestions that the DRV should have realized, once they saw that the *Maddox* was a regular U.S. Navy destroyer, that it was not involved in 34A operations, are simply silly. Nobody at the top levels of the U.S. government believed that it was unthinkable for a U.S. destroyer to get involved in 34A operations; those who are known to have discussed the possibility that DeSoto patrols and 34A operations might be associated or "intertwined" include the Joint Chiefs of Staff, the secretaries of state and defense, and Ambassador Maxwell Taylor;[65] Admirals Sharp and Felt had actually recommended, back in May, that this be done (see above). Why on earth might Hanoi have decided it was unthinkable for a U.S. destroyer to participate in 34A operations?

Apologists for the U.S. government often write and talk as if the *Maddox* was, visibly and obviously, an innocent reconnaissance vessel. Thus General Wheeler, Chairman of the Joint Chiefs of Staff, later commented:

We had a couple of destroyers that were in international waters. They had been doing this for some time, going up the coast of North Vietnam but out in the [waters]. In fact, we even avoided going in closer than about thirteen miles. They claimed twelve miles as their territorial water. We only claim three, as you probably know. But we stayed outside of what their claim of territorial waters was. Now, I'm not trying to mislead you. These ships were equipped with electronic equipment so that we could keep an eye on the naval order of battle, the air order of battle, and so on in North Vietnam, and also to pick up other interesting tidbits of information. I don't regard this as a provocation, unless you want to take it as a provocation that we have a Soviet intelligence collector that sits right off the port of Charleston all the time. We have another that sits right off the runway in Guam. In fact, I've seen it myself. They stay outside of our territorial waters, which is three miles. Now, is that a provocation, or isn't it?[66]

Aside from the falsehood of Wheeler's claim that the DeSoto patrol stayed thirteen miles from the North Vietnamese coast, one might note that the Soviet intelligence collectors carried little or no armament. Had the Soviet Union stationed a vessel equipped with five-inch guns right off Charleston harbor, Wheeler would have treated this as a serious provocation. Had the Soviet Union put such a vessel off Charleston during a week when the Soviet Union was also sending Cuban gunboats to shell the South Carolina coast, it is unlikely that it could have remained there even twenty-four hours without being attacked by U.S. forces.

The *Maddox* spent the afternoon and early evening of July 31 orbiting between Tiger Island and the North Vietnamese mainland, just north of the seventeenth parallel. The island is about thirteen miles from the mainland, so this could just barely be done without violating the limits that had been set for the DeSoto patrol (no approaches closer than eight miles from the mainland or four miles from islands). There may have been some carelessness; the navigation log shows that at 2100G, just before leaving the area, the *Maddox* passed slightly less than four miles from the island. This was the closest approach to the territory of the DRV at any time during the patrol. (Two recent books state, erroneously, that the closest approach of the *Maddox* to any island was five miles.)[67]

The destroyer then moved slowly northward, at a distance from the coast that varied between eight and twenty miles. On August 1, its closest approach to the mainland was eight miles, and the closest to an island (Hon Mat, offshore from Hon Ngu and high on the list of planned targets of OPLAN 34A raids) was about four and a half miles. Information of various sorts was gathered according to plan.

By the afternoon of August 1, the *Maddox* was increasingly being tracked by radar. Gerrell Moore does not recall any sign, however, that the coastal defense forces were seriously disturbed by the presence of the destroyer. Everything still seemed calm that evening; Moore thinks that he probably watched a movie in the wardroom. Afterward, at about 2130 or 2200 ship's time (1930G or 2000G), he went to the comvan to check on the situation, as he always did before going to bed. He found the men on duty very happy; they were getting useful information. Coastal stations were making reports that included the bearing of the *Maddox*, and when the men in the comvan intercepted such a report, "back plotting" from the actual location of the ship enabled them to locate the coastal station that had originated the report. These were only observation reports, however; there was nothing threatening about them.[68]

The Destroyer Approaches Hon Me

The DRV was in fact disturbed about the presence of the *Maddox*, often deep within what it considered its territorial waters. Only on the evening of August 1, however, did a real crisis arise, apparently triggered by the approach of the *Maddox* to the island of Hon Me shortly after sunset. The picture of Vietnamese actions that night one gets from Vietnamese sources is rather different from the picture one gets from the American side, based on intercepted messages, but both pictures are probably correct; they represent different facets of what must have been a confused whole.

For the Americans, the first indication of trouble came when the comvan intercepted a message stating that a decision had been made to attack that night. An officer who saw the intercepted message states that it was very short, probably only a single sentence, and did not specify what target was to be attacked. It came from very high in the People's Navy, and was directed down the chain of command, not up. Captain Herrick was immediately awakened to see this message.[69]

Shortly afterward, the comvan intercepted another message, giving the location of an "enemy" vessel; the location specified was that of the *Maddox*. Gerrell Moore's recollection is that this was not just another routine tracking report from a coastal radar station: "It came from a higher authority and gave a specific location, rather than the range and bearing from an observation post." Officers on the destroyer put the two messages together, and concluded that the enemy to be attacked that night was their destroyer.[70]

Next came a much longer message, perhaps one-half to three-quarters of a page. The men in the comvan did not find its meaning immediately obvious even when it had been decrypted and translated into English, but Captain Herrick interpreted it, on the basis of his experiences off Korea years before, as indicating that small vessels were to strap explosives to their bows and attack by ramming. As in the first message, the target of the attack was not specified.[71] There was not then, and is not now, any reason to doubt that this referred to the *Maddox*. The tactic of ramming would have been preposterous against the small, fast vessels used in the OPLAN 34A raids against the North Vietnamese coast. It made sense only against a larger target such as a destroyer, and the *Maddox* was the only such target in the area.

Gunner's Mate 2d Class Ronald Stalsberg was in charge of one of the five-inch gun turrets. He recalls having been told that night that there was information indicating a danger from junks with explosives strapped to them, or mines on cables strung between junks. This information was not circulated to the crew in general—it did not go to anyone below Stalsberg—but people in key positions on the ship were informed about it.[72]

Captain Herrick decided the risks close to shore had become unacceptable. Between 0236G and 0248G he increased speed, turned eastward out to sea, and set General Quarters (ordered the ship made ready for combat, with all men at their battle stations).[73] It is difficult to be sure of the exact sequence of events. At least one of the three messages, perhaps two, had been reported to Captain

Herrick before 0236G, but the third probably did not come in until after his turn away from the coast.

Commander Ogier comments that the explanation usually given for the decision to move further from shore, a concentration of junks, is in a sense false. There was indeed a concentration of junks, but the real reason for the decision was the ominous radio intercepts. The fact that the United States was intercepting enemy communications was highly secret, so the move away from shore was explained publicly as having been caused by the concentration of junks.[74] Patrick Park also recollects a huge number of local vessels, presumably fishing boats, strung out in a tremendously long line that night—an "awesome, intimidating, and strange" sight. Ronald Stalsberg says that the line of fishing junks was strung out roughly parallel to the coast, moving outward from the coast.[75]

Gerrell Moore believed, and still believes, that the *Maddox* would have been attacked that night if Captain Herrick had not turned out to sea.[76] To get one or more small vessels properly fitted with explosives and detonators, however, on short notice in the middle of the night, would not have been quick or easy tasks. The order for this to be done was not given until well past midnight. It should not be assumed that the boats' crews would have managed to complete the job, sortie, and then locate the destroyer before dawn (bearing in mind that there were no radar-equipped vessels available in the area) even if Herrick had remained close to shore.

From the viewpoint of the Vietnamese on shore, the crisis had begun several hours earlier. The island of Hon Me had been shelled from the sea two nights before. The *Maddox*'s five-inch guns had a range of 18,000 yards. When the destroyer approached within gun range of Hon Me around dusk on August 1, coming within 12,000 yards by 2030G, it must have seemed very likely that it intended to repeat the attack with heavier weapons. The idea of strapping explosives to the bows of boats and ramming sounds like a desperate expedient, contrived by men trying to figure out some way of defending Hon Me from the destroyer during the hours it would take for properly armed military vessels to reach Hon Me from their base at Van Hoa, 145 miles to the north.

The DRV possessed no large warships. Its naval strength was mainly in Chinese-built gunboats of a type the United States called "Swatow boats." These eighty-ton vessels, about eighty-three feet long, were armed with 37-mm[77] cannon—weapons lighter than would really have been desirable even for dealing with the PTFs that conducted OPLAN 34A raids against the North Vietnamese coast, and absurdly inadequate for use against a destroyer.

The only North Vietnamese vessels that would have a chance in a fight against the *Maddox* were twelve torpedo boats, referred to informally in American sources as PTs and formally as P-4s. These twenty-four-ton aluminum-hulled vessels, built in the Soviet Union, were about sixty-six feet long and twelve feet across the beam. Each was armed with two torpedoes suitable for attacks against large vessels, plus a pair of heavy machine guns (14.5 mm) intended primarily for defense against air attack. The effective range of the machine guns was about 2,000 meters horizontally or 1,000 meters vertically. The boats' diesel engines could drive them to a maximum speed of fifty-two knots; normal cruising speed was about thirty-five knots.[78] (By August 1964, the U.S. Navy had realized that these twelve vessels were the only torpedo boats the DRV had.[79] There had earlier been a mistaken report that the DRV also had four somewhat larger P-6 torpedo boats; this had probably arisen from the fact that some of the men serving aboard the P-4s in North Vietnam had trained aboard P-6s in China.)

Each torpedo carried 550 pounds of TNT in its warhead, adequate to cripple and perhaps sink a destroyer.[80] The problem was that the effective range of the torpedoes was much shorter than the effective range of the *Maddox*'s five-inch guns. Doctrine in the People's Navy, as described by officers and men captured and interrogated by U.S. forces in 1966,[81] called for firing torpedoes from a range of 1,000 yards or less. This meant that a torpedo boat attacking a destroyer would be under fire from the destroyer for several minutes before it got close enough to fire torpedoes in return.

Neither the information available in Washington nor that published in the standard reference work *Jane's Fighting Ships*—probably the source the men on the *Maddox* would have checked to learn what they were up against—gave a particularly accurate picture of North Vietnamese torpedo boats. There are minor variations, but in general the picture in the sources available to Americans was of a vessel intermediate in characteristics between the P-4 and the Swatow: larger, slower, and carrying heavier guns than the actual North Vietnamese torpedo boats—25 mm instead of 14.5 mm.[82]

The P-4 was a highly specialized design. Its lack of cannon made it almost useless against small vessels like the PTFs used in OPLAN 34A raids, unless it imitated the technique that the 34A raiders were just beginning to use at this time, and mounted on its deck a recoilless rifle—a weapon originally built for land warfare—to supplement its regular weapons. It was well qualified, however, for its intended function—attacks on vessels much larger than itself, such as destroyers. Its very high speed gave it a real chance, in the proper circumstances, of dashing in on a destroyer too suddenly for the guns of the destroyer to be able to stop it from reaching torpedo range and scoring a hit.

At the time the idea of strapping explosives to the bows of small vessels and ramming the destroyer was raised, the DRV had already decided to send three torpedo boats to Hon Me—boats T-333, T-336, and T-339, which together constituted Section 3 of Torpedo Boat Squadron 135. The order given by the commander of the People's Navy at 2120G—less than an hour after the closest approach of the *Maddox* to Hon Me—was conditional, however. The torpedo boats were not at this time given the order actually to attack the destroyer; they were being put in a position where they *could* attack, if the destroyer continued to behave in a fashion that the People's Navy considered an intolerable infringe-ment of Vietnamese territory. Two Swatow boats, T-142 and T-146, were also sent to Hon Me.[83] The People's Navy was thinking about the possibility that the destroyer would work together with the PTFs from Danang in an attack on the coast of North Vietnam, in which case the torpedoes of Section 3 would be the appropriate weapons to use against the destroyer, but the 37-mm cannon of the Swatows would be needed to deal with the PTFs.

From this point onward, the *Maddox* was far more cautious. It headed back toward the coast after dawn, but its closest approach to any island on August 2 was ten miles, and its closest approach to the mainland was thirteen miles. Cap-tain Herrick reported at 1015G, "Approx 75 junks in area. No other craft visible. Will deviate from track as necessary to avoid passing thru junk concentration."[84]

The comvan was probably intercepting more reports by coastal stations tracking the *Maddox* during the morning and early afternoon of August 2, but such intercepts would not have been particularly memorable and there is no available information about them.

Around noon on August 2, when the *Maddox* was about ten miles from the island of Hon Me and fifteen miles from the mainland, the crew observed the three torpedo boats of Section 3, and also the two Swatow boats, traveling southward along the coast. The closest approach of the torpedo boats to the destroyer was seven miles; they arrived at Hon Me at 1222G.[85]

At this point, the record of events becomes confused. An after-action report dated August 5 said that the torpedo boats emerged from Hon Me at fifteen knots and were acquired on radar at 1257G, but soon afterward disappeared into a concentration of fishing junks.[86] This is probably not correct. No such report appears in other U.S. records including the ship's logs, and the range given in the report (76,000 yards) is far too great to be reconciled with other information in the same report. A detailed chart of the movements of all the vessels involved in the action of August 2, constructed by the People's Navy,[87] indicates that the three PT boats and the two Swatow boats remained at Hon Me until about 1400G.

The First Incident, August 2

The official history of the People's Navy states that Section 3 received an order to attack the destroyer at 1350G.[1] The history does not, however, explain who gave this order, and there had in fact been a misunderstanding; the commander of the People's Navy had not ordered an attack. Vietnamese officers interviewed in 1989 seemed to believe that the commander would have issued such an order within a day or two, when the *Maddox* was in a location making an attack appropriate, but the *Maddox* was not in such a location at 1350G on August 2. These officers stated that a recall order was sent when it was realized that the torpedo boats were going out to attack the *Maddox*, but that this recall order, which was supposed to be relayed to them by T-146 (one of the Swatow boats near Hon Me), never reached them.[2] Reports written a few days or weeks after the incident state that a recall order actually did reach the torpedo boats, but only when their battle with the *Maddox* was over or almost over.[3]

The attack order was intercepted by the comvan; less than half an hour should have been required for it to be translated and shown to senior officers on the destroyer. It specifically ordered an attack using torpedoes, but once again did not say explicitly what was to be attacked.[4] Officers on the destroyer had no difficulty deducing that their ship was the objective; no other possible target for a torpedo attack was in the area.

Until this message was intercepted, things had been rather relaxed on board the *Maddox*. Gerrell Moore's recollection is that the events of the previous night had not prevented the destroyer from going to "holiday routine" that day—it was Sunday—and that as he emerged from the comvan to carry the message to Captain Herrick, he saw sailors sunbathing on the decks.[5]

The patrol schedule called for the *Maddox* to orbit from 1000G to 1800G in the vicinity of a point designated "D," northeast of Hon Me at 19°47′ N, 106°8′ E. For the first two hours or so, the destroyer in fact orbited to the south of point "D," going no farther north than 19°42′. (The suggestion by Joseph Goulden that the *Maddox* spent the morning in the vicinity of the Red River Delta, considerably farther north, is unfounded.)[6] At 1222G, however, the three torpedo boats arrived at Hon Me, to the southwest of the destroyer. The *Maddox*, instead of approaching to observe, headed northeast away from the island, reaching 19°48.8′, about fifteen miles from the coast, by 1415G. At that time, the CIC log surprisingly reports that the ship was proceeding to point "E"; the orbit around point "D" was being terminated almost four hours ahead of schedule. Presumably Captain Herrick had decided that for the destroyer to remain near Hon Me almost until dusk, as contemplated by his schedule, would not be wise with three torpedo boats there.

Most accounts state that the radar of the *Maddox* acquired three torpedo boats, coming toward the destroyer at thirty knots from Hon Me, at 1400G.[7] All three of the relevant ship's logs, however, indicate that the three torpedo boats were acquired on radar about half an hour afterward. The entries for acquisition of the three PT boats on radar show times of 1435G in the Surface Search Radar Contact Sheet, 1435G in the CIC (Combat Information Center) log, and 1438G in the deck log. An after-action report dated August 5 gave the time as 1433G.[8] It is likely that the log entries were made only after a few minutes had been taken to compute the course and speed of the PT boats, and that their first acquisition on radar was at about 1430G. The ship went to General Quarters at 1430G, which would not have been likely to occur without something having been acquired on the radar.

The PT boats needed every possible advantage if they were going to attack a destroyer (the very name "destroyer" is derived from "torpedo-boat destroyer"). What they needed to do was to make their attack run on the destroyer from the southeast, pinning their enemy against the coast. Safety for the destroyer lay to the southeast, away from the Vietnamese coast and toward other U.S. Naval units. If it came to a fight, Captain Herrick would have had to head away from the coast even if there had been enemy vessels in his way. If the PT boats could approach him from the southeast, therefore, they and the destroyer would be coming at one another head-on. The range between them would close very rapidly, and from the time they were close enough for the destroyer to shoot at them effectively, it would be only a short time—under four minutes if the destroyer did not prolong it by trying to dodge around them—until they were close enough to have a reasonable chance of hitting it with torpedoes.

What actually happened is that while the PT boats were heading *northeast* toward the point where the *Maddox* would have been if it had not intercepted their orders, it was heading *southeast* away from that point. By the time the PT boats realized their mistake, they were approximately west of their target, and they ended up chasing the *Maddox* southeast, being shot at for an extended period as they tried to overtake the destroyer. Under these conditions they were not likely to win the fight, and they did not. Figures 1a, 1b, and 1c illustrate the different results of approaches from different angles.

Interception of the message ordering the PT boats to attack had given the destroyer a crucial advantage, and may in fact have determined the outcome of the combat that followed. As Commander Ogier commented long afterward, "The PT boats were behind us because we had already started moving away from them as a result of the messages we received. They approached from astern because that was the only option that we gave them."[9]

Records of the *Maddox* indicate no detection of radar use by the torpedo boats, and the men on the destroyer saw no radar masts when the PTs got close enough for such details to be observed. They reached the entirely justified conclusion that North Vietnamese PT boats possessed no radar.

In fact, all North Vietnamese PT boats were equipped with the Soviet-made Type 253 radar that the United States called "Skinhead," capable under good conditions of detecting a destroyer-sized target at ranges out to about fifteen miles. It was designed, however, to allow the radar mast to be folded down when the radar was not in use. With the radar mast erect in its working position, the profile of the boat was considerably higher, allowing it to be detected by possible enemies, either visually or by the use of their own radar, at a greater distance. Also, with the mast erect the radar was subject to vibration damage as the boat pounded through the waves on high-speed runs.[10] On August 2, the visibility was good enough so that radar seemed unnecessary, and the boats were planning to make their attack run at absolute maximum speed. All three boats therefore had their radar masts folded down.

An article in *Hai Quan* about the commander of T-339 says that the vessel detected the destroyer by radar before making a visual sighting.[11] The article does not in general seem reliable, and may simply be wrong on this point. It is possible, however, that the torpedo boats used their radar briefly when they first left Hon Me, to verify the location of the *Maddox*, and then folded the radar masts down for their high-speed run toward the destroyer.

Nominal doctrine in the North Vietnamese navy was that radar should be used in all torpedo attacks, but there was a general understanding that this doctrine would be ignored in situations where visibility was good. The radar was not good enough to tell a torpedo boat captain more than he could learn by naked eye, once the range got close, and the disadvantages of trying to use it were considerable.

As was stated above, the *Maddox*'s logs indicate that the torpedo boats appeared on the radar, coming out from Hon Me, at about 1430G. By this time the *Maddox* was at least sixteen and probably about eighteen miles from the North Vietnamese coast. It seems likely that reports of radar acquisition at 1400G arose

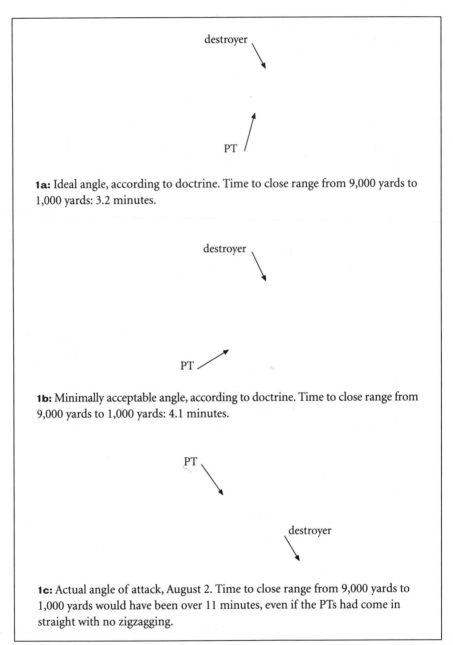

1a: Ideal angle, according to doctrine. Time to close range from 9,000 yards to 1,000 yards: 3.2 minutes.

1b: Minimally acceptable angle, according to doctrine. Time to close range from 9,000 yards to 1,000 yards: 4.1 minutes.

1c: Actual angle of attack, August 2. Time to close range from 9,000 yards to 1,000 yards would have been over 11 minutes, even if the PTs had come in straight with no zigzagging.

Figure 1. Possible angles of attack by PTs against a destroyer

from the navy's desire to explain the destroyer's turn out to sea at 1423G without revealing U.S. radio intercept capabilities.

Admiral Sharp has given another incorrect explanation of the *Maddox*'s turn out to sea, suggesting that simply as a matter of luck the *Maddox* "had reached the northern extreme of her patrol" and had turned southward before the PT boats began their approach.[12]

Information about radio intercept capabilities was supposed to be guarded with stricter secrecy than almost any other category of information the U.S. government possessed. Information about the design of nuclear weapons was not treated with such care. In this case the secrecy did not hold; political colum-nist Jack Anderson had learned something of the *Maddox*'s capabilities, and even published details of information from one intercepted message, within two weeks.[13] William Bundy says he has no recollection of any strong reaction within the U.S. government to Anderson's revelation. The ability of the United States to intercept such messages was widely enough known that the revelation that some actually had been intercepted may have been too minor a breach of security to inspire massive outrage.[14] But official sources avoided acknowledging the *Maddox*'s capabilities for years thereafter. This should not be treated as proof of some conspiracy to conceal information that would be embarrassing to the government. Refusing to say anything, even to confirm what was com-mon knowledge, was and is standard procedure for matters of communications intelligence.

The importance of such an attitude is supported by the actual events of August 1964. If the DRV had understood the situation, code procedures could have been put in place that would have been beyond the ability of the men on the *Maddox* to decipher, and the torpedo boats would have had a much better chance of sinking the American vessel.

Later in the war the People's Navy displayed a great deal of concern for communications security, with people monitoring the wavelengths used by naval vessels and issuing written reprimands to anyone heard making careless transmissions.[15] Communications security is said already to have been quite tight even in 1964, but not tight enough to keep the Americans from finding out what was going on.

Once the PT boats had in fact appeared on the radar, approaching at high speed, the *Maddox* informed the Seventh Fleet that an attack seemed imminent. When they reached a range of 9800 yards, at a time that was variously recorded as 1505G or 1508G, the *Maddox* fired three or four shells. Commander Ogier gave the order, after obtaining permission from Captain Herrick. Herrick has made it clear that he intended these as warning shots, not to be aimed at the PT boats, and his recollection is that they fell short, or ahead of the torpedo boats.[16] There may have been, however, a failure of communication with his subordi-nates. Commander Ogier states that although these were intended as warning shots, they were aimed directly at the PT boats, since a direct hit on the first salvo was so unlikely that it did not seem necessary to offset the shots. Lieutenant Raymond Connell, who as weapons officer passed on the order, has also said that these shots were aimed directly at the PT boats. Ensign Richard Corsette, who carried out the order, has stated recently after searching his memory that he did try to offset the shots to the left, but by such a small margin that they actually fell to the right of the target vessel.[17]

The torpedo boats continued to approach. The destroyer began rapid fire at a time variously recorded as 1508G or 1511G, range about 9,000 yards, using a standard mix of explosive shells. Some ("AAC" shells) were set to explode on impact, which could cause devastating damage to a PT boat, but only with a direct hit. Others ("VT-frag") were set to explode in the air near the target and spray it with metal fragments; this was less devastating but did not require such accuracy. VT-frag shells, however, were designed primarily for use against aircraft, and the fuzes were intended to set them off when they came close enough to a plane for the fragments to destroy or cripple it. To be fully effective against a PT boat, much less fragile than a plane, they would have needed fuzes set to detonate them closer to the target. The VT-frag shells fired by the five-inch/ thirty-eight-caliber guns had a "nominal detonation distance" of seventy feet; those fired by the three-inch/fifty caliber guns had a "nominal detonation distance" of fifty feet. A total of 283 shells were fired. Of these, 71 were five-inch AAC. In the only available copy of the ship's report on ammunition expenditure the section describing the remaining 212 is partly illegible, but it appears to indicate that all were VT-frag—132 three-inch and 80 five-inch. An account by Dr. Samuel Halpern, who had come aboard the *Maddox* with Herrick, indicates that the destroyer fired 71 five-inch AAC, 132 three-inch VT-frag, 68 five-inch VT-frag, and 12 five-inch star shells.[18] The destroyer was about twenty-eight miles from shore—the torpedo boats considerably less—at the time the shooting began.

The torpedo boats of Section 3 were commanded by three brothers; their father had been a navy man, and they had followed his career. Nguyen Van Bot, commander of Section 3, also commanded boat T-333. His brother Nguyen Van Tu commanded T-336, and Nguyen Van Gian commanded T-339. Several officers who were not normally assigned to Section 3, including Le Duy Khoai (commander of Squadron 135), were also aboard one or more of these vessels. (It was standard for extra officers to be aboard when the PTs went out on a mission.)[19] DRV accounts state that the three torpedo boats initially approached the *Maddox* in numerical order—the command vessel (T-333) led, followed by T-336 and T-339.

The captain of a P-4 could, and normally would, fire both of his torpedoes by a single push on the firing lever. The torpedo tubes did not point exactly forward; each tube was angled slightly outward (one and one-half degrees), to spread the torpedoes far enough apart so it would be difficult for the target ship to dodge both torpedoes. Doctrine called for three torpedo boats to fire at approximately the same time, so there would be enough torpedoes to create a really broad spread, and for firing to occur at a range of 600 to 1,000 yards. This procedure would give reasonable assurance of at least one hit.[20]

This was not what actually happened on August 2. As the three torpedo boats neared the *Maddox*, T-333 tried to pass the destroyer, to get into position to attack from the beam, while T-336 and T-339 headed straight in from the rear. The commander of T-336 launched first, at much farther than the recommended range, having decided that the fire of the destroyer was too intense for an approach to close range to be practical. The commander of T-339 held his fire until he was considerably closer, but not close enough.[21] Firing at long range meant that the angle of the spread would have put the two torpedoes of each attacker so far apart that at most one of them could seriously threaten the destroyer; firing at different times meant that the destroyer would only have to worry about the torpedoes of one attacker at a time. The deck log of the *Maddox* indicates that the destroyer maneuvered to avoid torpedoes at 1518G and again at 1521G.

T-333 turned toward the target only after T-336 and T-339 had already fired. Tran Bao, the Executive Officer of Torpedo Boat Squadron 135, said later that T-333 had fired its torpedoes.[22] Observers on the *Maddox*, however, got the impression that at least one torpedo had been jarred from the launcher of T-333 by a hit from one of the shells of the *Maddox*. There is no record that they saw any torpedoes being deliberately fired at them by T-333.

The main armament of the *Maddox* was in its three five-inch gun turrets, designated (in order from bow to stern of the ship) Mount 51, Mount 52, and Mount 53. GMG2 Ronald Stalsberg was mount captain of Mount 51. He recalls that his turret fired on the leading PT boat until that boat was crippled; after that the mount shifted fire to the other PTs. What crippled the lead boat looked to Stalsberg like an AAC round, fuzed for impact detonation, hitting the water very close to the PT; the detonation seemed to lift the PT up and then drop it. This may be the incident that other sources describe as a direct hit, but Stalsberg does not think that the shell he saw actually struck the boat. If it had done so he would have expected to see flying fragments, and he did not. For the shell actually to have struck the boat would have been unusual; on a target the size of a PT, "to get a direct hit is pretty hard to do."[23]

The only damage to the destroyer was one hole made by a bullet from a 14.5-mm machine gun; Richard Corsette believes the bullet was fired by T-333. Men on the destroyers thought they saw a 25-mm cannon, such as the description of P-4 torpedo boats in *Jane's Fighting Ships* would have led them to expect, on one of the boats. They reported that it was not in use. DRV sources deny the presence of such a weapon on any of the boats.[24]

The boats turned away, whether because the *Maddox*'s fire was too hot to endure, because they had no more torpedoes, or because they had received a recall order. They did not, however, turn away simultaneously; T-339 had lost contact with the other two, and continued to fight at close range for a few minutes after T-333 and T-336 had turned away.[25] The *Maddox* turned and pursued the torpedo boats, still firing at them.

According to Patrick Park, there were serious problems with the gunnery of the *Maddox* on August 2; the overall effectiveness of the five-inch guns was less than half what it should have been. He was in the sonar room on August 2, but at an earlier stage of his career on the *Maddox* he had worked in the main gun director, so he had some knowledge of what was involved. The confusion was bad enough that even from his position in the sonar room, while the action was going on, Park knew from experience that everything was probably going seriously wrong. He learned more later, talking with various people including the captains of the five-inch gun turrets.

> The entire *ship* was caught off guard—in practice we were always briefed (you know, like a quiz *before* the "big test"). But *now* (unlike before where everybody had been prompted and should know their part) damage control parties, fore and aft, were not prepared to stock or restock magazines in gun tubs, as ammunition was needed. . . .
>
> There was also a lack of information and communication from the gunnery officer on the bridge who should have gotten the word to the damage control party to get up more ammo.
>
> Damage control parties did finally start getting ammo moving up to the gun mounts—but the *time delay* was a serious factor and never should have happened.[26]

Another large portion of the problems with gunnery were traceable to a very inexperienced pointer/communicator in the Main Gun Director. "You've got a kid up there who doesn't know diddley-squat about anything, not even the correct jargon." The pointer/communicator was responsible not only for elevating the director to align it with targets, but also for keeping the mount captains, in the gun mounts, informed of the type of shells and type of powder they should be firing, and keeping them informed about the movements the gun turrets were about to make. (It was not desirable to have the crews of the gun turrets caught by surprise when power machinery under the control of the gun director suddenly rotated their turrets, or suddenly stopped rotating them.) An inexperienced man could not begin to perform all these tasks, as Park was well aware, as he had been in this job at an earlier stage of his career on the *Maddox* and had felt totally inadequate until he learned how to do it.[27]

On August 2, the men in the five-inch turrets were badly banged around by unexpected movements of their turrets, and they were not getting an adequate flow of shells from their respective magazines in the bottom of the ship. For lack of proper shells, they were putting anything available into the guns. Park says that even dummy rounds were fired—just metal, with no explosive in them— since being harmless, they were kept permanently in the turrets, while real ammunition was kept in the magazines.[28]

Portions of Park's account find support from other sources. Ronald Stalsberg says that the ride in his turret was rougher than it needed to be—the man in the director neglected to disconnect Mount 51 when rotating the ship's turrets to targets on which Mount 51 could not bear, and thus he banged Mount 51 into the stops that prevented the gun barrels from smashing into the superstructure of the ship, or from being aimed at the superstructure of the ship—but "the ride is never smooth."[29]

Richard Corsette feels that Park seriously exaggerates the gunnery problems, but he confirms Park's statement that dummy rounds were fired. Halpern says that the five-inch shells fired at the PT boats included a dozen star shells—totally inappropriate for the situation. Stalsberg also believes that some star shells were fired, probably by Mount 52 (the turret that would have been assigned to fire them in a situation that really called for them). No blue shells (star shells) came to Mount 51 during the action. Stalsberg thinks some of the people handling ammunition might not have understood the color-coding system, and might not have realized that the blue-painted shells were star shells; Halpern says "they were in the handling room and there wasn't time to weed them out."[30]

Most important, all sources indicate that the average rate of fire of the five-inch guns was far below what it should have been. According to Stalsberg, if everything went smoothly, each of the two-barrel five-inch gun mounts could put out forty rounds per minute for a brief period, but then the ammunition in the upper handling room would be used up. After that, the need to bring up ammunition from the magazines would slow the rate of fire to twenty-eight or thirty rounds per minute, at best.[31] The figures on ammunition expenditure indicate that in more than ten minutes of firing,[32] the three five-inch turrets, between them, managed to get off only 151 shells, an average of less than five shells per minute per turret, even including star shells.

As Stalsberg comments, "We certainly could have fired at a much more rapid rate than that." He says he can no longer recall this action in great detail, but he believes that the main problem was that the gun director was not keeping the guns locked onto the PTs. He does not recall a serious problem with the supply of ammunition to the guns, holding the rate of fire to an abnormally low level when the guns *were* locked on.[33]

The ammunition supply to his turret (Mount 51), however, was better than that to others. The root of the problem was that the U.S. Navy was suffering from a serious manpower shortage at this time, and was routinely sending ships out to the Pacific with fewer men aboard than would be needed to operate them properly in combat. Richard Corsette's recollection is that the theoretical wartime complement for the *Maddox* was 296 men, but that the destroyer actually had about 212. When the shooting began on August 2, the magazines were not manned, which created a serious problem once the "ready service" shells had all been fired. Lieutenant Connell, the weapons officer, ordered the crew of Mount 52 to go below and assist in hoisting ammunition from the magazines to Mount 51: "Until the ready service rings were replenished, only MT 51 could fire."[34]

As soon as the ship secured from General Quarters, Park ran topside to find out what had happened. There he met the gun captains from the five-inch turrets, who were already discussing the problems. There was a general agreement that something had to be done. Before August 4, the assignments for General Quarters were rearranged; Park was assigned the station of pointer/communicator in the main gun director.

Air Attack on the PT Boats

Shortly after the torpedo boats turned away, four F-8E Crusaders from the carrier *Ticonderoga* arrived and attacked the retreating vessels. The *Maddox* ceased fire and turned southward again as the planes arrived;[35] Captain Herrick felt he could let the planes handle the PT boats from that point onward. Herrick received orders to retire from the area rather than pursuing, but these were sent to him only after he had already turned southward for reasons purely involving the local situation, and reported to his superiors that he intended to retire from the Gulf of Tonkin "at best speed" unless otherwise directed.[36]

By the time the planes arrived, all three PT boats were heading for shore, but in two groups; T-333 and T-336 were together in the lead, and T-339 was trailing.[37] The American aircraft split up to attack all three, firing Zuni rockets and strafing with 20-mm cannon. Initially, Commander James Stockdale and Ltjg. Richard Hastings attacked the two lead boats (it is not clear which attacked T-333 and which attacked T-336), while Commander R. F. Mohrhardt and Lt. Commander C. E. Southwick attacked T-339. Mohrhardt and Southwick later also attacked the two lead boats.

All indications from U.S. Navy sources are that no hits were scored with Zuni rockets. Stockdale, Mohrhardt, and Southwick each specifically saw their own Zuni rockets miss their targets.[38]

Hastings himself may not have seen where his rockets went; he was distracted by damage to his own plane. He had been diving to fire; as he was pulling out of the dive, he felt a sharp jolt, and when he looked he saw that a substantial piece of his port wing was missing. He had seen the flashes of gunfire aimed at him by the boat at which he was diving; he assumed he had been hit, and so reported to the other aircraft. He was apparently mistaken. Stockdale "had a good look at that damage" when he and Hastings rejoined. He is confident it was caused simply by the stress on the wing when Hastings was pulling out of his dive; the F-8 was easy to overstress.[39]

It is very unlikely that either of Hastings' Zunis hit. A Zuni is a large rocket, five inches in diameter, over nine feet long, weighing 107 pounds, and with a motor powerful enough that it is usually moving at supersonic speed by the time it reaches its target.[40] If a hit had been scored with such a weapon, one of the pilots would have noticed the fact. None did, however, and the description of the attack on the two lead boats in the after-action report filed from the carrier states baldly, "the Zunis did not hit the targets."[41]

Stockdale escorted Hastings south to the location of the *Maddox*. Hastings orbited there, where he would have rescue available if he had to bail out, while Stockdale headed northward again after the torpedo boats. The men on the torpedo boats did not realize, when he arrived back on the scene of the combat, that he was one of the participants in the initial air attacks on them, coming back for a second time. They thought he was a new arrival on the scene; this explains why North Vietnamese accounts say that five American aircraft attacked the torpedo boats, while American accounts make it clear there were only four.

The pilots scored hits on all three boats, with 20-mm guns. T-339 was the hardest hit; when the American jets were finished, it was dead in the water and smoke was pouring from it. The damage, however, was not as serious as some accounts suggest. The vessel's engines were crippled, but much of the smoke, at least, came from a smoke generator. One Vietnamese account implies that the smoke generator had been turned on deliberately to screen the torpedo boat from the Americans, and while acknowledging that it did not provide much concealment, the account suggests that it may have given the American pilots the impression that the boat was heavily damaged, and thus encouraged them to shift their attack to the other vessels. Another states that it was set off accidentally by a 20-mm shell from one of the American aircraft. Both Mohrhardt and Southwick say that someone on the boat threw a smoke bomb into the water.[42]

The torpedo boats fired back at the planes as best they could, but their 14.5-mm machine guns were not working reliably. Those on T-339 jammed. A bearing in the gun mount on T-333 broke, making it impossible to train the gun for several crucial minutes. The radarman grabbed a light automatic weapon— probably an AK submachine gun, a shorter-barreled version of the famous AK-47—and provided what must be considered subliminal air defense by firing it at the attacking aircraft.[43]

The DRV eventually decided that one American plane had been shot down and one damaged. There was confusion for a while, however; the officer who was responsible for keeping track of American aircraft losses was unable to file any report on the question because he had been severely wounded and was unconscious.[44] No DRV source says how many aircraft the DRV believed had been shot down during this period of confusion, but it seems likely that two were claimed. James Stockdale has commented on the way his and Hastings's aircraft must have looked when they left the scene, one in fact seriously damaged and both "heading south over the horizon right on the deck belching the inevitable black smoke of J-57 engines at 100% military [power]."[45] If the crews of the boats noticed and reported this, the DRV could easily have concluded that gunners on the boats had shot down two U.S. planes.[46]

T-339 would probably have been sunk, and perhaps one or both of the others in addition, had it not been for a failure of communication between Rear Admiral Robert Moore (on the *Ticonderoga*) and Vice Admiral Johnson (Commander of the Seventh Fleet). Moore had sent a second flight of aircraft with orders to sink the PT boats. This was exactly what Admiral Johnson both expected and wanted him to do. Johnson authorized pursuit by the aircraft as far as the North Vietnamese coastline, although he is not certain that this was within his authority; there may have been a policy he was violating that would have required pursuit to stop at the three-mile limit. Admiral Johnson ordered the *Maddox* not to pursue the PT boats, because he felt this task could better be left to aircraft. Admiral Moore, however, when he saw the order that the *Maddox* not pursue the PT boats, interpreted it as meaning that Admiral Johnson had changed his mind and did not want the PT boats to be sunk; he therefore ordered the second flight of aircraft not to fire on them, when they reached the area.[47]

There is a great deal of disagreement between different sources about how much damage was inflicted on the torpedo boats, and by what American weapons. U.S. sources, except for Stalsberg, state that the destroyer scored at least one direct hit with a five-inch shell. All U.S. sources state that the aircraft scored no hits with Zuni rockets. Vietnamese Naval officers interviewed in 1989 said that there was no direct hit by a five-inch shell, but that there was a direct hit with a rocket. Despite doubts raised by Stalsberg's recollection, this author is inclined to accept the American version, on the grounds that (1) the people firing such weapons are in a much better position to keep track of what weapon was fired at what moment than the people being hit by them; and (2) the hit scored on the torpedo boat seems to have occurred before the time the aircraft joined the action.

The Vietnamese accounts are most convincing about the total amount of damage suffered by Vietnamese forces. The Americans believed they had sunk at least one torpedo boat, T-339, but they were mistaken.

When the shooting was over, T-333 and T-336 were unable either to locate T-339 or to raise it on the radio. They headed for the mouth of the Song Ma (the mouth of the river was marked as Lach Chao on American maps, but was called Lach Truong by the Vietnamese). They reached shore at the beach of Sam Son just south of the river mouth. The choice of this location may have been based on the need to beach T-336 to keep it from sinking; it had been seriously damaged and had taken on a lot of water. They reported that T-339 had been lost in action. T-339, however, was only badly damaged. The radios and the engines had been knocked out, and water was coming in through a hole in the hull six or seven centimeters in size. The hole, however, was soon patched. After several hours' work one of the two engines was running again, and the vessel limped to shore on the island of Hon Ne, a few miles north of the river mouth.[48]

This account seems consistent with the last American sighting report from the afternoon of August 2. Lt. Commander Donald Hegrat, a photo-reconnaissance pilot operating from the *Ticonderoga*, had already been in the air when Herrick requested air support for the *Maddox*. Hegrat asked for permission to go to the scene, but he had to hold north of the *Ticonderoga* for a least an hour before permission was granted. During this interval he did an in-flight refueling. By the time Hegrat reached the scene of the action, most of the units that had been involved in the combat were gone. There was only one Vietnamese vessel in sight. It was at least ten miles from the *Maddox*, and was heading for shore at what Hegrat recalls as fairly high speed. Hegrat cannot now recall the exact heading of this vessel; he has only a faint impression that it was something between east and northeast. A report filed a few hours after the end of his mission says he saw it going north.[49] He photographed it, but the bad light conditions of the late afternoon made the photographs sufficiently unclear that the exact type of vessel could not be identified.[50]

The Americans faced a considerable amount of conflicting information about DRV losses in this battle. When the four jets had finished their attack, and they and the *Maddox* left the area, one torpedo boat had been dead in the water and apparently sinking. Soon after, the Americans intercepted the incorrect report from T-333 and T-336 that T-339 had been lost in action.[51] It is almost certain that an American reconnaissance plane took photographs of Lach Truong within the next few days, which would have shown T-333 and T-336 but not T-339 there. There was thus some justification for the conclusion of Edward Marolda and Oscar Fitzgerald that one torpedo boat, T-339, was sunk.[52]

Some people who did not have full access to the above information have suggested that there were two torpedo boats sunk; their view may have been derived from the fact that Lt. Commander Hegrat, when he searched late in the afternoon, after T-333 and T-336 had already reached shore, had been able to find only one vessel still in the area of combat. It is hard to figure out what support there may have been for the way Secretary McNamara told members of key Senate committees on August 6 that he believed all three boats had been sunk.[53]

The question was conclusively settled in July 1966, when a group of three torpedo boats again came out for action in the Gulf of Tonkin, and all three were sunk by American aircraft. American naval vessels picked up nineteen officers and men from the vessels that had been sunk, and discovered that these had been torpedo boats T-333, T-336, and T-339. They were in fact the same vessels, not replacements serving under the numbers of lost vessels. Most of the men captured were recent recruits who had not been involved in the incident of 1964, but two of them knew a great deal about it. Senior Lieutenant Tran Bao had probably not been present at the incident of August 2 (see above) but had been executive officer of PT Squadron 135 at the time, and in that capacity had written the after-action report on the incident. Mid-Lieutenant Nguyen Van Gian (the American interrogation report lists his name as Giang), commander of T-339 in 1964, was still commanding it in 1966 despite the belief of the Americans that it had been sunk in the attack on the *Maddox*.

Tran Bao said that no torpedo boats had been lost in the attack on the *Maddox*, and described for his captors when, where, and how each of the three vessels involved had reached shore. It seems clear in fact from the overall report on the interrogation of the nineteen men that no North Vietnamese torpedo boats had been lost under any circumstances during the year 1964.[54]

Another prisoner, Senior Captain Nguyen Van Hoa, captured in July 1967, described an incident in 1966 (presumably the one in which the nineteen men discussed above were captured) in which three PT boats were sunk. An officer in Washington later misread one of the reports on Captain Hoa's interrogation and thought Hoa had said that three PT boats had been sunk in the attack on the *Maddox* in August 1964. The original interrogation report not only says no such thing, it conveys a clear impression that no PT boats were sunk at any time during the year 1964. (For further details see Chapter 8.)

Evaluation

When Secretary of Defense McNamara and JCS Chairman Wheeler briefed key senators on the incident four days later, they gave the senators a simple picture of unprovoked attack against U.S. ships on the high seas. According to this picture, the attacks on the islands of Hon Me and Hon Ngu, three nights before the August incident, had had nothing to do with the U.S. Navy. McNamara testified:

Our navy played absolutely no part in, was not associated with, was not aware of, any South Vietnamese actions, if there were any. I want to make that very clear to you. The *Maddox* was operating in international waters, was carrying out a routine patrol of the type we carry out all over the world at all times. It was not informed of, was not aware of, had no evidence of, and so far as I know today has no knowledge of, any possible South Vietnamese actions in connection with the two islands that Senator [Wayne] Morse referred to.[55]

McNamara described a force of junks, owned and operated by the RVN (though some had been paid for by U.S. military assistance funds), that had been set up to block maritime infiltration into South Vietnam. He described this force as having been so completely a South Vietnamese operation that he said he did not believe the U.S. had any advisors aboard any of the junks even when they were operating south of the seventeenth parallel. He described the raids against North Vietnam as having been carried out by this force of patrol junks.

> In the process of that action, as the junk patrol has increased in strength they have moved further and further north endeavoring to find the source of the infiltration.
>
> As part of that, as I reported to you earlier this week, we understand that the South Vietnamese sea force carried out patrol action around these islands and actually shelled the points they felt were associated with this infiltration. Our ships had absolutely no knowledge of it, were not connected with it; in no sense of the word can we be considered to have backstopped the effort.[56]

(The idea that the PTFs at Danang were part of a force set up to combat infiltration was the standard cover story for their operations. This idea had been discussed in detail, and specifically described as a "cover story," in a message written by General Paul Harkins, commander of MACV, in late May.)[57]

The senators were further told that the *Maddox* had been about thirty miles from the North Vietnamese coast at the time torpedo boats were first sighted heading south toward Hon Me, a few hours before the shooting started. They were told that when the torpedo boats approached with apparent intent to attack, the *Maddox* fired three warning shots, but did not attempt actually to hit the boats until they themselves had fired torpedoes. (Secretary McNamara and General Wheeler each said in their testimony that the fire from the *Maddox* was a response to torpedoes being fired by the PT boats, but Secretary McNamara also presented a prepared statement indicating, not very clearly, that the *Maddox* had actually fired first. No senator seems to have noticed the discrepancy; they all seem to have accepted as true the statements that the North Vietnamese fired first.)[58] What was passed to the main body of the Senate was a simplified version, in which the warning shots were omitted and the *Maddox* was said to have taken no action until the North Vietnamese craft had fired torpedoes.[59]

They were given the impression that, in accord with the rules of engagement as then understood, the U.S. forces had only driven off the attackers instead of pursuing and trying to sink them.[60]

This picture was false in almost every detail. U.S. Naval officers had not only known about the attacks on the two islands, they had given the PTFs the orders for those raids. The *Maddox* had not been thirty miles from the coast, but fifteen, when the torpedo boats were first sighted. The *Maddox* had been trying its best to sink the torpedo boats, and scoring hits with the shrapnel from exploding shells if not with the shells themselves, for several minutes before any torpedoes were launched. Finally, when the boats turned away, the *Maddox* pursued and attempted to sink them. The *Maddox* broke off only when the four planes from the *Ticonderoga* arrived and took over the pursuit, using rockets and 20-mm cannon. The greatest restraint shown was that after the first four jets had exhausted their rockets and ammunition, the additional jets that arrived later on the scene did not renew the attack. And that, as has been explained, happened because Admiral Moore had misunderstood Admiral Johnson's orders, not because any American commander wanted to avoid the use of excessive force.

The way the executive branch misled the Congress may to some extent have reflected a desire to conceal genuine military secrets. The *Maddox* had not been on a "routine patrol," but on a fairly sensitive intelligence-gathering mission.

One must also remember that not all of the incorrect statements made about these events arose from deliberate dishonesty. McNamara in particular was suffering both from lack of knowledge—his ignorance of the weapons carried by PT boats was conspicuous in his statements of August 1964—and lack of sleep. On two important points—the question of who had fired first, and the number of PT boats sunk in the August 2 incident—his verbal testimony was much less accurate than the prepared statement that he brought to the hearing and gave to the senators in written form.

A draft of a report on the Tonkin Gulf incidents written soon after by Assistant Secretary of Defense for International Security Affairs John McNaughton gives the impression that the overall planned patrol track of the *Maddox* was less provocative than it was—staying farther from shore and not going so far north in the gulf—and is flatly wrong in placing the destroyer farther from shore than was actually the case in the August 2 incident. This implies that McNaughton, and by inference McNaughton's boss, McNamara, did not know what the *Maddox* had been doing. There is the possibility that this was simply a classified preliminary draft of something intended for eventual public release, in which case its errors might have represented deliberate deception rather than ignorance. A later summary of the events written within the Pentagon, however, that was classified "top secret" and very definitely was not intended for broad dissemination even within the government, likewise places the destroyer much farther from the coast than was actually the case on August 2, and gives the impression that the planned patrol track did not go nearly so far north into the gulf as was actually the case. This summary also states that "no hot pursuit was attempted" against the torpedo boats that had carried out the August 2 attack.[61]

McNamara denies to this day that there was any dishonesty in his testimony. At times his defense has seemed a bit strained, as when he argued in 1968 that his statement that "our Navy was not aware of any South Vietnamese actions" should be regarded as true, because all it had really meant, in context, was that Captain John Herrick had not known enough details about the "South Vietnamese actions" to have been able to coordinate his ship's movements with them. He denied that he had said in 1964 that the *Maddox* did not know anything about the raids.[62] In his memoirs he acknowledges that he had said in 1964 that the *Maddox* did not know anything about the raids, and admits that this was "totally incorrect" since Captain Herrick did know about 34A; but he continues to claim that he was correct in saying that "our Navy . . . was not aware of any South Vietnamese actions." Captain Herrick was not part of the U.S. Navy? He also continues to claim that "the U.S. Navy did not administer 34A operations."[63]

Thomas Hughes has commented that as Director of the Bureau of Intelligence and Research (INR) at the State Department, he was cleared to know about covert operations such as OPLAN 34A. Allen Whiting, head of the Far East Division of INR, also was cleared to know. Most intelligence analysts, however, were not cleared to know, and the written reports on such matters as North Vietnamese motivations and behavior would not have reflected knowledge of these things. Mr. Hughes gave his superiors oral briefings in which his full knowledge of such matters was factored in, but he does not believe he would have made written reports reflecting the full extent of his knowledge. The written reports were prepared on the assumption that they would be seen by people not cleared for such matters.

Mr. Hughes does not know how much lower-level analysts figured out about OPLAN 34A on the basis of information from Radio Hanoi via *FBIS*, from the *New York Times*, or other media channels. If they did figure out part of it, they would have known it was only part, and they would have known it was information they were not supposed to have. They might have engaged in self-censorship, keeping it out of their reports, but the decision whether to factor it into their reports would have been an individual one.[64] The problem this posed for analysis of the Tonkin Gulf incidents, in which OPLAN 34A was central to DRV motivations, is obvious.

Some DRV sources have suggested that the torpedo boats were not actually approaching in order to attack, and that the destroyer had started a fight unnecessarily by firing on them. The DRV would later claim that the torpedo boats had been "compelled to take action in self-defense" after they had been fired upon by the *Maddox*.[65] It is quite clear, however, that this was not actually the case.

It would be difficult to pick either side as having been wholly to blame for this incident. If the United States had wanted to avoid a violent incident, then during a week when the United States was sponsoring repeated raids against the North Vietnamese coast, it would not have sent a U.S. destroyer so close to that coast, under conditions where the captain would feel he had no choice but to fire first when approached. Captain Herrick wanted to avoid an incident, but his orders made it impossible for him to do so. If the DRV had wanted to avoid a violent incident, the orders with which the torpedo boats headed south to Hon Me would have been different, and the misunderstanding that sent them out from Hon Me to attack the *Maddox* could not have occurred.

The U.S. forces in fact felt that they had shown restraint in deciding not to retaliate against North Vietnamese forces other than the three boats that had carried out the attack on the destroyer, and not even sending more planes to attack those three boats once the planes immediately on the scene had exhausted their rockets and ammunition. This sense that restraint had been shown may have predisposed the United States to react more violently after the second incident, two days later.

Premier Khanh, in Saigon, urged the United States to take some retaliatory action to avoid being branded a "paper tiger."[66] Ambassador Taylor shared Khanh's view; he urged retaliation against North Vietnam, and later expressed surprise in his memoirs that no such action was taken. He even suggested to Washington that the United States adopt, and publicly announce, a policy of attacking any North Vietnamese Swatow boat that ventured into international waters.[67] This would have been so imprudent politically, especially given its inconsistency with America's public posture of defending the freedom of navigation in international waters, that it is hard to believe Washington could have accepted the idea. Possibly Taylor was engaged in the standard bureaucratic maneuver of proposing an unrealistic action in order to get a less drastic one accepted as a compromise. Undersecretary of State George Ball told Robert McNamara that the action Taylor was suggesting would have amounted to a declaration of war. McNamara said he thought Taylor was overreacting, and that Taylor's message would just have to be ignored.[68]

President Johnson decided not to retaliate for the incident; he explained in his memoirs that this decision had been based on doubt that the attack on the *Maddox* had actually been ordered by the government of the DRV.[69] This surely must represent American interception of the recall message that, according to officers of the People's Navy, was sent when the commander of the People's Navy realized that the torpedo boats were attacking the *Maddox*.

It is also crucial to note the way the Americans had been filling in the blanks on intercepted messages during the hours before the August 2 incident. The United States had intercepted three North Vietnamese messages containing attack orders. In no case was the target of the attack specified, but officers on the *Maddox* believed that their ship was the intended target, and the actual attack on August 2 confirmed their judgment. This left them with a predisposition to interpret any later intercept dealing with operations against an unspecified target as referring also to an attack on their ship.

This tendency was accentuated by the way the first of the three ambiguous messages had been interpreted. First, officers on the destroyer had seen an intercepted message indicating that the North Vietnamese navy was to attack an unspecified enemy. Then, they had seen a report on the location of an enemy vessel, the location being their own. They deduced that the enemy to be attacked was their destroyer. They were entirely correct in this case, but there existed a possibility of future misunderstanding. The DRV coastal defense forces regarded the *Maddox* as an enemy vessel, and made periodic reports on the destroyer's movements. If some future message dealing with action against an unspecified target were intercepted, the chances were good that a message reporting the location of the *Maddox* would also be intercepted shortly before or afterward. Putting the two together, the Americans would see a repetition of the pattern they had seen on the night of August 1–2, and be sure that they had intercepted an order for an attack against the *Maddox*.

DRV Accounts of the Incident

The DRV gave this incident much less publicity, at first, than did the United States. The misunderstanding that had sent the torpedo boats out to attack the *Maddox* at the wrong time and the wrong place, well beyond even the twelve-mile limit claimed by the DRV, had created an embarrassing situation. The August 3 and August 4 issues of *Nhan Dan* said nothing about the incident. On the front page of the August 5 issue there was finally an article, but it was rather inconspicuous near the bottom of the page; it did not portray the incident as very important and indeed did not make it clear that either side had actually done any shooting. It said that the *Maddox* had been behaving in a provocative fashion and that DRV naval units had "acted" to drive the ship out of Vietnamese territorial waters. The lead stories in the paper that day dealt with agricultural production.

After the United States launched airstrikes against North Vietnam on the afternoon of August 5, DRV public statements became less restrained. A *Nhan Dan* editorial published August 6 said that the DRV vessels had fought valiantly against the *Maddox* on August 2. Such accounts, however, still made the actions of the DRV vessels seem less aggressive than they had actually been (note the parallel with the way U.S. accounts made U.S. actions seem less aggressive than was actually the case). The typical DRV account praised the torpedo boats for showing great heroism in driving the *Maddox* out of Vietnamese territorial waters, while obscuring the fact that the torpedo boats had attempted actually to sink the *Maddox*. These accounts usually included several of the following elements:

1. Many stated that the combat had occurred much closer to the coast than had actually been the case; in one version the shooting began only eight miles from the coast.[70]

2. Many described the Vietnamese vessels involved as "patrol boats" (in other words Swatow boats, which would have been incapable of sinking a destroyer), rather than torpedo boats.[71] Articles appeared even in the Army newspaper *Quan Doi Nhan Dan* and the navy journal *Hai Quan* conveying the absurd impression that patrol vessels had defeated a destroyer with superior gunfire.[72] A later article on the August 2 incident included diagrams showing the ways a destroyer could dodge a torpedo after it had been fired, but still avoided the use of the word "torpedo" (*ngu loi*).[73]

3. When DRV statements admitted that the Vietnamese vessels had been torpedo boats, they did not mention any torpedoes actually having been fired (though one account, while not specifying the type of vessel, did have a very clear hint: it described the vessels first using gunfire, and then using all types of weapons with which they were equipped).[74]

4. The impression was often conveyed that the Vietnamese vessels did not decide to attack the *Maddox* until after the *Maddox* had fired at them. The greatest extreme to which this line was carried was a claim (made in a speech by a naval officer to a youth group) that the *Maddox* had made a "surprise attack" against the Vietnamese vessels.[75]

5. The impression was often conveyed that the encounter between the *Maddox* and the DRV vessels had occurred by chance, rather than because the DRV vessels had deliberately set out after the American destroyer.

The DRV, and in particular the navy, went into ecstasies of patriotic pride about this incident. Some of it was based on exaggerated claims that the relatively small and low-technology vessels of the DRV had inflicted serious damage on the *Maddox*, had killed (*tieu diet*, a verb often used during the war in DRV accounts of casualties inflicted on the enemy, which could be translated "annihilated," "destroyed," or "wiped out") officers and men on the destroyer, and had shot down one of the jets that attacked them just after their fight with the destroyer.[76] There was also, however, some very real basis for the pride. The torpedo boats had fought first against a vessel much larger than they, and then against jet aircraft. These were enemies having much more advanced technology than they, belonging to the strongest navy in the world. They had not gotten off unscathed—there had been four men killed and six wounded—but no torpedo boats had been sunk, and if they had not really inspired the panic they claimed aboard the *Maddox*, they had gotten Washington to pull the U.S. Navy back farther from their coast. U.S. statements emphasized that the United States had not been driven out of the Gulf of Tonkin, but after August 2, U.S. ships stayed farther out toward the middle of the gulf; it would be more than six months before Washington would again permit any U.S. destroyer to make the sort of close approach to the coast—within the range of five-inch gunfire—that the *Maddox* had been making on July 31 and August 1. These were impressive accomplishments for a navy so small and so recently established. And if the People's Navy (not knowing about Admiral Moore's misinterpretation of Admiral Johnson's orders) chose to interpret the failure of the Americans to push their pursuit of the torpedo boats at the end of the battle as meaning that the Americans had been intimidated by the fighting qualities of the torpedo boats,[77] the mistake seems understandable.

The DeSoto Patrol Resumes

Captain Herrick suggested that his mission be terminated, but his superiors rejected the idea. Admiral Johnson, commander of the Seventh Fleet, probably represents a typical reaction; he considered it important as a matter of principle not to allow the impression that the U.S. Navy could be driven out of the area.[1] He was, however, willing to have the return of the DeSoto patrol to the gulf be rather brief, ending well before the originally scheduled date.[2] When the DeSoto patrol resumed on August 3, it did so under new rules, keeping the patrol farther from the coast; this reduced its ability to gather useful intelligence (see below). The admiral did not want his ships wasting too much time in the gulf, if they were no longer going to be doing anything useful other than demonstrating that they could not be driven out.

A second destroyer, the *Turner Joy*, was ordered to join the *Maddox*. The *Turner Joy* had up to this time been a "watchdog picket" for the *Ticonderoga*, stationed at the mouth of the Gulf of Tonkin to give warning of anything coming out.

Radarman Second Class Chad James was a CIC watch supervisor, and also ECM coordinator, on the *Turner Joy*. When the *Turner Joy* was chosen to join the *Maddox* and go into the gulf after the August 2 incident, James took this as a reflection of the fact that the *Turner Joy* was the best ship available, in fact the best destroyer in Destroyer Squadron 19. When interviewed in 1990, he returned to this point repeatedly. "We knew we were better. . . . We were going to take care of business." Before entering the gulf the *Turner Joy* was ordered to take ammunition from another destroyer (James thinks this was the *Edson*, but he is not sure), which was very unusual and annoyed the men on the other destroyer.[3]

The two destroyers entered the gulf to resume the DeSoto patrol on August 3.

The Joint Chiefs of Staff had directed that the closest approach of the destroyers to the North Vietnamese mainland was to be "11 miles, repeat 11 miles."[4] Michael Forrestal, Special Assistant for Vietnam Affairs in the State Department and also chairman of the Vietnam Coordinating Committee, reported that the eleven-mile limitation "reflects the fact that NVN probably claims that her territorial waters extend 12 miles off her coast. We do not admit this claim, and the theory is to show this by penetrating it to the extent of one mile."[5]

Marolda and Fitzgerald incorrectly state that the Joint Chiefs had "advised that the ships now could approach no closer than twelve nautical miles to the North Vietnamese mainland."[6] Joseph Goulden, on the other hand, in a misunderstanding that has been repeated by some later authors, says that when Captain Herrick wanted to end the patrol after August 2, "the Pacific command ordered him to resume the patrol, and on a course even more provocative than before." Herrick's new orders in fact made his course much less provocative, not more. Goulden's error arose partly from the fact that he was working from a preliminary draft of the orders, which allowed closer approaches to the coast than the version under which Herrick actually operated when he resumed the DeSoto patrol on August 3, but Goulden was applying an exaggerated interpretation even to that preliminary draft.[7]

Herrick had been told his closest approach to the North Vietnamese coast was to be eleven miles, but the schedule gave him five days, and he seems to have been in no hurry. On August 3 and again on August 4, his closest approaches to the coast were about sixteen miles. The amount of actual intelligence collected was much lower than before August 2.[8] The Joint Chiefs, however, when they extended the limit on approaches to the coast from eight to eleven miles, had left the limit on approaches to islands at four miles, and Herrick actually did approach to within about nine and a half or ten miles of islands on August 3 and 4. This should have satisfied Washington's desire that he demonstrate nonrecognition of any claim the DRV might make to a twelve-mile limit, since the DRV would certainly claim territorial waters extending the same distance from islands as from the mainland.

Two of Captain Herrick's messages from this period (the first of which has sometimes been attributed mistakenly to Admiral Moore, on the *Ticonderoga*) reveal his perception of the situation, based on his experience August 2 and on the intercepted DRV radio messages that he was getting from the comvan:

It is apparent that DRV has cut [*sic*] down the gauntlet and now considers itself at war with us. It is felt that they will attack U.S. forces on sight with no regard for cost. U.S. ships in the Gulf of Tonkin can no longer assume that they will be considered neutrals exercising the right of free transit. They will be treated as belligerents from first detection and must consider themselves as such, DRV PTs have advantage especially at night of being able to hide in junk concentrations all across the Gulf of Tonkin. This would allow attack from short range with little or no early warning.[9]

Evaluation of info from various sources indicates that DRV considers patrol directly involved with 34-A ops. DRV considers US ships present as enemies because of these ops and have already indicated their readiness to treat us in that category.[10]

Ronald Stalsberg says that when the *Maddox* went back into the gulf, "I felt pretty sure that we were probably in for some more problems." The men in his gun mount, however, were on the average less tense than they had been before the August 2 attack; they had gained confidence that they could handle trouble if it came.[11]

Commander Robert C. Barnhart, Jr., captain of the *Turner Joy*, had much less information about the overall situation than Herrick did. There is really no way Barnhart could have been given full information. Much of what Herrick knew involved intercepts of North Vietnamese radio messages, and since nobody had expected that Barnhart would be part of the DeSoto patrol, he had not been given the special security clearance required for access to such information. Even if Barnhart had been cleared for the information, it could not have been transmitted to him because the *Turner Joy* did not have the code systems used for communicating information from radio intercepts.

The *Turner Joy* was, like the *Maddox*, seriously shorthanded in August 1964. Sonarman Second Class Richard Bacino was in charge of the visual watch on the *Turner Joy*. He recalls that the men under him were on "port-and-starboard" watches, half of them on duty at any given time. (When the ship was at General Quarters, of course, all the men were on duty.) Bacino himself had nobody to whom he could hand over responsibility for the visual watch; he was on call twenty-four hours a day. He had installed a mattress pad in a corner of the deck so he could snatch bits of sleep there, having learned by experience that if he tried to go below to his regular bunk, he would almost always be called topside again to evaluate some sighting before he had gotten any significant amount of sleep.[12]

On board the *Turner Joy*, crewmen were briefed on the enemies they were likely to face and shown pictures of DRV aircraft and PT boats.[13] Ensign Douglas Smith, first lieutenant of the *Turner Joy*, says the general attitude aboard the ship was positive:

Most of us hoped something would happen, but few really expected anything. Especially after the boats were resoundingly defeated the previous day.

This first day was almost as if it had been taken from a story book. The crew was more thrilled than one can imagine at finally having the opportunity to play at war. Everyone carried a survival knife, not necessarily because it was considered necessary, but because it was fun to carry. In the Navy this is not necessarily unusual—but to see the display of weapons carried this day was indeed hilarious. One fire control technician in the forward director carried a full size Gurkha knife, which proved nearly as dangerous as the threat itself.[14]

On August 3, there were many junks in the area patrolled by the two destroyers, most of them probably fishing junks. The destroyers repeatedly passed quite close to these junks. To Ltjg. John Barry, ASW Officer of the *Turner Joy*, "the water seemed cluttered." There was no sense of tension; Barry saw a couple of people on the small craft wave at the destroyers.[15]

By the morning of August 4, these small craft had disappeared. That afternoon, a small tanker, of a sort that could have been used to refuel PT boats, emerged from behind an island, saw the destroyers, turned abruptly around, and went back behind the island. To Barry the contrast with the previous day's relaxed atmosphere seemed striking, but he still did not think that there would be another incident like that of August 2.[16]

The August 3 Raid

On the afternoon of August 3, another four-boat raiding party (PTFs 1, 2, 5, and 6) left Danang, this time heading for mainland objectives about seventy-five miles north of the DMZ, at Cape Vinh Son and at Cua Ron (the mouth of the Ron River). PTF 2 had to turn back with engine problems. PTFs 1 and 5 shelled a radar installation at Vinh Son for twenty-five minutes starting at about 2300G; PTF 6 shelled what is usually described as having been a security post on the riverbank at Cua Ron (though one officer suggests the target may actually have been a group of Swatow boats moored at a dock just inside the mouth of the river). A DRV patrol vessel, presumably a Swatow, pursued PTF 6 for forty minutes but was too slow to catch it.[17]

MACV requested that Herrick keep the destroyers north of latitude 19°20' until the morning of August 6, to avoid mutual interference between the DeSoto patrol and OPLAN 34A operations. The request from MACV did not specify the nature, location, or timing of the OPLAN 34A operations in question.[18] In fact, aside from the shellings on the night of August 3 described above, there were two other raids planned: capture of the crew of a fishing boat in the vicinity of Vinh, and shelling buildings on the island of Hon Mat. The schedule of raids for the month of August indicates that these were to occur concurrently on August 5.[19] It seems probable but not certain that this meant they were to occur not long after midnight of the night of August 4–5.

Admiral Sharp suggested that the American destroyers far to the north might serve as decoys to distract the DRV's coastal defense forces from coastal raids further south.[20] As it turned out, the message telling Herrick to stay up to the north did not reach him in time, and during the raids of the night of August 3–4, the destroyers were closer to the target area than they had been intended to be, though not really close. The nearest approach of the PTFs to the destroyers was about fifty miles, and occurred more than an hour before the actual attacks.

Vietnamese naval officers interviewed in 1989 said that the DRV had not been able to track the movements of the destroyers during the night of August 3–4. The *Maddox* reported being shadowed by a vessel using a "skinhead" radar—standard for small vessels of Communist navies—starting at about 1930G.[21] It was heading southeast across the gulf when first spotted. Its commander was curious enough about the destroyers to deviate slightly from his original course and stay with them, observing from a distance, as long as they also were going approximately southeast. But when the destroyers turned north around midnight, he continued toward whatever his original destination may have been. His vessel was near the southwest corner of Hainan when the destroyers lost it on their radar, several hours later. Given this pattern of movement, the vessel was surely Chinese. Officers of the Vietnamese People's Navy in 1989 gave this author the impression that the Chinese had passed some report of this to Vietnam,[22] but there is no way to tell how fast the Vietnamese got this report, and when they did get it they might not have been sure that the vessels whose movements it described were the *Maddox* and *Turner Joy*.

The Vietnamese who checked the facilities that had been bombarded in the OPLAN 34A raids on the night of August 3–4 are said to have found 125-mm shell fragments.[23] This was approximately the size that would have been fired by the main guns of the *Maddox* and *Turner Joy* (estimates of the size of the guns on the *Maddox*, in DRV sources, range from 123 mm to 127 mm; the actual size was 127 mm).

The basis for this report is difficult to explain. The largest weapon that the Americans even considered mounting on a PTF, in 1964, was a 106-mm recoilless rifle. This was a large enough weapon that its shell fragments might have been mistakenly evaluated as having come from a 125-mm weapon, by Vietnamese soldiers who were probably not familiar with the exact appearance of the fragments from either 106-mm or 125-mm guns (neither having been used against targets in that area of Vietnam for at least ten years), but who had spent many hours watching an unfriendly vessel armed with guns of approximately 125 mm maneuvering offshore on August 1. When the Americans tested the idea in South Vietnamese waters, however, they had discovered that a 106-mm weapon was too large to be used safely aboard a PTF; the muzzle blast damaged the vessel.[24] Even these tests apparently did not take place until slightly after the August 3 operation.[25]

By the time of the August 3 operation, PTFs 7 and 8 had been equipped with 81-mm mortars, and it was intended that these be used for bombardments of shore targets in the fairly near future.[26] PTFs 7 and 8 were not, however, among the vessels that carried out the August 3 operation.

There is no good evidence from the American side that any weapon larger than 57 mm was used on the night of August 3. Cathal Flynn comments that recoilless rifles are similar enough to regular naval guns in their rate of fire and trajectory that if they were used from the sea at night, the people fired upon might believe that a destroyer had come in close to shore and shelled them. This could occur, according to Flynn, even with recoilless rifles as small as 57 mm.[27] To mistake 57-mm shell fragments for 125 mm in daylight, however, would require a considerable degree of carelessness.

The DRV had not accused the *Maddox* of involvement in the raid on Hon Me and Hon Ngu on the night of July 30–31, but the DRV did accuse the *Maddox* and *Turner Joy* of having participated in the raid of August 3–4. The available DRV accounts indicate that the raiding force was believed to have comprised four PTFs from Danang, plus the two American destroyers.[28] If the DRV had difficulty figuring out how many vessels had been involved in the operation, one reason would have been that the radar on Vinh Son really had been heavily damaged; it was out of service for probably five days or more.[29]

Were the Destroyers Set Up?

General Vo Nguyen Giap recently suggested, in a conversation in Hanoi with Robert McNamara, that the United States had sent the DeSoto patrol into the Gulf of Tonkin for provocation, hoping to get an excuse for escalation of the war. A number of people in the United States government have, at various times over the years, expressed similar suspicions. Many men aboard the *Maddox* apparently ended up suspecting that the U.S. government, or some people very high up in the government, had wanted the *Maddox* sunk or badly shot up, to provide the United States an excuse for retaliating against North Vietnam. According to stories circulating on the ship, several men on the *Maddox* saw a fleet tug with the American task force just outside the Gulf of Tonkin, a tug that would not normally have been with this task force. This would have been a suitable vessel to go in and help haul the *Maddox* out, if the *Maddox* were badly shot up. A member of the crew of the tug is rumored to have said to someone on the *Maddox* that the *Maddox* had been expected either to be sunk or to suffer heavy casualties.[30]

George Ball, undersecretary of state at the time of Tonkin Gulf, expressed very similar suspicions shortly after the war in an interview with British journalist Michael Charlton.

Ball: At that time there's no question that many of the people who were associated with the war . . . were looking for any excuse to initiate bombing.

Charlton: And this may have been the incident that those people were waiting for.

Ball: That's right. Well, it was: the 'de Soto' patrols, the sending of a destroyer up the Tonkin Gulf was primarily for provocation.

Charlton: To provoke such a response in order to pave the way for a bombing campaign?

Ball: I think so. I mean it had an intelligence objective. But let me say, I don't want to overstate this, the reason the destroyer was sent up was to show the flag, to indicate that we didn't recognize any other force in the gulf; and there was *some* intelligence objective. But on the other hand I think there was a feeling that if the destroyer got into some trouble, that would provide the provocation we needed.[31]

On February 20, 1968, testifying before the Senate Foreign Relations Committee, Secretary McNamara said:

I must address the suggestion that, in some way, the Government of the United States induced the incident on August 4 with the intent of providing an excuse to take the retaliatory action which we in fact took. . . .

I find it inconceivable that anyone even remotely familiar with our society and system of Government could suspect the existence of a conspiracy which would include almost, if not all, the entire chain of military command in the Pacific, the Chairman of the Joint Chiefs of Staff, the Joint Chiefs, the Secretary of Defense, and his chief assistants, the Secretary of State, and the President of the United States.[32]

Like so much of what McNamara told the senators, this was nonsense. It is not at all hard to suspect these people of formulating such plans (they would not have thought of this as "conspiracy") if one has read some of the documents in the files of the National Security Council. Such notions were in the air at this time and were regarded as legitimate. On August 3, the very day that the PTFs were sent northward to attack Vinh Son and Cua Ron, Ambassador Taylor proposed to Washington that if in the near future the DRV acquired MIG jets, the United States should deliberately invite them to attack U.S. reconnaissance aircraft. As he put it, if the United States sent reconnaissance aircraft over the DRV with strong fighter escorts, the MIGs would "have to stay down in humiliation or rise to be destroyed."[33]

If Taylor's superiors were shocked by his proposal, they have left no available record of their outrage. Many of them were involved in the planning that had begun in late July (see Chapter 2) for possible airstrikes against targets in Laos, to be carried out on the excuse of protecting American reconnaissance aircraft against Communist anti-aircraft guns. Early in September, John McNaughton, in a draft "Plan of Action for South Vietnam" that suggested the United States prepare to take actions that would be likely "to provoke a military DRV response" that could in turn "provide good grounds for us to escalate if we wished," included DeSoto patrols among the potential ways of provoking DRV action. He did not seem actually to want a DRV attack on a DeSoto patrol destroyer to be successful, but he did note that if the DRV managed to sink a U.S. ship, this would make a massive U.S. retaliation appropriate.[34] A few days later, Taylor, Secretary of State Rusk, General Wheeler, and McNamara himself approved a paper suggesting that in the not very distant future the United States might wish deliberately to invite an attack on a U.S. naval patrol—they seem to have been referring specifically to a DeSoto patrol, though they did not use that phrase—in order to have an excuse to retaliate against the DRV (see Chapter 10).

The enormous conspiracy that McNamara derided did not exist at the time of the Tonkin Gulf incidents. Had the people he listed all been working together to provoke an attack on U.S. ships at the beginning of August 1964, they would have been far better prepared than they were (see Chapter 9) to carry out their retaliation if the North Vietnamese did in fact take the bait and give them the excuse they needed.

To arrange a provocation, however, would by no means have required the huge number of conspirators McNamara suggested. The men in Saigon who were making requests and recommendations to the Navy about what the De-Soto patrol should do, and then scheduling OPLAN 34A raids in the light of the schedule of the DeSoto patrol, could have decided to maximize the chances that the North Vietnamese would think that the destroyer was somehow involved in the raids, and attack it. It is not necessary to suppose that such a group would have included even General Westmoreland or Ambassador Taylor, much less all the other individuals McNamara listed.

If one examines the OPLAN 34A raids, the times and places of which were set by SOG in Saigon, and the track of the *Maddox*'s movements (which SOG knew, and was supposed to take into account when scheduling OPLAN 34A raids), it appears that the DeSoto patrol was always far away when a raid occurred, to give the United States the ability to deny any provocation, but in other ways the relationship between the DeSoto patrol and the raids was quite provocative.

The OPLAN 34A operation of the night of July 30–31, just before the *Maddox* entered the Gulf of Tonkin, has already been discussed. Three more were scheduled for the period the destroyer was to be in the gulf. Scheduled for the night of August 3–4 were bombardment of a radar installation on the cape of Vinh Son, and of the security post at Cua Ron, just south of the cape. This was the first time in OPLAN 34A that targets on the mainland of North Vietnam had been bombarded by gunfire from the sea. The *Maddox* had been very conspicuous to observers on the cape, steaming back and forth reconnoitering the area on August 1 (two and a half days before the raid).

The next two operations, the seizure of the crew of a fishing boat and the shelling of Hon Mat, were scheduled for August 5. The fact that PTFs are known to have been out on operations on the night of August 4–5 resolves what would otherwise have been a difficult question: whether August 5 in the schedule meant after midnight on the night of August 4–5, or before midnight on the night of August 5–6. The August 5 raids have been almost ignored in the literature on Tonkin Gulf, because the PTFs never reached their targets; they were recalled when the *Maddox* and the *Turner Joy* reported being attacked by North Vietnamese torpedo boats that night. It is likely that DRV preparations to defend against this raid were misinterpreted as preparations to attack the destroyers, and that this misunderstanding played an important role in convincing the Americans that an attack on the destroyers had actually occurred (see discussion of radio intercepts in Chapters 6 and 8).

The only North Vietnamese vessels suitable for combat against a destroyer, the torpedo boats, were based at the port of Van Hoa (which the Americans called Port Wallut), far up at the northern end of the Gulf of Tonkin. On the night of August 3–4 while a 34A raid was going on further south, the original DeSoto patrol schedule had called for the destroyer to be cruising past Van Hoa, going northeast along the coast. The daylight hours were to be spent in the vicinity of the Chinese-Vietnamese border. On the night of August 4–5, again a night of a 34A raid, the destroyer was to come back southwest along the coast, reaching what was designated Point India, less than thirty miles from Van Hoa, an hour after midnight local time. The destroyer was to orbit around Point India for the next eight hours.

The incident of August 2 proved that the DRV was in a dangerous temper. When the United States decided nonetheless to continue carrying out 34A raids while the *Maddox* and *Turner Joy* were in the gulf, SOG requested that the destroyers remain fairly far north in the gulf—north of the area where the *Maddox* had been attacked on August 2, even if not as far north as had been contemplated in the original schedule—for several days while the 34A raids were going on further south.[35]

This pattern of decisions does not prove that anyone in the U.S. government was consciously hoping for a torpedo boat attack, waving a destroyer (in the original plan) or two destroyers (in the modified plan after August 2) under the collective nose of the People's Navy in the northern part of the gulf, but the pattern does seem suggestive.

During the past few centuries there have been a number of provocative incidents arranged in order to give great powers excuses for military action against weaker countries in Asia. These incidents often have been arranged not by the home governments of the great powers involved, but by officers on the scene, sometimes of quite modest rank.

A good example involving the U.S. armed forces occurred in 1971. Many U.S. military men were very frustrated about the limits on U.S. bombing of North

Vietnam in effect at that time. General John D. Lavelle, commander of the Seventh Air Force, requested permission from Washington to bomb some important targets and was turned down. Late in 1971, he arranged for officers under his command to begin filing false reports of North Vietnamese attacks on U.S. reconnaissance planes, and his forces were then able to bomb targets in North Vietnam in retaliation for the imaginary incidents. There is no firm evidence that those above Lavelle were involved in his actions, knew about them, or even deliberately looked away so as not to know about them.[36]

It must be emphasized, however, that only circumstantial evidence exists suggesting a deliberate plan to provoke an attack on the destroyers. Commander Robert Laske, who as communications officer of the maritime section of SOG would have been in a better position to know than anyone else whom this author has interviewed, believes that SOG quite genuinely tried to keep the OPLAN 34A raids far enough from the DeSoto patrol for the DRV to be able to tell that these were separate operations.[37]

A further complicating factor, very difficult to evaluate, is the way senior civilian officials who were aware of the 34A raids kept their knowledge almost completely out of the sort of records that ended up in the files on Tonkin Gulf.

At the end of 1964, a memo of the Chairman of the Joint Chiefs of Staff summarized the procedures for the control of raids against the North Vietnamese coast; a later SOG official history treats this as having been the procedure throughout the year 1964:

a. COMUSMACV was required to submit a monthly program for approval by CINCPAC, the Joint Chiefs of Staff, and higher authority.

b. After receipt of the monthly program approval, COMUSMACV requested approval for execution of each individual maritime mission.

c. Individual mission requests were coordinated for execution approval by the Special Assistant for Counterinsurgency and Special Activities, Joint Staff, with the Deputy Secretary of Defense [Cyrus Vance]. The Assistant Secretary of Defense for International Security Affairs [John McNaughton] then coordinated approval with the State Department and the White House. Consideration for approval of each mission was undertaken only after the results of the previous mission had been received and evaluated.[38]

Approval of specific raids by civilian authorities seems in fact to have been occurring in August 1964, but the only available record came from Michael Forrestal, who had not been involved in the process and indeed did not approve of it. Around noon on August 2, at the White House, President Johnson discussed the American response to the August 2 incident with Secretary Rusk, George Ball, Cyrus Vance, and Tom Hughes of the State Department; General Wheeler; Colonel Ralph Steakley of the Joint Staff; and Winston Cornelius of the CIA. At this meeting the president not only confirmed the decision that sent the *Maddox* back into the Gulf of Tonkin along with the *Turner Joy*, he authorized the continuation of OPLAN 34A raids (definitely the one scheduled for the night of August 3–4, and perhaps also those for the night of August 4–5; the procedure of waiting for the results of each raid to be evaluated, before approval of the next was initiated, described in the last sentence of the memo quoted above, would not have been practical when there were to be raids on consecutive nights). But if Michael Forrestal had not written a memo six days later to Secretary Rusk, strongly hinting that the approval of the raids had been a mistake, and protesting the fact that he (Forrestal) had not been consulted about the decision or even informed of it—he had had to find out by asking people on August 4—we would not know that OPLAN 34A had been discussed at the meeting at all, or that President Johnson had any knowledge of the August 3–4 OPLAN 34A raid.[39] Forrestal had also written a memo to Rusk on August 3, mentioning more vaguely that there were 34A raids scheduled for the period August 3–5.[40]

When reports came in on August 4 that North Vietnamese torpedo boats had attacked the *Maddox* and *Turner Joy*, however, and top officials were discussing the incident, there was a strange silence about OPLAN 34A. William Bundy has stated that when senior officials were trying to figure out why the DRV would have attacked U.S. vessels on the night of August 4, nobody in Washington suggested that the 34A raid against North Vietnam the previous night might have been Hanoi's motivation, because nobody in Washington knew, up to about August 10, that there had been any 34A raid on the night of August 3.[41]

MACV had sent to Washington, late in July, a precise schedule of the maritime operations to occur under OPLAN 34A for the entire month of August, with date and target for each operation: COMUSMACV to JCS, 301107Z July 1964. Bundy, however, says that he was unaware of this. Indeed, he was under the impression that no advance schedule was sent or could have been sent in July, because the raids had not been scheduled so long in advance. He is reasonably sure, though not absolutely certain, that he did not get any information about these raids until at least August 10.[42]

Several other sources convey a similar impression. Robert McNamara, in a statement he prepared for the Senate Foreign Relations Committee in 1968, said that he had not learned of the August 3–4 raids until after August 6:

> I learned subsequent to my testimony of 6 August 1964 that another South Vietnamese bombardment took place on the night of 3–4 August. At the time of that action, the Maddox and the Turner Joy were at least 70 miles to the northeast. The North Vietnamese attack on the Maddox and the Turner Joy on the night of 4 August occurred some 22 hours later.
>
> I think it important, too, in dealing with the issue, to recall that the President had announced publicly on 3 August that our patrol would continue and

consist of two destroyers. It is difficult to believe, in the face of that announcement, and its obvious purpose of asserting our right to freedom of the seas, that even the North Vietnamese could connect the patrol of the Maddox and the Turner Joy with a South Vietnamese action taking place some 70 miles away.[43]

When the National Security Council met to consider reports that the *Maddox* and *Turner Joy* had been attacked in the Gulf of Tonkin on the evening of August 4, CIA director John McCone interpreted the supposed North Vietnamese action as defensive, a response to the 34A raids, but the only available record indicates that he was referring to the attacks on Hon Me and Hon Ngu, which had occurred on the night of July 30–31; no reference appears to the attack on the North Vietnamese mainland on the night of August 3–4 or to the aborted raids scheduled for the night of August 4–5, which would have been far more relevant.[44] At least three men at this meeting had been present when the president had authorized the August 3–4 raid (and perhaps also the August 4–5 raid) two days before—President Johnson himself, Secretary Rusk, and General Wheeler. Yet the record shows not a word from anyone. Was this because, like McNamara according to his statement quoted above, they could not imagine that shelling of the North Vietnamese coast could have influenced the attitude of the Vietnamese toward unfriendly warships cruising off that coast, and neglected to mention the August 3–4 shelling because they could see no relevance in it? Or was it that they saw all too clearly the relevance of the August 3–4 shelling, and wished to avoid undermining Secretary Rusk's contention, at this meeting, that the North Vietnamese had made an "unprovoked" attack on the two U.S. ships? (This logic could apply either as a motive for not discussing it, or as a motive for omitting it from the record if it were discussed; Allen Whiting, head of the Far East Division of the State Department's Bureau of Intelligence and Research, thinks it more likely that the August 3–4 raid was discussed at this meeting but omitted from the record than that it was never mentioned at all.)[45] If indeed they felt on August 4 that the shelling had been provocative, we may also wonder whether any of them had felt the same on August 2 at the meeting at which the shelling had been approved.

After the United States had bombed North Vietnam on August 5, with much public indignation about the unprovoked North Vietnamese attack on the U.S. destroyers, those who knew about the August 3–4 shelling had even more motive to avoid candid discussion of the subject.

The Second Incident, August 4

On the night of August 4, all seemed quiet near the North Vietnamese coast. Far out in the gulf, however, about halfway between Vietnam and the Chinese island of Hainan, something clearly was happening. There was the sound of gunfire, the glare of star shells, and much air activity. Senior Vietnamese officers sent an urgent message to their allies across the gulf, asking: Were the Chinese comrades fighting with the Americans? The Chinese, meanwhile, had seen the same signs of battle and sent an equally urgent message to Hanoi: Were the Vietnamese comrades fighting with the Americans? The answer, in both cases, was negative.[1]

Tonkin Spook

The two destroyers had spent August 4 cruising from north to south along the coast; their closest approach to the shore was sixteen miles. They were at General Quarters for most of the day. Chad James recalls that shore radar locked onto the *Turner Joy* often during this period.[2] The destroyers were also shadowed by a vessel equipped with a "skinhead" radar for at least four hours, starting at about 0900G or 0930G. This vessel was to their west, between the destroyers and the shore, though it was at one point mistakenly reported as having been to their east.[3] For the North Vietnamese navy actually to have placed a shadower to the east of the destroyers, in a position to cut them off from the open sea, would have been a highly aggressive move.

The two destroyers headed out to sea as evening approached. The night was very dark and most of those involved say that the weather was poor, from drizzle to thunderstorms, though Commander Ogier is an exception; he does not recall weather as bad as some others have suggested.[4]

The DRV message traffic Captain Herrick had been seeing had warned him he might be attacked again. He did not have adequate warning, however, that his radar might prove deceptive.

Destroyers normally use a highly automated procedure for controlling gun-fire. Automatic devices continually adjust the aim of the fire-control radar to follow the movements of the target being tracked. Other devices adjust the aim of the guns, to keep them aimed at whatever target the fire-control radar is tracking. For all this to work, however, the fire-control radar must first "lock onto" the target—the fire-control radar must be aimed at the target and get an echo that is clearly enough defined for the automatic devices to be able to identify it as the thing that must be tracked. Surface-search radar, which simply displays targets as blips on a screen for the operators to interpret as they choose, can show targets that are not clear enough for fire-control radar to lock onto them.

It is well known that certain types of weather have the ability to generate radar images. Television weather reports, indeed, routinely show radar plots of rain clouds. An experienced radar operator should not have much difficulty distinguishing a dense cloud from a ship on his radar screen. The large size and fuzziness of the weather-generated image will prevent it from looking much like a surface vessel to a human operator looking at the screen of a surface-search radar, and will prevent a fire-control radar from locking onto it.

It is a mistake, however, to assume that this takes care of the problem of radar ghosts. For one thing, weather of the sort that occurred on the evening of August 4 can do odd things to the radar images of genuine objects. Normally one would think it impossible for airplanes to be confused with surface vessels on radar, since the slowest airplane moves so much faster than the fastest surface vessel. Commander George Edmondson, nevertheless, confirms that such confusion can occur in weather of the sort he remembers encountering on the night of August 4. He served as Navigator of the aircraft carrier *Kitty Hawk*, operating in this area not long after the Tonkin Gulf incidents, and states that there were "numerous times" when weather anomalies caused the carrier's radar to mistake the carrier's own aircraft for surface vessels. He comments that on the night of August 4, the radar operators on the destroyers tended to report surface vessels in just the locations where he and his wingman were flying low and slow over the water; he concludes that it is very likely the radar on the destroyers was mistaking aircraft for surface vessels.[5] This should be considered, at the very least, as a serious possibility. If the radar operators on a carrier could mistake aircraft for surface vessels, those on a destroyer could presumably make the same error.

Aside from possible confusion involving aircraft, there is the phenomenon sometimes called "Tonkin Gulf Ghost" or "Tonkin Spook," a radar anomaly found in the Gulf of Tonkin and (under other names, of course) a few other limited areas. The phenomenon generates radar images that are much smaller and more clearly defined than those normally generated by weather. One officer recalls that the median duration of one of these images is about four minutes, but he adds that the duration can be several times this long.[6]

It is not even clear that Tonkin Spook arises from weather, although it tends to occur in conditions of high humidity and temperature inversion. Another hypothesis that has been suggested within the U.S. Navy is that the spooks are generated by flocks of seabirds.[7] This hypothesis seems especially good in as much as it would be consistent with the high speed of Tonkin Spooks; one reason Ogier rejects the idea that they could be generated simply by weather is that he has seen them move at high speed when the wind conditions could not move a weather anomaly at the correct speed and direction. A much less likely hypothesis is that the spooks are rough areas on the surface of the water, capable of reflecting radar waves, caused by schools of fish on the surface.

Not even the most experienced radar operator can simply look at a Tonkin Spook on a radar screen and realize from its appearance that it does not represent an actual surface vessel. A man sufficiently familiar with this phenomenon can probably learn that the image on the radar screen does not represent a real vessel by watching the way the image changes when he adjusts the settings on the radar. A man accustomed only to distinguishing actual vessels from the sort of images generated by weather in more typical areas of the world, not aware of the special characteristics of Tonkin Spook, will probably accept without question that what appears on his screen is the image of a genuine vessel, and not attempt to adjust his radar.

Radar ghosts of this sort are characteristic, not of Asian waters in general, but of certain limited areas in Asia. Paul Schratz, an American submariner, found himself late in 1944 in an area near Okinawa where radar ghosts were very frequent and "terribly nerve-racking." "The pips were clear and distinct, generally tracking at about twenty-four knots and, more often than not, heading directly for the submarine. Too close for a plane, too fast for anything but a PT boat—or a hostile seagull."[8]

When U.S. Navy operations in the upper gulf became extensive, the area would become known for the frequency with which spurious images appeared on radar.[9] Commander Richard Schreadley comments that false radar targets in the Tonkin Gulf were "widely noted, but never adequately explained." He has described how in January 1973, as commanding officer of the USS *Blakely* (DE-1072), he observed on his radar a group of rapidly closing contacts realistic enough that his weapons officer wanted to open fire:

> I hesitated. The contacts were speeding across the radar scope faster than any surface contact I had ever seen. Could they be low-flying aircraft? If so, whose? Even as I watched, the contacts, sharp and well-defined one moment, vanished the next.

From conversations I later had with other ship captains, I am convinced that the *Blakely*'s experience was far from unique. The Tonkin Gulf ghosts most often were attributed to freak weather conditions or "ducting" of electromagnetic waves.[10]

Up to August 1964, however, the United States had not been going much into the Tonkin Gulf, and Tonkin Spook was a local phenomenon of the upper gulf; off the coast of South Vietnam, even as far north as the latitude of Danang, radar was much more reliable.[11]

Different officers have expressed different conclusions about what appeared on their screens during the night of August 4. Ensign Richard Corsette, who directed fire from the two forward gun mounts on the *Maddox* that night, later commented, "I know the way our radar was acting, my firm belief was that everything I locked onto was weather."[12]

Corsette can evaluate the events of August 4 in the light of later experiences in this area, in which radar showed firm and convincing images of surface vessels when the visibility was clear and he could simply verify by eye that no surface vessels were present. Another officer aboard the *Maddox* described similar encounters; he stated that some of the radar ghosts he encountered in this part of the world, at later dates, were so realistic that no radar operator would be able to distinguish them from real vessels. He said that an acquaintance of his, an officer who had not been aboard the *Maddox*, once told him of encountering a Tonkin Spook so convincing that there was an eerie temptation to open fire at it, despite the fact that the weather was clear and the officer could easily see that there was no vessel of any sort at the location where the spook showed on the radar.[13] They had had no warning *before* the 1964 DeSoto patrol, however, that they should expect such things in the Gulf of Tonkin.

It is likely that one of the daylight incidents mentioned above occurred on August 5, 1964, only a few hours after the second Tonkin Gulf incident. Once again, the radar screens showed small contacts; at one point (the time has unfortunately been garbled in the message) the *Maddox* reported nine contacts closing fast. At least one report mistakenly indicated that the *Maddox* had actually opened fire on one or more of these contacts. A message from the *Maddox* denying that the destroyer had actually opened fire on a radar contact at 1518H, said that the *Maddox*, while being approached by a high-speed radar contact that turned out to be "negative," had radioed to the *Turner Joy*, "Will open fire when in range."[14]

Toward the August 4 Incident

The destroyers secured from General Quarters at about 1720G. They had been at General Quarters, though it may have been a modified state of combat readiness, for about six hours. One may assume that there was a certain amount of fatigue on both destroyers. Douglas Smith later recalled, "After dinner, the tone had significantly died down to the point where most felt there would be no further action during this patrol. Needless to say, everyone was sorely disappointed. Without being able to fathom the element of danger—and therefore subconsciously forgetting it—we felt we had been cheated of all the anticipated fun (action)."[15]

The night of August 4 was, as already stated, very dark; to Ensign Smith it seemed "one of the moonless/starless nights mariners dread. Visibility was almost zero."[16] For many personnel on the destroyers, wind-blown spray impaired vision even further. Captain Herrick, whose position on the *Maddox*'s bridge was out of the path of the spray, has estimated he could see to a maximum of about 300 yards. The records of the destroyers indicate fluctuating winds averaging about seventeen knots, though they disagree on the timing of the fluctuations. The *Maddox* reported waves of five to six feet throughout the crucial period that evening.[17]

Senior officers on the two destroyers had agreed in advance about how certain tasks were to be shared in the event of trouble. The *Turner Joy*, holding station 1,000 yards astern of the *Maddox*, was responsible for ensuring that the two destroyers not collide. This meant that the *Turner Joy*'s radar had to be tuned for short-range operation; the *Maddox* was responsible for long-range radar observation of any potential enemies.

With the radar at high power, it could pick up targets at long range, but the amount of "surface clutter" (reflections of the radar off the tops of nearby waves) tended to mask closer targets. Reducing the power reduced the amount of reflection off wave tops and thus allowed nearby targets to stand out more clearly on the radar screens, but made it difficult or impossible to detect targets at long ranges.

The *Maddox* was to be responsible for illuminating targets with star shells. A chronology drawn up aboard the *Maddox* nine days after the action (referred to hereafter as the joint chronology) by officers from both ships, plus Captain Andy Kerr, a lawyer from Seventh Fleet staff,[18] states that the *Turner Joy* did not have any star shells; but both the CIC log and the after-action report of the *Turner Joy* give the impression that the ship did have star shells. The problem was that the *Turner Joy* would have had difficulty firing them at the times they were needed. The *Turner Joy*'s guns were more modern than those of the *Maddox* and could maintain a very rapid rate of fire—thirty shells per minute from each five-inch gun. (A little later in the war, a television news crew filmed the *Turner Joy* shelling the Vietnamese coast. The rate of fire shown in the film is truly astonishing to this author's civilian eyes.) What made this possible, however, was that the guns were loaded by automatic machinery; shells were placed in ammunition drums several decks below the actual guns, and the machinery loaded these shells into the guns in the order they had been placed in the ammunition drums. It would have been pointless to include star shells when loading the ammunition drums before the action, because there was no way to tell, ahead of time, at what points in the action star shells might be needed. And with the gun crews short of personnel, it would not have been easy to bypass the automatic machinery and insert a star shell into the system on short notice.

If the two destroyers were attacked simultaneously by both aircraft and surface vessels, the *Maddox* would concentrate on the surface vessels, and the *Turner Joy*, whose five-inch guns were the best anti-aircraft weapons on either destroyer, would use those against aircraft and use only its three-inch guns against surface vessels.[19]

The *Turner Joy* had only three five-inch guns (half as many as the *Maddox*), each in a separate turret. Mount 51 was at the front of the ship, Mount 52 and Mount 53 in the rear. In action these could be controlled by either of two gun directors. Director 51, the main gun director, was at the front of the ship; Director 52 was at the rear.

One can seldom expect to find all the machinery working perfectly on a naval vessel. On the *Turner Joy* there was one problem that may have reduced the accuracy of the guns, and several problems affecting the ship's rate of fire. Mount 51 was out of action throughout the evening of August 4, due to malfunctions in the system for elevating the gun. The loading crews of the other two were seriously undermanned. There should have been nineteen men working on the loader deck and magazine associated with each gun; there were in fact eleven. Problems in the loading machinery took both Mount 52 and Mount 53 out of action for brief periods during the action of August 4; the manpower shortage was at least to some extent a contributing factor. On the three-inch guns, for which the loading was not so mechanized, the loading crews suffered from inadequate training.[20] These problems did not affect accuracy, but they reduced the ship's overall firepower by at least a third.

The main gun director, Director 51 at the front of the ship, was also out of action on the night of August 4. This was partly because of a bad end reflector on its radar feedhorn. Fire control and electronics personnel had made a new reflector by modifying the lid of an oxygen canister from a firefighter's oxygen breathing apparatus, and had attached this to the feedhorn. This jury-rig allowed the radar to work, but imperfectly. John Barry, director officer, comments that this problem was not severe enough to have prevented the director from being used on the night of August 4, and in fact he believes that it was used to control gunfire from the forward three-inch gun at least once. The main reason the forward gun director was not used to control five-inch gunfire was that the forward five-inch gun mount was out of action. With all five-inch gunfire coming from Mounts 52 and 53, at the rear of the ship, it made sense to have the fire controlled by Director 52, which was also at the rear and did not have its field of view astern blocked by the funnels of the destroyer. "Director 52 had not previously been used to control fire in surface gunnery exercises, because its computer [was] not as accurate for surface fire" as that of the main director, and because the rules for gunnery competitions did not require use of the alternate director.[21]

Mount 52 was loaded with VT-frag; Mount 53 was loaded with AAC. The after-action report states that the AAC rounds loaded before the action were fuzed for proximity detonation at fifty feet from a target,[22] which makes excellent sense. The *Turner Joy* had the primary responsibility for air defense, and shells fuzed for detonation on impact would have been almost useless against aircraft. With Mount 51 out of action altogether and Mount 52 seriously undermanned, it is hard to see how Mount 53 could have been loaded with shells that would not do anything to an aircraft unless they came in physical contact with it. Fuzing the AAC rounds for detonation at fifty feet made them effective against both air and surface targets; indeed the Pacific Fleet recommended soon afterward that AAC rounds be fuzed for detonation on proximity even when the targets were to be small surface targets such as PTs.[23]

An Imminent Threat

Years later, Secretary of Defense McNamara gave the Senate Foreign Relations Committee summaries of four intercepted messages, which he claimed constituted proof that the August 4 incident had been real. The first, a message sent from Naval Headquarters in Haiphong to Swatow boat T-142 at 1610G, had specified the location of the destroyers as of 1345G.[24] McNamara used this, without stating the location or the time, as if the report had given the location of the destroyers close enough to the time of the supposed attack that night to have constituted guidance for the attacking vessels. But the destroyers' cruise along the coast took them twenty-seven miles to the southeast from the position specified in the message, before they turned out to sea at 1604G. Only a report of their position after 1604G would have been able to convey even a clue as to where the destroyers were likely to be found that night.

The second message, about which Herrick was informed at 1915G (the Pentagon had been informed by a phone call from NSA a few minutes earlier), included an order to make ready for military operations, using Swatow boats T-142 and T-146, and perhaps torpedo boat T-333 if it could be made ready in time.[25]

It is hardly surprising, given the way the attack on August 2 had been preceded by an order for an attack against an unspecified target, that officers on the *Maddox* decided their ship was going to be attacked again. When what seemed to be another attack actually occurred, this was taken as further confirmation that the interpretation had been correct.

Almost certainly it was not correct; this time the message about action against an unspecified target had nothing to do with any destroyer. T-333 was the least damaged of the three torpedo boats that had attacked the *Maddox* on August 2; T-142 and T-146 were the two Swatows that had observed that attack from a distance. If the mission referred to in the message had been an attack on two destroyers far out to sea, it seems unlikely that the DRV would have chosen for the mission a pair of Swatows, which had no weapons capable of doing serious harm to a destroyer, and a torpedo boat that was still not finished repairing engine damage from its last combat (and that probably had no usable weapon more powerful than a machine gun, since it seems most unlikely that torpedoes to replace those fired in the combat of August 2 would have been available in the Sam Son area, where T-333 had reached shore on the afternoon of August 2 and where it remained at least until August 5).

It is far more likely that the "military action" for which these vessels were being told to prepare was defense against an OPLAN 34-A raid. The Swatows would have had primary responsibility for local defense, if the PTFs from Da-nang had attacked any target in their area. T-333, while not very useful for defense against an OPLAN 34-A raid, would have been the best unit available to back up the two Swatows, and would have needed to prepare for action regard-less, being a possible target for attack by the PTFs. The PTFs were in fact on their way north that evening; Commander Robert Laske recalls having been on duty that night as communications officer at the maritime section of SOG, to moni-tor the progress of the operation.[26] There is no way to be sure whether the DRV knew where the intended targets of the raid were (in fact about thirty to thirty-five miles south of Hon Me).

At about 1930G, the destroyers increased speed from twelve to twenty knots. At 1940G, Captain Herrick reported to the *Ticonderoga* that he had received "info" indicating that an attack by Swatow and/or torpedo boats was "immi-nent"; he said he was proceeding southeast at best speed.[27] The euphemistic reference to "info" from an unspecified source, and the mention of both Swatow and torpedo boats as possible attackers, suggest that the main source of his worry was the intercepted message he had gotten a few minutes before. It is also possible, however, that his radar screen had begun to show faint images far to the northeast, which during the next ten minutes would firm up to become three clear radar contacts.

At 1946G, the *Maddox* recorded radar contact with a vessel traveling at thirty-three knots, bearing 070°, range 36.4 miles, course 320° according to logs kept at the time, course 170° according to a later report. Following normal procedures, the "skunk" (possibly hostile radar contact) was assigned the code letter "N." Two additional contacts were recorded at 1948G and 1950G, skunk "O" at 34 or 38 miles, bearing 044°, speed 28 knots, and skunk "P" at 36.6 miles, bearing 060°, speed 40 knots.[28] (The times would represent not the moment each skunk first appeared on the screens, but the time a minute or two later when its course and speed had been computed, and these facts could be entered into the logs.) Records kept on the *Maddox*, dating from August 4, indicate that there were three of these skunks. Some reports of later dates suggest that there may have been as many as five. Thus there is a statement by Captain Herrick that there were five contacts, of which three paralleled the course of the destroyers southeastward while two headed northwest, and also a statement by Ltjg. Frederick M. Frick that the exact number was impossible to determine—between three and five—and that they had faded on the radar approximately three minutes after the destroyers changed course to the southeast. The discrepancies have not been explained.[29]

Radarman Second Class Chad James had stayed on watch in the CIC when the *Turner Joy* secured from General Quarters and most other men went to eat. He was confident nothing would happen, "because we were well out to sea." Then a radio message came from the *Maddox* stating there was information indicating the possibility the destroyers would be attacked that night by a significant number of enemies. Without waiting for the ship to be ordered formally to General Quarters again (which happened soon after), James began switching people around in CIC, putting at each crucial station the man best qualified for the job.[30]

Ltjg. John Barry took the watch on the *Turner Joy*'s bridge at 2000G. He recalls that there was no sign of trouble—everyone was relaxed, and many of the crew were watching a movie. The people handing over the watch did not mention that there had been, during the previous few minutes, any escalation in tension or any indication of imminent trouble. They could have mentioned distant radar contacts, but if so they did not discuss the contacts in threatening enough terms to make their statements memorable. The first indication of trouble that Barry received was a message from Captain Herrick just after the watch had changed, instructing the *Turner Joy* to go to General Quarters and expect a possible torpedo attack. Barry hit the button sounding General Quarters instantly;[31] the logs say that this happened at 2004G. The men got to their stations unusually fast. Barry, like James, said in his interview that the officers and men of the *Turner Joy* were considerably better than average.

The account that follows is based on the assumption that the destroyers' records of the movements of skunks "N," "O," and "P" were reasonably accurate. It should be borne in mind, however, that this was not necessarily the case. If these skunks represented surface vessels, they must have been small—approximately the size of PT boats or Swatows. They were, for the whole of the time they were tracked, beyond the range at which the destroyers' radar would have been able to track such vessels if the weather conditions had been such that radar waves traveled in straight lines; they could be tracked only if atmospheric conditions were making the radar waves curve, following the curvature of the earth. This is called "ducting." Ducting may occur in a reliable and consistent fashion in very calm weather, when a blanket of warm moist air sits just above the surface of the sea, and is not dispersed by wind action. That was not the case on the night of August 4. Rain squalls of the sort that seem to have been present that night can allow targets to be tracked *intermittently* out to very long ranges, but as an expert on radar has commented, "With a number of 'intermittent' returns it is possible to construct a radar track that goes almost anywhere at any speed you want to imagine."[32]

The records of the destroyers give the range and bearing of skunks from the destroyers at various times on the night of August 4. If we are to plot the movements of the skunks, we must first plot the movements of the destroyers. Unfortunately, the records of the destroyers are inconsistent. Figure 2a is based on the specific positions—latitude and longitude—of the destroyers at specific times as recorded on the *Maddox*. Figure 2b is based on the courses and speeds of the destroyers as recorded on the *Maddox*. Figure 2b will be used as the basis for the account that follows. That the *Maddox*'s officers would have made errors in computing their ship's latitude and longitude when out of sight of land seems inherently more probable than their recording seriously inaccurate courses; additionally, the *Turner Joy*'s records come much closer to matching Figure 2b than 2a. (The specific latitudes and longitudes marked on the track charts in the *Turner Joy* action report are so inconsistent with one another that no usable information can be obtained from them. The courses and speeds indicated by these track charts, however, and the courses and speeds given in the *Turner Joy*'s logs, are close to those from the logs of the *Maddox* that were used as a basis for Figure 2b.)

Either in the message of 2004G that first alerted the *Turner Joy* or in another message soon afterward, the *Maddox* reported the locations of "N," "O," and "P." The radar on the *Turner Joy* was briefly retuned to long range to check this report, which must have seemed rather improbable; the range was very long for detection of small surface vessels. The skunks were right where the *Maddox* had said they were.[33] By this time the skunks were no longer scattered; they had come together at 2007G, at a point about halfway between the original positions of "N" and "O."

To get into position to attack the destroyers, which were located southwest of them but on a southeast course, the skunks would have needed to go approximately due south. What their convergence on a common point actually did was to bring "N" northwest (actually getting farther from attack position), "O" south (toward attack position), and "P" west (neither toward nor away from attack position). Once they had joined together, they headed approximately west, on a course taking them nowhere near the destroyers.

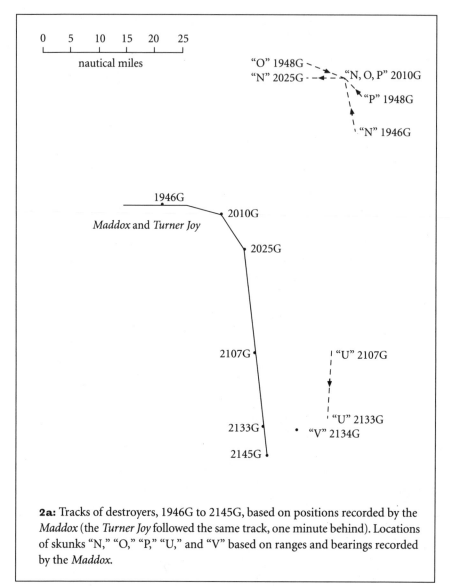

2a: Tracks of destroyers, 1946G to 2145G, based on positions recorded by the *Maddox* (the *Turner Joy* followed the same track, one minute behind). Locations of skunks "N," "O," "P," "U," and "V" based on ranges and bearings recorded by the *Maddox*.

Figure 2. First and last recorded locations for skunks, 1946G to 2134G

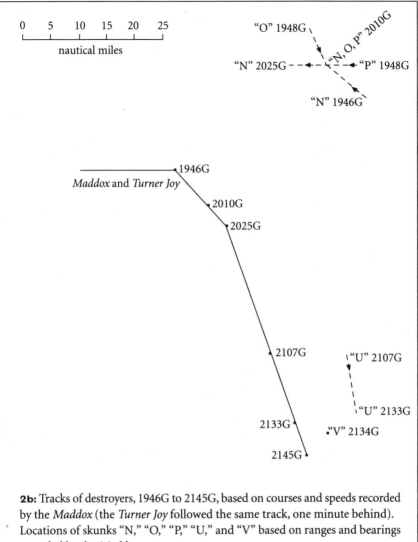

2b: Tracks of destroyers, 1946G to 2145G, based on courses and speeds recorded by the *Maddox* (the *Turner Joy* followed the same track, one minute behind). Locations of skunks "N," "O," "P," "U," and "V" based on ranges and bearings recorded by the *Maddox.*

It is not clear how long the three contacts remained together. Radio messages from the *Maddox* to the *Turner Joy* reported on the movements of "P" at 2018G and of "N" at 2019G and 2025G (in none of these reports were the course and speed consistent with the idea that the skunk was attempting to close, or shadow, the destroyers).[34] Such reports on the movements of individual skunks imply, though they do not prove, that the skunks were no longer together and their movements needed to be reported separately. An after-action report, however, states that they were still together at 2030G.[35]

There is an early after-action report from the *Maddox*, which states that at 1946G, the *Maddox* had "detected three to five contacts 40–[4]2 miles to east and in intended night steam area. These contacts appeared to attempt pursuit but broke off after about ten minutes at range 40 miles."[36] The reasons this should be discarded as a product of the confusion and fatigue that was prevailing five hours after the shooting ended include: (1) it seems confused even as to the number of contacts; (2) it gives no exact location for any of these contacts at any time; (3) its vague description of the location of these contacts at 1946G, forty to forty-two miles to the east, contradicts the data in all the more detailed reports that do give exact locations; (4) if the contacts had attempted pursuit, then regardless of where they had started out—forty to forty-two miles to the east as stated by this report, or in the locations given by other, more detailed reports—they would not at the end of ten minutes still have been as far as forty miles from the destroyers.

The *Maddox* acquired an additional object on radar at 1955G, designated skunk "R," bearing 104°, range twenty-nine miles, course 270°, but it was moving much more slowly (ten knots) and therefore seemed less threatening.[37] Radar operators seem to have taken over an hour to decide that skunk "R" was in fact a spurious image generated by weather.[38] Skunk "S," initially detected at 2039G, bearing 092° range twenty-two miles doing speed of thirty knots, and skunk "T," initially reported at 2103G, bearing 091°, range thirty-nine miles, were evaluated as weather after much less delay.[39]

Records are incomplete for four contacts detected at 2059G, bearing 093°, range twenty-nine miles. The fact that they were never assigned any letter or letters, and their omission from the after-action reports, suggests that they must have been evaluated as weather. There is no record of such an evaluation, however, and the presence of these skunks does seem to have been reported to the *Ticonderoga*, which passed up the chain of command a report that they were holding a distance of twenty-seven miles from the destroyers.[40] As a result of this report, these skunks played a conspicuous role in some summaries of the action written in Washington.

At 2015G, three "bogeys" (unidentified aircraft) were detected to the northwest, bearing 287°, range twenty-eight miles.[41] (A report from the *Maddox* several hours later stated that these contacts had been evaluated as land.)[42] Captain Herrick reported to the *Ticonderoga* that he had both unidentified vessels and unidentified aircraft on his radar screens.

The *Ticonderoga* responded to the reports from the *Maddox* by launching six aircraft—two Skyraiders (George Edmondson and wingman), two F8 Crusaders (James Stockdale and wingman), and two A4D Skyhawks (Wesley McDonald and wingman)—in support. The Skyraiders were slower because they were propeller-driven, but they carried a heavier bomb load than the jets, and also had a greater fuel capacity so they could remain over the destroyers for a longer period. Stockdale's wingman suffered an immediate electrical failure and had to return to the carrier, but Stockdale went on without him.

The destroyers had been going due east when skunk "N" first appeared to their northeast. The speed of the skunks implied that they were military vessels, and Captain Herrick would have had to assume that they were unfriendly even if he had not been attacked two days before. Promptly after the first detection of skunk "N," the destroyers changed course to the southeast and increased speed in order to evade the threat. The *Maddox* went to General Quarters at 1958G and the *Turner Joy* at 2004G. Ensign Smith, when thinking earlier in terms of daylight attack, had assumed that dealing with PT boats would be like shooting fish in the barrel. He was no longer so confident: "Since I was now cooped up inside CIC, I no longer carried this 'fish in the barrel' feeling—unless it was that the shoe had reversed feet. Giving far more credit to the enemy than their equipment allowed them, I felt that the night cover was to their advantage. Once again, sweat started to trickle down my body."[43]

As it turned out, skunks "N," "O," and "P" remained well to the north; none of them ever got significantly south of the position at which "N" had first been recorded at 1946G. With the destroyers moving southeast at maximum speed while the skunks moved west, the range opened rapidly. Most reports state that radar contact was lost at "about" 2045G, but there is one report that the *Maddox* still held skunk "N" at 2046G, heading northwest away from the destroyers at twelve knots.[44]

When the skunks were first detected, they lay directly across the track that the two destroyers had followed the previous night while steaming northward through the eastern part of the gulf. Officers on the destroyers, who even before this had been more than half expecting another attack, decided that the North Vietnamese, knowing where the destroyers had spent the previous night, had sent PT boats to lie in wait in the same area and ambush them. The first full-scale after-action report describes how the destroyers had intended to spend the night of August 4 maneuvering within a square, twenty-four miles on a side, in the eastern gulf about 100 miles from the Vietnamese coast.[45] It then states that when the three skunks were acquired, "CTG 72.1 evaluated the situation as a trap, since these relatively high speed craft appeared to be waiting in the area used on prior occasions, and most recently, the night before, by the *Maddox* and *Turner Joy* as a night-steaming area."[46]

This scenario is not quite as plausible as it appears on the surface, for two reasons:

1. The suggestion that this area had been used repeatedly in the past for night steaming simply is not correct. The two destroyers had passed through the area once, without lingering, during a long (sixty-five mile) south-to-north run the previous night. Aside from this, neither destroyer had ever come near the area.

   The North Vietnamese, indeed, surely must have been tracking the DeSoto patrol with enough care to know that the *Maddox*'s night-steaming pattern had never repeated itself. The *Maddox* had remained close to shore on the night of July 31, had withdrawn a moderate distance (about thirty miles) toward the middle of the gulf on the night of August 1, had left the gulf entirely for the night of August 2, and had gone far out into the middle of the gulf (it is not clear whether the North Vietnamese knew just how far—in fact about ninety miles) on the night of August 3. The destroyers' daytime patrol on August 4 had followed a pattern (north to south) directly opposite to the daytime pattern of August 3 (south to north). If the North Vietnamese did know just where the destroyers had spent the night of August 3, it is hard to see why they would have expected the destroyers to follow the same path on the night of August 4, and in fact the destroyers were not planning to do so.

2. If the DRV had managed to figure out just what the night steaming track of the destroyers had been the previous night and, wanting to attack them, had for some reason decided to gamble on their following the same track a second time, then putting vessels at the location of skunks "N," "O," and "P" (to await the destroyers on their way north) would not have been a sensible way to do the job. Such a maneuver would, predictably, lead to exactly what did happen on the night of August 4: the destroyers would detect the vessels by radar while well to the south of them, would turn southward away from them, and would successfully evade them. (The fact that "N," "O," and "P" never got within twenty miles of the destroyers has been downplayed or completely ignored by most of the authors who have interpreted these skunks as North Vietnamese PT boats waiting in ambush for the destroyers.) As has already been stressed in connection with the incident of August 2, for a PT boat attack on the destroyers to have much chance of success it had to come from the south.

These points do not prove that "N," "O," and "P" were not North Vietnamese PT boats waiting in ambush for the destroyers. The behavior of military commanders does not always conform to what a historian will later decide to call "sensible." But an ambush in this location makes little enough military sense that it should not be treated as the obvious explanation for the appearance of these skunks on the radar screen of the *Maddox*. We should look for other possibilities.

Captain Herrick has recently suggested that some of the vessels that appeared on his radar on the night of August 4 may have been Chinese rather than North Vietnamese.[47] In regard to skunks "N," "O," and "P," this possibility should be taken seriously, if we assume that these skunks represented real vessels of some sort. They were closer to the island of Hainan, a part of China, than to any part of the Vietnamese coast. (Secretary McNamara, at a press conference August 5, said that there was no doubt the PT boats that attacked the two destroyers came from North Vietnam: "The radar made it quite clear that they were coming from North Vietnamese bases."[48] This was totally false; to the limited extent that the radar gave any indication of the source of the supposed attacking vessels, it suggested China.)

The only night for which there is clear evidence that the Chinese had tracked the destroyers, and thus knew their night steaming path, was August 3; it would have made reasonable sense for the Chinese to put some patrol vessels on that path on the night of August 4, to warn the destroyers off or at least observe their actions if they were to come the same way again.

Skunk "U"

At 2108G, radar on the *Maddox* detected a new skunk, designated "U," bearing 090°, range fifteen miles, course 214°, speed approximately thirty knots. This was an intercept course, but the skunk continued to close for only a few minutes; it then turned southeastward to parallel the destroyers. It was held by the radar of both destroyers, and the records of its movements, coming from the two ships, are as consistent as one is entitled to expect. Within five minutes, radar operators had decided that skunk "U" was actually three or four vessels in close formation.[49]

The distance from the last reported location of skunk "N" was great enough to make it absolutely impossible that "N" could have reached this location in the available time. The locations of "O" and "P" are not so extensively documented in the ships' records, but even if we ignore the statement in the after-action report that they were still together with "N" at 2030G, it is not plausible that they could have gotten far enough south, quickly enough, to have been among the vessels making up "U."

By this time, Captain Herrick had air cover overhead. Commander Stockdale came in sight of the destroyers, whose highly luminous wakes were clearly visible, at about 2108G. He remained within sight of the destroyers, always below 1,000 feet, for about the next hour and a half. He was operating without

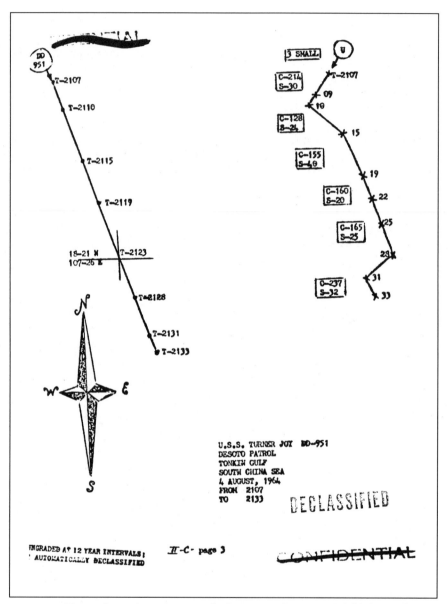

Figure 3. *Turner Joy* action report track chart, 2107G to 2133G. This image has been reduced by 55 percent from the original document.

lights, so the Skyhawks were ordered to remain above 2,000 feet unless otherwise specified. He had good visibility and could see the destroyers very clearly. Water conditions made the wakes of the destroyers luminescent; the extreme darkness of the night made the glowing wakes very conspicuous. It appeared to him that the destroyers, in choppy seas, spray, and what looked like at least twenty knots of surface wind, probably had poor surface visibility.[50]

Commander McDonald, flying just under the cloud ceiling (much higher than Stockdale), did not have so clear a view. He was only able to see the wakes of the destroyers when he was fairly close to them, and they were not highly conspicuous even then.[51]

At 2117G, immediately after the radar operators had decided that skunk "U" was actually several vessels, the aircraft overhead were vectored (guided by radio) to the location of the skunk. The aircraft were unable to find anything there, but skunk "U" continued to appear as a radar image, and by about 2133G it had approached to 23,200 yards (11.5 miles).[52] It then disappeared,[53] a fact that most later accounts neglect to mention.

At about 2131G, the *Turner Joy* and apparently also the *Maddox* picked up another group of two to four contacts thirty-six miles to the southeast, dead ahead of the two destroyers. These, however, were quickly evaluated as weather.[54]

The Action Begins: Skunks "V" and "V-1"

The most important part of the action came between 2134G and 2145G; this is the period that provides the most plausible case that a North Vietnamese attack on the U.S. destroyers actually occurred. Unfortunately, as will appear below, Captain Herrick himself seems not to have regarded the records of what happened during this period as being reliable in all details. The following paragraphs, summarizing what was observed aboard the two destroyers, are based mainly on the joint chronology, drawn up aboard the *Maddox* by a number of officers including the executive officer of the *Turner Joy*, and formally signed by Captain Herrick on August 13. Most paragraphs of this chronology were incorporated word-for-word into both the DeSoto patrol report and the *Maddox* action report, dated August 24 and 25 respectively, both signed by Commander Ogier.

At 2134G, the surface-search radar of the *Maddox* detected a new threat, designated skunk "V." It was 9,800 yards (4.8 miles) away, bearing 093°, approaching at thirty-five to forty knots. The records indicate that the fire-control radar of the *Maddox*—the radar of the gun directors—locked onto this target, but only very briefly; lock-on was lost before they had time to open fire. After heading toward the *Maddox* for several minutes, it made a quick turn to the left, range 6,200 yards, at 2137G.[55] This seemed, to the men watching the radar scopes, similar to the turns that had been made by PT boats after torpedo launches on August 2, although it is hard to explain why a torpedo boat would have launched a torpedo at such an absurd range when it had not come under fire. All of the torpedo boats that attacked the *Maddox* on August 2 pressed in considerably closer than this before launching, even though they *were* under fire.

Patrick Park was stationed in the main gun director, with Ensign Corsette. He says that he may well have locked onto this target, though he can no longer remember specifically. If so, he doubts that the lock-on lasted more than twenty seconds: "Tops was thirty seconds" for lock-on of any target during this general period, "and during those 20–30 seconds what we were on was classified by us as either sea conditions or rain squalls."[56]

The *Maddox*'s forward three-inch gun mount fired briefly at 2140G.[57] Apparently this was done without assistance from fire-control radar, simply on the basis of a range and bearing supplied by surface-search radar.

Meanwhile, radar on the *Turner Joy* had locked onto a skunk also approaching from the same direction. The joint chronology gives the impression that it was detected at 2134G, immediately after detection of "V" by the *Maddox*, and states that it was slightly closer than the skunk "V" detected by the *Maddox*, slightly to the right, and faster (moving at fifty knots rather than thirty-five to forty). The corresponding chronology from the *Turner Joy*, however, says the skunk was acquired at a range of 8,000 yards, bearing 086°, speed fifty knots, course 210°, at 2137G; this suggests that this skunk was not closer to the destroyers than the skunk "V" detected by the *Maddox*, but more distant. The track chart attached to this report indicates that "V-1" was acquired at 2137G at a range of about 11,500 yards, much more distant than any location recorded elsewhere for either "V" or "V-1." The discrepancy between the chronology and the track chart has not been explained.[58] This skunk was designated in the after-action reports as "V-1."

The *Turner Joy* opened fire at 2139G, using the aft guns under the control of Director 52.[59] There may well have been an interruption in the lock-on of the fire-control radar. The destroyer opened fire at 2139G, ceased fire at 2141G, and then opened fire again. Lock-on was lost and firing ceased for the second time at 2142G; the after-action reports indicate that the surface-search radar continued to track skunk "V-1" until 2144G.

Chad James's recollection is slightly different. When the ship was at General Quarters, James's job was long-range air control. He was responsible for aircraft from the time they left the carriers up to the time they reached the immediate vicinity of the destroyer. When they reached the destroyer, he would hand responsibility for them to Chief Radarman Robert Johnson, who sat next to him in CIC, and who was responsible for close-range air control.

As "V-1" approached, Chief Johnson had the surface-search radar showing on his radar screen, and he had expanded the view to show a large-scale image of objects close to the ship. At this expansion, the target showed on the screen as a blob of considerable size. James was looking at Chief Johnson's screen.

James said, when interviewed, that at the time the *Turner Joy* was firing at "V-1," there was not yet any air support—no planes had yet been assigned to the *Turner Joy*. James and Chief Johnson were therefore able to pay closer attention to surface radar targets than would have been possible if they had been busy controlling aircraft. The headphone of the radio Johnson would have used for communicating with aircraft was not even over Johnson's ears. Johnson was a man who always paid attention to the whole picture even when he was controlling aircraft, but in this case he was able to give his full attention to surface targets.

James said that the radar will not show a five-inch shell in flight toward the target, nor will it show the explosion of the shell itself; rather what appears is a hazy patch, the radar image of liquid water thrown into the air by the detonation of a shell. James recalls that Johnson's screen showed three shells going off, right on top of the target. "All three were clearly visible when they hit. You could see each one individually."

The surface-search radar was doing twelve sweeps a minute, or one every five seconds. The hazy patches from the shells going off were visible for perhaps two sweeps. After that, the blob that indicated the target went dead in the water, and with each sweep it was smaller on the screen than on the previous sweep. In three or four sweeps it was gone, making a total of five or six sweeps, which would represent a total of twenty-five or thirty seconds from the time the three hits were scored on it to the time it disappeared. According to James: "As I recall there was no [further] reason to fire at that target, it didn't exist. We switched to other contacts." James is completely sure that this radar target was a surface contact, and that the shells of the *Turner Joy* had sunk it.[60]

Various sources disagree as to the range of skunk "V-1" at 2139G, when the *Turner Joy* initially opened fire. A figure of 4,000 yards is given by the chronology in the *Turner Joy* action report. The track chart attached to the report, however, indicates that "V-1" was at about 8,000 yards, and the joint chronology gives the range as 7,000 yards.[61] A plausible hypothesis is that the range was 7,000 to 8,000 yards when the *Turner Joy* opened fire for the first time, and 4,000 yards the second time.

David Mallow was a sonarman third class. He had been in the navy for slightly more than two years, and he had been aboard the *Maddox*, as a sonarman, for slightly more than one year. On the evening of August 4, he had just gone off watch when the destroyer went to General Quarters. He returned to his station in the sonar room, where he was the sonar operator. On the *Maddox* the sonar room was not adjacent to the combat information center; the only information that came to Mallow about the targets being tracked on radar was what came by phone, and that was not a lot of information.[62]

Shortly after the *Maddox*'s radar showed skunk "V" turning sharply at 2137G, range slightly over 6,000 yards, Mallow heard noises on the sonar. He cannot now recall what he had been told about radar targets approaching to close range, or whether he had been told anything about such targets, in the preceding minutes.

It was assumed on board the *Maddox* at the time that the noises Mallow was reporting were incoming torpedoes. Some sources indicate that he reported them as such. Mallow, however, says that he simply reported noise spokes; he did not try to decide whether these were the sounds of torpedoes or of the propellers of hostile vessels. The *Maddox*'s ASW officer (Ensign John Leeman) and weapons officer (Lieutenant Raymond Connell) have confirmed that Mallow simply reported "noise spokes" or "hydrophone effects," and that the decision to translate this to "torpedoes" was made higher up the chain of command.[63] In an account written two days later, Captain Herrick reported that when he heard (over a speaker system) the report from the sonar room to the bridge that noises had been detected, he could hear in the background over the same speaker the actual noises, which "sounded to me like torpedo noises."[64] Captain Herrick has recently confirmed this account, adding that what he interpreted at the time as the sound of torpedoes was possibly the beat of the destroyer's own propellers.[65] Of course anyone hearing sonar noises as background sounds over a speaker system, and trying to sort them out from the words being carried over the same speaker system and also from the voices of other people on the bridge, would have been far less able even than Mallow to distinguish reliably between sounds generated by torpedoes and sounds generated by the destroyer. But if people on the bridge (Herrick's location at the time) and perhaps also in CIC were deciding for themselves that the sounds they could dimly hear over speakers were torpedoes, this would completely have nullified the effect of Mallow's caution in not using the word "torpedo" when he reported sonar noises.

Mallow did not and does not disagree with the interpretation that was placed on his reports: "Anytime you have high-speed noise, you have a probable torpedo out there." He does not believe that every noise spoke he reported during the action was the sound of a genuine torpedo, but he is "absolutely convinced a majority of them were."[66]

The joint chronology states that the first reported torpedo was on a bearing of 051°. The *Turner Joy* was warned by radio that a torpedo had been detected, and both destroyers turned to starboard to evade. Either during the turn or just after the *Turner Joy* had steadied onto the new course, 210°, at least three men saw what they believed to be a torpedo passing up the port side aft to forward. The *Turner Joy*'s sonar did not, however, detect any torpedo. (Questions about this sighting will be dealt with in Chapter 7.)

All major after-action reports written aboard the *Maddox* contain the same strangely phrased statement: "A comparison of the proximity of *Maddox* and

Turner Joy DRT marks, in plotting 'V-1' and 'V', respectively at time 2139 indicate a possibility that this might have been only one contact which launched at time 2137, turned back, and launched another torpedo at 2142."[67] Taken on its face, this statement seems to deduce the possibility that the two radar skunks represented the same vessel from the fact that there was a single moment—2139G—when their tracks came close to one another. All other records including the track charts, however, indicate that these were two entirely separate targets, the tracks for which did not even vaguely resemble one another. Skunk "V" headed continuously *away* from the destroyers from 2137G until radar contact was lost at 2142G, range 9,000 yards and opening, bearing 090°. "V-1" headed continuously *toward* the destroyers from 2137G onward and was approximately at its closest point of approach—less than 4,000 yards from the *Turner Joy* and less than 5,000 from the *Maddox*—when radar contact was lost at 2144G.[68] Certainly the officers who produced the *Maddox* action report, incorporating in it the language quoted above, did not really believe that the two contacts had represented a single vessel; they stated it was "probable that at least three torpedoes" had been launched by the two vessels.[69] This would have been impossible for a single torpedo boat.

Several witnesses from the *Turner Joy* have clearly indicated that they believed the disappearance of "V-1" from the radar screens at close range meant that it had been sunk. It was not claimed as a sinking, however, in the after-action reports. The joint track chart indicates that skunk "V-3," acquired on radar at 2220G, was believed to be the same enemy vessel as the skunk "V-1" lost at 2144G.

Spurious Continuities between Skunks, "N" to "V-1"

The *Turner Joy* action report, without giving precise details about the movements of skunks "N," "O," and "P," makes them seem more like actively hostile vessels than do the corresponding reports from the *Maddox*. Describing the period immediately after the skunks were first detected northeast of the destroyers, the *Turner Joy*'s report states:

These contacts were tracked on a southerly course at speeds up to 33 knots. . . .

Upon detection and evaluation, CTG 72.1 turned the formation on a southeasterly course (130T) [this occurred at 1946G] to open the threat and ordered maximum boiler power. Approximately one half hour later, when the OTC altered the formation course to 160T [this occurred at 2020G], the contacts were tracked on a parallel course, but were held to be adjusting speed in an attempt to gage the destroyers' track.

In the ensuing action standard evasion doctrine was employed for torpedo evasion.[70]

Almost all of this is without foundation. The skunks were not even all on various southerly courses, much less the same southerly course, at the time this report says they were "tracked on *a* southerly course." The statement about the skunks paralleling the destroyers at about 2020G not only cannot be found in any available report from the *Maddox*, it is in striking contrast to the available reports, which give courses for the skunks at 2019G, 2025G, and 2030G.

Even more striking is the way the *Turner Joy*'s report fails to mention that these skunks drifted aft and faded from the radar due to long range, a fact made clear in the corresponding reports from the *Maddox*. Instead, the paragraph describing the skunks paralleling the destroyers and gauging their speed is immediately followed by a paragraph in which the destroyers are under torpedo attack; the uninformed reader would surely assume that the contacts described in the previous paragraphs were responsible.

The fact that the movements of the skunks appear so much more threatening in the report from the *Turner Joy* than in the reports from the *Maddox* has to reflect the attitudes of the respective authors, not the information available to them, since tracking of these skunks had been done almost entirely by the *Maddox*. As has been stated above, the radar of the *Turner Joy* was set for close range during almost all of the relevant period, and on the one occasion when the *Turner Joy* did record a position for these skunks based on its own radar observations, this position corresponded perfectly with the reports of the *Maddox*, and contradicted the threatening picture in the paragraphs quoted above.

Accounts written in later years by people who believe that there really was an attack on the two destroyers often present a picture showing much more consistency even than can be found in the after-action reports.

Edward Marolda has published a paper indicating not only that skunks "N," "O," and "P" attempted to pursue the destroyers, but that their pursuit brought them to the area where the destroyers were attacked—that they were the same vessels as the ones collectively known as skunk "U" that were shadowing the destroyers at relatively close range shortly before the shooting started.[71] He and Oscar Fitzgerald had laid the foundation for this linkage of what were in fact two widely separated sets of contacts—the southernmost position ever recorded for "N," "O," or "P" was at least forty miles from the northernmost position ever recorded for "U"—with an account of the movement of the skunks that not only repeated the most extreme exaggerations of the after-action reports about the supposed efforts of "N," "O," and "P" to pursue the destroyers as they withdrew to the southeast, but also relocated "U" to the north in a fashion that no after-action report ever attempted to do, describing "U" as having first been detected "thirteen miles behind" the destroyers, making it seem very reasonable that the vessels making up "U" were the ones away from which the destroyers had been moving.[72] In reality, "U" appeared on the screens not behind them, but slightly ahead of them—approximately due east of the destroyers, which were heading southeast.

The account in Marolda and Fitzgerald also amalgamates "V" and "V-1" into a single contact called "V1," which is described as if the movements of "V" as recorded on the *Maddox* and of "V-1" as recorded on the *Turner Joy* had been consistent with one another (see Figures 4a and 4b).[73]

The amalgamation of separate contacts reaches its greatest extremes in statements suggesting a continuity stretching all the way from "N," "O," and "P" to "V-1." Commander Barnhart, in response to the idea that what appeared on the radar might have been ghost images, has been quoted as saying: "Was it a ghost? A ghost doesn't go 32 miles in toward you, make a turn and then make a perfect torpedo attack against you."[74] (The phrase "a perfect torpedo attack," used to describe a supposed torpedo firing from a very unfavorable angle, at a range much too great to have produced a reliable hit even from a good angle, is as odd as the rest of Barnhart's statement.) Admiral Ulysses S. G. Sharp, Commander-in-Chief, Pacific, at the time of the incidents, has made a similar exaggeration.[75]

The Apparent Incident Continues

There followed about two hours of apparently intense combat, during most of which the two destroyers were miles apart. Captain Herrick reported at 2142G that he had opened fire, and at 2152G that he was under continuous torpedo attack.[76]

The two destroyers fired over 300 rounds. The *Turner Joy* was responsible for most of this; the *Maddox*'s gun directors achieved no satisfactory lock-ons to radar targets, though quite a few shells, mostly three-inch, were fired without lock-on. Most sources indicate that the *Turner Joy*'s radar contacts looked good at least while they lasted, though they tended to be brief. One officer from the *Turner Joy*, however, told Joseph Goulden in 1968: "We were getting blotches on the radar screen—nothing real firm, so we were whacking away at general areas with proximity fuzes, hoping to get something."[77]

Patrick Park this time was in the main gun director of the *Maddox*. Park says that from the time the ship went to General Quarters, the fire control radar only locked onto one clear, genuine target the whole night: the *Turner Joy*. The gun director officer (Ensign Corsette) was given many targets by the surface search radar, but with the exception of the one that turned out to be the *Turner Joy*, all of them were just "nature in action." They did not have the characteristics attributed to vessels on the radar screen—this was particularly noticeable when Park elevated or depressed the radar, looking for a clearly defined top and bottom of the target. Also, they didn't last. "Surface returns such as sea swells

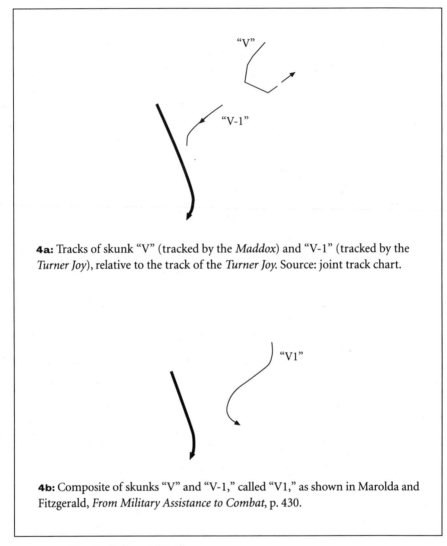

4a: Tracks of skunk "V" (tracked by the *Maddox*) and "V-1" (tracked by the *Turner Joy*), relative to the track of the *Turner Joy*. Source: joint track chart.

4b: Composite of skunks "V" and "V-1," called "V1," as shown in Marolda and Fitzgerald, *From Military Assistance to Combat*, p. 430.

Figure 4. Skunks "V" and "V-1"

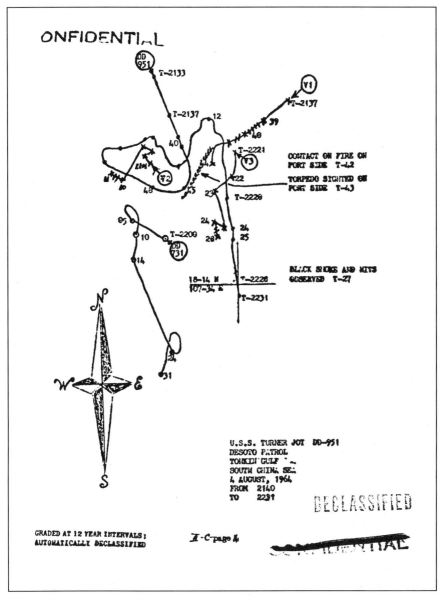

Figure 5. *Turner Joy* action report track chart, 2133G to 2231G. This image has been reduced by 55 percent from the original document.

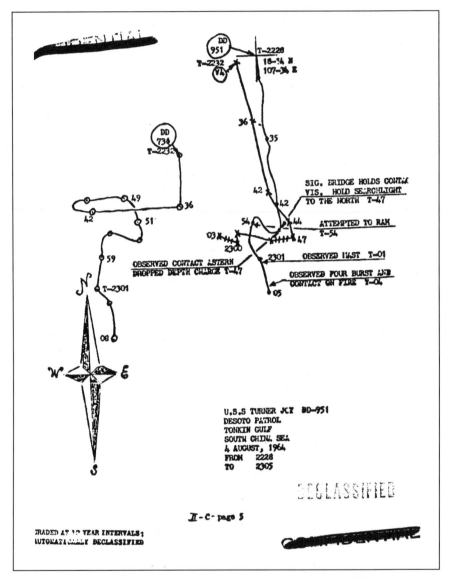

Figure 6. *Turner Joy* action report track chart, 2228G to 2305G. This image has been reduced by 55 percent from the original document.

would roll under and we'd lose contact; air returns such as sheets of rain would hold but without clear definition as I elevated or depressed the radar."[78]

Statements made shortly after the action indicate that after skunk "V," the radar contacts acquired by the surface-search and fire-control radars of the *Maddox* were "random and intermittent"; the gun directors of the *Maddox* were unable to lock onto any of them.[79] Park remembers something slightly different:

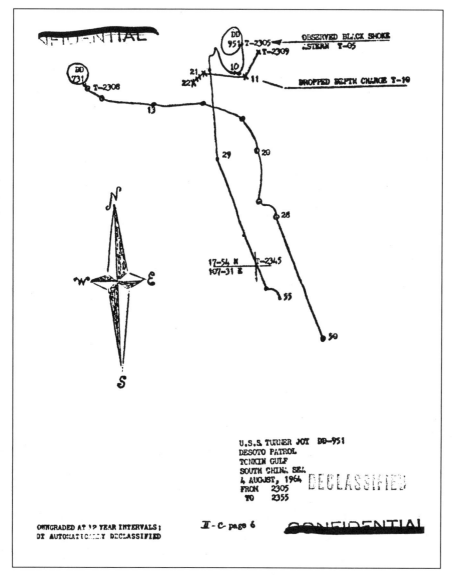

Figure 7. *Turner Joy* action report track chart, 2305G to 2355G. This image has been reduced by 55 percent from the original document.

We locked onto quite a few of them. You can lock onto these sea swells. You can hold it for up to twenty seconds and then it will disappear as it rolls under. Rain squalls will last longer, but signals are very weak and hard to hold. . . .

Several times that night, because we had not established a viable contact early on, control of the guns was turned over to other gun directors. Then . . . we'd get a strong (natural cause) contact, and simultaneous to our classifying

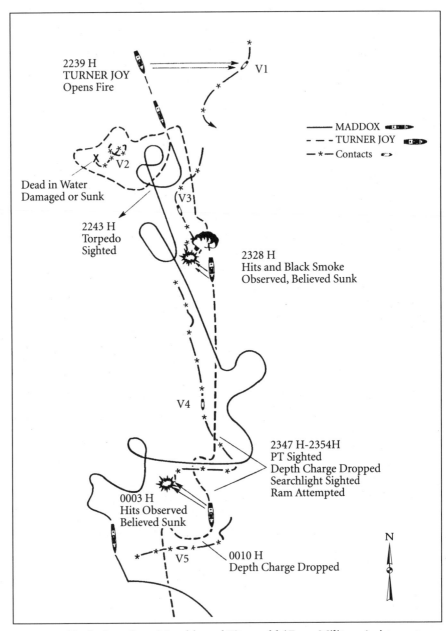

Figure 8. Track chart from Marolda and Fitzgerald (*From Military Assistance to Combat*, p. 430).

the contact, gun control would be coming back on the line to me, only to learn that it was more of the same. Mount captains, the entire bridge, CIC, [the] director officer, even I was mad at myself for not having a skunk to shoot at. But I'd be damned if I was gonna shoot a wave just to say I'd sunk something.

Park is convinced that there could not have been a PT boat without the fire-control radar being able to pick it up and identify it as a genuine target: "There couldn't have been a canoe out there."[80]

The *Turner Joy*, which was able to obtain lock-ons and was doing most of the shooting, claimed to have sunk two of the attacking vessels. Ensign Douglas Smith was functioning as gunnery liaison officer in the CIC of the *Turner Joy*. He operated the MK 5 target designation system. This had a square console, with a radar screen in the middle and a joystick at each corner. To designate a target, Ensign Smith would use the joysticks to move a circular cursor on the screen. When the cursor lay on top of the radar blip for the target selected, Ensign Smith would direct the fire-control radar to lock onto that radar target. If the lock-on were successful, the gun director (and guns, if so engaged) would then follow that radar blip automatically, without the need for any further manual tracking with the joysticks. All gunfire by the *Turner Joy* on the night of August 4 was automatic; it occurred only when there was a successful lock-on, and the fire-control radar was tracking a target without the need for manual tracking.

The radar targets that he was designating for gunfire that night seemed to him completely genuine: "When I tracked those things, there was no question in my mind that they were not phantoms." He was obtaining good firm lock-ons; the system did not "chatter" (locking on for a few seconds, then repeatedly losing and regaining lock-on) as he would have expected the system to do if the contacts had been spurious. Nor does he recall contacts breaking up or disappearing in such a fashion as to make him think they had been spurious. When radar contacts were lost, however, he did not have time to think much about whether the way they had disappeared might suggest that they could have been spurious; he had to turn his attention immediately to other contacts.[81]

The *Turner Joy*'s radar showed contact after contact. During the two hours of apparent combat, there is not a period of five minutes for which one cannot find, somewhere among the track charts, logs, and after-action reports, at least one reference to a contact having been held. There are five major sources of data on the contacts: (1) the track charts attached to the *Turner Joy* action report, which trace the movements of both destroyers, and of five radar contacts; (2) the chronology also forming part of the *Turner Joy* action report, which includes some contacts that were omitted from the track charts, and also reveals that some of the contacts that are shown on the track charts by uninterrupted lines were in fact held only intermittently on the radar; (3) a very large track chart (now in the Naval Historical Center) prepared by Radarman Second Class Koplin, probably with the assistance of one or more other members of the crew of the *Turner Joy*, on an unspecified date probably in the first half of August; (4) a track chart in the Naval Historical Center that this author believes to have been the chart prepared aboard the *Maddox* as an attachment to the joint chronology dated August 13, 1964(hereafter the joint track chart); and (5) the quartermaster log, deck log, and CIC log of the *Turner Joy*. The listing that follows will include comments on the differences between these various sources.

For "V-1," the impression conveyed by the *Turner Joy* action report track chart—that the contact was held without interruption by the surface-search radar from 2137G to 2144G, moving continuously toward the destroyer in a most threatening fashion—is supported by the other sources. A number of sources state that the fire-control radar also locked onto this target very firmly. The fire-control radar of Director 52, however—the director actually controlling gunfire that night—cannot have had lock-on for all of this period. The action report track chart shows, and other sources confirm, that the guns fired at this target only rather briefly. It was not a matter of ceasing fire because the target no longer seemed a threat, either; the chart track shows "V-1" continuing to close the destroyer, and indeed firing a torpedo, after the point at which *Turner Joy* ceased fire. If this track chart is accurate, there has to have been some problem with fire-control radar lock-on.

For the period from 2147G to 2213G, the record is very unclear. The various track charts contradict one another, the *Turner Joy* action report chronology contradicts all the track charts, and the relevant page of the *Turner Joy* CIC log is simply missing.

A radar target was acquired at 2147G, at close range almost directly ahead of the destroyer, and was held on the radar for probably about five minutes thereafter. When it first appeared it was off the port bow of the destroyer, already closer to a good torpedo launch position than skunk "V-1" had ever gotten. Commander Barnhart, however, seems not to have taken it seriously as a threat. Instead of taking evasive action, he continued on a straight course that soon placed the contact in what would have been, if it had really been a hostile PT boat, a near-perfect attack position—the joint track chart indicates a range of only about 1,000 yards—off the starboard bow of the destroyer. This does not appear to have resulted from any effort on the part of the target. While Koplin's track chart and the joint track chart are not in precise agreement as to the movements of this target, they both make it clear that the target made no effort to launch a torpedo attack when in a near-perfect position to do so, and in fact both suggest that the target was oblivious to the presence of the destroyer. The *Turner Joy*'s course also "masked" the five-inch guns during most of the approach—made five-inch gunfire against the radar target impossible by placing the ship's superstructure between the target and the gun turrets. The destroyer did fire on this target with the forward three-inch gun during at least part of the approach. The lack of any evasive action by the destroyer, and the way the contact was eventually omitted from the action report track chart and the action report chronology, suggest that the contact did not have the appearance of a genuine PT boat.

Sometime between 2201G and 2204G, a new contact was acquired, not far from where the last had been lost; this was eventually designated "V-2." Various sources differ as to where it was first acquired, and whether it was held continuously or intermittently. The joint track chart and Koplin's track chart treat this as a continuation of the contact originally acquired at 2147G. Like the contact acquired at 2147G, "V-2" moved in an apparently random fashion; there is no suggestion in any of the track charts of any deliberate effort by the contact to close with the destroyer. "V-2" had wandered out to a range of 10,000 yards by the time radar contact was lost at 2213G.

During the last minutes that "V-2" was being tracked, between 2210G and 2213G, the joint track chart shows another contact suddenly appearing much closer to the destroyer. This contact, however, was omitted from the action report track chart and the action report chronology.

The *Turner Joy* fired on some target at 2210G, fired again at 2212G or 2213G, and in the CIC log at 2214G triumphantly recorded, "Believe we sunk contact"; but the records are so contradictory and confused that it is not even possible to be sure whether the contact believed to have been sunk was "V-2," which by that time was about five miles southwest of the destroyer, or the contact that had suddenly appeared on the radar screens at 2210G less than one mile west of the destroyer, or possibly yet a third contact, never shown on any track chart, which may perhaps have been held three miles north of the destroyer. (For more detailed discussion, see Chapter 7.)

The action report track charts show nothing happening between 2214G and 2220G, but the quartermaster log reveals a brisk flurry of combat.

2216 Commenced firing to port 5 in. power . . .
2217 Steady on 185° PGC
    Ceased fire
    One contact appears dead in water
2218 R[ight] 5° rudder
    Receiving assistance from aircraft
    Commenced firing to port & stbd
    C[hanged] c[ourse] to 210° PGC
2220 Believed one contact sunk & one dead in water[82]

The contact at which the destroyer fired at 2216G was held on the radar for only two minutes, and the action report chronology evaluated it as "possibly a false echo."[83]

No track chart shows any contact to port at 2216G or 2218G, and only one—Koplin's—shows the one to starboard.

Contact "V-3" was acquired at 2220G, range 4,800 yards. The destroyer fired on it for an unknown length of time between 2224G and 2228G. Other records confirm the impression that it was held continuously until it disappeared at 2228G, range under 3,000 yards, believed to have been sunk. By this time the range had been under 4,000 yards for seven minutes.

The *Turner Joy* action report track chart shows "V-4" as an uninterrupted line from 2232G to its disappearance (believed sunk) at 2303G. Other records indicate that it was intermittent at least until 2242G; the joint track chart shows real tracking for this target beginning only at 2246G. Aircraft were reported making a strafing run at this contact, astern of the destroyer, at 2237G.[84]

Contact was lost at this point, range about 3,000 yards; the CIC log reported "hold no active surface contacts" at 2238G. Contact was regained at 2242G, range under 2,000 yards, but there is no indication that any shots were fired for five more minutes. The *Turner Joy* fired on "V-4" briefly at about 2247G or 2248G. Contact must then have been briefly lost, judging by the entry "regain contact" at 2251G in the CIC log. Shortly afterward, the destroyer attempted to ram the contact. Joseph Schaperjahn, the *Turner Joy*'s chief sonarman, remembers people on the destroyer bracing themselves for the impact, but there was no impact. The after-action report shows:

> 2254: Hard left rudder to attempt ramming contact. Contact lost in sea return at 700 yards.
> 2259: Regained contact bearing 320T, range 1500 yards. Contact appeared on starboard side, having evaded ram. Fire control radar locked on.[85]

The *Turner Joy* resumed firing at 2300G, and when contact was lost at 2303G, "V-4" was evaluated as having been sunk.

It is not clear what the target to port was at which the *Turner Joy* fired briefly at 2305G; nothing shows on the track charts. The direction was wrong for this to have been belated fire directed at the position of "V-4."

A contact that the after-action reports leave undesignated, but which will be treated here as "V-5" to fit the nomenclature in Marolda and Fitzgerald, shows on the track chart as having been held from 2309G to 2322G. Other sources, however, indicate that out of this thirteen-minute period, radar contact was only held for two brief intervals of about two minutes each.

The action report track chart indicates that "V-5" was to starboard of the *Turner Joy* at 2310G and roughly astern at 2312G. The action report chronology states that it was fired upon astern at 2310½, and that firing ceased when radar contact was lost at 2311G. The quartermaster and deck logs, however, each state that the destroyer opened fire briefly at 2310G and then opened fire again at 2312G. It seems possible that the fire at 2312G was directed at something other than "V-5," which does not show on the track chart.

What was believed to be the same contact was reacquired at 2321G and fired upon briefly from 2321G to 2322G. The chronology simply says "contact opening" at 2322G; the action report track chart suggests contact was lost at 2322G.

The assumption that the contact held from 2309G to 2311G or 2312G was the same vessel as the contact held from 2321G to 2322G seems inadequately founded. If we accept the track on the action report track chart as an accurate picture of the movements of the vessel during the period when radar contact was not held, it would appear that contact was lost when "V-5" was less than two miles away, and that the distance remained under two miles (sometimes less and sometimes more than one mile) for the whole of the nine or ten minutes until contact was regained at 2321G. It might be added that the track shown on the chart for this contact also shows it passing about two miles to the north of the *Maddox* during that ten minutes of invisibility. The failure of the *Maddox* to track it on radar compounds the oddity of the *Turner Joy's* failure to do so.

The action report track chart covering the period from 2308G to 2350G shows no radar contacts after 2322G. Other records indicate a number of brief, close-range contacts during this period (see Chapter 7), at two of which the *Turner Joy* fired. The records are so scanty that it is difficult to be sure how many of these contacts there were, how long they were held, or at which of them the *Turner Joy* fired. Firing ceased for the last time at 2344G, and the last records of contacts being held on the radar give times of 2347G and 2348G. The two destroyers then retired from the gulf.

Various stations throughout the ship communicated with one another via telephone talkers. Information could get distorted when one man repeated by telephone things he thought he had heard from another man by telephone. There were a few reports from various places that got into logs, but not into the after-action reports. For example, the CIC log entry for 2321G, "2 fish down starboard side," clearly refers to a report of a torpedo sighting, but no torpedo sighting at or near this time appears in later chronologies.

Commander Barnhart's station on the bridge was not an ideal position from which to command the ship during a night action. He later told his superiors:

It is recommended that a Captain's Battle Station be established in the ship's CIC and that Commanding Officers be authorized and directed to utilize this space as the tactical situation dictates.

Comment: This entire battle was fought in pitch darkness where almost all Combat Information was processed in CIC. The Commanding Officer's Battle Station on the Bridge was completely darkened, had no status boards, only two radar repeaters, no DRT etc. In a night battle, the Bridge station is one of the poorest on the ship insofar as facilities are concerned. CIC has sufficient equipment, facilities and status boards to function efficiently as the Captain's Battle station.[86]

Both destroyers dodged torpedoes reported by the sonarman on the *Maddox*. The "*Maddox* evaded at least 26 suspected contacts evaluated as torpedoes on the AN/SQS 32A sonar system."[87] Sonar on the *Turner Joy* could detect no torpedoes, however, and radar on the *Maddox* could not detect the vessels appearing on the radar of the *Turner Joy*. Commander Ogier later commented on this portion of the incident: "The *Maddox* did not have any unidentified blips on its radars. . . . We were relying on reports from the *Turner Joy*. I was very concerned about our inability to pick up the *Turner Joy's* radar targets. I have since concluded that false targets may be picked up by some radars and not by others because of the difference in their frequencies or other differences."[88]

Another factor that might be considered is that the fire-control system of the *Turner Joy* was more modern and more automated than that of the *Maddox*. Patrick Park says that he distinguished PT boats from wave tops on the fire-control radar of the *Maddox* by raising and lowering the beam, and observing the results; other people experienced with radar have told the author how they have sometimes been able to distinguish genuine from spurious radar targets by manipulating the power settings. The fire-control radar of the *Turner Joy*, however, operated automatically once assigned a target. The operators did not fiddle with the controls to the same extent as was the case on the *Maddox*.

The *Turner Joy* also dropped depth charges, set for detonation at a very shallow depth; this is among the standard tactics for defense against torpedo attack. The depth charges had not been armed before the action began. Joseph Schaperjahn later recommended a medal for the senior torpedoman, who had to remove the safety bars and set the depth charges for shallow depth by feel, working in the dark, leaning over the rear of the ship with five-inch guns going off overhead.[89]

Ensign Smith heard later that at some point during the action, the fire of the *Turner Joy's* forward three-inch guns had jarred open one of the windows on the open bridge. In the darkness this was not noticed until a spray of water from a wave breaking against the bow came through the open window and hit a junior officer in the face. The man thought he had been hit by enemy fire, and dropped to the deck, yelling. A medic actually arrived before anyone figured out what had happened.[90]

Eventually, Commander Ogier realized that the number of noise spokes reported by his sonarman had become ridiculous, and that what had been interpreted as torpedo noises had to be something else. He stopped dodging, and the incident came to an end.[91]

There is dispute over another event that may have helped put an end to the incident; Patrick Park tells the story but Richard Corsette denies it. According to Park's version, through most of the action he had been able to find nothing on the fire-control radar firm enough to be a target. Both Park and Ensign Corsette, the director officer, were very tense; Corsette was being chewed out by the gunnery officer (on the bridge) for the director's inability to lock onto targets.

Then the director did lock onto a target, and the order came to open fire. Park now feels as if God intervened at that point; despite the anxiety and tension that could very easily have made him accept the order without thought, he suddenly realized that what he was aimed at was the *Turner Joy*. Another man in the director, Fire Control Technician Timothy Deyarmie, had the same feeling at the same time. Corsette, as anxious as everyone else, repeated the order to open fire. Park refused to fire until he knew where the *Turner Joy* was. He and Corsette were yelling at one another loudly enough that Ogier heard them, and yelled, "Cease fire."

Ogier then asked CIC where the *Turner Joy* was. CIC did not know; they had lost track of the *Turner Joy* some time before, when changing sheets on the track chart. When the *Turner Joy* was asked to give a bearing for the *Maddox*, it turned out that the *Turner Joy* had similarly lost track of the *Maddox*. Ogier then asked the *Turner Joy* to flash truck lights, and there they were: right where Park had the five-inch guns targeted. Over the next fifteen minutes, people calmed down and the incident ended.[92]

Meanwhile, the planes overhead were repeatedly directed to locations where the destroyers' radar showed enemy vessels, but no pilot ever saw a PT boat. Lieutenant Commander Donald Hegrat, flying combat photo-reconnaissance, said he could see the destroyers and their wakes very clearly, but no torpedo boats. His photos showed the same. The night was very dark, cloudy and moonless.[93] Stockdale could not understand why, under conditions where he felt his visibility was excellent, he could see no torpedo boat wakes and no sparks from the hits supposedly being scored on torpedo boats by the guns of the destroyers.[94] Such sparks would have been terribly conspicuous in the darkness; he had been able to see sparks from hits by 20-mm shells on PT boats even in daylight on August 2.

A number of pilots have commented on the impression of panic and confusion they received from the destroyers' radio transmissions. Ltjg. Everett Alvarez, Jr., flying an A-4 Skyhawk from the *Constellation*, has said:

> When we switched over to the destroyers' frequencies I was startled to hear so much bedlam and confusion. There were bursts of frantic commands and shouted reports from both ships as they desperately gave ranges, courses and torpedo bearings. Pilots from the *Ticonderoga* were trying to pin down the destroyers' positions in the rain and thick overcast. "What's your position?" the

pilots asked. We had to strain to catch the reply because three or four people on the ships were shouting simultaneously: "Torpedo bearing . . . ," "Turning hard to port," "Sonar bearing . . . ," "Radar contact! Radar contact!"[95]

Alvarez describes how Stockdale managed to impose some order on the situation, getting one of the destroyers to fire a flare to mark its location, and later guiding Alvarez to the correct location to drop some flares. The transmissions from the destroyers, however, remained confused and in one case dangerously inaccurate.[96]

John Barry recalls that at one point a fighter plane made two passes, firing at some target close astern—too close to the ship for safety. Barry got on the phone and said something along the lines of "Get that thing out of here!" Richard Bacino also recalls an aircraft firing a pod of rockets that passed over the *Turner Joy* and then hit the water, close enough to the destroyer to make him very nervous.[97] Barry and Bacino would have been even more disturbed if they had known how close some planes had come to targeting a strike on their ship. Lieutenant Commander John Nicholson, who led a flight of three A-4 Skyhawks (including Alvarez's plane), tells of his arrival over the destroyers, comparatively late in the action:

We began searching for ships, and I saw two high-speed wakes heading 180 degrees, heading south. The guy in the CIC said, "That's not us, we're heading 000," and I recall him calling that heading because 000 is 360. Aviators use 360 and blackshoes [surface ship personnel] 000. Boch was with me, and he said, "Roger, I've got the two wakes; they're heading 180." The voice in the CIC said, "Those must be the PT boats, take them under attack." We armed, and I said, "One in," as we went into our run, and all of a sudden I heard, "Hold fire, hold fire"—it was the two destroyers heading 180—and the attack was broken off.

Talk about history being made; we were within split seconds of dumping on those two tin cans—I mean split seconds. From that point on, I lost total faith in who the hell was controlling down there.[98]

The Evidence from the Destroyers

7 Captain Herrick developed doubts about the incident very quickly. The more than twenty torpedoes supposedly heard on sonar seemed preposterous, given the total number of torpedo boats the DRV possessed. Experimentation revealed that during high-speed maneuvers, the destroyer's own propeller and/or rudder produced the sort of noise spokes that had been interpreted as torpedoes.

At 0027G, Herrick reported: "Review of action makes many reported contacts and torpedoes fired appear doubtful. Freak weather effects on radar and overeager sonarmen may have accounted for many reports. No actual visual sightings by *Maddox*. Suggest complete evaluation before any further action taken."[1] At 0054G, he sent a strikingly self-contradictory message laying out some of the information available to him, and his doubts about it:

> *Maddox* and *Joy* now apparently in clear further recap reveals *Turner Joy* fired upon by small calibre guns and illuminated by search light. *Joy* tracked 2 sets of contacts. Fired on 13 contacts. Claims positive hits 3, 1 sunk, probable hits 3.
>
> *Joy* also reports no actual visual sightings or wake. Have no recap of aircraft sightings but seemed to be few. Entire action leaves many doubts except for apparent attempted ambush at beginning. Suggest thorough reconnaissance in daylight by aircraft.[2]

He later commented on the reluctance with which he had sent these messages: "You wonder how they're going to react to that. . . . There's a sort of gung-ho spirit in any of the services, and not many people like to admit they're wrong or have been wrong, but the stakes were too great in this case. I couldn't stonewall this thing then and pretend—you know, yeah, damn it, it really happened, I can't just take that chance."[3]

During the first two days after the supposed incident, there was a great deal of message traffic back and forth across the Pacific, with Washington frantically calling for information about what had occurred. An officer who saw the messages later commented that communications discipline seemed to have broken down completely. "Everybody and his dog" was addressing questions directly to Captain Herrick, bypassing the chain of command.[4] There was considerable information coming from the *Turner Joy* that suggested a real attack,[5] but much less from the *Maddox* and apparently none at all from the aircraft carriers.

Phil G. Goulding, later the assistant secretary of defense for public affairs in the Johnson administration, once wrote: "A cardinal rule in an establishment as large as the Department of Defense is to assume that first reports are always wrong, no matter what their security classification, no matter to whom they are addressed. Beware of them. Ignore them. File them. Do not, under any circumstances or conditions, share them with the press, for they will come back to plague you."[6]

In this case, however, Washington decided upon a very public retaliation for the supposed attack without waiting for detailed accounts of what had happened on the night of August 4. Once this retaliation had been carried out, the policymakers responsible very badly needed evidence that the first reports from the *Maddox* and the *Turner Joy*, indicating an attack, had been correct.

Secretary McNamara believed (mistakenly—see Chapter 8) that North Vietnamese communications intercepts proved there really had been an attack. As he explained to the National Security Council and the president on the evening of August 4, however, this information was too secret to be released to the public. Other forms of evidence would have to be found to prove that there really had been an attack.[7] On August 6, Director of Central Intelligence John McCone spoke with Secretary of State Rusk about this. "M[cCone] said he had gone into the question of the use of some of the sensitive information to prove the night attack and disprove Hanoi's allegation that it did not take place; it just cannot be used; we will have to have eyewitness accounts and things of that kind."[8] Awareness of this problem may well have lain behind the "flash" message, classified "top secret," that the Joint Chiefs of Staff had sent half an hour before this conversation, to the commanders of all the U.S. units involved in the action: "An urgent requirement exists for proof and evidence of second attack by DRV naval units against TG 72.1 [the destroyers] on night 4 Aug as well as DRV plans and preparation for the attack, for previous attacks and for any subsequent operations. Material must be of type which will convince United Nations Organization that the attack did in fact occur."[9] The deadline for response to this message allowed less than nineteen hours for gathering the required evidence. After receiving this demand, the commanders in the Pacific provided far more support for the idea of a real attack than most of them had provided before.

It should not be assumed that this was simply a matter of telling whatever lies Washington wanted to hear. Captain Herrick and Commander Ogier both state that at the time they wrote their replies to the JCS on August 7, the review they had made of the sighting reports had left them convinced that the attack had been real.[10] Both men have established records of honesty that entitle them to belief, though it seems permissible to note that the message from the JCS would have given them an incentive to convince themselves that the attack had been real.

Richard Corsette made a statement, included in a response to the JCS message, discussing various targets he had acquired on his radar the night of August 4. He tried, however, to phrase his descriptions of those targets so as to convey his actual belief: that the targets he was describing had been just weather.[11] The *Ticonderoga*'s response to the JCS message seems to have contained deliberate exaggeration of the evidence (see below). In general, it seems wise to place more reliance on statements that appear in records dating from before the JCS message than on statements that appear in the record for the first time on or after August 7.

It might also be noted that when senior civilians from the Pentagon came out to Asia and started interviewing personnel on August 10, the officers and men furnished to them for these interviews seem to have been selected to include only those who would provide evidence that there really had been an attack.

The Search for Consistency

When one is trying to decide whether the evidence in an affair such as that of August 4 is reliable, one of the most important criteria is its consistency. If different instruments and different witnesses all give approximately the same report of the movements of a supposed attacking vessel, this suggests, though it does not fully prove, that their reports constitute an accurate record of the movements of a real vessel. If different witnesses and instruments give conflicting accounts of the movements of the supposed vessel, then some of them must be wrong, and it is quite possible that they are all wrong and that there was no vessel.

Captain Alex A. (Andy) Kerr, a U.S. Navy attorney, has cited the consistency of the reports of the night of August 4 as evidence that an attack on the U.S. destroyers really occurred on that night. Kerr was involved in several stages of the process by which the U.S. government formulated its view of the events of that night. Shortly after the incident, he went by helicopter to the *Maddox* and participated in a meeting involving officers of the *Maddox* and also the operations officer of the *Turner Joy*. The report produced by this meeting—the joint chronology—was the basis of all later after-action reports produced on the *Maddox*, and heavily influenced the after-action report of the *Turner Joy*. Kerr carried this report with him when he returned to the *Oklahoma City* (flagship of the Seventh Fleet), and was there while Admiral Johnson evaluated it. Finally, at a much later date, he helped Secretary McNamara prepare for his famous 1968 testimony before the Senate Foreign Relations Committee.

Kerr comments, not unreasonably, that "false contacts are usually random and do not persist for long periods. The same false contact would seldom be sensed by two ships that were in different positions."[12] Of the analysis in which he participated, carried out aboard the *Maddox* about a week after the incident, Kerr later wrote: "We carefully constructed a composite chart. It reflected all of the information available on both ships during the incident. The tracks of both ships were plotted. All radar, sonar, and visual data, with times, ranges, and bearings were entered. The chart showed remarkable correlation. . . . There was great consistency between all the contacts made by both ships. Furthermore, the tracks of the attacking vessels, as plotted independently by both the *Maddox* and *Turner Joy*, coincided and were precisely what one would expect from attacking torpedo boats."[13]

The formal report of the analysis Kerr claims to be summarizing, however, the joint chronology signed by Captain Herrick August 13, does not confirm this. The impression it conveys, in fact, is that while skunk "U" showed in approximately the same location on the radar of both destroyers, shadowing them at a range of ten miles or more, contacts at closer ranges were tracked either by the *Maddox* only or by the *Turner Joy* only—never by both.[14]

What appears to be the chart itself is now in the Naval Historical Center. One looks in vain on this chart for even a single place where tracking by both destroyers of a single radar target is shown. Skunk "U" was in fact tracked by both destroyers, but the chart shows only the track as recorded by the *Maddox*, not the slightly different track recorded by the *Turner Joy*.[15]

Kerr's statement is an example of a widespread problem: many of the accounts of this incident make the record seem much more consistent than it really was. Part of the reason is that the records of any complex event, even a genuine one, always contain errors and inconsistencies. Anyone trying to write an account must "smooth" the record to produce something that fits together and makes sense. The various records of the location of the *Maddox* at various times are not always consistent. When different records, or consecutive entries in the same record, are impossibly inconsistent, the historian must choose which to believe and which to modify or ignore, to produce an account in which the *Maddox* is never in two locations at the same time, and does not move from one location to another at a higher speed than was actually within the capabilities of the destroyer.

There is a danger, however, that the events can be made to appear more consistent than they actually were. If one has a number of entries in various documents, describing the locations or movements of radar targets at various times, and one reconstructs the movements of an enemy vessel, then one must choose which entries to emphasize and which to downplay or ignore, and choose how to interpret the ambiguous ones, in such a fashion as to produce a consistent and meaningful picture. But after doing this, one cannot use the consistency of the picture one has constructed as evidence that the vessel in question was real.

It is difficult to trace the process by which the records of the events of August 4 were "smoothed." On many questions the original records cannot be found; only later, reworked versions are available. Also, the smoothing process occurred on a piecemeal basis. One man would eliminate one inconsistency from the record, often operating in complete good faith, on the principle that if two reports are contradictory, one of them must be wrong and should be ignored. Later, someone else would eliminate another inconsistency.

It seems to have been widely regarded as bad form to allow doubts as to whether there had been an attack against the destroyers to appear on paper. The interviews this author has conducted suggest that a great many U.S. Navy personnel felt such doubts, in the immediate aftermath of the incident; but only a few (mostly informal) reports exist expressing such doubts. This would have left each individual with the impression that the others believed there really had been an attack, and thus discouraged efforts to place in the record evidence that there had not been an attack.

The after-action reports written a few days or weeks after the incident present an impression of more consistency than was actually present in the available evidence. Some of the strongest comments on this issue come from Joseph Schaperjahn, chief sonarman on the *Turner Joy*. He believes that the after-action reports of the *Turner Joy* were "gundecked." They were written so as to make the evidence of an attack seem stronger than it actually was, both by the omission of negative information such as Schaperjahn had tried to present, and by the adjustment of information to make it present a meaningful pattern. Schaperjahn does not believe that the pattern of movement of PT boats, as charted in the after-action reports, corresponds with the actual data collected during the action. "What I remember seeing is haphazard contacts all over the damn place. . . . I saw the original DRT and it was nothing but chicken scratches."[16] It should be stressed that the data from a real incident could in some cases look a lot like chicken scratches; the fact that the data needed adjustment in order to achieve consistency would not, by itself, constitute proof that the incident had been spurious. It is plain, however, that the final reports on the August 4 incident reflected very substantial adjustment of the data.

During the incident, the *Turner Joy* held a huge number of short-range radar contacts, mostly lasting five minutes or less. One of the earliest after-action reports, sent about an hour after the end of the shooting, said that the *Turner Joy* had fired on thirteen contacts.[17] The track charts incorporated in the *Turner Joy* action report (Figures 5, 6, and 7), however, show no contacts lasting less then seven minutes. The difference partly reflects the omission from the action report track charts of tracks that seemed indecently brief, including at least five at which the destroyer actually fired. Even more important is the way brief contacts that were not omitted were instead linked together to create the illusion of prolonged ones.

The action report track charts show exactly five contacts held on the destroyer's radar between 2137G and 2350G. Each of these is represented on the chart by an uninterrupted line; the average duration shown is thirteen minutes. In reality, however, none of these contacts had ever been tracked continuously for as long as thirteen minutes. "V-1" and "V-3," shown as having been tracked for seven minutes each, seem in fact to have been tracked continuously for the indicated periods. "V-4," "V-5," and probably also "V-2" are composites, produced by linking brief radar contacts together to create the impression of prolonged ones.

The arbitrary nature of this process is most clearly visible in the case of "V-5," since different men on the destroyers chose to make the linkages in different ways, producing inconsistent composite chart tracks. *Turner Joy* acquired a brief contact at 2309G. The action report chronology states that this contact was lost at 2311G. There were a variety of others, also brief, at various locations during the next half hour. A partial chart has been constructed (Figure 9a), based primarily on ranges and bearings recorded in the action report chronology and the CIC log. Schaperjahn's phrase—"haphazard contacts all over the damn place"— seems appropriate. Koplin's track chart brought order out of this chaos by linking the contact held from 2309G to 2311G with later contacts to the south, to create a single continuous track lasting from 2309G to about 2344G (Figure 9b). The action report track chart for this period, however (Figure 9c), completely omitted the contacts to the south, and linked the brief contact held from 2309G to 2311G with an even briefer one (2321G to 2322G) to the west, creating a thirteen-minute track for a contact that has been referred to in this manuscript (following the nomenclature of Marolda and Fitzgerald) as "V-5"; no formal designation was given to this contact in any report from the destroyers.

The twenty-six minute track for "V-2" in the joint track chart (Figure 10a) is explicitly marked as a composite; the chart shows two tracks, with a dotted line linking the point at which the first contact was lost with the point at which the second was acquired. Even the much shorter track shown for "V-2" in the action report track charts, beginning sometime between 2201G and 2204G, and ending at 2211G (Figure 10c), is probably a composite. The sections of this track for the minutes from 2204G to 2208G are so inconsistent with the corresponding sections of the tracks on the joint track chart and Koplin's track chart

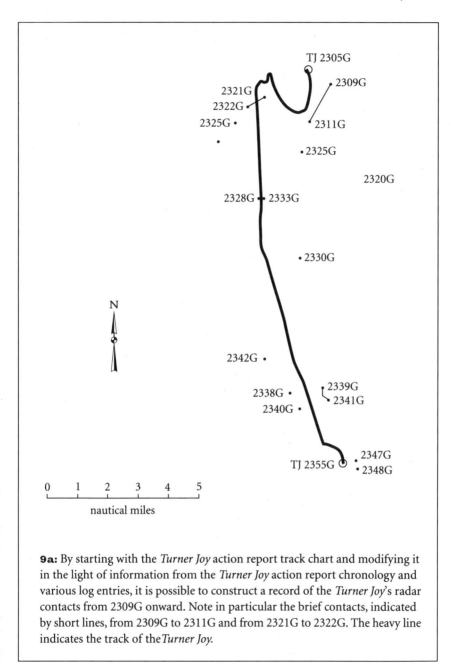

9a: By starting with the *Turner Joy* action report track chart and modifying it in the light of information from the *Turner Joy* action report chronology and various log entries, it is possible to construct a record of the *Turner Joy*'s radar contacts from 2309G onward. Note in particular the brief contacts, indicated by short lines, from 2309G to 2311G and from 2321G to 2322G. The heavy line indicates the track of the *Turner Joy*.

Figure 9. Skunk "V-5"

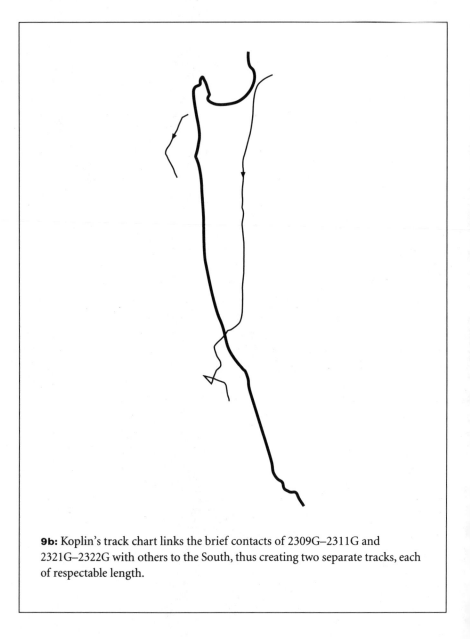

9b: Koplin's track chart links the brief contacts of 2309G–2311G and 2321G–2322G with others to the South, thus creating two separate tracks, each of respectable length.

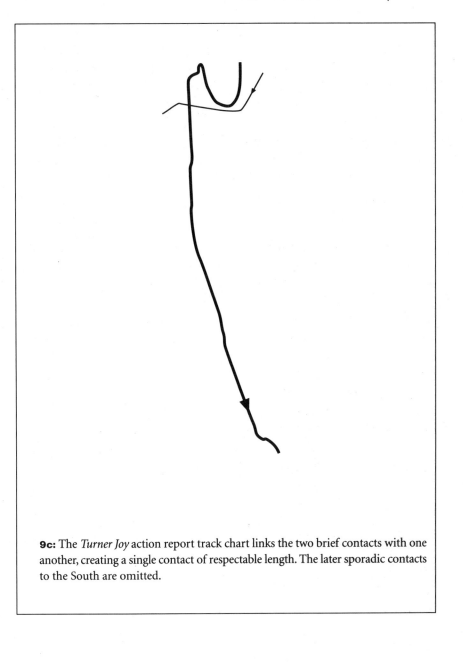

9c: The *Turner Joy* action report track chart links the two brief contacts with one another, creating a single contact of respectable length. The later sporadic contacts to the South are omitted.

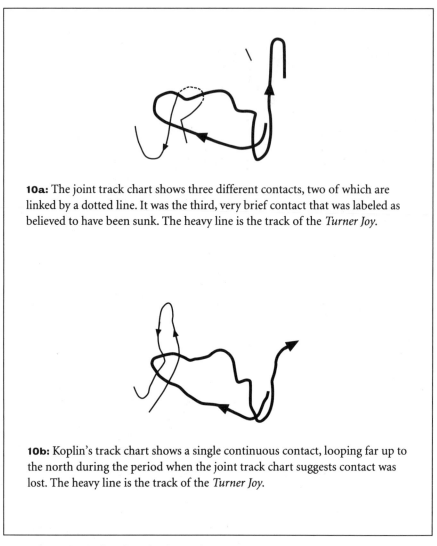

10a: The joint track chart shows three different contacts, two of which are linked by a dotted line. It was the third, very brief contact that was labeled as believed to have been sunk. The heavy line is the track of the *Turner Joy*.

10b: Koplin's track chart shows a single continuous contact, looping far up to the north during the period when the joint track chart suggests contact was lost. The heavy line is the track of the *Turner Joy*.

Figure 10. Skunk "V-2" and other radar targets

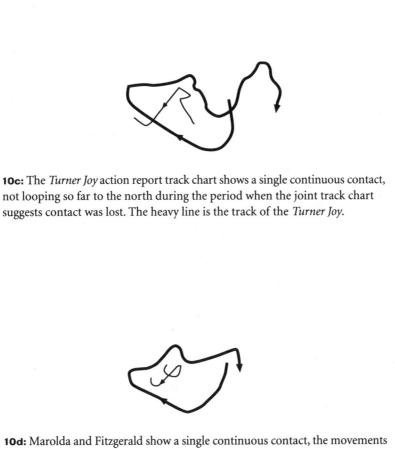

10c: The *Turner Joy* action report track chart shows a single continuous contact, not looping so far to the north during the period when the joint track chart suggests contact was lost. The heavy line is the track of the *Turner Joy*.

10d: Marolda and Fitzgerald show a single continuous contact, the movements of which do not correspond to those shown on any chart from the destroyers (*From Military Assistance to Combat*, p. 340). The heavy line is the track of the *Turner Joy*.

(Figure 10b) as to carry a strong implication that in this case, as with "V-5," there had been several brief contacts in different locations, and different people had made different decisions about how to link them together.

For the last four minutes that "V-2" was tracked, from 2210G to 2213G, the joint track chart also shows an entirely separate target at very close range (less than 2,000 yards when first acquired; see upper right section of Figure 10a). This contact is labeled on the chart "contact believed sunk (2213)."

In the action report chronology, the story of "V-2" appears as follows:

2201—Hold surface contact bearing 278T, range 2,000 yards. Fire Control Radar locked on. Contact held opening to the West. Designated skunk "V-2."

2204—Changed course to 010T.

2210—Changed course to 060T, to unmasked [sic] batteries. Continued to course 180T. Commenced firing at skunk "V-2."

2211—Ceased firing. Lost radar contact.

2212—Regained contact. Range 6000 yards. Resumed firing.

2212½—Ceased firing. Estimated three hits on contact. Changed course to 160T.

2216—Changed course to 185T.[18]

Certainly the *Turner Joy* had fired at something at 2210G and 2212G; in fact the CIC log entry for 2214G reads, "Believe we sunk contact." But was the target "V-2"? To put it bluntly, the account in the chronology is preposterous. If the *Turner Joy* had acquired on radar something believed to be a hostile torpedo boat, range 2,000 yards, the destroyer would not have waited nine minutes to open fire, doing so only after the range had become so long that the supposed torpedo boat was no longer much of a threat and also would have been so hard to hit as to make the claim of its sinking an absurdity. (The range to skunk "V-2" at 2210G and 2212G, incidentally, was not 6,000 yards as is suggested by the chronology, but about 10,000.) The explanation for the delay given in the chronology—that the destroyer was only able to fire after making a course change to unmask batteries—is spurious; the batteries had not been masked on the previous course.

The joint track chart shows the gunfire at 2210G and 2212G directed not at the distant "V-2," but at another target (call it "V-2A"), which had suddenly appeared on the radar at 2210G less than 2,000 yards from the destroyer. The joint track chart has a label indicating that this target, rather than "V-2," was what had been believed to have been sunk at 2214G. Rather than accept the action report chronology's account of gunfire directed at "V-2," demonstrably inaccurate in detail and grossly implausible overall, it seems better to accept the much more reasonable joint track chart. After "V-2A" was edited out of the record because of its brevity (it was only held from 2210G to 2213G), the gunfire directed at it, and the claim it was sunk, could have found their way into the account of "V-2," the target of more respectable duration that had been held on the radar at the same time.

The quartermaster log, which is the only available record of the radar targets or the gunfire between 2210G and 2213G that was actually written down at the time of the events, rather than hours or days later, suggests yet another possibility: that the *Turner Joy* actually fired at a third target to the north, not found on any track chart. The quartermaster log indicates gunfire at 2210G and 2213G; these times are close enough to those given in the other sources (2210G and 2212G) that they probably refer to the same incidents. For the fire at 2213G, however, the bearing of the target is specified as "astern." This cannot possibly refer to "V-2," but it hardly fits the location of "V-2A" any better. If the target had been indeed directly astern of the destroyer at 2213G, in other words directly to the north, then the turn initiated at 2210G really would have been needed to unmask the batteries (not the case for either "V-2" or "V-2A") and the range really could have been 6,000 yards (completely wrong for either "V-2" or "V-2A"), just as the chronology had said. (See the 180-degree turn, from a northbound to a southbound course, in the upper right section of Figure 10a.)

The Radar Evidence

If we consider the first six (possibly seven) high-speed contacts acquired on the radar of the destroyers on the night of August 4, these being "N," "O," "P," and the three (or possibly four) collectively known as "U" that ran parallel to the destroyers for about twenty minutes and then vanished just before the shooting started, the record of their movements indicates the following:

—All of them disappeared from the radar without ever having approached much closer to the destroyers than they had been when first acquired.
—None of them ever got any further forward of the destroyers—got into a better attack position—than it had been when first acquired.
—None of them can have been the "V" and/or "V-1" that supposedly approached the destroyers and launched a torpedo at about 2139G; the available sources all indicate that the distance from the last known location of "U" to the first known locations of "V" and "V-1" were incompatible with any speed possible for a PT boat.[19]

We can discard absolutely the usual notion about these contacts—that they represented PT boats that were substantially faster than the destroyers, knew the location of the destroyers, and were trying to close and attack. The hypotheses that make some sense are that they did not represent vessels at all; that they represented vessels that were unaware of the location of the destroyers; or that they represented vessels that were not interested in closing to attack the destroyers.

"N," "O," and "P" may well have been genuine vessels. We have no negative pilot reports for these three skunks. The single position report based on radar tracking by the *Turner Joy* is completely consistent with the position reports based on tracking by the *Maddox*. The available records indicate that radar contact with them was held for approximately an hour, and was lost only at a range at which it would have been surprising if contact had not been lost.

The negative reports of the pilots overhead, and the unexplained disappearance at moderate range of the three (or four) skunks that made up "U," make it very unlikely that these can have been vessels of any sort. They were "Tonkin Spooks," or they were the radar images of the aircraft, being misinterpreted as surface vessels.

Consider now the vessel or vessels that supposedly made the first torpedo run against the destroyers, "V" and/or "V-1." "V" appeared at 2134G, and was held for eight minutes. If it had been a real vessel, why was it not noticed until 2134G? For many minutes before this, the attention of radar observers on the destroyers had been focused on the east. There, they supposedly had clear radar contact with PT-sized vessels at a range of about ten miles. Are we really to suppose that they did not notice a vessel of the same size, on approximately the bearing on which their attention was concentrated, until it was less than five miles away? Radar waves follow an inverse-square law, but radar echoes follow an inverse-fourth-power law. Other things being equal, the radar echo from a target half as far away will be sixteen times as strong.

The discrepancies between the positions recorded for "V" by the *Maddox* and for "V-1" by the *Turner Joy* were great enough that the farthest Captain Herrick was willing to go, even knowing his superiors' desire for evidence of a real attack, was to say that there was "a possibility" that "V" and "V-1" could have represented the same vessel. In fact, if we compare the after-action reports from the two destroyers (see Chapter 6), it is hard to see even a possibility. The incompatibility is too great to be explained by any differences in the calibration of radars, or by any plausible degree of carelessness in recordkeeping; "V" and "V-1" cannot have been a single vessel. In order to believe that "V" was a real PT boat, then, we must believe that this PT boat spent several minutes within four miles of the destroyer *Turner Joy*, without the *Turner Joy*'s radar operators, who were alert and looking for trouble, having detected any sign of it. In order to believe that "V-1" was a real PT boat, we must believe the same thing about the *Maddox*'s radar operators.

The fact that the surface-search radar of the *Maddox* was able to track "V," but the main fire-control radar was not (see Chapter 6), takes on special interest in the light of a comment by Captain James Barber, who later in the war had "extensive personal experience" with the radar ghosts of the Gulf of Tonkin: "a fire control radar is less likely to be fooled by a Tonkin Gulf Ghost than is a search radar."[20]

There are similar problems in regard to all the later contacts. "V-2" was not detected until it was within two miles of the *Turner Joy*. "V-3" was not detected until it was within three miles of the *Turner Joy*. "V-4" was not detected until it was within about three miles of the destroyer, and radar contact was twice lost for significant periods at ranges of two miles or less. "V-5" was not detected until it was within two miles of the *Turner Joy*. It is supposed to have spent all of the thirteen minutes immediately after it was detected within two miles of the *Turner Joy*, but for most of this period it was not held. It also is supposed to have passed about two miles to the north of the *Maddox* during this period; it was not tracked by the *Maddox* while doing so.

If a PT-sized vessel approaches within attack range of a destroyer, it does not seem too much to ask that the radar operators of the destroyer track it continuously for fifteen minutes, or at least have little trouble tracking it—they should achieve something close to continuous tracking—for as long as it is within five miles of their destroyer. Of the six contacts "V," "V-1," "V-2," "V-3," "V-4," and "V-5," none met or even almost met either criterion.

The reports of the destroyers claim that the *Maddox* had been able to track what were believed to be PT-sized vessels continuously for about an hour at ranges of over thirty miles (skunks "N," "O," and "P"), and that both destroyers had been able to track what were believed to be PT-sized vessels continuously for over twenty minutes at a range of about ten miles (skunk "U"). If we take these claims seriously, it is very hard at the same time to take seriously the idea that objects as difficult to track at ranges of one to five miles as "V," "V-1," "V-2," "V-3," "V-4," and "V-5" can actually have been PT boats.

Radar and Gunnery

The tendency of the *Turner Joy*'s radar contacts to disappear shortly after they were acquired has in some cases been explained by the claim that they had been sunk by the destroyer's gunfire.

Thus we have "V-3," acquired by the *Turner Joy* at 2221G. The destroyer opened fire at 2224G, and the contact disappeared from the radar at 2228G. It was believed that this meant the target was a PT boat, and that it had disappeared from the radar because it had been sunk. This interpretation was strengthened by the report (in fact quite dubious; see below) that black smoke was seen at the correct time and approximately the correct location.[21]

"V-4" was acquired by the *Turner Joy* as an intermittent contact about 2228G, and a firm one at 2242G. The destroyer fired at it from 2247G to 2248G, and lost it on radar at 2254G. What was believed to be the same contact was reacquired at 2259G, and the destroyer resumed fire at 2300G. When the contact disappeared at 2303G, this was interpreted as meaning it had been sunk.[22]

Comparison with the events of August 2, however, makes this interpretation very implausible. Real North Vietnamese PT boats, on August 2, showed no tendency to disappear even when subjected to prolonged pounding with five-inch guns.

Admittedly the guns of the *Turner Joy* were more modern than those of the *Maddox* and should have been more accurate, but the difference was not great enough to make it plausible that a genuine PT boat would have sunk almost immediately when the *Turner Joy* fired at it.[23]

The shells fired by the 5″/54 guns of the *Turner Joy* were longer and heavier than those fired by the 5″/38 guns of the *Maddox*, and contained about 24 percent more explosive. Ronald Stalsberg comments, however, that the 5″/54 gun had not had all the bugs worked out of it by 1964; it was not a great gun. Considering all the factors—number of five-inch guns available for use (six on the *Maddox* August 2, two on the *Turner Joy* August 4), rate of fire per gun, weight of shells, and accuracy—he feels that the destructive power of the fire the *Maddox* put out on the afternoon of August 2 was at least as great as the destructive power the *Turner Joy* would have been able to put out on the night of August 4.[24]

The *Turner Joy*'s guns were not operating under anything like optimum conditions; indeed Commander Barnhart later wrote a remarkable report on the handicaps under which his gunners had operated, including undermanning of the loading crews; reliance on Director 52, which had never been used to control fire against surface targets during gunnery drills because it was not as accurate as Director 51 (out of service that night); and "a large number of premature bursts" of VT-frag shells.[25]

It must be borne in mind that the *Turner Joy*'s shells—the ship fired 258— were fuzed for proximity detonation. The three-inch guns fired 28 rounds; all were VT-frag with a nominal detonation distance of fifty feet. The five-inch guns fired 220 rounds. Of these, the 134 fired by Mount 52 were VT-frag with a nominal detonation distance of seventy feet; the 86 fired by Mount 53 were AAC rounds. All the after-action report says is that the AAC rounds loaded before the action were fuzed for proximity detonation at fifty feet.[26] In purely technical terms it would have been possible to change the fuze settings between the time the shells were placed in the ammunition drums and the time they were actually fired, or to use a different fuze setting when loading shells into the drums during the action, to replace those that had been expended. But given the care and thoroughness with which the *Turner Joy*'s after-action report analyzed the performance of ship's ordinance, and suggested lessons to be learned from it (including, specifically, what types of shells were most appropriate for use against small surface craft), it is hard to believe that its authors would have written it in such a fashion as to give the impression that all shells fired were fuzed for proximity detonation, if this had not been the case.

VT rounds had two disadvantages for short-range fire against a target like a

PT boat. One was that the fuzes were very sensitive, so sensitive that it was possible for them to detonate on proximity to a dense cloud. They could work pretty well against surface targets at long range, following a high trajectory. But if they were aimed at a surface target at short range, they had to be fired on relatively flat trajectories, which kept them close enough to the surface of the water that the fuzes sometimes detonated on proximity to the surface, before reaching a point where they might detonate on proximity to the target.

The other disadvantage was that they had been designed for use against aircraft, which are much more fragile targets than torpedo boats. Even when they did not detonate prematurely, the fragments they produced, going off seventy feet from a torpedo boat, were not likely to inflict crippling damage.

When ship's officers reported having observed (on their radar) shells scoring "direct hits" on radar targets, what this meant was that shells had been seen to have headed straight for the target and detonated when they came within the set distance.

Even in the unlikely event that the *Turner Joy* fired some AAC shells fuzed for detonation on impact, the phrase "direct hit," as applied to these shells by observers using radar, would in most cases mean that the shell had detonated on contact with the surface of the water a few feet from the target. The radar was not precise enough to enable anyone to tell whether a shell had actually hit an enemy vessel or only hit the water next to it. If the destroyer had fired shells fuzed for impact detonation, the officers watching the radar would not always have known which of the shells appearing on the screens were fuzed for detonation on proximity to the target and which were fuzed for detonation on impact, but they would have known that a majority were fuzed for detonation on proximity. They would naturally have thought of any shell that showed on the radar as having detonated close enough to a target that it would have detonated by proximity fuze, if it had had such a fuze, as constituting a direct hit. When both tired and excited, they might perhaps have evaluated as a "direct hit" even a round that only came almost as close as would have caused it to detonate by proximity to the target.

The *Maddox*'s gun directors had not been locked onto the three PT boats for as much time as they should have been during the incident on August 2. This held down the total number of shells fired during the period the PT boats were within close range. This problem on the *Maddox*, however, seems modest if we compare it with the problems the *Turner Joy* had on August 4, gaining and keeping lock-on with the radar of Director 52.

The *Turner Joy*'s five-inch guns were loaded and fired by automatic machinery that cranked out shells at a uniform rate of thirty rounds per minute per gun. Mounts 52 and 53, both at the rear of the ship, had essentially the same field of fire and they were normally operated in tandem, firing simultaneously on the same target under the control of the same director, at a combined rate of sixty rounds per minute. At approximately 2230G, malfunctions developed in both mounts. From that point onward there were times when only one gun was able to fire, and times when Mount 52 was firing at a rate of only fifteen rounds per minute. Mount 52 fired a total of 134 shells on the night of August 4, and Mount 53 fired 86.

They did not normally fire continuously for anything close to a whole minute. The problem was that the fire-control radar could lock onto the water thrown into the air by bursting shells. After a few seconds of fire, the gunners would not know whether their director was locked onto its original target, or to the water thrown up by their own shells. Standard procedure was therefore to fire a burst of shells, wait for the water to subside so they could reconfirm lock-on (either verify that the fire-control radar was still locked onto the proper target, or shift it back to the proper target if it had drifted off), and fire another burst. Douglas Smith describes seven shells per gun as representing a burst of "average, minimum" length, but stresses that the actual number could vary widely.[27]

This may provide the explanation for the only reported incident when the *Maddox* ever had clear radar contact, even briefly, with any of the *Turner Joy*'s radar targets. At one point Captain Herrick was called over to a radar screen, on which he could see a radar target and the pips of shells in flight from the *Turner Joy*, going out to the target. The pips for the shells merged with that for the target, and then the target disappeared. The time from when he came to the screen until the disappearance of the target was not more than one minute. Since he presumably would have been called to the screen promptly after anything that seemed to be a PT boat was detected, he believes that the total length of time the target was held on the screen, including the time before he reached the screen, was probably not more than two minutes. When this author suggested to Captain Herrick that the target he had seen on the screen, with shells heading toward it from the *Turner Joy*, might have been water droplets thrown into the air by the detonation of previous shells from the *Turner Joy*, he said this seemed possible.[28] It is impossible to tell which of the *Turner Joy*'s radar contacts this was, since the incident is not mentioned anywhere in the *Maddox*'s records. Presumably the brevity of the contact persuaded the officers who compiled the records that it was obviously spurious.

The track charts in the *Turner Joy* action report show supposed PT boats within relatively close range for a total of about sixty-nine minutes. During those sixty-nine minutes the destroyer fired an average of less than three five-inch shells per minute. (The *Turner Joy* fired 220 five-inch shells on August 4, but fewer than 200 of these were fired during the period when the track charts show valid targets to have been available. The remainder were fired at targets that even the *Turner Joy*'s officers later recognized as having been probably spurious, and therefore did not include on their track charts.) In comparison, the *Maddox*, even with the serious problems described in Chapter 4, fired five-inch AAC and VT-frag at an average rate of about ten rounds per minute during the period targets were available on August 2.

The malfunctions in the loading systems of the guns on the *Turner Joy* cannot begin to explain an apparent rate of fire of less than three rounds per minute. Other relevant factors: (1) The skunks in question were not actually held for sixty-nine minutes; the action report track charts seriously exaggerate the lengths of time "V-4" and "V-5" were tracked; (2) it sometimes took a startlingly long time to attain fire-control radar lock-on and open fire when a contact actually was held by the surface-search radar; and (3) the guns could not go on firing for very long, because the lock-ons did not last.

The *Turner Joy*'s records indicate fifteen occasions when the destroyer opened fire; on ten of these occasions the target appears to have been one of the contacts that show on the track charts attached to the ship's action report. There are two pairs of times that are close enough together that they may represent consecutive bursts in what were essentially single incidents of fire; eliminating these possible duplications leaves thirteen separate incidents of fire (which fits well with the after-action report, mentioned above, which said the destroyer had fired on thirteen contacts). The total of 220 five-inch rounds fired gives an average of seventeen rounds per incident. This would represent two to three bursts of normal length if they all came from a single gun mount; one to two bursts if both Mount 52 and Mount 53 were firing together. The apparent implication is that targets at which the *Turner Joy* was able to fire a burst, reconfirm lock-on, fire another burst, and reconfirm lock-on again, were unusual.

A number of sources have been quoted here with descriptions of firm, uninterrupted radar lock-ons by the *Turner Joy*'s fire-control radar. The ship's total ammunition expenditure indicates that the lock-ons of Director 52, at least—the director that controlled the five-inch guns that night—cannot have been uninterrupted for long periods. Given the normal psychology of a combat situation, brief lock-ons might have felt longer than they were.

The most spectacular cases of failure to fire that one finds in the *Turner Joy* action report are skunks "V-2" and "V-5." "V-2" is supposed to have come in to a range of 2,000 yards, and then wandered out to a comparatively long range before the destroyer managed to fire a shot. "V-5" is supposed to have spent the entire period from 2312G to 2321G within 4,000 yards of the *Turner Joy* without having been fired upon during that period.

The *Turner Joy* seems to have fired on ten or more different targets ("V-1," "V-2," "V-3," "V-4," "V-5," and at least five others never given formal designations). Dividing total ammunition expenditure by ten gives an average of twenty-two five-inch and three three-inch shells per target. (If we were to accept the after-action report stating that thirteen targets were fired upon, this would give still lower averages.) All targets vanished from the radar screens under this not very impressive amount of fire, usually within five minutes of the first shells aimed in their direction, and usually at ranges of less than 5,000 yards. In the end the *Turner Joy* only claimed two sinkings, skunks "V-3" and "V-4," but it is hard to see why this claim was so modest. Skunks "V-1" and "V-5" had also disappeared from the radar at such close range that it would be hard to find any other explanation besides sinking, if one assumes that they were PT boats in the first place; two men with whom the author has spoken clearly believed that the *Turner Joy* had sunk skunk "V-1." Possibly the officers who decided on the final claim had somehow heard about the communication intercept that had been interpreted to mean that two PT boats had been sunk, and they were trying to fit their claim to this intercept.

The *Maddox*, attacked by three PT boats on August 2, had fired an average of forty-seven five-inch and forty-four three-inch shells per PT boat, not counting star shells. The *Maddox* had scored several "direct hits," and there is evidence of at least one actual impact detonation, probably by a five-inch AAC round from the *Maddox*, possibly by one of the Zuni rockets, larger than a five-inch shell, fired by the aircraft. At the time the *Maddox* ceased fire, none of the PT boats had sunk, or was visibly sinking, or had even gone dead in the water. After four jet aircraft had worked the three PTs over with 20-mm gunfire, one was left dead in the water; but the best evidence indicates it did not sink, and even the more optimistic American sources do not claim that it sank quickly.

If the *Turner Joy* had scored direct-impact hits with AAC shells on August 4 (as probably did happen on August 2), it would remain unlikely that genuine PT boats would have disappeared within four minutes ("V-3") or three minutes ("V-4"). We can be virtually certain that the *Turner Joy* scored no direct-impact hits.

It should also be noted that interrogation of DRV torpedo boat personnel captured later in the war indicated that no DRV torpedo boats were sunk in any incident in 1964 (see Chapter 8). All North Vietnamese torpedo boats belonged to a single squadron and had a single home base at Van Hoa; the sinking of boats from this squadron could hardly have been kept from the rest of the squadron. If any of the *Turner Joy*'s radar skunks *were* North Vietnamese PT boats, then, they were not sunk.

The radar contacts tended to appear and disappear at frequent intervals; in only a few cases did this occur soon enough after the destroyer had fired at the contact for the conclusion to be reached that the contact had disappeared as a result of having been sunk by the gunfire. A good case could be made that there was no connection between the gunfire and the disappearances; that with the targets appearing and disappearing intermittently, and the ship firing intermittently, the relationship between firing and disappearances was purely chance.

We should ask, however, whether there was anything that could have generated a radar image and that (unlike a PT boat) really *would* have been likely to disappear quickly after being fired upon. A flock of birds would be very likely to vanish from a radar screen following detonation of five-inch shells in their midst. This author doubts that flocks often fly over the middle of the gulf at night, but seagulls resting on the surface of the water could have been startled into flight by the excitement.

Commander George Edmondson is of the opinion that both "V-3" and "V-4" were the radar images of his and/or his wingman's aircraft, distorted by weather conditions to the point that they were being interpreted as surface objects.[29]

It must be borne in mind that the U.S. Navy, up to 1964, had not had much experience of operations in the Gulf of Tonkin, and scarcely anyone[30] on the two destroyers had been exposed to the remarkable realism of the spurious radar images sometimes encountered there. Within weeks after the incident, Richard Corsette repeatedly had the experience of acquiring clear and convincing images on his radar, in the daytime at ranges close enough so he could simply look and see that there was nothing whatever in the location where his radar showed a vessel. This altered his attitude toward even the skunks that had appeared on his radar at the very beginning of the August 4 incident, which (unlike those a little later) had seemed clear and real at the time.[31] Corsette was not the only man on the destroyers to have such an experience after August 4, but there is no indication that anyone had had it before August 4.

Detection of North Vietnamese Radar

The idea that torpedo boats could have attempted to aim torpedoes without radar assistance at relatively maneuverable targets such as destroyers, on a dark night with poor visibility, strains credibility. The after-action reports are clear, however: "there were strong indications that the boats did not have radar. . . . USS TURNER JOY verified on ECM equipment (BLR) that contacts had no radar in operation by complete absence of normal CHICOMM or DRV seaborne radars." "The boats were not using radar."[32]

It has been argued that surprise is a major factor in warfare, and that the North Vietnamese would surely have had sense enough to want to achieve surprise in an attack against the destroyers.[33] This would have meant maintaining electronic silence when possible, and when forced to use either radar or radio, using them in short bursts, to make detection by the destroyers difficult.

There are two things wrong with this argument. One is that a desire to preserve secrecy does not automatically confer an ability to preserve secrecy. Regardless of what anyone would have preferred, an attack by a widely scattered group of vessels, far out to sea on a dark night in poor weather, would have required a great deal of use of radio and radar.

The other problem is that a desire for surprise only explains why attacking vessels would have restricted radio and radar use up to 2139G, the moment when the *Turner Joy* opened fire. If "V-1" and the others were real PT boats, some explanation other than a desire to catch the destroyers by surprise must be found for their willingness to maintain for two additional hours a degree of electronic silence that would have crippled their efforts to sink the destroyers, and made it difficult for them to obtain rescue when damaged or sinking, when the five-inch shells falling on them would have made it impossible for even the most blindly optimistic to suppose that the Americans were not aware of their location and intentions.

"Passive" radar use, sometimes called ECM, could have helped hypothetical PT boats to some extent if they carried the radar themselves, and were not depending on radar guidance from Swatows. A radar set can spot the signals of another set, without sending out any signals of its own and thus without being detectable. Passive radar, however, can only indicate the bearing of an enemy vessel, not its range. From a series of bearings taken at different times, one can sometimes deduce the range to an enemy vessel, and its course and speed, but the enemy vessel must be holding a constant course and speed, and one must not, oneself, be shadowing the enemy vessel by moving on the same course and at the same speed. If one did happen to be paralleling an enemy vessel, on the same course at the same speed, passive radar would not even enable one to know for sure that one was doing so. Nor could it provide an adequate basis for aiming torpedoes on a dark night in poor weather.

As was stated in a previous chapter, the U.S. Navy was under the mistaken impression that North Vietnamese PT boats lacked radar. If this impression had been correct, then an attack on the American destroyers would have been so difficult as to strain credibility. Given the fact that the PT boats did have radar, it strains credibility even further to suggest that in a battle conducted in bad weather and total darkness, they would have made little or no use of it.

After describing the movements of skunks "N," "O," and "P," Marolda and Fitzgerald state in a footnote: "Another contact, possibly equipped with radar, was detected as close as twenty miles to the east and paralleling the American ships' passage south but made no attempt to close with them. This was perhaps the Swatow motor gunboat that Captain Herrick and Commander Barnhart believed used its radar to vector the P-4s toward the destroyers."[34]

This statement quite simply is not true. The sources cited for it, reports by Captain Herrick and Commander Barnhart, had indeed acknowledged the obvious fact that the North Vietnamese navy could not have located the two destroyers, in order to attack them, without using radar: "some radar or ECM assistance must have been involved in vectoring the PT boats into the proper position."[35] Neither these reports nor any others, however, mention signs of such a radar-equipped vessel actually having been *detected* on the night of August 4. Neither these reports nor any others, furthermore, mention the detection of *any* vessel, with or without radar, behaving in the fashion described above by Marolda and Fitzgerald. Both Herrick and Barnhart understood the importance of this issue. If on the night of August 4 they had detected a shadowing vessel that they suspected of having possessed radar, it hardly seems likely that they would have neglected to mention it in their reports.

It should be noted that the hypothesis in the quote that PT boats could have been vectored to the destroyers (given directions by radio, telling them in which direction to steer) by a vessel that was using ECM (passive radar) is not tenable. For a vessel using active radar to have vectored PT boats toward the destroyers would have been a clumsy and difficult procedure. For a vessel using ECM (passive radar) to have vectored the PT boats to the destroyers would have been completely impossible.

When questioned about this, Edward Marolda explained that the source for the statement about a vessel having been detected was a letter by A. C. Lassiter, Jr., Commander Ogier's successor as commander of the *Maddox*, modifying the DeSoto patrol report. Unfortunately for Marolda's case, what the letter described was not a vessel detected on the night of August 4, but the radar-equipped vessel, probably Chinese, that shadowed the destroyers on the night of August 3 (see Chapter 5). The letter was very clear on this; it gave the date August 3 not once but twice, and also gave numerous other details (e.g., latitude and longitude of the destroyers at the time the vessel was detected) that fit the records for August 3 but not those for August 4.[36]

The Torpedo Reports and the Sonar Evidence

It was obvious, as soon as Captain Herrick and others had time to think, that the comparatively inexperienced sonarman David Mallow, who had been operating the *Maddox*'s sonar on the night of August 4, and who was not accustomed to trying to interpret underwater noises while the ship was at high speed, had repeatedly reported noise spokes that actually represented the sounds of his own destroyer.

There was a peculiarity in one of the rudder motors of the *Maddox* that made a noise, which would be picked up on sonar, whenever the ship made a turn either to port or starboard. Patrick Park says that Mallow had not been familiarized with this problem. Park was much more experienced with sonar, and although he had been transferred to the main gun director after the August 2 incident, he realized on the basis of what he was hearing on August 4 that Mallow was picking up the sounds of the rudder motor. Park tried to report this but was unable to get the message through.

The *Maddox*'s sonar had a tape recorder, which had recorded all sounds picked up during the action. As soon as the ship secured from General Quarters, Commander Ogier told Park to evaluate the tape recordings.[37] He was interviewed about this in 1970 or 1971:

Q: Tell me, do you think that night, August 4, in that pitch black, in that heavy swell, rain storms—was there anything to shoot at?

A: No, I don't. I am certain that there was not anything to shoot at, right from the beginning.

The Captain asked me immediately after the attack to go down and evaluate all the recordings that had been made of noise that was—that sonar was reporting, and I kept myself pretty busy for the next three days, really, trying to evaluate these things and determine if we had heard anything that might have been, even a question mark that it might have been a torpedo or anything else in the water, not related to the two ships or noise of either one of them.

Q: Then what was your evaluation?

A: Absolutely nothing.[38]

Park's initial finding, which he reported on the morning of August 5, was that the only noise spikes on the tape recordings were from the rudder motor. Ogier was upset. He ordered Park to evaluate the tape again, checking the noise spikes on the tape against the ship's turns as recorded in the quartermaster log. Park did this; *all* noise spikes on the tape corresponded to turns of the ship as recorded in the quartermaster log. Mallow, however, had reported more noise spikes than could be accounted for by turns of the ship; "A court steno couldn't have kept up with Mallow's reports." As explained in Chapter 6, Mallow's very first report came when the ship was on a straight course. Park suggests (this is something he believes now, not necessarily something he reported in 1964) that this arose when Mallow, who because of what he had heard from the bridge was "no doubt already looking for a spoke . . . found the 'port after quarter' noise spoke characteristic to our ship."[39]

Park's memory of the number of Mallow's reports was not exaggerated. In the Naval Historical Center in Washington there is a chart labeled *Maddox* track #23, showing the *Maddox*'s path with lines radiating out from it to indicate the bearings on which Mallow had heard noise spokes at particular times. It is undated, but it appears to be the original chart on which Mallow's bearings were recorded as Mallow reported them, during the action. It shows 178 noise spokes, recorded between 2143G and 2324G. There were intervals when none were recorded; the longest such interval was seventeen minutes, from 2205G to 2222G. During the times when Mallow *was* hearing these sounds, which add up to almost two-thirds of the period from 2143G to 2324G, he was reporting an average of two to three bearings per minute. It is hard to tell how anyone could have looked at these 178 bearings and decided that they represented twenty-six torpedoes, or any particular number of torpedoes.

If we are to decide whether Mallow's reports represented sounds generated by his own ship, the orientation of the sounds in relation to the destroyer is crucial.

Of the 178 recorded bearings, 43 were recorded at times (2146G to 2153G and 2243G to 2249G) for which the line representing the destroyer's path and the lines representing torpedo bearings overlay one another in such a confusing fashion that this author has been unable to discern even approximately the course of the destroyer at the time the bearing was recorded. The analysis that follows is based on the 135 bearings for which it is possible to discern at least approximately the relationship between the orientation of the destroyer and the direction from which the sounds seemed to come.

This analysis strongly confirms that Mallow was hearing a port-after-quarter noise spoke generated by his own ship. At least two-thirds of his reports were for noises at relative bearings of 225° to 270°. For the first seventy-six minutes that he was hearing presumed torpedo noises, in fact, *all* of his 104 bearings were to port, and 88 percent were on relative bearings between 225° and 270°; he did not report any noise spokes at all to starboard until 2259G. Figure 11 shows the distribution of relative bearings up to 2259G. This clearly represents noises generated by the destroyer being mistaken for torpedo noises. The way the destroyer was twisting and dodging would have turned one side and then the other of the destroyer toward any real torpedo boats that might have been present, and any torpedoes they fired would have been distributed among a great variety of different bearings. Given the suggestions that have sometimes been made that the very first sonar report was valid, and that only the later ones were based on the destroyer's own sounds, it is crucial to note that the very first report was on almost precisely the average bearing of the spurious ones detected during the next seventy-five minutes.

When Mallow was asked about Patrick Park's analysis of the sonar tapes, he said that Park was not qualified to do such an analysis. The analysis that Mallow takes seriously was not done on the ship; the tapes were sent away for it. Mallow says that he did not get to see the results of this analysis, but that he heard from Ensign John Leeman, the ASW officer on the *Maddox*, that the tapes had indicated numerous torpedoes.[40]

One has only to look at the after-action reports, and the embarrassment they show about the lack of good sonar evidence, to realize that this cannot be correct. The failure of the *Maddox*'s sonar tapes to reveal any torpedo noises made them such an embarrassment that their very existence is barely acknowledged in Navy records. When the author requested from the navy, under the Freedom of Information Act, all reports of the analysis of these tapes, the navy's response was that no such reports could be located. The only known document that even mentions the tapes is a message stating that they were being forwarded up the chain of command, and expressing hope that analysis of them would provide proof that a torpedo attack had occurred. This message did not mention the analysis that had already been performed, with negative results, aboard the *Maddox*.[41]

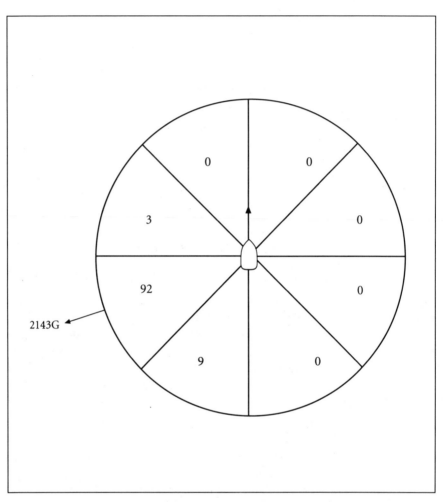

Figure 11. Bearings of sonar reports, relative to orientation of the *Maddox*, 2143G to 2259G. The number of sonar reports in different sectors has been noted inside the circle. The relative bearing for the very first sonar report, at 2143G, has been added as an arrow outside the circle. Source: *Maddox* track #23 (NHC).

Most of Mallow's sonar reports are no longer taken seriously. A large number of torpedoes necessarily implied a large number of PT boats at very close range to fire them, and no PT boats had shown on the *Maddox*'s radar screens after 2142G. It is claimed, however, that those at the very beginning of the action, around the time skunk "V" was disappearing from the *Maddox*'s radar screens and "V-1" from the *Turner Joy*'s, were valid.

During the night of 4 August 1964 *Maddox* evaded at least 26 suspected contacts evaluated as torpedoes on the AN/SQS 32A sonar system. Of these, only the first three were considered valid (time 214[2?]–2144). The sonar system was being operated in the passive mode at speeds in excess of 30 knots. The internal noise, aircraft flying low near the ship, possible patrol boat noise, and highspeed propeller noise reflected from the rudders accounts for the great number of false torpedo contacts generated. . . .

It is probable that at least three torpedoes were launched between 2142 and 2144 since it was heard on the *Maddox*'s sonar at a time when self noise should not have been generated.[42]

(The statement that "self noise should not have been generated" during this period, with the aging destroyer pounding through the waves at thirty knots, is odd to say the least.)

Mallow made numerous sonar reports at the beginning of the action—at least eight reports over a period of about three minutes. Most accounts mention only a single sonar report in this period, but different accounts select different ones of Mallow's eight. This has confused matters considerably, but the various bearings shown on *Maddox* track #23 make the sequence clear. Mallow first reported noises on a bearing of 051°, next on a bearing of 037.5°, and then on various other bearings gradually shifting to about 160°. This is a fairly wide diversity of bearings. If one considers the bearings relative to the destroyer, however, the diversity is much less; seven of the eight reports were on the port after quarter. As the destroyer turned to starboard, the noises also shifted to starboard, staying on approximately the same bearing relative to the ship.

If Mallow's first eight sonar reports were all genuine torpedo noises, they would not of course have represented eight torpedoes; in some cases several reports would have represented the bearings of the same torpedo at different times. It is impossible, however, to reconcile all of these reports as a series of bearings for a single torpedo, and it would be difficult to fit all the reports even to two torpedoes. The report quoted above evaluating Mallow's reports during these minutes as having indicated "at least three torpedoes" seems reasonable, if one assumes that what Mallow was hearing was actually the sound of torpedoes at all.

A number of people have used Mallow's initial sonar report—they all mention only a single report—as a crucial piece of evidence that there really was a PT boat attack, because just after Mallow began to report noise spokes, and the two destroyers turned to evade, a torpedo is said to have been seen just missing *Turner Joy*. The early reports list three witnesses: Ltjg. John J. Barry and Seaman Larry O. Litton, both in Director 51, and Seaman Edwin R. Sentel, the port side lookout.[43] Later reports added Seaman Rodger N. Bergland, in Director 52 (the director actually controlling five-inch gunfire that night, with a good view aft and to the sides), to the list of witnesses. The torpedo is supposed to have passed up the port side of the ship, aft to forward, at a distance that was estimated differently by different witnesses. One hundred yards is the estimate usually accepted. The times given for the sighting vary from 2143G to 2145G.

The following three passages, from the *Turner Joy*'s "Proof of Attack" message August 6, from the *Turner Joy* action report, and from the chronology incorporated in all major reports written aboard the *Maddox*, describe how the sonar report and the visual sighting fit together. The suggestion that the torpedo heard by the *Maddox* was the same as that seen by the *Turner Joy*, a suggestion that adds to the apparent credibility of both reports, is especially clear in the first and second passages.

> Most convincing proof was sighting of torpedo wake by [John Barry, Larry Litton, and Edwin Sentel] for fol[lowing] reasons:
> A. Torpedo was reported by *Maddox* coming from initial contacts which ambushed task group.
> B. *Turner Joy* maneuvered to avoid completed torpedo was sighted passing abeam to port abt 300 feet aft to fwd on exactly the course (bearing) reported by *Maddox*.[44]

> At time 2143 *Maddox* reported a torpedo in the water bearing 047T from her. After plotting the torpedo bearing, *Turner Joy* altered course to starboard and successfully evaded the torpedo. The standard torpedo evasion doctrine is to turn away from a torpedo fired abaft the beam and steady on a course 30° short of the reciprocal of the original torpedo bearing. The torpedo wake was sighted by four personnel on the port side about 300 feet from the ship, travelling from aft to forward.[45]

> *Maddox* lost contact on "V," bearing 090, 9000 yards and opening, after an apparent quick turn of "V" to the left. At the same time that this maneuver was noticed, *Maddox* sonar reported hydrophone effects bearing 051, which was classified torpedo. . . .
> *Maddox* changed course to the right with full rudder to avoid the torpedo, transmitting a warning to *Turner Joy*. . . . At about 2144 *Turner Joy* received the *Maddox* report of a torpedo in the water bearing 040. This bearing was plotted on *Turner Joy* DRT and a right course change was immediately recommended by CIC to the bridge to avoid the torpedo in accordance with standard torpedo evasion doctrine which is: If the torpedo is fired from abaft beam then ship turns away and stops 30° beyond the reciprocal of the torpedo bearing. *Turner Joy* came right and just after steadying on course 210°, a torpedo wake passed up the port side aft to forward, at a distance of about 300 feet.[46]

If we consider these statements in the light of the track charts showing the movements of the two destroyers and their radar targets, a problem emerges. The *Turner Joy* action report (second passage quoted above) assumes that the torpedo reported by the *Maddox* was the same as that seen by the *Turner Joy*; the track chart accompanying the report shows the torpedo as having been fired by skunk "V-1." But the track for the torpedo shown on the chart indicates that this could not have been the same torpedo. It is in fact impossible to construct any track for a torpedo fired by skunk "V-1" that passes up the side of the *Turner Joy* after having been detected by the *Maddox* on a bearing of 040°, 047°, or 051°. Such a track can be constructed for a torpedo fired by skunk "V" (the contact never tracked by the *Turner Joy*'s radar), but only by assuming that the torpedo was heard at very long range, and that it was running at significantly less than its forty-two-knot designed speed.

Of the four reported witnesses, John Barry is the only one this author has been able to locate for an interview. Barry and some other junior officers rotated through certain positions on the destroyer during 1964. Although Barry was anti-submarine warfare (ASW) officer by August, he had been gunnery officer not long before, and he was still the best qualified director officer on the ship. In a situation where the potential enemies were surface vessels rather than submarines, Commander Barnhart had decided that Barry's General Quarters station should be in the main gun director rather than in sonar.

One of Barry's duties was to be ready to control the guns visually, if the radar were not working. He stood, therefore, with his head sticking up out of the director, with an excellent view ahead and to both sides of the ship. Larry Litton, inside the director, could also see out to some extent, but not as well as Barry.

There was no radar screen in the director, no display capable of showing multiple targets. All the fire-control radar could do at any given time was to lock onto one target designated for it by the Target Designation System in CIC, and keep track of the range and bearing of that target for as long as lock-on was held. There were dials indicating the range and bearing of the target onto which the radar was locked. A computer controlled the aim of the fire-control radar, keeping it locked on without active intervention by the men in the director.

When the approaching skunk "V-1" was getting close to the *Turner Joy*, a report came from the *Maddox* of a torpedo in the water. Both destroyers turned to starboard to evade. This was the only report of detection of a torpedo by the *Maddox*'s sonar that reached Barry during the action.[47]

While the *Turner Joy* was in the middle of the turn, Barry saw a thin white line in the water off the port side of the ship. In a statement recorded three days later he estimated the distance from the ship at 500 feet.[48] A journalist who interviewed him about three years later quoted him as having said: "I looked down off our port side and I saw like a white streak, just coming right through the water, right at us, and fortunately we had started to turn. I grabbed the man next to me [Litton] to show it to him."[49] When interviewed recently he estimated the range at 100 yards but said that after so long he could not be sure, and indeed he doubted that even at the time he could have made a precise estimate of the distance to a phosphorescent white line in the total darkness of the night. When he looked forward, he saw that the line had a front end, and that the front end was advancing—it was lengthening as he watched. He believed, and believes today, that the white line was the wake of a torpedo, and that it would have hit the *Turner Joy* if the destroyer had not been turning. He believes that it was the same torpedo seen by Litton and Sentel. He adds, however, "I have never been confident that the torpedo was what the *Maddox* reported."

Barry's recollection is that he did not report this during the action, "because it was over before I could have," and he did not want to clog the phone circuits with unnecessary reports.

The target that the fire-control radar had been tracking had been taken under fire by the aft guns. Barry saw the detonation of the shells, and what looked to him like secondary explosions. This must have been before he saw the white line in the water; the track charts make it clear that the location on which the guns were firing would have been blocked from his view as soon as the destroyer began to turn.

Barry does not now recall anything about Larry Litton's sighting of the white line, or anything either of them may have said to the other. He doubts they would have discussed it; their focus was on the next task: "What's over is over." There was another radar target to worry about soon after the loss of lock-on to "V-1."[50] Although Barry has no recollection of another radar target having been acquired already at the time he saw the white line, it is likely that this had in fact occurred; his director "was at that time trained about five degrees off the port bow,"[51] and this corresponds too precisely with the bearing on which the joint track chart shows the next target after "V-1" for coincidence to seem likely. If the director's radar had not yet locked onto the new contact, it must at least have been searching for it, following detection of the new contact by the surface-search radar.

Seaman Sentel, the portside lookout, reported the torpedo wake to the bridge; he was probably the only one to do so at the time. According to the joint chronology the originally planned evasive maneuver—changing course from 160° to 210°—had already been completed when Sentel saw the torpedo; as a result of his report, *Turner Joy* then turned further to the right.[52]

Ensign Douglas Smith, in CIC, says he remembers hearing Barry describing the torpedo over a telephone circuit linking people involved with gunnery; this circuit did not go to the bridge. The description was frightening; Smith remembers Barry saying, in a steadily rising voice, "I see a torpedo wake in the water, and it's coming right at us. . . . Here it comes, it's coming right at us, here it comes, here it comes. . . . There it goes." The total time elapsed was on the order of fifteen to thirty seconds.[53] Barry, who does not believe he said this, suggests a possible explanation. He remembers that another officer was on the telephone circuit at the time, saying in a very excited fashion, "There's a PT boat out there!" Barry had to ask that officer to stop tying up the phone circuit this way. He feels that he and the other officer could have mixed together in Smith's memory.

Of all the personnel on either destroyer on the night of August 4, the one best qualified to evaluate the sonar evidence was Chief Sonarman Joseph Schaperjahn, on the *Turner Joy*. He was the only chief sonarman on either destroyer; he had been operating sonar on destroyers since the Second World War.

While the two destroyers were cruising uneventfully along the North Vietnamese coast August 3 and 4, Schaperjahn was not particularly tense or excited. The cruise seemed "routine" to him. When word came on the evening of August 4 that hostile contacts had appeared on the radar and that a torpedo attack was actually expected, however, he got psyched up.

During this part of the evening, his concern was listening for torpedoes. He had a small radar repeater screen, but he was not paying much attention to the radar contacts. They were not within torpedo range, and thus not his business. His concern was what was happening in the immediate area of the ship. He had the impression that a torpedo might come at any minute; he had to be ready to detect it in time to give a useful warning. He heard nothing.

Schaperjahn does not believe that what Barry and the others saw can really have been a torpedo; he feels the V-shaped bow wave, made conspicuous by the luminescence in the water, is a likelier explanation. He spoke to Barry not long after the incident. Despite Schaperjahn's skepticism, Barry stuck firmly to his claim that he had seen a torpedo.[54]

It has sometimes been said that the failure of the *Turner Joy*'s sonar to detect this torpedo is not surprising, given the failure to detect torpedoes in practice exercises in the past. Schaperjahn comments "That's a lot of baloney." The beat of a torpedo's screws shows up clearly on sonar. The witnesses reported this one passing close by the ship, aft to forward. Since the torpedo would not have been much faster than the ship, it would have been close beside the ship for a significant time before it finally pulled ahead. Even with the destroyer at high speed, a sonar apparatus in proper working order could not have failed to detect such a torpedo. Schaperjahn is sure his apparatus was in working order, because after the incident the Navy had it checked by experts, who rated it "4-0" (working perfectly). If what Barry and the others saw had been a torpedo, there is "no way" the sonar could have failed to pick it up.[55]

Douglas Smith commented later that a torpedo passing up the side of the ship 100 yards away "should have been very clearly audible" even when the destroyer was at thirty knots. A torpedo is very loud, "like a locomotive right outside your living room," and the *Turner Joy* had about the best sonar then available in the U.S. Navy.[56]

Suggestions that the *Turner Joy*'s sonar lacked sensitivity seem to have appeared only in reports written aboard the *Maddox*. These state that the failure of the *Turner Joy*'s sonar to detect torpedo noises "is a general characteristic of this type sonar and, in fact, *Joy*'s sonar has in the past failed to detect torpedo noises when, during exercises, torpedoes were known to have passed close aboard."[57]

In fact the *Turner Joy*'s sonar was substantially *superior* to that of the *Maddox*, not inferior. It is not clear how the notion that the *Turner Joy* had inferior sonar crept into the reports written on the *Maddox*, when the senior sonarmen on both ships knew better.

No such notion can be found in the *Turner Joy* action report,[58] which mentions only a single incident when the sonar had failed to detect a torpedo in a practice exercise, and does not say that the torpedo in this incident had come close to the destroyer. In general, according to this report, "equipment performance was not a factor" in the failure of the *Turner Joy*'s sonar to detect torpedo noises. There were three explanations that the report *did* consider credible for the failure of the sonar to detect the torpedo that Barry and the others had reported:

1. The report argues that the *Turner Joy* was following only 1,000 yards behind the *Maddox*, so the turbulence of the *Maddox*'s wake would have masked sounds. John Barry also says that it is not surprising the *Turner Joy*'s sonar failed to pick up this torpedo. He believes, and other knowledgeable people whom he has consulted agree, that the *Maddox*'s wake, together with the *Turner Joy*'s speed, could have masked the sounds of a torpedo.[59]

   Barry is sure that the *Turner Joy* was still within the *Maddox*'s wake when he saw the white line. The most reliable record now available of the relative movements of the two ships, the joint track chart, at least makes it very plausible that the *Turner Joy* could have been within the *Maddox*'s wake. If we accept this as fact, however, the question should be asked which is more probable: that fifty-five seconds after the *Maddox* passed the point at which the torpedo is supposed to have been seen, the water there was still so turbulent that the rather loud noise of a torpedo propeller could not be heard 100 yards from a destroyer moving at high speed—could not be heard even intermittently—or that fifty-five seconds after the *Maddox* passed, the turbulence of the wake was generating white lines on the surface, one of which was mistaken for the track of a torpedo. To this author, the latter seems more likely.

2. The report argues that there was a zone to the rear of the ship where the *Turner Joy*'s own noise would have masked the sounds of a torpedo, and the

torpedo "probably was in the blind zone." This is absolute nonsense; while different versions of the torpedo sighting contradict one another in several ways, all of them, including the one in this very report, agree that it passed up the side of the destroyer. This means that it was well outside the "blind zone."

3. The report argues that sonar "operators are not familiar with high speed noises. Normal ASW speeds are between 18 and 22 knots, and operators have not become sufficiently acquainted with noise responses at speeds in excess of 27 knots to distinguish otherwise detectable echoes and noise spokes."[60] This argument would have more credibility if the man operating the sonar on the night of August 4 had had less than twenty years of experience.

If what appeared alongside the *Turner Joy* was in fact a torpedo, comparison of its course with the movements of the two destroyers shows that this torpedo could not possibly have been as close to the *Maddox* as 1,000 yards, at the time Mallow heard noises that are supposed to have been generated by this torpedo. Probably it would have been over 1,500 yards from the *Maddox*.

If what appeared alongside the *Turner Joy* was in fact a torpedo, then Joseph Schaperjahn, a very experienced sonarman with good equipment, was unable to hear it at a range of 100 yards even when it was not behind the ship. We can hardly be asked both to believe this and to believe that Mallow, a much less experienced sonarman using inferior equipment, was able to overcome the handicap of thirty-knot speed so well that he could hear and identify this torpedo at a range of well over 1,000 yards. Sound operates under an inverse-square law; the noise of a torpedo at 100 yards would be *one hundred times as loud* as that of a torpedo at 1,000 yards. The way these facts have been ignored or distorted in many accounts of the event, in order to give superficial plausibility to Mallow's report, constitutes one of the most important examples of the "smoothing" of the records.

If we wish to believe both in Mallow's report and in the torpedo wake passing the *Turner Joy*, we must suppose that there were two entirely different torpedoes, one that passed close enough to the *Maddox* for Mallow to be able to hear it, and one that passed close to the *Turner Joy*. These could not even have been fired simultaneously by a single PT boat; they would have had to be fired independently, either by two different PT boats or by one boat that fired two torpedoes at different times and from different locations. (Note that for a PT boat to fire both of its torpedoes simultaneously, by a single push on its firing lever, was standard procedure, as well as the only sensible thing for the boat's commander to do in the circumstances existing that night.) We must then suppose that the *Turner Joy*, getting by radio a report of detection by Mallow of a torpedo that was not in fact any threat, took evasive action that just happened to save the ship from being hit by an unrelated torpedo. John Barry says that he believes this is what actually happened.

Considering the night of August 4 overall, Schaperjahn states that if there had actually been PT boats attacking the destroyer, there is "no way in the world" that his gear could have failed to pick up the sounds of torpedoes, and the screw beats of the attacking PT boats themselves, especially the number that were reported. He would have been able to detect the screws of PT boats out to a range of 4,000 or 5,000 yards. He never even turned on the sonar recorder; there was nothing worth recording.

Repeatedly during the incident—perhaps half a dozen times—Schaperjahn picked up the beat of the *Maddox*'s propellers on his sonar. The first couple of times this happened he reported it immediately as a sonar contact, giving the bearing; only after reporting it did he figure out, with help from CIC, that it was actually the *Maddox*. After that he started keeping better track of the *Maddox*'s location, so when he picked up its sound again, he could either specify that it was the *Maddox* when reporting it, or simply not bother to report it.

Some of the claims Schaperjahn has made for the capabilities of his sonar seem extreme. Patrick Park has expressed doubt that Schaperjahn would really have been able to pick up the screws of PT boats out to a range of 5,000 yards when his destroyer was going thirty knots.[61] Schaperjahn's belief that he would have been able to hear a torpedo at 100 yards, however, seems solidly founded.

Schaperjahn was hesitant to decide that the failure of his sonar to detect torpedoes or PT boats proved that none were present, because they could not have been detected if directly behind the destroyer. The turbulence of the destroyer's wake would have shielded them from sonar detection. And in fact, according to Schaperjahn, several of the radar contacts that were believed to be hostile PT boats stayed (unlike the supposed torpedo wake) directly behind the destroyer as it weaved through the darkness. The precision with which these contacts held station behind the destroyer, however, was too good. Even if there had been a rational reason for a PT to want to stay exactly behind a destroyer—which there was not—a PT would not have had the ability to do so with such precision: "Even with radar they couldn't anticipate our turns, and to my knowledge they had no radar." Schaperjahn believes that a contact holding station so exactly behind the destroyer, through drastic changes of course, had to be the "knuckle" generated on the surface of the water by the destroyer's own screws: "Fire control radar was famous for picking up knuckles astern."[62] Schaperjahn's statements about targets following precisely in the wake of the *Turner Joy* cannot be substantiated from the track charts, but some other sources also state that radar contacts seemed to trail in the destroyer's wake.[63]

As time went on, he stopped believing that his ship was actually under attack: "Finally I called the bridge and said 'Bridge, there's nothing out there.'" The ship continued to dodge and fire at supposed attackers. Schaperjahn continued to report to the bridge that there were no attackers. Finally he was told by the bridge that they didn't want negative reports, only positive reports. So he stopped sending reports to the bridge. He does not know to whom he was speaking on the bridge, except that it was definitely not Barnhart. He does not know who told him to stop sending negative reports. He does not know whether Barnhart even knew of his negative reports; whoever on the bridge received those reports might not have passed them on. The only record of Schaperjahn's reports is in the *Turner Joy*'s quartermaster log at 2156G: "sonar reports no contacts in water." (Schaperjahn made it clear in the interview that he regarded Barnhart as a good commanding officer, and was not criticizing Barnhart's conduct during the incident. Barnhart acted to protect his ship and crew, on the basis of the information he received. Schaperjahn was disturbed, and still is, about the way the evaluation of the incident was handled afterward.)

At the time the shooting began, Schaperjahn had been psyched up for combat, as noted above. By the later portions of the supposed incident, however, he had relaxed completely, and indeed he was laughing at the situation.

After the action, Lt. Commander Robert B. Hoffman, the executive officer of the *Turner Joy*, started gathering information. John Barry comments that Hoffman had the wisdom to start taking statements from people very quickly, before they could have their memories altered by conversations with one another. Schaperjahn, however, comments that Hoffman said he wanted to hear from anyone who had seen anything indicating the presence of PT boats. He did not send for Schaperjahn. Schaperjahn states, "I went to him, and wanted to put my two cents in, and he refused it." Hoffman said he did not want negative reports. "If anyone should have been at this briefing or info gathering session, it should have been the senior sonarman. After all, it's said we were under torpedo attack, and this is sonar business. I feel I could have changed the minds of several V.I.P.s if allowed to attend."[64]

It became apparent, as soon as people had time to think, that many of Mallow's sonar reports had to have represented something other than torpedoes. Captain Herrick took the very first of these reports much more seriously than the others, however, both because he believed that the *Maddox* had not yet begun the high-speed maneuvers that later caused so many spurious reports, and because of the supposed correlation with the report that a torpedo had been seen by four men on the *Turner Joy*. Herrick felt that visibility was good enough that a report of a sighting of a torpedo wake at 300 feet had to be taken seriously.[65] Twenty years later, however, Herrick learned that his notes and the ship's log showed that the destroyer had been traveling at thirty knots; this seriously undermined his faith in the sonar report.[66]

It is clear from the statements given three days later by the men on the *Turner Joy* that when they looked out into the darkness they were at least half expecting to see a torpedo wake on the port side of the ship:

John Barry: "I held no [radar] contacts at time when bridge reported torpedo in the water port side. . . . I immediately started looking for torpedo wake so as to pass possible helpful information to the bridge."

Larry Litton: "We were alerted of a torpedo attack on the ship. As we were warned I came up out of the hatch to observe anything I might be able to see. Upon being where I could see, the director officer [Barry] at this time yelled to me of a torpedo off our port side. I then caught sight of a wake in the water that was definitely that of a torpedo."

Edwin Sentel: "I was informed by CIC to be on an alert for torpedoes in the water. I looked over the port side and saw a torpedo wake approximately 110 feet out from the ship."[67]

The first report giving any details about the sighting reads: "Torpedo wake sighted by Dir 51 officer [Barry] reliability good. Also seen by one member Dir crew [Litton] reliability good and port lookout [Sentel] reliability fair. All agree torp wake came up from astern passing thru wake then up port side. Distance abeam approx 300 ft. Torpedo was fired by one of two contacts which initiated action."[68]

The statement about all witnesses agreeing the torpedo had passed through the wake is very strange. Not only is it contradicted by all other accounts of the incident, but anyone who knew the *Turner Joy* should have been able to recognize that it was impossible, since the two witnesses whose testimony was rated most reliable, Barry and Litton, were both stationed just forward of the destroyer's funnels, which totally blocked their view to the rear. If a torpedo had passed through the destroyer's wake, they could not have seen it do so. Barry's only hypothesis is that a later report of a radar target in the wake, which prompted the *Turner Joy* to drop a depth charge, could somehow have gotten mixed in with the report of the torpedo sighting.[69]

Eugene Windchy has argued that some or all of the four accounts of torpedo sightings do not refer to the time of the first supposed torpedo firing, but refer to later in the evening, and that the timing has been adjusted to make them all seem to refer to the same incident. This argument is based partly on great discrepancies in the different witnesses' accounts of the distance, partly on discrepancies as to the length of time the supposed torpedo was visible, partly on the fact that some of the witnesses do not seem at all sure just when they saw it, and partly on the fact that several people who had access to the early reports from the *Turner Joy* spoke of *two* torpedoes having been sighted.[70] The first two arguments are very weak. If various people all saw a single torpedo, from various vantage points, it would be surprising if they all had it in view for the same length of time, and not surprising if they made various estimates of its distance from the ship. Barry's comment on the difficulty of estimating distances on such a dark night seems very reasonable.

The last of Windchy's arguments, however, looks stronger now than it did when Windchy's book was published. Now that some of the relevant records have been declassified, it appears that there must indeed have been reports of torpedo sightings at more than one time. In the CIC log of the *Turner Joy*, there is an entry—"2 fish down starboard side"—for a much later hour, 2321G, that disappears from later accounts; the sighting that produced this entry may well have been amalgamated into the report of sightings by multiple witnesses at the beginning of the incident. There is also an entry "torpedo in water" in the quartermaster log at 2318G. The *Turner Joy* radioed to the *Maddox* at approximately 2335G, "Two torpedoes fired evaded same."[71]

John Barry says he believes that he, Litton, and Sentel "all reported the same occurrence"; that these three sightings "were the same torpedo."[72] The evidence seems clear that these three sightings all did occur right at the beginning of the action, just after Mallow's first torpedo report. Bergland's sighting, however, may well have occurred at a considerably later hour.

Other Visual Sightings on the Destroyers

Many men on the *Turner Joy* and a few on the *Maddox* said that they had glimpsed one thing or another during the incident. Some of these sightings, including a column of black smoke at one point and a searchlight in the distance at another, can be verified from the logs of the *Turner Joy*. Others, most importantly sightings of actual PT boats silhouetted in the night, appear not to have been reported until considerably after the incident.

The very dark night was punctuated by a great variety of lights, most of them moving. Nature provided "occasional flashes of lightning all around the horizon."[73] The U.S. Navy provided the muzzle flashes of the destroyers' own guns, the detonation of the shells over the targets, the truck lights that the destroyers turned on and off intermittently, the wing lights that some aircraft turned on and off intermittently, at least two different types of rockets fired by the planes, 20-mm tracers fired by the planes, at least two types of airdropped flares, and the star shells fired by the *Maddox*. Given tension, fatigue, and a firm belief that the ships were under attack, the opportunities for deception of the eye seem almost limitless. Herrick himself later said, of two men who claimed that they had seen the cockpit lights of a PT boat passing their ship, "A Marine aboard ship can see almost anything."[74] More concretely, he comments that what appeared to be a searchlight in the distance could actually have been light from one of the destroyers' star shells reflecting off the clouds.[75]

A considerable number of men on the *Turner Joy* saw what they believed to be a searchlight in the distance. The after-action reports give the time as 2247G; the CIC log gives what is probably a record of this sighting—"hold search light on contact"—at 2245G. There is no report giving an exact bearing for this searchlight. The after-action report indicates that it was to the north of the *Turner Joy*, nowhere near the direction of the *Maddox*. Statements made by witnesses a few days after the incident place it off the starboard bow of the *Turner Joy*. Various men estimated relative bearings of 030°, 060°, 040° to 070°, and 045°.[76] If the destroyer had been on a course of about 210° at the time, as shown on the action report track chart, these relative bearings would be about right for the location of the *Maddox* at this time. If the destroyer had been on a course of about 310° at the time, as indicated by Koplin's track chart and the action report chronology, these relative bearings would be wrong for the *Maddox*.[77] It seems possible that the *Maddox* turned on a searchlight at this time, but there is no evidence to support this possibility. Commander Barnhart told an interviewer a few years later that he had asked the *Maddox* at this time whether a light had been shown and had received a negative response.[78]

The only witness the author has been able to interview at length about the searchlight is Richard Bacino. The statement he signed a few days after the incident said that it was clearly a searchlight, that it seemed to be 2,000 to 5,000 yards away, off the starboard bow, and that it "seemed to be searching."[79]

When this author read that statement to him, he said he did not remember it, and in regard to the bearing of the light, he said flatly that the statement was wrong. He stated very firmly that the light was not off the starboard bow. It was off the starboard quarter, at a relative bearing of about 100°. The bearing might have shifted a bit forward during the period he was watching the light, but he does not recall such a shift, and he is sure it did not shift far enough forward to be describable as being off the starboard bow. Bacino happened to be facing the right way when the light went on, so he was able to watch it for the whole time it was on: "I saw the light come on, and I saw it go off. At no time did I take my eye off that light."

He was and is convinced that what he saw was a twelve-inch incandescent light of the sort used by many ships, including the *Turner Joy*, for exchanging messages between ships by Morse code. Bacino was very familiar with the appearance of such lights at night; reading messages sent to the *Turner Joy* by other American ships, using this type of light, was among his regular duties.

The beam emitted by a twelve-inch incandescent light spreads out quite a bit. This makes the transmission of messages easier, at any reasonable range; the light does not have to be aimed precisely at the receiving vessel in order for the message to be understood. The spread of the beam, however, means that the twelve-inch incandescent light is not much use for illuminating a distant object at night. An American destroyer would use the much brighter and more concentrated beam of a xenon light for illumination. Bacino doubts, however, that a PT boat would have an electric generator powerful enough to operate a xenon light. A PT boat, having nothing brighter than a twelve-inch incandescent light, might attempt to use it for illumination.

When Bacino saw this light, he assumed that it came from the *Maddox* and that the *Maddox* intended to send a message to the *Turner Joy*. He phoned CIC to verify that the bearing of the *Maddox* matched that of the light. CIC told him that the *Maddox* was off the port bow. This startled him, since the light was off the starboard quarter. Bacino asked the CIC again; the CIC repeated that the *Maddox* was off the port bow.

The light remained on for more than just a few seconds; there was time for Bacino to report it to CIC, to ask twice about the bearing of the *Maddox*, and have his question answered twice. There was also time for some people who had not been on deck when the light appeared to emerge on deck to look at it.

The light was aimed approximately at the *Turner Joy* for the whole of the time it was on. Bacino accepted as accurate the portion of his 1964 statement saying that the light seemed to be searching, but only in the sense that there were small changes in the angle of the light, too small ever to put the *Turner Joy* outside the spread of the beam. All that could be seen, therefore, was the light itself. If it had been aimed up in the air, or off to the side, Bacino would have been able to see it as a beam in the air, but this did not occur. He is very firm on this point; at no time did the light shine up in the air, or swing around either toward or away from the destroyer, or show a visible beam in the air.

It should be noted that judging the direction in which a twelve-inch incandescent light was pointed was a familiar task for Bacino. When other American ships were signaling to the *Turner Joy* with such lights, part of his job was to signal to the man sending the message asking that man to correct his aim, if he did not have his light pointed properly at the *Turner Joy*. At no time did the light Bacino saw on August 4 wander far enough from the *Turner Joy* that Bacino would have felt inclined to ask for correction of the aim, had this light been sending a Morse code message that Bacino was trying to read.

The light did not in any effective sense illuminate the *Turner Joy*, but the reason was that a twelve-inch incandescent light is not capable of illuminating a distant object the way a xenon light can.[80]

No firm conclusions can be reached about this light, but it at least seems likely that the various versions of the sighting of the searchlight refer to the same actual incident, and that the times given in the records for this incident are accurate to within a couple of minutes. The same is not true, however, of the reports that smoke was seen, believed to come from a PT boat hit by the *Turner Joy*'s gunfire.

In the *Turner Joy* action report, the sighting of smoke by Commander Barnhart and at least four other men fits neatly into the logic of the action, appearing at the location of "V-3" just after the time (2228G) when radar indicated that the target had been sunk. It should be noted, however, that none of the records of smoke sightings in the CIC log fits this timing. There is in fact no relationship between the hours at which smoke sightings appear in the CIC log (2218G, 2220G, and 2248G) and the hours at which these sightings appear in the after-action report (2227G, 2228G, and 2305G).[81] Barnhart's description of the incident in an interview about three years afterward makes it clear that the smoke appeared before "V-3" was acquired by radar, as the CIC log says, rather than at the time "V-3" disappeared, believed to have been sunk, as the action report says.[82]

It also seems unlikely that a PT boat could have put out enough smoke for it to be visible, on a dark night, without there having been any visible flames. The explanation offered in the after-action reports—that the PT boat sank immediately instead of burning on the surface—makes little sense. Even a brief moment of burning on the surface could have produced visible flames; only an extended period of burning on the surface could have produced "a thick column of smoke."[83]

Several sailors on the *Turner Joy* said that they had seen vessels in the darkness. The clearest sightings seem to have been made by three of the loaders in Mount 32 (the aft three-inch gun mount), who said they had seen a PT boat lit by a flare. Many of the details are unclear. Donald Sharkey said it was to starboard, Kenneth Garrison said it was to port, and Delner Jones did not say anything about the bearing. None of the three men said how far away it had been. Kenneth Garrison's statement that it was visible for about two minutes seems extremely implausible, given the failure of the lookouts to notice it. Delner Jones made a drawing of the vessel the following day; Kenneth Garrison confirmed that the drawing matched what he had seen. It is said that the drawing closely resembled the actual appearance of North Vietnamese PT boats. It was claimed that these men had never seen North Vietnamese PT boats, or pictures of them, with the implication that they would not have been able to make accurate drawings unless they had really seen PT boats on the night of August 4. (Schaperjahn describes this claim as "a lie." When the *Turner Joy* was ordered to join the *Maddox* in the patrol the *Maddox* was conducting off the North Vietnamese coast, members of the crew of the *Turner Joy* were briefed on potential enemies that might be encountered in the area. Members of the crew were shown pictures—Schaperjahn cannot recall whether these were drawings or photographs—of North Vietnamese PT boats and aircraft. Schaperjahn himself was the man who showed the pictures to the sonarmen and torpedomen.)[84]

No copy of the drawing can now be located, but it might be noted that the claims that were been made for its accuracy have particularly emphasized that it showed no visible radar on the PT boat.[85] Given the likelihood that in an action on a very dark night, torpedo boats would have had their radar masts erect in the working position, the lack of a radar mast on the drawing seems to this author a count against it, rather than a count in its favor. When the mast was erect, the dome housing the radar antenna at its top was remarkably conspicuous, as can be seen in the photo of a North Vietnamese torpedo boat published in a recent U.S. Navy history.[86] For some reason the caption mistakenly identifies the vessel as a Swatow boat, although a clearly visible torpedo launching tube, and the fact that the vessel has only one rather small twin gun mount, should have left no doubt that it was a torpedo boat. Possibly the U.S. Navy was still using lack of a visible radar mast as an identifying characteristic for North Vietnamese torpedo boats.

The Report of Automatic Weapons Fire

When Secretary of Defense McNamara briefed the press about twelve hours after the end of the August 4 incident, he said the *Turner Joy* had reported that "the destroyer had been fired upon by automatic weapons while being illuminated by searchlights."[87] He had already given this story to the National Security Council;[88] he repeated it again when he and General Wheeler spoke to key Senate committees August 6. Queried, he explained that the automatic weapons fired by the Swatow and/or PT boats were believed to have been three-inch guns.[89]

This was impossible—the biggest guns in the whole North Vietnamese navy were about one-and-a-half-inch, and the biggest guns even mistakenly credited to North Vietnamese torpedo boats in exaggerated western reports were one-inch—but it sounded so convincing that not even the most suspicious of the senators, Wayne Morse of Oregon, thought to question it. A three-inch gun fires a rather powerful explosive shell, and in the absence of an actual attack, it would be very difficult to imagine being fired at by such a weapon. It is also difficult to imagine that one is being illuminated by a searchlight.

This weird story does have some foundation in events aboard the *Turner Joy*. The sighting of an apparent searchlight by personnel aboard the *Turner Joy* has already been discussed. There are also a number of reports dating from during or soon after the action indicating that men aboard the *Turner Joy* thought they had seen signs of machine gun fire directed at them. An entry in the CIC log of the *Turner Joy* for 2305G reported, "Flashes from [bearing] 155 believed to be firing at us." An after-action report written around noon the following day (interesting for its total omission of silhouette sightings and for its statement that the searchlight illuminated the *Turner Joy* and was bright enough to impair night vision), after there had been time for "extensive interviews along with action reconstruction to determine how much imagination and reality" there had been in earlier reports, stated:

Most machine gun fire observations confused and too varied for evaluation. Two rpts were significant: (1) Mt 51 ROMC observed initial contacts on port side spraying a flash fore to aft as they approached for initial attack. No hits as believed firing extreme range. This is in agreement with ranges on initial contact. Eval rpt fair unsubstantiated. (2) MT 31 gun capt and one crew saw water splashed stbd side being directed from ahead at time orig was attempting ram one PT boat. Eval poor. No hits were received from small arms fire.[90]

The reports of the searchlight and of the gunfire were passed by voice radio to the *Maddox*, probably while the action was still going on. At some point in the chain of oral transmission they were combined into a single incident.

Captain Herrick doubted the accuracy of this story, but he had no way to be sure it was inaccurate, and he certainly had no right to refuse to pass it on to Washington.[91] Immediately after the apparent attack, the *Maddox* reported that "further recap reveals *Turner Joy* fired upon by small calibre guns and illuminated by search light."[92] A report sent by the *Maddox* at 0558H stated: "CO *Turner Joy* claims sinking one craft and damage to another with gunfire. Damaged boat returned gunfire no hits. CO Turner Joy and other personnel observed bursts and black smoke from hits on this boat. This boat illuminated *Turner Joy* and his return fire was observed and heard by *TJ* personnel."[93]

Statements about North Vietnamese gunfire having been seen persisted for several days; the last such statement is in a report of interviews with crew members of the two destroyers, carried out at the U.S. base at Subic Bay on August 10.[94] While in Subic, however, these men were questioned by U.S. naval officers who concluded that men on the two destroyers had been seeing one another's gunfire and thinking they were seeing the muzzle flashes of enemy gunfire.[95] The interpretation must have been convincing; references to enemy gunfire having been seen disappear abruptly and completely from the reports of the destroyers, at that time. Three years later, when interviewed by David Wise, Commander Barnhart no longer remembered that there ever had been any report of gunfire directed at his ship.[96]

The Problem of Excited Witnesses

Gerrell Moore has described the situation aboard the *Maddox* during the action of August 4 as one of "mass confusion all around."[97] Patrick Park says, "We had people screaming and yelling all night long."[98] Others have also described confusion aboard both the *Maddox* and *Turner Joy*.

By coincidence, this author's interview with Joseph Schaperjahn took place shortly after the completion of the U.S. Navy's report on the incident in which the U.S. cruiser *Vincennes* mistook an Iranian airliner for a fighter plane and shot it down. Schaperjahn drew parallels between the two incidents. In each case, he said, men finding themselves for the first time in an apparent combat situation became so excited that they could not interpret their instruments accurately. In circumstances such as existed on the two destroyers, every momentary contact made by radar or sonar—clouds, birds, knuckles, fish, bottom echoes—gets reported. Schaperjahn particularly noted the number of very brief contacts recorded on the *Turner Joy*. What shows on the radar has to be interpreted. When men are as tense as those in the CIC of *Turner Joy* on the night of August 4, according to Schaperjahn, they will identify everything that shows on their radar screens—every seagull, every knuckle on the surface of the water—as a hostile vessel. "I could go into any ship in the Navy, walk into CIC and sonar, psych people up, and cause an incident."[99]

Hardly anyone on the *Turner Joy* had been in a combat situation before the night of August 4. Richard Bacino comments that he was excited at first, as indeed were a lot of men. He recalls that when an announcement came early in the action to "prepare for torpedo hit to starboard," half a dozen men all jumped to get into one small space that looked as if it might provide some shelter. He himself settled down after about fifteen or twenty minutes. "I was not so excited that I was confused about everything I saw." He says that he had been trained as a combat sailor and wanted combat; the fact that he later volunteered for two tours in Vietnam supports this claim. Not everyone had the same ability to calm down. The man who had the phone at Bacino's station was talking into it so excitedly, violating proper phone discipline, that Bacino had to take the phone away from him.[100]

By the time the most crucial incidents occurred, excitement must have been struggling with fatigue in many men. They had waited all afternoon, at General Quarters, for an attack that did not come. They had been somewhat tired by the time they secured from General Quarters as evening approached. The appearance of skunks "N," "O," and "P" sent them back to General Quarters and brought a rush of adrenalin, but there then followed another hour and a half of waiting. All of this cannot have been the best of preparation for the two hours of confusion that followed the appearance of skunk "V." The fatigue problem would have been worsened by the fact that both ships were seriously undermanned.

The witnesses are not unanimous on this issue. John Barry's impression is that the men on the *Turner Joy* were not tense, and were not expecting to be attacked, until it actually happened. He says the men on the *Turner Joy* stayed calmer than those on the *Maddox* during the action; the *Turner Joy* "stayed very well organized." He believes one reason for the difference is that people on the *Turner Joy* were not hearing all the reports from the *Maddox*'s sonar of torpedoes in the water.[101] Men on the bridge of the *Turner Joy* and in CIC, however, while they did not by any means hear all of Mallow's sonar reports—it seems unlikely that they can have heard even a quarter of them—did hear more of them than Barry did.

Evidence from Other Sources

The Testimony of the Pilots

There is no record of any sighting report filed on August 4 or 5 by any of the pilots who had flown over the destroyers on the night of August 4; the first message reporting significant sightings by the pilots was filed August 7 as a reply to the JCS message. What shows in the records for August 5 is that about two and a half hours after the end of the action, the *Ticonderoga* reported:

1. Returning pilots report no visual sightings of any vessels or wakes other than *Turner Joy* and *Maddox*. Wakes from *Turner Joy* and *Maddox* visible for 2–3000 yards.
2. Pilots fired ordnance in areas where skunks reported and in areas where directed by controllers.[1]

Commander George Edmondson and his wingman, Lieutenant Jere A. Barton, had piloted two A-1 Skyraiders launched from the *Ticonderoga* at the beginning of the incident. These propeller-driven planes were slower than the jets flown by most of the pilots over the destroyers that night, but could remain in the air considerably longer. Edmondson and Barton arrived over the destroyers before the shooting started on the night of August 4, and remained there until well after the shooting had ended.

Of the *Ticonderoga* pilots who were over the destroyers during the action, they were apparently the last to get back to the carrier. They arrived exhausted in the early morning hours of August 5. Commander Edmondson says, "The debrief was very short. As I recall the only question asked was did we see any enemy PT boats? The answer was no."[2]

After the "flash" message from the Joint Chiefs asking for evidence that could be shown to the United Nations, however, Edmondson and Barton were questioned again. A "redebriefing" on August 7 involved only officers of the *Ticonderoga*. Another on August 11 involved Deputy Assistant Secretary of Defense Alvin Friedman, and also another high-ranking civilian from the Defense Department, Jack Stempler. It is possible that part of the reason these men were chosen to be flown out from the United States to investigate Tonkin Gulf was that both of them were lawyers; the government seems to have been inclined to assign such tasks to lawyers. Edmondson had the impression they represented the United Nations Security Council. Two episodes during the night of August 4 were discussed in these redebriefings; Edmondson has described both of them to this author.

In the first of these episodes, Edmondson says that he and Barton were sent to investigate an object appearing on a destroyer's radar to the northwest of (astern of) the destroyers; he is not sure how far to the northwest. They had high-intensity flares, but the low cloud ceiling made it necessary to drop them from a very low altitude, and they landed in the water almost as soon as they started burning; they were thus almost useless. Edmondson decided to go down low while Barton dropped a flare from as high as was practical; this would give Edmondson his best chance of seeing something during the brief time before the flare landed in the water and went out.

While Edmondson was in his dive close to the surface, he saw bursts of light, which could have been muzzle flashes, a long way off, behind him and to the right. They seemed to be at surface level. Then, as he was pulling out of his dive, something that looked like tracers—moving lights—went past him, coming from behind him. He decided to dive again to see whether the same thing happened, with Barton waiting above to go after an enemy vessel if one could be seen firing at Edmondson. On the second dive Edmondson again saw what appeared to be tracers. Barton did not see them.[3]

Commander Edmondson's opinion today is that the tracers were fired by another U.S. aircraft some distance away, probably that of James Stockdale. The 20-mm tracer bullets used by the jets would indeed have created an appearance matching what Edmondson says he saw. Some pilots like McDonald did little firing, but Stockdale has said that when sent to locations where the destroyers' radar showed targets, he would "spray bullets around."[4] This author has found no evidence that either destroyer fired tracers that night. Commander Ogier says he cannot recall the *Maddox* having done so, and indeed he doubts the *Maddox* was equipped to fire tracers.

Edmondson believes that the muzzle flashes were the guns of the *Turner Joy*, and that the destroyer was firing at a location directly under him, the radar images of his and/or Barton's aircraft having been misidentified as a surface object, listed in the records of the destroyer as skunk "V-2." The confusion in the records of radar contacts held by the *Turner Joy* between 2147G and 2218G, and especially the ones at which the destroyer actually fired between 2210G and 2218G, indicates that there were a considerable number of brief radar contacts held at various locations during this period, rather than one or two prolonged ones (see Chapter 7). This gives considerable plausibility to the idea that at least some of these contacts might have been Edmondson's aircraft, sporadically dipping down low enough to pass through the beams of the surface-search and fire-control radars.

Edmondson says that at the August 7 redebriefing,

> Jere was very uneasy . . . therefore I answered all or most of the questions. As I recall, Jere didn't say anything during the debriefing, just nodded his head occasionally. I related to the staff that I had not seen anything that appeared to be a Vietnam PT boat but that I had seen surface gunfire at a distance which I took to be from our destroyers. I related that on two occasions I had seen what appeared to be tracers coming from the surface rising to my right and slightly below my aircraft. I believe I was asked if the tracers could have been anti aircraft fire. I said no because I had recently experienced AA gunfire at night over Laos and that anti aircraft shells will burst leaving a momentary flash of light.[5]

This would not have constituted an adequate response to the request of the JCS for proof that the destroyers had been attacked. The report of the redebriefing that was sent to Washington, however (which was not shown to Edmondson before it was sent), was rather different.

> At approx 041515Z [2215G] Cdr. Edmondson and his wingman were vectored to a reported surface contact northwest of *Maddox*. At a distance of 1½ to 2 miles, flying at 700–1500 feet, they report seeing gun flashes on the surface of the water and bursting light AA at their approximate flight altitude. Cdr. Edmondson and his wingman were at this time flying on opposite sides of a large circle, orbiting to the northwest of the *Maddox* attempting to visually sight the contact reported there. Firing would commence when one or the other of the aircraft had passed abeam or over the firing vessel, and would cease when the aircraft turned in toward it. Firing would only commence when aircraft lights were turned on. The two aircraft attempted unsuccessfully to get in a firing run on the vessel for about 10–15 minutes, after which they broke off and returned to their original position circling the *Maddox*.[6]

Since there will surely be those who will argue that the report of August 7 should be treated as a more reliable source than the twenty-three-year-old memories of the pilot involved, it should be pointed out that the report is inherently implausible; the fact that the pilot, having been shown the text of the report to refresh his memory, contradicted rather than verified it, is only a part of the evidence against it.

If Edmondson and Barton had seen gunfire as described, they should have succeeded in getting in a firing run; a North Vietnamese vessel that repeatedly marked its location to low-flying aircraft by conspicuous muzzle flashes, and could not move from the marked location without leaving a conspicuously luminous wake, should have been findable. It seems slightly surprising that North Vietnamese sailors would have been so stupid as to mark their location by blazing away at dimly glimpsed aircraft overhead, under conditions that gave them no realistic chance of hitting anything. It seems very unlikely that such trigger-happy fools would have then carefully ceased fire whenever the aircraft made themselves both more threatening and much easier to target, by turning in on an attack run.

Also, when Edmondson said that anti-aircraft fire would burst at his approximate altitude (as the report of August 7 then said he had reported seeing), he was thinking of the weapons that had been fired at him during his recent missions over Laos. The guns of North Vietnamese PT boats were not, however, nearly large enough to fire shells producing such bursts. The larger guns of Swatow boats could do so, but it is difficult to explain why the commander of a Swatow boat, with no armament that could do any serious harm to a destroyer, would have loitered within two miles of an American destroyer—well within the destroyer's gun range—to be shot at for an extended period.

If the pilots had actually seen such a clear indication of the location of enemy vessels as the report describes, it is hard to imagine why they would have abandoned the hunt after ten or fifteen minutes, without even bothering to inform the other pilots, who had not been able to spot any targets on the surface, of what they had seen. It is hard to imagine how such a sighting could have failed to appear in formal reports before August 7. There is also no indication that they said anything informally to other pilots aboard the *Ticonderoga*, before or after August 7. Stockdale has commented that ever since he learned (long afterward) of the August 7 report, "I have shaken my head in disbelief. Of course I knew George Edmondson well. We were fellow squadron commanders aboard *Ticonderoga*. We never discussed his 'sightings,' because I don't believe he ever mentioned them while I was with him aboard *Ticonderoga*. (If he had, it certainly would have caused a stir; Wes McDonald and I, the other two squadron commanders over the boats that night, were not keeping quiet our joint absolute conviction that there had been no boats out there.)"[7]

Edmondson's explanation for his failure to discuss his sightings with other pilots aboard the carrier—that other concerns quickly drove them from his mind—makes excellent sense, given the nature of the sightings as he describes them. It would be very implausible if he had seen the things the August 7 report claims that he saw.

At a later hour on the night of August 4, Edmondson saw an apparent high-speed wake, phosphorescent in the water. It appeared to have been made by a vessel moving in a straight line, but it was being broken up by wave action, so what looked as if it had originally been a linear wake had taken on a wavy, "snakelike" appearance. For a long time, he was positive it was a genuine wake that had been modified by wave action, but he now believes that the whole thing had "most probably" been created by wave action.[8]

It could not have been the wake of either of the destroyers. The two Skyraiders had just passed over the destroyers before coming to the location where the wake was seen, so he was able to know for sure that the destroyers had not been in a location to make this wake. Also, the "snakelike" wake was much narrower than the wake of a destroyer, though not narrow enough to be a possible torpedo wake.[9] It also, however, could not have been the wake of a PT boat, which would not have been narrower than that of a destroyer, but actually a little wider.[10] Edmondson recalls having said during his August 11 debriefing that the wake had been too narrow to have been made by a PT boat, and he presumably would have said it on August 7 had he been asked. What went to Washington, however, in the report of August 7 does not give the impression that there was any doubt it was a PT wake.

After comparing the movements of his and other aircraft with the account in Marolda and Fitzgerald of what had appeared on the screens of the destroyers, Edmondson concluded:

> If there were any PT boats in the area of V-1, V-2, V-3, V-4, or V-5 I should have been able to have seen the illuminist wakes during the three hours that Jere and I searched the area. . . . Jim Stockdale's holding close to the *Turner Joy* should have seen a V-2 and V-3 wake and Wes McDonald should have at least seen the V-3 wake. Had any of the radar contacts been hit by the *Turner Joy* gunfire as reported, one or all of us should have seen evidence of an explosion, fire, sparks, or something indicating that a PT boat had been damaged. . . .
>
> The two A-1 aircraft were in the very near vicinity of contacts V-1, V-2, V-3 and V-4 when the *Turner Joy* was firing at the radar contacts, and reporting PT boats damaged or sunk.
>
> There were no PT boats, therefore none could have been damaged or sunk.[11]

When Eugene Windchy and other nongovernment scholars began to investigate the Tonkin Gulf incidents a few years later, Barton refused to talk to Windchy about his experiences on the night of August 4. He died in 1970. Admiral James Stockdale, however, recently contacted a couple of the senior pilots who were with Barton in the squadron in 1964 to get an idea about Barton's motivation in these affairs. Their answers clearly indicated that Barton had been a very conscientious officer and had not liked being taken before the captain and asked to change his prior report of no sightings. Afterward, "He just wouldn't talk about it."[12]

Lieutenant Commander Donald Hegrat, again flying a photo-reconnaissance aircraft, arrived on the scene sometime in the middle of the action. He had not been among the first pilots to take off from the *Ticonderoga* because it had taken some time to load into his plane the magnesium flares used for night photography; they were too dangerous to be kept in the aircraft when there was no immediate likelihood they would be used.

Hegrat has described it as "an extremely stormy, low-ceilinged evening, with a lot of thunderstorms and lightning in the area." When he arrived over the destroyers, they were maneuvering "wildly." He could see their wakes clearly, glowing in the darkness, stretching behind the destroyers for a distance at least the length of the ships. He did not notice gunfire from the destroyers. The voice radio transmissions from the destroyers were "high-pitched and nervous"; he got the impression that "there was a great amount of tension" on the American ships.

Hegrat's aircraft carried a camera that took pictures on five-inch square negatives. For each shot with the camera, he would drop a photo-flash magnesium flare, which gave a brief, very intense light to illuminate the sea below the aircraft. He had forty of these photo-flash flares aboard.

The procedure he used was to get from one of the destroyers, by radio, a bearing and range to a target held on the radar of the destroyer. He would circle around to get in position, fly over the destroyer on the indicated bearing, and continue on that bearing. He would take a series of photos, overlapping one another, starting when he was over the destroyer and not stopping until he had passed the location where the target was supposed to be. He believes he made four or five such runs, using eight to twelve flares per run, during the thirty to forty-five minutes he was over the destroyers. He had no difficulty keeping track of the destroyers well enough to get into the correct position for the beginning of each run.

Each run covered a strip of ocean whose size depended not only on the number of photos taken, but also on the altitude of the aircraft, the size of the field of view of the camera, and the amount of overlap between photos. Hegrat was unable to furnish the author exact figures for any of these factors, but his best recollection suggests that a strip of eight photos might have covered an area a little more than 1,000 yards wide, and between 5,000 and 6,000 yards long.

When the photos were developed later, there was indeed a destroyer in the initial frame of each series, but no PT boats, or wakes of PT boats, in the later frames. Quite aside from the failure of PT boats to appear in his photos, Hegrat believes that, given the clear visibility of the wakes of the destroyers, he would have seen the wakes of PT boats with his own eyes if any had been present.

Standard procedure would have been for Hegrat to make all his photo runs under the guidance of one destroyer, but he does not recall whether he in fact got guidance from the *Maddox*, the *Turner Joy*, or both.[13] Probably all his runs were under the guidance of the *Turner Joy*, since it was the *Turner Joy* that had the convincing radar contacts during the period Hegrat was present. The statement in the *Maddox* action report, "Two photo-flash runs were made by aircraft,"[14] suggests a possibility, however, that two of Hegrat's runs may have been made under the control of the *Maddox*, and the others under the control of the *Turner Joy*.

Of all the Americans present on the night of August 4, James Stockdale eventually became the most vocal in saying that there had been no PT boat attack on the two destroyers August 4. His conviction was based essentially on the fact that he and the other pilots had not seen any PT boats, but it would be difficult to argue that he was not entitled to treat his lack of sightings as proof that there had been nothing to see. Two days before, on August 2, he had had the opportunity to compare the wakes of North Vietnamese torpedo boats with that of the *Maddox*. When PT boats were moving at high speed on August 2, they had left "long, foamy wakes, much more pronounced than the wake of a destroyer at full speed."[15] On the dark night of August 4, water conditions made wakes luminous. The wake of a destroyer was terribly conspicuous, "just a spotlight in a dark pit."[16] When Stockdale was guided to places where the destroyers' radar showed high-speed torpedo boats, and he saw no wakes, he had all the justification he needed to be certain that there had been no high-speed torpedo boats there. He is "sure" he would have seen anything within five miles of the two destroyers.[17]

It is not as if Stockdale, Hegrat, and Edmondson, using the conspicuously visible wakes of the destroyers as their base point, would have had to go a long distance in exactly the right direction in order to find themselves over the equally conspicuous wakes of attacking PT boats. The wakes of the destroyers are said to have been visible for 2,000 to 3,000 yards. The *Turner Joy*'s radar showed skunks "V-2," "V-4," and "V-5" approaching to within 2,000 yards, and skunks "V-1" and "V-3" approaching to within 4,000 yards. The situation was different for pilots operating at altitudes high enough that the weather impeded their view of the surface, and pilots newly arriving in the vicinity of the action, who had not yet located the destroyers.

Aircraft from the *Constellation* reached the scene later than those from the *Ticonderoga*. The *Constellation* had launched at 2200G, position approximately 18°07′ N, 112°00′ E.[18] This was on the far side of Hainan Island; the pilots had to detour southward in order to reach the scene of the action without overflying Chinese territory. Some of them, at least, then remained over the destroyers so long that they did not have the fuel to take the same detour on their way back;

they did overfly Hainan, which would have horrified Washington if the fact had become known.

When the pilots from the *Constellation* returned to their carrier at about 0100 on August 5, they (like the pilots from the *Ticonderoga*) reported having seen no clear evidence of the presence of torpedo boats near the destroyers. There does not, however, seem to have been any of them who felt the same degree of confidence as some of the *Ticonderoga*'s pilots that they would have seen torpedo boats if any had been present.[19]

Officers at higher levels in the navy apparently realized only slowly that the pilots were having trouble locating PT boats. Some seemed to be under the impression that the aircraft were finding and attacking PT boats even when the latter were not in the immediate vicinity of the destroyers. More than an hour after the shooting had ended, there was a report: "PT's have apparently broken off engagement. Air strikes are continuing and pursuit of PT's will continue until all efforts exhausted to destroy them."[20]

There is a variety of evidence suggesting that at least some men on the destroyers were strangely unaware of the fact that they had air cover overhead. Air cover was in fact present from about 2110G onward.[21] Chad James's account, however, indicates that the air controllers on the *Turner Joy* were still unaware of the presence of aircraft at the time his destroyer was firing at "V-1." After James had described this incident, explaining that there had been no American aircraft up at the time, this author said that the records of the incident indicated that there *had* been aircraft in the vicinity. After this, James at one point repeated his belief that there had been no aircraft up, but at another point he expressed anger over the possibility that the air traffic controllers might not have been informed of the presence of aircraft: "Why didn't we know?" In regard to James Stockdale's statements that he and other pilots had been over the destroyers, he asked, "If Stockdale is correct, where were they??? I know that they strafed us but that was [later in the action] when we were dropping depth charges aft and had already fired aft."[22]

James said that after the incident of "V-1," the air controllers on the *Turner Joy* "got very busy as CAP was on their way." Even half an hour after "V-1," however, a message from the *Maddox* at 2215G said "no air cover at present" and estimated that the nearest aircraft would not arrive for fifteen minutes. Eugene Windchy, interviewing personnel from the destroyers only three to seven years after the incidents, was also told repeatedly that no aircraft had shown up until after the shooting had started.[23]

These facts add greatly to the plausibility of what would otherwise seem an almost absurd hypothesis: that radarmen on the destroyers were mistaking the radar images of aircraft for PT boats. Both Edmondson and Stockdale were flying low enough so their aircraft must have been dipping, at least intermittently, into the beams of both destroyers' surface-search radar. If they were not recognized as aircraft, perhaps it really was because, as Edmondson has suggested, they were being mistaken for surface vessels.

Lieutenant Raymond Connell recalls that the radar of the *Maddox* held a number of brief contacts, which disappeared before the destroyer could get the guns aimed and commence firing. He says it was eventually realized that these were U.S. aircraft, "dodging through the periphery of our surface-search radar."[24] The *Turner Joy* had a more modern fire-control system, which should have enabled it to aim its guns at a target appearing on the radar, and open fire, in less time than the *Maddox* required.

Captured DRV Naval Personnel

Edward Marolda, discussing a report that the North Vietnamese had lost two vessels on the night of August 4, comments: "This coincides with the number of craft determined sunk by the *Maddox* and *Turner Joy* and with the report of a North Vietnamese naval officer captured in 1967."[25] In regard to the captured North Vietnamese officer, Marolda's statement simply is not true; no North Vietnamese naval personnel captured during the war suggested, under interrogation, that any DRV vessels had been sunk on the night of August 4, or indeed that any combat had occurred on that night.

The officer captured in July 1967 to whom Marolda was referring was Senior Captain Nguyen Van Hoa, a specialist in military law. The most complete report available from Captain Hoa's interrogation mentions the attack on the *Maddox* August 2, 1964, but not any incident on August 4, and does not suggest that any DRV torpedo boats were sunk in any incident during 1964. Captain Hoa described an incident in which three DRV torpedo boats had been sent out to attack the U.S. Seventh Fleet, and all three had been sunk, but according to the report he said this had happened in 1966. He was surely referring to the incident of July 1, 1966, in which three torpedo boats had come out and all indeed had been sunk, although Hoa's date was a bit off; his recollection was that this happened early in 1966.[26] One section of the interrogation report, summarizing the current strength of the DRV Navy, actually does the arithmetic, stating that there had originally been twelve torpedo boats, that three had been sunk, and that nine remained. This indicates clearly that Captain Hoa believed the 1966 incident he described was the only occasion on which DRV torpedo boats had ever been sunk.[27]

An officer in Washington, looking at an earlier draft (which cannot now be found) of the interrogation report, misinterpreted the statements about three torpedo boats having been sunk as referring to "the attack on the *Maddox* in August 1964."[28] Edward Marolda, believing incorrectly that one torpedo boat had been sunk in the August 2 incident, and hoping to find support for the

Turner Joy's claim that two had been sunk in the August 4 incident, decided to split the figure of three boats sunk, which his source had described as having occurred in a single engagement, and treat it as meaning that one boat had been sunk on August 2 and two on August 4.[29]

Nguyen Van Hoa was not a line officer and did not know much about torpedo boats; he would not even have known about the 1966 incident if word of it had not been spread by the arguments, among officers of the People's Navy, over who should be blamed for the orders that had sent torpedo boats T-333, T-336, and T-339 out to their doom on July 1, 1966.

The United States obtained far more useful information from interrogation of the nineteen torpedo boat personnel captured in that incident, particularly Tran Bao, who had been deputy commander of Torpedo Boat Squadron 135 in 1964. The overall report on the interrogation of the nineteen men makes it clear that no North Vietnamese torpedo boats can have been sunk at any time during the year 1964. The DRV had obtained twelve torpedo boats from the Soviet Union, which together made up a single squadron (Squadron 135), and there had been no additions to or subtractions from this force until 1966. No new torpedo boats had been acquired, and all of the twelve had been still in service—the captured men listed them by number, and specified the name of the current commanding officer of each one—until T-333, T-336, and T-339 went out and were sunk on July 1, 1966.[30] The notion that boats belonging to this squadron could have been sunk without the rest of the squadron learning about the fact does not deserve comment. It is almost as hard to argue that nineteen men, subjected to weeks of questioning (during which they showed hardly any ability to withhold from their interrogators military information that would obviously cause direct harm to the DRV), would have carried out a successful common deception on a subject for which their backgrounds would have given them no ability either to understand the importance of concealing the truth or to judge what they could reasonably hope to get the Americans to believe.

This overall report did not explicitly mention the question of whether there had been an encounter between torpedo boats and destroyers on August 4, 1964, because when the interrogators reported that they had obtained a detailed account of the attack on the *Maddox* August 2, 1964, and that they were trying to determine whether the prisoners knew anything about the August 4 incident, Pacific Headquarters ordered them "not repeat not" to ask further questions about this subject.[31] Other interrogators, presumably more trusted to deal with politically explosive material, later did ask about the August 4 incident, and reported:

Extensive interrogation of all potentially knowledgeable sources reveals they have no info concerning a NVN attack on U.S. ships on 4 August 1964. They state definitely and emphatically that no PT's could have been involved. . . .

The possibility that Swatows could have committed the 4 Aug attack has also been carefully explored. Here again, however, all sources disclaim any knowledge of such an attack. Based on the experience of interrogations thus far it is very possible that PT crews in general might not have heard of this attack since they apparently have little contact with other ship types. On the other hand, source [deleted][32] obviously has travelled in higher circles and has proved himself exceptionally knowledgeable on almost every naval subject and event of interest. Yet he specifically and strongly denies that any attack took place. When pressed further on this issue he states that if such an attack did take place, it could only have been committed by Swatows.[33]

The authors of this report were grasping at straws when they suggested that the reason PT boat crews knew nothing of a battle on August 4 was that it had been fought by Swatows. Even if we ignore such details as the fact that skunk V-1 was tracked at speeds impossible for a Swatow, it is hard to see how anyone could take seriously a notion implying the following:

—That the DRV, in a pre-planned attack against U.S. destroyers, chose to use Swatows, whose 37-mm or 40-mm guns would have given them no chance even to do serious damage to the destroyers before the destroyers sank them, and not PTs, which would have had a genuine chance in a battle against destroyers.

—That the weapons used in the attack on the destroyers were the guns of Swatow boats—rapid-fire cannon that fired exploding shells and that produced, on every shot, large bright muzzle flashes—but the men on the destroyers, looking out into the darkness, failed to see any evidence of this convincing enough for them to put it in the most complete and detailed versions of their after-action reports. Bear in mind that the radar contacts that are supposed to have represented attacking vessels are supposed to have conducted their attack at very close ranges—often within two miles of the *Turner Joy*, sometimes within one mile.

—That the crews of two types of coastal defense vessels had so little contact with one another that the officers and men of the PTs would never hear about a bloody battle fought by the Swatows. Bear in mind the level of bitterness that the personnel of the surviving Swatows would have had to feel, knowing that their comrades had been sent to pointless deaths on a mission that was properly the job of the PTs. It is hardly likely that they would have failed to mention this to the personnel of PT boats, if there were even minimal contact. Bear in mind also that the two types of vessels *did* work together. The force that assembled at Hon Me on August 2 before the attack on the *Maddox* was a mixed force of three PTs and two Swatows; the force alerted for action on the evening of August 4 was a mixed force of two Swatows and one PT.

The record on these men was confused when one of the interrogators, Sedgwick Tourison, published an account suggesting that Tran Bao had described the August 4 incident in the interrogation. He has since acknowledged that the date printed in this account as August 4 was actually August 2, and published another account in which he says Tran Bao denied knowing of any attack on the destroyers August 4.[34]

Communications Intercepts

The officers responsible for sending OPLAN 34-A raids against the North Vietnamese coast needed to know the movements of DRV naval vessels along the coast, and as Commander Robert Laske has commented, "We had a pretty good idea where those units were, on a continuing basis."[35] They must have paid especially close attention on nights such as August 4, when the PTFs based at Danang were on a raid to the North. Commander Laske recalls: "As the communications officer of the Military Assistance Command Special Operations Group (MACSOG) that night, I was in the group's communications center, monitoring maritime operations and related signal intelligence traffic with the chief of the group, Colonel Clyde Russell, U.S. Army. We wondered what could possibly be going on with the DeSoto (electronic intelligence) patrol when signal intelligence indicated that there were no North Vietnamese boats at sea. Colonel Russell's assessment was, 'The Navy is shooting at whales.' "[36] Commander Laske's opinion is that a PT boat attack on the *Maddox* and the *Turner Joy* could not have occurred without his knowing about it, from the communications intercepts he was monitoring.[37]

Every intelligence professional this author has been able to identify who has examined the intercepted North Vietnamese message traffic from that night (they were at CIA, NSA, and INR) has reached the same conclusion as the men in SOG: the intercepts did not indicate that there had been an attack on the destroyers. On August 4, however, senior officials were looking at the intercepts themselves instead of asking their intelligence officers what those intercepts meant. As CIA Deputy Director Ray Cline later put it, "Everybody was demanding the sigint [signals intelligence; intercepts]; they wanted it quick, they didn't want anybody to take any time to analyze it."[38] This phenomenon has been a problem for nearly as long as there have been radio messages to intercept. In 1916, when the German navy sortied for what was to become the Battle of Jutland, the British navy intercepted a German navy message. A British admiral, realizing that the intercept might be crucial, decided he must deal with it himself. He sat down with it alone, away from subordinates who would have been able to explain its significance to him, and misinterpreted it as meaning that the Germans had not sortied.

Very soon after the second Tonkin Gulf incident, Cline looked at the DRV communications intercepts considered relevant to that incident. There were about thirty or forty such intercepts in the file available to him at that time. He quickly began to wonder whether the messages that were being interpreted as DRV reports on the August 4 incident really referred to that incident, or to earlier events: "It was terribly difficult to figure out exactly what was happening." The main issue was timing. Key messages seemed to have been intercepted too early to fit the interpretations that were being placed on them. It was hard to be sure, however, because the information Cline had, about the times at which the messages had been intercepted, was seriously incomplete.

In 1964, there were "dozens" of intercept sites (counting mobile units as well as fixed sites) picking up DRV message traffic. When a message was picked up, it would be translated, then the officer in charge would have to approve it, and then it would be sent up the line. The length of time it took to get a message translated and sent out, and delays in transmission (especially if the intercept site routed the message to CINCPAC rather than directly to Washington), meant that it might be as much as five or six hours between the time a message was intercepted and the time it reached Washington.

When intercepts were distributed to users such as Cline in Washington, they did not always have even the date-time group for the time the intercept site had sent them up the line; users were not considered to need this information. When looking at the date-time groups that had not been deleted, it was not always easy to figure out which time zone had been used.

Cline went before the President's Foreign Intelligence Advisory Board to discuss those incidents. He believes he did this on August 6, 1964, but is not sure. Speaking to PFIAB, Cline was very positive about the PT boat attack on the *Maddox* August 2, but "rather negative" about the reported PT boat attack on the *Maddox* and *Turner Joy* August 4. He did not say that the second attack had not occurred, but he said the evidence was much less conclusive; the timing of the intercepts was the main thing that worried him. At this time he was "pretty confused" about the communications intercepts, he says, "but clear that no conclusive evidence had emerged that tied the intercepts to the 4 August incident. This view is what I passed on to PFIAB."

He took this position rather reluctantly. "I was trying to be upbeat, and say there was an attack." "I wasn't out to up-end the President," who had publicly announced that there had been an attack, "but I did feel an obligation to warn the PFIAB members, some of whom were my friends," that the evidence wasn't clear.[39] Clark Clifford, chairman of PFIAB at this time, states that if Cline made such a report to PFIAB, the information would have been passed on to President Johnson, and to no one else. He has no specific recollection of the matter, however.[40]

President Johnson was away from Washington from August 7 to August 9, but he spoke with Clifford on the phone on the morning of August 10, and met him briefly on August 11.[41] It seems likely that both conversations dealt with what Cline had told PFIAB; President Johnson stopped believing in the reality of the August 4 incident around this time, as he revealed in a comment to Undersecretary of State George Ball.[42]

In 1964 at CIA, Cline did not have time to make a more exhaustive analysis of the evidence. From 1969 to 1973, however, he was the director of the Bureau of Intelligence and Research at the State Department. At some point during this period—he thinks it was 1970 or 1971—he looked into Tonkin Gulf again as a result of renewed public discussion of the incidents. He worked this time from a file of intercepts that was much more complete, not only in the sense that there were "hundreds and hundreds" of intercepts instead of only thirty or forty, but also in the sense that the intercepts had date-time groups on them (though for many messages these still gave only the time the intercept unit sent the message up the line, not the time it had originally been intercepted). At first, Cline looked (as in 1964) mainly at the timing of the messages. Later his attention shifted to their content; he realized that the events they described did not fit what was supposed to have happened on August 4. In the end, he reached the "firm conclusion" that the communications intercepts that had been cited as evidence for the August 4 incident all referred in fact to the August 2 incident. "I became very sure that that attack [the one on August 4] did not take place."

In 1968, Secretary of Defense McNamara presented to the Senate Foreign Relations Committee summaries of four intercepted messages; he said that they proved the reality of the August 4 incident. The first and second of these have already been discussed in Chapter 6 ("An Imminent Threat").

McNamara summarized the third message as "indicating that the Swatow boats reported an enemy aircraft falling and enemy vessel wounded."[43] This author's Freedom of Information Act request to NSA for the texts of the messages McNamara had cited produced the following sanitized report: "At 041554Z [2254G on August 4] Swatow class PGM T-142 . . . to My Duc (19-52-45N 105-57E) . . . enemy aircraft was observed falling in . . . sea. Enemy vessel perhaps wounded."[44] The time mentioned in the report (probably the time the message had been intercepted) was in the middle of the period of apparent combat on August 4, but the location mentioned, My Duc, was more than a hundred miles away, on the coast of North Vietnam, a few miles from the places where the three torpedo boats had reached shore after the battle on August 2. It seems likely that T-142 had gone to assist the damaged torpedo boats and was still in that area on the night of August 4, sending information to higher headquarters about the results of the August 2 battle.

McNamara described a final message as "reporting that they had shot down two planes and sacrificed two ships, and adding further details of the engagement."[45] The text that follows was furnished by NSA. All words omitted were withheld by NSA; asterisks are used to represent letters that were illegible in the copy of the document furnished by NSA; and the material in brackets represents this author's interpretations of illegible or garbled sections:

> DRV entity . . . losses . . . two enemy aircraft shot down.
>   . . . *hoto own [shot down?] two enemy planes in the battle area. And one other plane was damaged . . . sacrificed t** [two?] ships . . . the restaretokay [rest are okay] . . . are starting out on the hunt. . . . Enemy ship . . . have been damaged.[46]

The message had been intercepted at 2259G on August 4. Although it looked like something that would have been sent from an operating unit to a headquarters, NSA said that it had been sent from North Vietnamese Naval Headquarters in Haiphong to an operating unit in the field.[47]

James Stockdale has analyzed the very close resemblance between the description of the shooting down of the two planes and what the North Vietnamese believed had happened on August 2.[48] The apparent statement that two ships had been sacrificed does not fit the battle of August 2, when no ships were lost, but neither does it fit the U.S. Navy's account of the incident on the night of August 4, in which the *Turner Joy* is supposed to have sunk two North Vietnamese vessels, the first at 2228G and the second at 2304G. It is hard to see how the author of the message, in Haiphong, could have learned even about the first of these fast enough to be reporting it in this message; certainly he could not have been reporting the second, which would not yet have taken place. Also, the statement about the rest being okay is the sort of thing one says after a battle, not during the shooting. The idea that a damaged American ship or ships had been seen is odd and the idea of two planes being shot down is even more so, on a totally black night that would have given the light, optically aimed guns of torpedo boats essentially no chance of hitting aircraft. On the other hand, the muzzle flashes of a futile attempt to do so should have stood out like beacons.

This intercepted message was the subject of not just one U.S. intelligence report, but two. The longer of the two, quoted above, was furnished to the author by NSA. There was also a shorter one, which included the shooting down of the two planes and the phrase about starting out on the hunt, but not the loss of the two ships.[49] This is extremely odd; the loss of two ships might have been expected to be too important to be omitted from any report of the intercept. The fact that the longer version has at various times not been found in two different files of the major intercepts in connection with Tonkin Gulf, each of which should have contained it, is also curious.

President Johnson's memoirs provide a possible resolution to the anomalies. Johnson said of an unspecified intercept, "The North Vietnamese skipper reported that his unit had 'sacrificed two comrades.' Our experts said this meant either two enemy boats or two men in the attack group."[50] Only the second interpretation is tenable. A Vietnamese Communist reference to sacrifice of two comrades (*hai dong chi hy sinh* or possibly *hai dong chi bi hy sinh*) would definitely mean that two men had been killed; it would not mean that two vessels had been sunk.

The following hypothetical reconstruction of events cannot be proved, but it makes sense: the message was a description of the battle of August 2, and it said that two comrades—two men on one of the torpedo boats—had been sacrificed. The first U.S. report of the intercept misinterpreted this as a statement that two boats had been sacrificed. Someone realized a few hours later that this might have been an error, and issued a second report, with the questionable statement about the sacrifice omitted. Copies of the earlier version were not included when some of the files on Tonkin Gulf were being put together, on the grounds that that version had been superseded.

It is hard to be sure which of the intercepts that McNamara discussed specified the name of the commander—Khoai—in whatever action it described.[51] This was presumably Le Duy Khoai, who had, according to the People's Navy, commanded the attack on the *Maddox* on August 2.

It cannot properly be argued that no enemy attack could have been carried out against the *Maddox* without the comvan having picked up communications among the enemy vessels. The comvan did not have that good an intercept capability, especially on the frequencies that torpedo boats used for voice communication with one another at relatively close ranges. The comvan had not picked up any messages from one PT boat to another during the attack of August 2, though there were messages being sent between those vessels. The airwaves were so crowded with the communications of the various American vessels and aircraft that the comvan was not able to pick any North Vietnamese messages out of the noise on August 2, and with even more American communications on the night of August 4, the comvan could easily have missed some North Vietnamese messages. But if one assumes that the radar targets reported by the destroyers really were North Vietnamese torpedo boats, they would have been far enough from shore so that reports to their superiors would have had to go by the HF wavelengths on which American monitoring capabilities were much better. Many of them were far enough apart that they would have had to communicate with one another by HF. Given this fact and the combined capabilities of the various American listening posts, there is ample justification for Gerrell Moore's evaluation: "I can't believe that somebody wouldn't have picked up something."[52]

Daylight Searches

Shortly after dawn, the U.S. Navy conducted a thorough aerial reconnaissance of the area where the incident had supposedly occurred. A group of two

F-8s, two A-4s, and one tanker for in-flight refueling, which landed back on the *Ticonderoga* at about 0800H, had apparently been involved in this search; some other unspecified aircraft apparently did not return until 1100H.[53] No signs of battle were found. It should be borne in mind that the torpedo boats on August 4 are supposed to have sunk as a result of explosions—either detonating shells from the *Turner Joy* or secondary explosions of fuel tanks or torpedo war-heads—that took place while the boats were on the surface. These should have broken loose many fragments and small objects. Lieutenant James Bartholo-mew was the Targeting and Reconnaissance Officer of the Seventh Fleet staff. He feels that the reconnaissance that was conducted would "definitely" have found wreckage or oil slicks if the destroyers had in fact sunk any PT boats there during the previous night.[54]

The two destroyers also went back later that day and searched for debris in the area of the supposed incident; the available records support Barry's description of this search as "cursory," and it was over by 1349H. Nothing was found. Schaperjahn recalls that the official explanation was that North Vietnamese fishing boats must have come out and cleaned up the debris.[55]

DRV Public Statements

The DRV was openly proud of having driven the *Maddox* away from the coast in the first incident, on the afternoon of August 2. For a few days, perhaps wishing to avoid inflaming the situation, Hanoi announced publicly only that the torpedo boats had chased the *Maddox* out of Vietnamese territorial waters, without saying that they had actually fired on the American vessel. After the U.S. bombing raids of August 5, however (see below), Hanoi said clearly that the boats had fired on the destroyer on August 2. Two torpedo tubes were on display for several years in a Hanoi museum, with a label reading:

TORPEDO LAUNCHING TUBE
Part of a torpedo boat of the 135th Naval Section which successfully chased away the US Maddox destroyer August 2nd 1964

Within hours after learning that the Americans were claiming there had been a second incident, the DRV issued a public denial of having attacked the Ameri-can destroyers on the night of August 4.[56] The DRV (and after 1976 its successor, the Socialist Republic of Vietnam) have stuck by this denial ever since.

Some authors suggest that Hanoi has admitted attacking the U.S. destroyers on the night of August 4. A book by Douglas Pike presents quotes from a PAVN official history in such a way as to make these quotes appear as an admission:

Today . . . PAVN Navy's anniversary, or "tradition day," is listed as 5 August 1964, the date of the Tonkin Gulf incident, "when one of our torpedo squadrons chased the destroyer USS *Maddox* from our coastal waters, our first victory over the U.S. Navy." . . .

The Tonkin Gulf naval clashes were on the nights of August 2/3 and 4/5; the second of these was chosen as the anniversary date apparently because that was the night "our torpedo squadrons chased the destroyer Maddox from our coastal waters," as the citation here puts it. If the Gulf of Tonkin Incident is a myth invented by the Pentagon, as some revisionist historians claim, the PAVN Navy is now part of the conspiracy.[57]

The extent to which Pike misrepresents his source can be seen if the words he quoted are shown in their original context:

On 2 August 1964 one of our torpedo squadrons chased the destroyer Maddox from our coastal waters, which is regarded as our first victory over the U.S. Navy. On 5 August 8 [*sic*] our People's Navy, along with the air-defense forces and people of Song Gianh, Cua Hoi, Lach Truong, and Hon Gai defeated the U.S. Air Force in a very glorious battle, shooting down many airplanes, capturing pilots, and defeating the first bombing raid by the U.S. Air Force in the North of our country.

For that reason, 5 August 1964 is regarded as the tradition day of the Vietnamese People's Navy.[58]

What the history Pike was misquoting really said about the incident of the night of August 4–5 was that the Johnson administration had "invented a story" of a North Vietnamese attack on U.S. warships.[59]

Summing Up

The evidence that is available on the American side does not support the Vietnamese charge that the Johnson administration knowingly faked the incident of August 4 in order to create an excuse to escalate the war, although the Vietnamese can hardly be blamed for making the accusation. If one considers only the evidence available to the Vietnamese, the case for a deliberate American plot appears very convincing.

Several participants in the incident who contend that there really was a PT boat attack on the night of August 4 have summarized for the author the reasons for their belief.

John Barry firmly believes that his ship actually was attacked by torpedo boats. He did not have much part in the later portions of the action, because CIC was giving the radar targets to Director 52 at the rear of the ship, rather than to his director. He did see what looked like secondary explosions from one of the later targets fired upon by the destroyer. His belief is based to a large extent, however, on the events involving skunk "V-1," which occurred at the beginning of the action "when minds were not yet confused." The thin white line that he saw in the water came from a direction compatible with the idea that it was the wake of a torpedo fired by the contact that had been tracked by both surface-search and fire-control radar of his destroyer, although he can no longer recall whether his own director—Director 51—tracked it. He saw what appeared to be secondary explosions when this target was fired upon by the aft guns.[60]

While the attack was going on, Ensign Douglas Smith was completely convinced, on the basis of what he could see on his radar screen, that the *Turner Joy* was under PT boat attack. Despite contrary evidence of which he has become aware since, he is still inclined to believe in the reality of the attack. He gave this author a written statement containing the following list of reasons for his view:

—The evidence of the radar screen returns was convincing then, as it is now.
—Even more convincing was the consistent lockons achieved; "phantoms" should not have resulted in consistent lockons and tracking.
—Various eyewitness reports speak of smoke, flashes of light and silhouettes. These came from a variety of sources and different locations. Especially convincing is the "Torpedo Report" by Ltjg. Barry.
—We know that the PT boats were in the area, and prepared to come out, from the action against *Maddox* on 2 Aug.
—The Intel unit aboard *Maddox* had warned of a possible attack—or at least of activity.
—The fact that no positive visual sightings occurred is curious, but not conclusive. Other than documentary evidence (from either side) to the contrary, which I am not aware of, there is nothing but hearsay and suppositions indicating that the attack did not occur.[61]

Richard Bacino is convinced, to this day, that there were PT boats near the *Turner Joy* on the night of August 4. The light he saw is the main reason for his belief. As he puts it, "Something was there. It was obvious as Hell."[62]

The case has been put just as strongly for the other side, however, by men who were also present at the incident. There are slightly more doubters than believers among those with whom this author has spoken. When the documentary evidence is added, the weight of the evidence is overwhelming: no attack occurred. There exist rational explanations of how all the evidence of an attack could exist without there having been an attack. There do not exist rational explanations of how all the evidence of no attack could exist if there had in fact been an attack.

The only major category of evidence that seriously tended to support the idea of an attack was naked-eye sightings from the destroyers. The radar evidence was at best very ambiguous. The sonar evidence was negative. The evidence from aerial photography was negative. The reports of the pilots—both those who were over the destroyers during the night, and those who searched for wreckage and oil slicks the following morning—were very powerfully negative.

The electronics intelligence evidence—the lack of detections of enemy radar use, or convincing communications intercepts—was negative. The results of interrogations of DRV naval personnel captured during the next few years were very powerfully negative.

The story of the incident of August 4 as it is usually given indicates that a number of North Vietnamese vessels stretched their attack out for two hours, when their armament was such that they could have fired in the first twenty minutes everything they had that was capable of harming a destroyer. All of them had the ability to remain invisible to the radar of the destroyers for large portions of the time that they spent within five miles of those destroyers. Their conspicuous phosphorescent wakes somehow remained invisible to the planes overhead. They kept track of the weaving destroyers and maintained their attack, in bad weather and extreme darkness, without either using active radar or communicating with one another by radio to an extent that would allow this to be detected by American listeners—this despite the fact that the shells falling on them from the *Turner Joy* could have left them in no doubt that the American radar had them spotted and that trying to hide by maintaining radar and radio silence was futile. They suffered heavy losses, but somehow the rest of the very small DRV Navy never heard (to judge by later interrogations of prisoners) that the incident had ever happened at all.

The reports of tired men under stress who, while looking out into a dark night that they were convinced hid attacking PT boats, thought that they had glimpsed those PT boats or evidence of their presence, cannot begin to counterbalance the impossibility of this version of events.

Donald Hegrat says he firmly believes that no PT boats were near the destroyers while he was in the area. He was not, however, among the pilots who were already over the destroyers when skunks "V" and "V-1" appeared on the radar screens. The lack of PT boats when he was over the destroyers does not prove that there had not been one or more PT boats near the destroyers earlier, touching off the incident and then departing before Hegrat arrived on the scene. He does not say he believes this is what occurred, but he thinks the possibility should at least be considered.

Douglas Smith has suggested something similar: "What is quite possible, if not perhaps most plausible, is that the boats were indeed in the Gulf—perhaps at long range—and that they made a half-hearted foray to attack, were driven away by the early gunfire (and the relative hopelessness of a night attack in the dark at high speeds), and that the ships continued to prosecute an attack that never really developed."[63]

This approach really provides the best argument that a genuine torpedo boat attack occurred. One key to Herrick's belief for the next few years, that there probably had been an attack, was based on the first apparent torpedo run. The behavior of the supposed attacking vessel was rational; it is said to have approached the destroyers, launched one or two torpedoes, and then departed at high speed. The radar of each destroyer showed what appeared to be a vessel making a torpedo attack from the east (even if not at the same exact location or at the same speed), giving at least a partial consistency to the incident. Several sources state that the *Turner Joy*'s radar tracked this vessel as a very firm, clear target. The sonar report of the torpedo it supposedly fired was taken seriously, since Herrick reported that the *Maddox* at that time had not yet begun the high-speed maneuvers that later caused so many spurious torpedo reports. Also, the visual sighting of the torpedo by men on the *Turner Joy* was among the more convincing of the visual reports.

By assuming that this initial attack by a single vessel really did occur, and that only the later portions of the supposed battle were figments of the imagination of over-excited men, one could construct a scenario that makes some kind of sense. It still is not probable. Much of the supposed evidence for the incident of August 4 applies only to the impossible scenario of the two-hour-long, multi-vessel attack. If this is subtracted, the evidence for the single attack at the beginning is not adequate to counterbalance the evidence that there was not an attack at the beginning. The conditions made wakes luminous in the darkness and gave aircraft (above the spray that the wind created at surface level) reasonably good visibility. James Stockdale, who *was* overhead at the time skunks "V" and "V-1" were detected, has stated very specifically that if a torpedo boat had made a long, straight run toward the destroyers at high speed, as reported by the ships' radar, he would have seen it. He did not.[64]

Some lines of argument that might have the ability to strengthen one portion of the evidence for a genuine attack weaken another portion. Thus the lack of intercepts of radio messages between the attacking PT boats could be partially explained by the hypothesis that the number of attacking boats was smaller than is usually supposed, but this would imply that some of what appeared on the radar to be attacking vessels were not; the credibility of all the radar evidence would be seriously reduced.

The only way to give even a shred of plausibility to the idea that PT boats could have sunk immediately after the detonation of proximity-fused shells a few feet away is to suppose that the shell fragments set off powerful secondary explosions of the fuel tanks, deck gun ammunition, or torpedo warheads aboard the PT boats, which blew them apart. This supposition makes the failure of the aerial search the following morning to find any oil slicks or wreckage twice as implausible.

If we suppose that there were in fact attacking vessels but that none were really sunk by gunfire from the destroyers, we resolve the difficulty of the lack of debris, and partially resolve the difficulty of the interrogation reports (since of the twenty prisoners whose interrogations were summarized earlier in this chapter, only two were in positions where they could not have failed to know about a combat incident involving torpedo boats even if no vessels were sunk in the incident), but we accentuate the problem of explaining why radar targets kept vanishing from the *Turner Joy*'s radar screens at close range.

Not all the evidence was available in 1964, and analysis even of the available data took time. Ray Cline later commented that in the immediate aftermath of the supposed incident he had doubts as to its reality, but that it took days before the actual flaws in the evidence became apparent.[65] Stockdale had reported immediately after his flight on the night of August 4 that he had seen no enemy boats; he was told that his report would go immediately to Washington, and later accounts indicate that it did so. However, Washington apparently waited until August 11 to follow this up by questioning him further.[66]

Herrick, faced with evidence both contradictory and incomplete, decided on the morning of August 5, 1964, that he could not be certain what had or had not happened the previous night. He has remained uncertain for most of the following years. He eventually concluded, however, that it was *unlikely* that any torpedoes were fired at any time on the night of August 4, unlikely that the radar image making the supposed first torpedo run was genuine, unlikely in fact that any enemy vessel came within 10,000 yards of the *Maddox* on that night.[67] Another officer of the *Maddox*, who also doubts that there was any attack on the destroyers that night, has explained that part of the reason for his present disbelief lies in experiences he had after the Tonkin Gulf incidents, which undermined his belief in what had seemed at the time good evidence. These experiences included seeing a very convincing spurious image on a radar set at close range in broad daylight, when he could verify by naked eye that there was no vessel where the radar showed one. On another occasion he also saw a porpoise leave a phosphorescent wake remarkably like that of a torpedo.[68]

Retaliation

At 0120H, about a half hour after the shooting ended, Captain Herrick asked the *Turner Joy*, "Did you actually see any craft?" and requested all positive information available.[1] The *Turner Joy*'s reply is not available, but at 0154H the *Maddox* informed Washington, "*Joy* also reports no actual visual sightings." Up to this time, however, there had been no opportunity for a systematic effort aboard the *Turner Joy* to gather reports of visual sightings; the destroyer was at General Quarters until about 0150H. Once the two destroyers had secured from General Quarters and the senior officers could begin questioning their crews, there would be reports of visual sightings aboard both ships.

Higher levels were continually pressing for information and evidence. For the first several hours, what Washington received came from the *Maddox*, which was sending and receiving almost continuously. The first known report sent directly by the *Turner Joy* went out at 0710H.

Commander Bryce Inman saw the message files a few days later. He has noted that communications discipline in the chain of command above the two destroyers had completely broken down in the hours following the incident. People at every level up to (and as best Inman can recall, including) the secretary of defense had addressed questions directly to the destroyers, instead of waiting for reports to come up the chain of command: "Everybody and his dog, right up the line."[2] Admiral Thomas Moorer, who was commanding the Pacific Fleet at the time, has described the way the communications system became jammed: "We were getting messages from Washington faster than we could decode them. Mr. McNamara would get impatient and send a message out in the highest classification asking what the hell happened to the other message. Our policy was that you always decode the one that came in last, just in case the situation had changed. So they never caught up."[3]

What did not show in the messages was the pressure McNamara himself was under. McGeorge Bundy has said that President Johnson decided at an early hour on August 4—from his description of the timing, this might even have been before the shooting started, when all Johnson had were reports that the destroyers might be attacked—to use the incident as an occasion to get Congress to pass what was to become known as the Tonkin Gulf Resolution. Bundy suggested taking a little more time to consider the matter, but Johnson (who Bundy believes had already discussed the matter with the chairman of the Senate Armed Services Committee) had made up his mind. He had done so without first asking whether it was absolutely certain that an attack had really occurred. "And we spent the rest of the day catching up with that," when that issue did arise. The reason question piled on question until the communications system overloaded was that McNamara was "asking on behalf of a president who had already committed himself to having a resolution and a speech and had the air time."[4]

Observing from Afar

Officers in the western Pacific, following the action in the gulf by radio, did not find the picture of enemy attack very convincing. James Bartholemew, for example, the intelligence officer on duty in the war room of the Seventh Fleet that night, says that he concluded while the supposed incident was still in progress that it was not genuine. Most of the other officers present, including Admiral Roy Johnson, the commander of the Seventh Fleet, seemed to share his opinion. He recalls that at one point, Admiral Johnson asked him how many torpedoes the *Maddox* had reported. Bartholomew does not now recall his reply—perhaps it was twenty-two, the total that was reported at 0042H—but from the look Admiral Johnson gave him, he was sure he shared his reaction: this was impossible.[5] Bartholomew felt the evidence showed clearly enough that the destroyers had not been attacked that he assumed Washington was probably aware there had not been an attack.

Admiral Johnson had not seriously considered the idea that the North Vietnamese would try to attack the DeSoto patrol a second time, after having been badly defeated when they tried to do so on August 2. He was "dumbfounded" by the report on the night of August 4 that they were trying again.

Aboard his flagship *Oklahoma City* on the night of August 4, getting information by radio from the two destroyers, Admiral Johnson could not tell whether an attack was actually occurring or not. The blips on the radar of the destroyers could have been radar ghosts. His recollection is that the pilots flying over the destroyers saw no indication of hostile vessels, and that there were no communications intercepts indicating the presence of hostile vessels.

During the hours following the incident, there were repeated queries from Washington, and from CINCPAC (Admiral Sharp) in Honolulu, asking whether there had actually been an attack. Admiral Johnson replied that he did not know, and that it would be necessary to wait for more information. One thing complicating the situation was that the *Maddox's* radio room did not have a coding machine, and the time it took to encode and decode messages by hand on the *Maddox* delayed communications.

Eventually, CINCPAC decided to assume that there really had been an attack. Admiral Johnson does not believe that CINCPAC had real justification for this decision in the information that had been coming to him from his subordinates.[6] In his telephone conversations with the Pentagon, Admiral Sharp made it clear that he doubted some of the details in the reports from the destroyers, especially the sonar reports. He told General Burchinal at 2:08 P.M. EDT, "Whenever they get keyed up on a thing like this everything they hear on the Sonar is a torpedo."[7] Sharp said roughly the same to Secretary McNamara two hours later, adding that the report that twenty-one torpedoes had been heard was "undoubtedly" an exaggeration.[8] The intercepted North Vietnamese messages analyzed in the preceding chapter played a key role in persuading Sharp that the attack had been genuine.

Officials in Washington, faced with a stream of reports, many of them inaccurate or conflicting, were unable to get a coherent picture of what had happened in the gulf. The level of confusion is illustrated by Secretary McNamara's statement to the National Security Council early on the afternoon of August 4 that the two destroyers had been attacked by three to six PT boats, which had fired nine or ten torpedoes.[9] An absolute minimum of five torpedo boats would have been required to fire nine or ten torpedoes.

Pierce Arrow: The Decision

President Johnson developed doubts about the August 4 incident a few days later; he told Undersecretary of State George Ball, "Hell, those dumb, stupid sailors were just shooting at flying fish!"[10] There is no evidence, however, that he had such doubts on August 4, when he ordered retaliatory strikes against North Vietnam.

Robert McNamara stated publicly in late 1995 that he had become almost certain that there was no attack on August 4, and had expressed doubt about the incident years earlier in conversations with journalist Henry Trewhitt and historian Randall Woods;[11] but there is no evidence that he had such doubts at the time the retaliatory airstrikes were ordered on August 4, or even by the time he spoke to the key Senate committees on August 6. When Admiral Sharp presented the evidence from North Vietnamese communications intercepts, the question seemed closed; there is no reason to suppose that Johnson or any of his advisors started worrying again about the reality of the attack until after Ray

Cline and other intelligence officers noticed the dubiousness of the interpretation that had been placed on the intercepts.

Even if there had been doubts about the reality of the August 4 attack, the political pressure on Johnson to react as if the incident had been real would have been very strong. He was in the middle of an election campaign. His opponent, Senator Barry Goldwater, was a conservative who advocated a very hard line against Communism; Johnson was campaigning as a moderate. Two American naval vessels had reported to Washington that they had been attacked by Communist forces. If Johnson had refused to take action on the grounds that he was not sure the report had been accurate, he could not reasonably have expected to keep the story from reaching the public. If it did so, then regardless of the final outcome (if the attack turned out really to have taken place, or if it turned out not to have taken place, or if the truth could not be established either way), at least some voters would have been convinced that the attack had been genuine, that there had never been serious grounds for doubting its reality, and that Johnson had attempted to cover up a Communist attack on U.S. fighting men either out of cowardice or out of political expediency. He would surely have lost votes; with bad luck he could have lost a great many votes.

The pressures President Johnson was under were illustrated the following month, when there was another incident in the Gulf of Tonkin (see Chapter 10), very similar to that of August 4 except that the evidence of an attack seemed even weaker this time. When Johnson expressed doubt that an attack had occurred in the September incident, Secretary of State Rusk criticized him to his face for failing to support the judgment of the officers on the scene.[12]

Secretary of Defense McNamara phoned Johnson at 9:12 A.M. (Washington time) on August 4 to report that an attack on the destroyers might be about to occur.[13] Johnson asked how quickly it would be possible to conduct a retaliatory airstrike. He did not actually order one at this time, but Alexander Haig, an assistant to McNamara and Deputy Defense Secretary Cyrus Vance, later said that after this conversation (which ended before the destroyers had even detected the long-range radar contacts "N," "O," and "P"), "there was never any realistic doubt that the air raid would take place."[14] By 10:00 A.M. McNamara had convened an "action group" in his office, including officers from the Operations Branch of the Joint Staff who had worked on the "94-Target List" and brought a copy of that list with them.[15] President Johnson was also discussing the idea of retaliation with his own subordinates. One of Johnson's aides, Kenneth O'Donnell, recalled that the president "was wondering aloud as to the political repercussions and questioned me rather closely as to my political reaction to his making a military retaliation. . . . The attack on Lyndon Johnson was going to come from the right and the hawks, and he must not allow them to accuse him of vacillating or being an indecisive leader."[16] Speaking to congressional leaders a few hours later, President Johnson described the option of not retaliating with the phrase, "We can tuck our tails and run. . . ."[17]

Admiral Moorer, commander of the Pacific fleet, reacted to the incident with a determination to sink the vessels that had actually participated in it. At approximately the time the shooting ended, he ordered: "Imperative that all NVN patrol craft which participated in tonight's action be destroyed. . . . At earliest feasible time, launch armed recce [reconnaissance] to attack and destroy positively identified NVN PT boats and Swatows along probable routes of retirement from tonight's action and in the DeSoto Patrol area. . . . Aircraft remain three repeat three miles from NVN coastline and twenty repeat twenty miles from Hainan."[18]

This was a fairly daring plan. The limit of only twenty miles on approaches to Hainan implied that the aircraft were to search areas between the scene of the incident and China, not just areas between the scene of the incident and Vietnam, and aircraft could not realistically have been expected to distinguish Chinese from North Vietnamese PT boats or Swatows.

Admiral Sharp and his superiors in Washington, meanwhile, were thinking of a different pattern of retaliation. Sharp was on the phone to General Burchinal, Director of the Joint Staff in the Pentagon, discussing the possibility of retaliatory airstrikes about twenty minutes after the shooting started in the Gulf of Tonkin. Twenty minutes after that, in another call, Sharp suggested that U.S. aircraft conduct an armed reconnaissance along the coast of North Vietnam, attacking any North Vietnamese naval vessels they could find. Burchinal said that actions stronger than this were being considered in Washington.[19]

There was discussion for a while of the possibility of mining North Vietnamese harbors, and at about 10:45 A.M. EDT an "action group" meeting in the office of the secretary of defense decided to have one hundred mines flown to the *Ticonderoga* from the Philippines. This was an unattractive option because of the time it would take to get mines out of storage, transport them to the aircraft carrier, and get ready to begin dropping them in North Vietnamese waters. The officers in the Pentagon preferred instant retaliation. But they were not sure how long it would take to get President Johnson to authorize action against North Vietnam. If the mines were ready by the time the president authorized retaliation, then mining might be a very appropriate form for that retaliation to take.[20]

Shortly after the shooting stopped in the Gulf of Tonkin, a consensus emerged among U.S. officials that airstrikes should be carried out against DRV naval forces, plus a petroleum storage facility at Vinh. Other types of targets, including airfields, industrial complexes, and bridges, had been considered but rejected. It took some time to settle on a precise list of targets. In addition to the ones that finally were hit, the PT boat base the Americans called Port Wallut, and the

Vietnamese called Van Hoa, had been considered until quite late in the planning process. It was finally dropped from the target list, partly because of weather problems and partly because it was uncomfortably close to China.

The American airstrikes were often discussed as if they were directed against PT boat bases, but in fact the bases hit were primarily Swatow bases; Port Wallut, the one finally dropped from the target list, was the place DRV torpedo boats were based. The only PT boats actually attacked in the U.S. airstrikes were those temporarily stationed elsewhere. These definitely included T-333 and T-336, which had remained in the vicinity of Lach Truong (Lach Chao, Loc Chao), not far north of Hon Me, since their combat against the *Maddox* on August 2. They were found and attacked there by Skyhawks from the *Constellation*. The report that aerial photography on August 5 showed three PT boats at Quang Khe[21] may be correct, but reports indicating that both PT boats and Swatows (different reports vary as to the exact numbers) were attacked at Hon Gay seem to have been mistaken. What seems to have happened is that U.S. pilots went in thinking only of two types of DRV vessels, the smaller PT boats and the larger Swatows. When they found at Hon Gay some Swatows and one still larger vessel, a Soviet-built submarine chaser of the S.O.I. class, they thought the Swatows were PTs and the sub-chaser was a Swatow.

Given the confused nature of the strike planning, it is uncertain how many of the men who dropped Port Wallut from the target list knew that this was the main base for DRV PT boats. Even in a study written in the Pentagon months later, it is not Port Wallut but Phuc Loi, the port adjacent to the town of Vinh, that is specifically identified as a "PT base."[22] This author has found no evidence that Phuc Loi was ever a base for PT boats.

There also may have been confusion over whether the strikes at DRV naval bases were to hit naval vessels only, or also hit anti-aircraft guns and other targets on shore. Initial discussions among senior military officers had presumed that at least some shore targets would be hit at these bases.[23] The Joint Chiefs of Staff completed a proposal at about 1:25 P.M. calling for attacks on both vessels and base facilities, at three DRV bases, and also destruction of the petroleum storage facility at Vinh. McNamara discussed this with President Johnson, who allowed the strike on the storage facility at Vinh and expanded the list of naval bases targeted from three to five but ordered that only vessels be hit at those bases—not base facilities. By 3:25 P.M., Secretary McNamara had discussed this with the Joint Chiefs.[24] At 4:35 P.M., Admiral Sharp passed the order to Admiral Moorer, commander of the Pacific Fleet, that the planes were to take "boats repeat boats as targets." Moorer had already instructed the Seventh Fleet, "It is emphasized that targets are boats only (at piers and at sea) plus Vinh oil storage."[25] At 6:07 P.M., however, Admiral Sharp and General Burchinal agreed that any anti-aircraft guns in a position to interfere with the attacks would be taken out.[26]

The Pierce Arrow Airstrikes

The retaliatory airstrikes of August 5, codenamed "Pierce Arrow," involved 64 sorties by carrier-based aircraft. Two planes were lost. (The DRV at first claimed to have shot down five, later increasing the claim to eight.)

There was a great deal of confusion in communications between Washington and the aircraft carriers off Vietnam. Plans for airstrikes were repeatedly modified in a fashion that must have made it very difficult to keep track of the changes, especially since many of the people involved were suffering from lack of sleep. Transmission of "flash" messages became much slower than usual, because there were so many such messages that the code clerks were unable to handle all of them promptly. Senior people sometimes got around the bottleneck by talking directly, over insecure telephone lines, using euphemisms in an effort to deceive any possible eavesdroppers. Thus when the cancellation of the strike on Port Wallut was being discussed, it was called "the one in the North."

A comparatively minor result of the confusion was that Washington did not understand exactly what targets were being struck. Secretary of Defense McNamara at first believed that there had been no attempt to attack anti-aircraft batteries—that the only targets had been vessels of the North Vietnamese navy, and petroleum storage tanks. When he realized that there had been some strikes against anti-aircraft batteries, he shifted to the other extreme and exaggerated the extent to which strikes had been made against these and other land targets.[27] From Secretary McNamara's description August 6, one might have thought that the strikes had been made primarily against land targets; he referred to strikes "against the bases from which these boats had come, against the boats themselves, and against certain support facilities, particularly a petroleum depot at Vinh."[28]

Much more important was the failure of communication over timing. The logs of telephone calls between Secretary McNamara, Admiral Sharp, and General Burchinal, during what was in Washington the evening of August 4 and in the Gulf of Tonkin the morning of August 5, show McNamara and Burchinal asking with increasing urgency whether the airstrikes had begun yet. The planes had been supposed to hit their targets at about 0900H (9:00 P.M. in Washington); the first of them did not actually do so until more than four hours later.

The delay has sometimes been attributed to the government's desire to make an aerial search of the Gulf of Tonkin in daylight, and find some debris from sunken PT boats to provide positive proof that PT boats had actually been present during the incident of the previous night. A desire for proof of attack probably was a factor in delaying Washington's approval of the strike until 0519H. At 0440H, General Burchinal told Admiral Sharp that there would be "'No go' till attack confirmed."[29] The delay in Washington's approval, however, had little if any effect on the actual timing of the strike, since the JCS order to execute the strike was sent so long before either the *Ticonderoga* or the *Constellation* was ready to launch that even after delays in transmission, it seems to have reached both carriers in plenty of time. A chronology probably prepared by the NSC staff states that the *Ticonderoga* actually received the strike execute message at 0722H, and the *Constellation* at 0750H.[30] The *Constellation*, which had only sailed from Hong Kong after the August 2 incident, was still racing westward, trying to get within a reasonable distance of the Vietnamese coast. The *Ticonderoga* was in position but was short of attack planes, so more were being flown in from the Philippines.[31]

At 6:07 P.M. EDT, Sharp said he expected the strikes to have been accomplished, with planes departing the target areas, by 9:00 P.M. EDT. General Wheeler, Chairman of the Joint Chiefs of Staff, telephoned Burchinal from the Cabinet Room of the White House at 8:05 P.M. Wheeler said he wanted to know as soon as word arrived that the aircraft had been launched. At 8:39 P.M., McNamara called Sharp and asked whether the launch had occurred yet; Sharp said it probably had, but he was not sure. McNamara reminded Sharp that "the President has to make a statement to the people and I am holding him back from making it, but we're forty minutes past the time I told him we would launch." At 9:09 P.M., Sharp told McNamara that the launch had not occurred, and would not occur for another fifty minutes; "they couldn't make the time." McNamara responded, "Oh, my God."[32]

The problem was that McNamara, and President Johnson, considered it important that the president announce the airstrikes to the American people on television, and for this to have its proper effect it had to occur before too large a proportion of the American public had gone to bed. Burchinal and Sharp had agreed at 6:07 P.M. that there would be no public announcement before the American planes were "off target," apparently meaning on their way home after making their attacks.[33] The full National Security Council, meeting a few minutes later, decided that there would be no public announcement until the planes were over their targets.[34] What Sharp told McNamara at 9:09 P.M., however, implied that it would be 11:00 P.M. on the east coast of the United States by the time the planes reached their targets. McNamara suggested that the enemy would be alerted as soon as the planes were launched, so it might not be necessary to hold the announcement until the planes actually reached their targets. Sharp was not happy with this idea. He seemed to think that the planes would be picked up on both Chinese and DRV radar as soon as they took off (this certainly overestimated the range of DRV radar, and perhaps also that of Chinese radar). But he told McNamara clearly, twice, that picking up the planes on radar would not tell the enemy where those planes were going.[35]

At 10:26 P.M., McNamara called Sharp again. Sharp said that he was sure the *Ticonderoga* had launched at 10:00 P.M., but he did not have actual confirmation. He said that the *Constellation* would not be able to begin launching until

1:00 A.M., and would not have aircraft over targets until after 3:00 A.M. McNamara again said, "My God."[36]

Sharp was mistaken—the *Ticonderoga* had been nowhere near ready to launch at 10:00 P.M. (1000H)—but soon after this telephone conversation, a quirk of fate intervened. The effort to get a large number of planes fueled, loaded with bombs, and ready for takeoff might have caused a certain degree of congestion on the *Ticonderoga*'s deck at the best of times; the landing of the planes that had been searching without success for any debris or oil slicks from sunken PT boats, and the process of landing the aircraft coming in from the Philippines, made matters worse. To cut down this congestion, four A1H Skyraiders, scheduled to participate in the airstrike on Vinh, were launched simply to get them out of the way, at a time that has variously been reported as 1043H or 1049H, and ordered to orbit in the vicinity of the carrier. Their fuel endurance was much greater than that of the jets making up the majority of the strike force; they could afford to loiter in the air for an hour or so while waiting for word that it was time to set out for their targets.

At 11:20 P.M. EDT, Sharp telephoned McNamara again and told him that planes had launched at 10:43.[37] Although Sharp also said the planes would not be over their targets for another one hour and fifty minutes, McNamara decided it had been long enough since the launch that he could assume the North Vietnamese had realized what was coming at them, and that the president could go on radio and television to make the long-delayed announcement.

It is plain from the record that Secretary McNamara did not have a clear picture of what was happening on the far side of the Pacific. The president probably knew considerably less. One tends to assume that when the U.S. armed forces go into combat the president is able at least briefly to focus his entire attention on the crisis. That was not the case on the evening of August 4. During the hours while he was waiting for word that the American airstrike had begun, President Johnson was informed that the bodies of three murdered civil rights workers had just been found in Mississippi. This was a very touchy situation. Racial violence—both attacks by whites against blacks in Mississippi (of which the triple murder was an outgrowth) and riots by blacks in Detroit in late July, in the course of which forty-three people had died—seemed likely to have a significant impact on the 1964 presidential race, and President Johnson would have had to devote some genuine attention to the latest news from Mississippi. The first word he got was a phone call from the FBI at 8:01 P.M. He spoke with the governor of Mississippi at 9:35, and with the FBI again at 9:40.[38]

The four Skyraiders circled the *Ticonderoga* for about an hour. They started for their target, the petroleum storage facility at Vinh, at 1135H.[39] The carrier was at that time at about the latitude of Danang, well south of the seventeenth parallel (the line separating North from South Vietnam). This was over 100 miles from the nearest Chinese territory, and about 200 miles from the nearest point in North Vietnam. Computing the precise time at which the four Sky-raiders crossed the seventeenth parallel would require better data than this author has been able to find, but they surely did not do so before 1145H, and probably not before 1150H. According to a time chart apparently prepared by NSC staff, the four Skyraiders entered the area of DRV radar coverage at 1212H. The *Ticonderoga* began launching a dozen jets, slated to attack the petroleum storage facility and also DRV patrol boats and torpedo boats nearby, at 1216H (12:16 A.M. of August 5 in Washington); these entered what the United States believed to be the area of DRV radar coverage at 1232H.[40]

The first American planes actually to reach their targets were six F-8s sent to attack DRV vessels at Quang Khe. They had taken off from the *Ticonderoga* later than the jets attacking Vinh, and penetrated DRV radar coverage later, but because Quang Khe was well to the south of Vinh, and thus closer to the carrier, they were able to begin their attacks at 1315H;[41] the four Skyraiders and twelve jets attacking Vinh did not commence their attack until about 1325H.[42]

The *Constellation* began launching a first wave of strike aircraft at 1300H and a second, larger wave at 1430H. These aircraft did not reach DRV airspace until long after the strikes by the *Ticonderoga*'s aircraft had begun.[43]

President Johnson went on television at 11:37 P.M. EDT to announce U.S. airstrikes against "gunboats and certain supporting facilities in North Viet-Nam." At this time, the only planes in the air were the four Skyraiders heading for the petroleum storage facility. No planes targeted on naval vessels took off until more than half an hour after Johnson announced those attacks; no attacks were actually made against any target until an hour and a half after Johnson's announcement. This was enough time to give the DRV a useful degree of advance warning. The public announcement that Johnson would be going on television that evening, released even earlier,[44] might have been an adequate clue for an alert observer.

Early in a press conference beginning at 12:02 A.M., McNamara said, "U.S. naval aircraft . . . have already conducted air strikes against the North Vietnamese bases from which these PT boats have operated."[45] This was odd phrasing, since Sharp had told him quite clearly that the strike aircraft would not yet have reached their targets by this time. In McNamara's defense, it must be said that he may have been suffering from a certain degree of fatigue and confusion. In the same press conference, he described the two-hour incident on the night of August 4 as having lasted about three and a half hours.

Four years later he told a Senate committee that the launch had been at about 10:00 P.M., Washington time.[46]

Secretary McNamara tried to justify the way strikes on different targets had occurred at different times by saying that the United States had expected that enemy radar would pick up the aircraft at the time of their launch from the carriers, and that this turned out actually to have occurred. The best that could be done to maximize surprise, therefore, had been to have simultaneous launches from both carriers rather than to arrange for simultaneous arrival at different targets. The planes from the *Constellation* had to fly farther than those from the *Ticonderoga* and therefore arrived at their targets later.[47]

McNamara's suggestion that the two aircraft carriers launched at approximately the same time is false. If one interprets "enemy radar" to include Chinese radar on Hainan, it is possible that the American aircraft were picked up on radar immediately after launch, but given what is known about communications linkages in the area, it seems unlikely that Chinese radar operators would have notified Hanoi of every aircraft that appeared on their screens, and virtually certain that any message they did send would have suffered serious delays in transmission.

Early in September President Johnson was assured that he had not tipped off the attack; the "North Vietnamese *did* have the aircraft on their screens" before he spoke.[48] This statement was apparently based on a chronology prepared in the Department of Defense, dated August 28, 1964, and still classified today because it contained information from NSA.[49] This author suspects that when the chronology is finally declassified, it will turn out to be mistaken; reports on Tonkin Gulf prepared in the Department of Defense in this period contain numerous errors in time zone conversions.

Even if we were to assume that the DRV had both total radar coverage and perfect communications, however, so that air defense officers knew the movements of all aircraft at all times, the suggestion that this would have told them that an American airstrike was coming, by the time of President Johnson's announcement, would remain ludicrous. Aircraft carriers launch aircraft, frequently, as a part of normal peacetime operations. The *Constellation*'s deck log indicates that in the six hours before the carrier began launching aircraft for the strike against North Vietnam, fourteen aircraft had been launched for other purposes. Comparable figures for the *Ticonderoga* are not available, but would probably be as large. It can hardly be argued that at the time of Johnson's speech the presence of four Skyraiders in the air off the coast of *South* Vietnam (and that is where they were at the time of Johnson's speech) could have conveyed even a strong hint that the coast of North Vietnam was about to be bombed.

On the *Constellation*, planning had been based on the sensible premise that launches should be staggered so as to have aircraft actually hit all targets simultaneously; the recommended time on target was 1545H, which would require launches staggered from 1300H to 1430H, with the *Constellation*, more distant from the targets, beginning launches well before the *Ticonderoga*.[50] The intrusion on these plans at 1154H of word that the *Ticonderoga* had already begun to launch, and would have aircraft arriving on target at about 1310H,[51] may have been something of a shock.

It is possible that President Johnson was partially insulated from the political effects of his premature announcement by the fact that Senator Goldwater had also jumped the gun. President Johnson had wanted to obtain Goldwater's public approval of the airstrikes against North Vietnam, and had gotten in touch with Goldwater by phone at 10:06 P.M. EDT on the evening of August 4. Goldwater indeed supported the president, but he issued his statement of support almost an hour *before* President Johnson went on television, and it went out to the world via UPI wire almost immediately: "I am sure that every American will subscribe to the actions outlined in the President's statement. I believe it is the only thing he can do under the circumstances. We cannot allow the American flag to be shot at anywhere on earth if we are to retain our respect and prestige."[52] This would surely have been enough to alert any DRV intelligence officers who learned of it that the United States was about to take some military action against the DRV, though there is no indication that Goldwater's statement in fact came to their attention in time to do them any good.

Stockdale has described his portion of the airstrike in some detail. He was awakened early on the morning of August 5 and told he was to lead the strike against Vinh. No adequate maps of the target were available. Four Skyraiders and two Skyhawks would hit petroleum facilities; six Crusaders and four Skyhawks would do flak suppression. There was one photo Crusader. The plan was for a simultaneous surprise attack by all aircraft, going in low along paths believed to be in radar shadow. Stockdale, certain there had been no attack on U.S. ships the night before, assumed the North Vietnamese would not be expecting retaliation, and decided not to carry missiles suitable for air combat.[53]

Jet pilots manned their planes shortly after 1200H; they heard that Johnson had gone on television a half hour before and announced the raids. The first jet was launched at 1216H. The jets joined the Skyraiders close to shore; they broke radio silence to start their run-in on the target at 1328H. After the initial attack in which the jets hit anti-aircraft guns and the Skyraiders destroyed the petroleum tanks, the aircraft proceeded to attack DRV naval vessels in the area. One or two jets also strafed and fired rockets at the wharf area along the riverbank adjacent to the petroleum storage facility.[54]

None of the *Ticonderoga*'s aircraft were lost at Vinh or Quang Khe. At other targets farther north, however, two of the *Constellation*'s aircraft were shot down.

Ltjg. Everett Alvarez, Jr., flying an A-4C Skyhawk, was attacking vessels in the harbor at Hon Gay—four Swatow boats and one considerably larger Soviet-built submarine chaser of the S.O.I. class. He expended his ammunition in two passes and was departing the area, but he had to cross a peninsula between the harbor and the sea, and while over it his plane was crippled by anti-aircraft fire. He had to eject almost immediately; he landed in the sea a short distance off shore. He was quickly pulled from the water by five armed men in a small boat.[55]

Ltjg. Richard C. Sather, in a Skyraider, was attacking Swatow boats T-130 and T-132 in the vicinity of Lach Truong when his plane was hit, presumably by fire from one of the vessels, and crashed into the sea between the Swatows about two miles offshore. There was no indication that he had managed to bail out of his plane before it crashed, and it was assumed, correctly, that he had been killed. The water was shallow, and local authorities were able to recover the wreckage of Sather's aircraft. His body was returned to the United States after the end of the war.

If it had seemed practical, an amphibian aircraft would have gone in to try to rescue a downed pilot (the plane in fact took off from Danang and was orbiting near the mouth of the gulf), but there was no realistic chance of success for either of the pilots downed on August 5. Alvarez was believed to have gotten out of his plane alive; his rescue beeper had been heard by other pilots. Their reports, however, indicated that rocks and shoals, and the presence of enemy forces, precluded any rescue effort for him. Also, they were not sure exactly where Alvarez had come down, or even whether he had come down on land or in the water. Sather's plane had crashed between two enemy vessels and there was no indication he had survived the crash. At 1940H, therefore, plans for a rescue were called off.[56]

McNamara also said, "We think there were very few civilian casualties because these bases and the depot were in isolated portions of North Vietnam."[57] The depot in question was certainly not in an isolated area; it was in Vinh, the capital of Nghe An province. The pilot who commanded the strike commented long afterward that what had sometimes been described as "a neat little package of a certain number of oil tanks blown up, translates quite differently when you're up there and they are in a city of forty-four thousand people. Our marksmanship was uncanny. The bombers got the bombs down into the tanks and nothing outside the fence surrounding it, but there were still people around."[58] In order to protect the planes actually bombing the depot, other planes hit anti-aircraft guns apparently not within the fenced area.[59]

Despite the falsehood of McNamara's specific words, however, the American pilots seem to have done a good job—better than they sometimes did in later years—of limiting their attacks to military targets. Some DRV accounts were phrased as if the U.S. airstrikes had targeted innocent civilians, but such statements were for the most part quite vague;[60] the only specific claims of harm to civilians were in statements that the American aircraft had hit a ferry landing, wounding three people inside, and that they had attacked a coal barge (both incidents at Hon Gay).[61] These specific claims are probably true; pilots sent to attack small military vessels in an unfamiliar harbor, lacking good information about where in the harbor those vessels would be located (see comments by John Nicholson quoted below) and lacking time to take a thorough look around due to the intensity of the anti-aircraft fire, would not have had to be grossly careless for some of their fire to strike such targets.

The Americans claimed, optimistically, that eight PTs and Swatows had been destroyed and many more damaged. It is difficult to tell, from the available records, the exact basis for the claim of eight vessels destroyed.[62] The report from the interrogation of Tran Bao in 1966, indicating that at least one (and possibly three) Swatows were sunk, but no PT boats, seems more convincing. On board the two PT boats that were among the vessels attacked at Lach Truong, there were approximately four men killed and some others injured; these casualties were caused primarily by rocket fragments.[63] Nothing is known about casualties aboard Swatows, but the numbers must have been considerably higher than the numbers Tran Bao gave for casualties aboard the PT boats; most of the vessels attacked were Swatows, and at least one Swatow was actually sunk.

An article about the lessons that had been learned about the repair of damage to vessels during a battle gives the impression that rockets had also been the main source of hull damage during air attacks; this was probably based mainly on the experience of Swatows attacked at various locations on August 5. The damage must in many cases have been quite severe; the article describes briefly the best methods of patching holes in the hull less than fifteen centimeters across; holes fifteen to thirty-five centimeters across; and holes more than thirty-five centimeters (fourteen inches) across.[64]

Defending against the American Airstrikes

Wheeler and McNamara said that the DRV had been caught totally by surprise; "It is inconceivable that a military force expecting an attack would have its boats lying dead in the water at the base, and this is exactly the way we found most of the North Vietnamese."[65]

This picture was greatly exaggerated. Anti-aircraft gunners on land seem indeed to have been surprised, and generally did not fire during the first pass made by attacking aircraft. Vessels of the North Vietnamese navy, however, were not surprised. In mid-August, responding to a request from the Joint Chiefs that he state whether surprise had been achieved and explain the basis for his response, Admiral Moorer, commander of the Pacific Fleet, commented on Quang Khe, Hon Gay, and Lach Truong separately:

Little or no initial surprise of boats apparent at Quang Khe. Boats were getting underway from pier at time first run was commenced. Boats fired upon attacking aircraft on first and subsequent runs. . . .

[At Hon Gay]: Complete initial surprise not repeat not achieved. Rationale: no unit is capable of anti-aircraft response to air attack in 4–6 seconds in any but alert posture. . . . Fact that PGM/PT boats not underway may indicate period of alert before attack very short.

[At Lach Truong]: Initial surprise not repeat not achieved. Rationale: A1/A4 aircraft taken under fire two minutes before attack.[66]

The DRV had observed extensive American air activity over the Gulf of Tonkin during the night of August 4–5. Toward morning the American aircraft disappeared, at least from the sections of the gulf close enough to North Vietnam to be within the range of coastal radar, but they were back, in considerable numbers, by about 0710H. A U-2 high-altitude reconnaissance aircraft made a leisurely pass over North Vietnam itself from 0924H to 1253H.[67]

All along the coast, anti-aircraft gunners manned their weapons, at a maximum alert status, and waited to see what would happen. Their commanders tried to figure out what the Americans might be doing. According to a history published long afterward, the commander of the air defense forces was able to come up with one hypothesis: that the Americans were partly conducting reconnaissance, and partly keeping a lot of planes in the air simply to keep the DRV air defenses at maximum alert for a prolonged period; when the anti-aircraft gunners had become tired and bored, the Americans could be hoping to carry out a surprise attack.[68]

The suspense was ended for some by President Johnson's broadcast announcing the American airstrikes. It was monitored in Hanoi by a radio listening unit under the Foreign Ministry, and reported to the PAVN high command. From there, General Van Tien Dung telephoned the headquarters of the air defense forces with news of the impending American air attack. Shortly after air defense headquarters received this warning based on Johnson's speech, it was confirmed by a report from a radar station near Dong Hoi that American aircraft were heading north over the gulf.

There was no evidence of unreasonable delay in the dissemination of the warning from air defense headquarters to anti-aircraft units in the area near Hanoi and Haiphong. The warning also seems to have reached the gunners on Swatow boats in most places. It certainly should have reached them, since every Swatow had its own long-range radio, and every gunner would have been within shouting distance of his vessel's radio operator. The DRV, however, while it had reasonably good long-range radar to provide general warning of an impending attack, had long been deficient both in the local, short-range radar that would provide immediate guidance to anti-aircraft gunners, and in air defense communication systems. MACV had said in mid-July that improvements in the communication systems had recently been reported,[69] but if so the new equipment may have gone mostly to the Hanoi-Haiphong area. The American aircraft were coming from the south; the targets they reached first were the southernmost ones, far from Hanoi. No alert message, either from Hanoi based on Johnson's speech or from the long-range radar near Dong Hoi that had picked up the aircraft on their way north, reached anti-aircraft gunners at Vinh before the American bombs started to fall there. At Quang Khe, which was even farther to the south and was attacked before Vinh, a DRV source gives the impression that no alert message had reached anyone, even on the Swatows (though Admiral Moorer had a contrary impression; see above).[70]

The anti-aircraft forces at Vinh, though they did not get warning on August 5, had been preparing for months for the possibility of air attack. Vinh was a major transshipment point for supplies heading to Laos, and down the Ho Chi Minh Trail to the battlefields in South Vietnam. This was probably the real reason the Americans chose to bomb the fuel storage facility at Vinh. American statements on the subject refer only to the role of this fuel facility as a support facility for the North Vietnamese navy, but this role was in fact rather minor. Few DRV naval vessels, and no PT boats, were based in the vicinity. When the U.S. Navy made the Vinh petroleum facility its number one priority, the destruction of which was treated as more urgent than the destruction of PT boats or other naval vessels,[71] it seems legitimate to deduce a concern for the major role of this facility as a supporter of the Ho Chi Minh Trail, rather than for its minor role as a supporter of the North Vietnamese navy. (Another possible explanation should however be considered: there may have been some awareness among naval commanders of how difficult it would be for aircraft to sink small, maneuverable vessels like PTs and Swatows. By making the Vinh petroleum tanks the top priority, the U.S. Navy at least ensured that it would be able to say, afterward, that its top priority target had been destroyed.)

Vinh lay near the eastern end of Road 7, which ran northwest, crossed the border into Laos at Nam Can, and led to the Plain of Jars. Other roads running south from Vinh led to the Ho Chi Minh Trail. These facts made the town an obvious target for American air attack. In June 1964, anti-aircraft artillery units (Regiment 234 and Battalion 24) had been sent across the border into Laos to defend the stretch of Road 7 on the Laotian side of the border against air attack.[72] This was an area where anti-aircraft units were in direct combat, often against the T-28s flown by Thai or Lao pilots, and sometimes against U.S. jets. It is likely that the dispatch of these anti-aircraft units to that section of Laos had been prompted by incidents in the vicinity of the Plain of Jars, in which anti-aircraft guns shot down U.S. Navy jets on June 6 and 7, and the United States flew retaliatory airstrikes on June 7 and 9.[73]

This movement of PAVN anti-aircraft units from Nghe An province into the combat zone in Laos had been followed at the beginning of August by a spillover of the war in the opposite direction: the bombing of Nam Can and Noong De August 1 and 2, by T-28 aircraft that had been assigned to bomb the section of Road 7 on the Laotian side of the border. These incidents must have given military commanders in the province capital (Vinh) an exceptionally clear sense that air attack really was something that could happen at any time. The whole town had carried out a major air defense drill, with what are said to have been good results, on August 4.[74]

For much of the morning of August 5, as numerous American aircraft criss-crossed the gulf, searching for some evidence of the previous night's "battle," the anti-aircraft gunners manned their weapons on maximum alert. Toward noon, the American aircraft returned to their carriers, and the alert was relaxed. It was not relaxed very much, however; the gunners went only a few steps from their weapons to sit and eat their lunches.

James Stockdale led the planes assigned to flak suppression—attacking the anti-aircraft guns, to clear the way for the ones attacking the petroleum facility. The flak suppression planes made two passes. He says the anti-aircraft gunners did not open fire until near the end of the first pass; "We didn't start to get flak till we were pulling out of that first run; all we could see was hundreds of guys coming out of nowhere diving into those gun emplacement abutments."[75] Anti-aircraft fire was considerably heavier during the second wave of U.S. attacks at Vinh than during the first wave.[76]

Everett Alvarez, one of the pilots who hit Hon Gay at a considerably later hour, has described how he "flew through streams of black flak peppering the sky from the naval craft and AAA batteries on the hills behind. This was heavier flak than we'd anticipated and they opened up so quickly it was obvious they'd been on alert."[77]

The Americans had been drawing up contingency plans for airstrikes against North Vietnam for months, but they were not ready to carry them out on August 5. Indeed, one of the first things that the Joint Chiefs did after the August 5 airstrikes was order CINCPAC to formulate the detailed plans that would be necessary if the United States should finally decide to launch airstrikes against the "94 target list" that had been under desultory discussion for several months.[78] If one looks at the American sources, one sees clear signs of the way the Pierce Arrow airstrikes were launched on short notice, in response to an unexpected and ambiguous event. The strikes from the two aircraft carriers were not properly synchronized with each other or with President Johnson's announcement. Stockdale has commented on the lack of adequate maps of the target he was assigned at Vinh. Alvarez says that the briefing he was given for his attack at Hon Gay, further north, "was so scant it left gaping holes in vital information on target layouts and area defenses."[79] John Nicholson said that the problem was especially great for the pilots like himself who had originally been briefed for the strike on Port Wallut that was canceled.

> Just before launch, our target was changed to Hon Gai. We had to regroup and frantically look on the map to [see] what this damn Hon Gai looked like. There really was no time to study the target; and then off we went in this mass gaggle. The flight leader did brief us on the way, saying the target would be PT boats tied up at the southeast pier, or wherever the hell it was. . . .
>
> The boats at Hon Gai weren't visible as we approached, and the lead called

up and said, "I see no PT boats tied to any pier," and we were now a mass of planes in enemy territory. Alvarez came up and said, "The boats are out in the bay. They're anchored in the bay."[80]

Little sign of this was visible, however, to the North Vietnamese. A well-trained pilot, operating in daylight against coastal targets having very conspicuous terrain features to mark them, can navigate without difficulty to a place he has never heard of two hours before the mission. The Vietnamese were accustomed to a style of land warfare in which any effort to send men deep into strange territory would predictably lead to disastrous failure unless the men in question were first given many days to memorize the terrain and plan their movements. They tended to assume that the skillfully conducted attack on them represented the product of careful advance planning and preparation. Thus a description of the U.S. attack at Quang Khe said the planning showed in the way the aircraft dove right in to attack, not wasting any time searching around for their targets, and interpreted the timing as a calculated effort to catch the defenders during their lunch break.[81] How could the author have guessed that the Americans had wanted to attack at dawn, and that the attack at the lunch hour simply reflected how far they had fallen behind schedule? Who in Hanoi, noting the way a U-2 reconnaissance plane had passed over the targeted areas a few hours before the airstrikes, could have dreamed that the Americans had not had any communications channel through which information from the reconnaissance flight could be sent to the aircraft carriers in time to do the strike pilots any good?

The leadership of the DRV obtained a closer personal look at the events of the crisis than might have been expected. Men wanting to escape from the heat of August in Hanoi often went to the seashore; some key men happened to be in seaside locations close to the combat of August 2 and 5. General (and Politburo member) Nguyen Chi Thanh was at Sam Son, in Thanh Hoa, when torpedo boats 333 and 336 came ashore there after their attack on the *Maddox* August 2.[82] Premier Pham Van Dong apparently witnessed the American aircraft attacking Hon Gay on August 5.

The Tonkin Gulf Resolution

There was overwhelming public support for the way President Johnson handled this crisis; a Harris survey showed that 85 percent of the public approved while only 3 percent disapproved. This led to a major shift in the way the public perceived Johnson's handling of the war in general. Shortly before, Americans had disapproved of Johnson's general handling of Vietnam by a margin of 58 percent to 42 percent. Following the incidents at sea and the U.S. airstrike, the Harris organization found the public approved of Johnson's handling of Vietnam, 72 percent to 28 percent. Before Tonkin Gulf, when asked whether the United States should put military pressure on North Vietnam, and reminded that this might involve the risk of conflict with China, people had generally been negative (31 percent in favor, 37 percent opposed). After Tonkin Gulf, the same question drew strongly positive responses (50 percent in favor, 25 percent opposed).[83]

On August 7, Johnson obtained easy passage through both the Senate and the House of Representatives for the Tonkin Gulf Resolution, which granted him very broad powers to conduct combat operations in Southeast Asia. His staff had been wanting for some time to get such a resolution passed by the Congress; the August incidents allowed them to do so. The crucial passages read: "Congress approves and supports the determination of the President, as Commander in Chief, to take all necessary measures to repel any armed attack against the forces of the United States and to prevent further aggression. . . . The United States is . . . prepared, as the President determines, to take all necessary steps, including the use of armed force, to assist any member or protocol state of the Southeast Asia Collective Defense Treaty requesting assistance in defense of its freedom."[84]

The message President Johnson sent to Congress, asking for passage of this resolution, gave the impression that he was asking the Congress to write it, not sending over a text written in the executive branch.[85] This impression must have been widely accepted; a UPI dispatch stated specifically that the president had left the wording of the resolution to Congress.[86] The wording had in fact been negotiated between the executive branch and a few key leaders in Congress, starting from a draft that Secretary of State Rusk had presented to the National Security Council at about 6:30 P.M. on August 4.[87]

President Johnson felt that Harry Truman, in 1950, had erred by going into the Korean War without first getting a firm commitment of support from the Congress. He did not wish to make the same mistake. Robert McNamara quotes him as saying, "By God, I'm going to be damned sure those guys are with me when we begin this thing, or they may try to desert me after I get in there. . . . I'm gonna get 'em on the takeoff so they'll be with me on the landing."[88]

After many members of Congress had turned against the war, Johnson protested, "I don't even criticize them for taking that position if that's what their conscience dictates. But I just wish their conscience had been operating when they were making all these other decisions. Because Congress gave us this authority. In August 1964, to do whatever may be necessary. That's pretty far-reaching. That's—the sky's the limit."[89]

The president was deceiving himself; he had not really gotten the Congress in with him on the takeoff. Not having believed when they voted for the resolution that the president intended to use it as authority for massive escalation of the war, many members did not feel committed later to support him in putting it to such use. William Fulbright, who as chairman of the Senate Foreign Relations Committee became a major spokesman for the resolution, acknowledged during Senate debate that the resolution could be used as authorization for the United States in effect to go to war, but he was not worried about this possibility because everything he had heard indicated that President Johnson did not intend to use it for any such purpose.[90] He discussed the OPLAN 34A raids against North Vietnam, but treated them as purely South Vietnamese operations.

Debate in the House of Representatives showed less awareness of the theoretical possibility that the resolution could be used as authority for a major escalation of the war. Thomas Morgan, chairman of the House Committee on Foreign Affairs, said in that debate that the resolution was "definitely not an advance declaration of war. The Committee has been assured by the Secretary of State that the constitutional prerogative of the Congress in this respect will continue to be scrupulously observed."[91] The debate in the House also involved less discussion of the actual facts either of the incidents in the Gulf of Tonkin or of the OPLAN 34A raids that had preceded them.

The problem of persuading the Congress not to think of such a resolution as a predated declaration of war had been under consideration for months. A talking paper for the June 10 meeting discussed in Chapter 2, considering what would happen if the resolution were brought before the Congress, listed some of the questions that would be asked and the answers that should be given to them. First on the list was the following:

Q. Does this resolution imply a blank check for the President to go to war over Southeast Asia?

A. The resolution will indeed permit selective use of force, but hostilities on a larger scale are not envisaged, and in any case any large escalation would require a call-up of Reserves and thus a further appeal to the Congress.[92]

The difficulty of explaining to members of Congress why the administration was asking them to vote for the resolution, if no major escalation was envisaged, was probably the main reason the June 10 meeting had decided not to bring the resolution before Congress at that time. The reports of attacks on U.S. ships furnished the necessary explanation.

Some members of Congress realized before many months had passed that they had been too quick to accept assurances that there had been no American provocation before the Tonkin Gulf incidents, and that the Johnson administration would not use the Tonkin Gulf Resolution as authority to escalate the war. It would be years, however, before they began to doubt that the two destroyers had actually been attacked on the night of August 4. Democratic senator Ernest Gruening of Alaska, a strong critic of the Vietnam War and one of the two senators who actually voted against the Tonkin Gulf Resolution in 1964, published in 1968 (with a co-author) a book entitled *Vietnam Folly*, bitterly critical of the war. The chapter on Tonkin Gulf, fifteen pages long, listed many ways in which the Johnson administration had deceived the Congress and the public about the incidents, but even at this point (writing had been completed during 1967), it did not occur to Senator Gruening to say that there was any question about the reality of the August 4 attack.[93]

Denying Provocation

In the immediate aftermath of the August 2 incident, senior people in Washington seem to have understood that the action by the torpedo boats had been motivated by the recent attacks on the North Vietnamese coast. Secretary of State Rusk, on August 3, told Ambassador Taylor in Saigon: "We believe that present OPLAN 34A activities are beginning to rattle Hanoi, and *Maddox* incident is directly related to their effort to resist these activities. We have no intention yielding to pressure."[94]

George Ball's telephone logs show that Ball, Secretary McNamara, and Mc-George Bundy were all considering the idea of explaining to the press that the DRV had been confused and had believed the *Maddox* had been involved in a raid against the North Vietnamese coast.[95]

At that time, the administration had needed to persuade the public and the Congress that the president's decision not to retaliate for the August 2 incident had been correct. After the August 4 incident and the American retaliation of August 5, it became much more convenient to forget that there had ever been any provocation, or anything that the DRV might have regarded as provocation. What the administration told the Congress was that there was no connection between the DeSoto patrol and any raids against the North Vietnamese coast, and that Hanoi was aware that there was no connection.

After the August 4 incident, when senior officials discussed with one another why it was that the DRV had (they supposed) sent torpedo boats out to attack two U.S. destroyers, the available record shows very little consideration of the possibility that recent attacks against the North Vietnamese coast might have been a part of the motive. This may have been pure expediency; they may have been pretending not to see the obvious because such a pretense was politically convenient. We should seriously consider the possibility, however, that something more was involved. The available evidence presents a convincing impression that most administration officials (the main exception being Director of Central Intelligence John McCone—see below) really did not regard defensive concerns as a likely motive for DRV action, perhaps because they did not have adequate information about the American actions that would have inspired such defensive concerns in Hanoi. It is not clear how many senior officials in Washington knew about the August 3 shelling of the North Vietnamese coast (see Chapter 5). A secret report on the Tonkin Gulf incidents written by John

McNaughton, assistant secretary of defense for international security affairs, conveys the impression that the planned patrol track of the *Maddox* would have kept the destroyer about twelve miles off the coast and would not have gone far up into the northern gulf.[96]

But aside from possible lack of information, there is a sense of unreality in some of the internal communications of the executive branch, a belief that the North Vietnamese would ignore rational considerations when deciding whether to attack American ships. Senior policymakers often wrote as if Hanoi's decisions would not be affected by the question of whether the American ships were engaged in actions Hanoi found objectionable, or even by whether they were in a location where an attack on them would be militarily practical, but solely by whether the United States was acting tough enough to retaliate. Thus when top officials in Washington discussed whether the next DeSoto patrol should be ordered not to approach within twenty miles of the North Vietnamese coast, the consensus was that "the 20-mile distance would not appreciably change chances of a North Vietnamese reaction, while it would deprive them of a propaganda argument."[97] Given attitudes like this, even men who were aware that the United States had behaved very provocatively just before the August 2 attack on the *Maddox* might have regarded this as coincidence rather than cause and effect.

The public, of course, was not told even as much as the senators about the possibility that the North Vietnamese could have had some reason to fear U.S. Navy activities off their coast. When the DRV made its first public protests about attacks on Hon Me and Hon Ngu, the United States issued a denial.[98] McNamara, asked by reporters about attacks by South Vietnamese vessels against the North Vietnamese, gave an ambiguous denial on August 5, and clearly denied having knowledge of such attacks on August 6.[99]

Press Coverage: The Facts of August 4

It is hard to blame the American press for accepting, unanimously, the government's claim that American destroyers had been attacked on the night of August 4. The information released by the U.S. Navy and the Defense Department seemed to leave no room for reasonable or even unreasonable doubt. This showed more clearly in the weekly magazines than in the newspapers, since the magazines had more time to select the most impressive items from the plethora of information available.

U.S. News & World Report picked up, presumably from Secretary McNamara's press conference, the report that the attacking vessels had fired on the *Turner Joy* with automatic weapons while illuminating the destroyer with a searchlight so as to be able to see what they were shooting at. In *Life* magazine's version, the automatic weapons were upgraded to 37-mm cannon, and a clear impression was conveyed that this cannon fire had actually struck the American destroyers: "The PTs continued to harass the two destroyers. A few of them amazed those aboard the *Maddox* by brazenly using searchlights to light up the destroyers—thus making ideal targets of themselves. They also peppered the ships with more 37 mm fire, keeping heads on the U.S. craft low but causing no real damage."[100]

The reality of the attack seemed just as clear in the account published by *Time*:

> There were at least six of them, Russian-designed "Swatow" gunboats armed with 37-mm. and 28-mm. guns, and P-4s. At 9:52 they opened fire on the destroyers with automatic weapons, this time from as close as 2,000 yds.
>
> The night glowed eerily with the nightmarish glare of airdropped flares and boats' searchlights. For 3½ hours, the small boats attacked in pass after pass. Ten enemy torpedoes sizzled through the water. Each time the skippers, tracking the fish by radar, maneuvered to evade them.[101]

Readers in this Tom Clancy era may be tempted to snicker at the journalists who wrote this story, so ignorant of the technology that they thought torpedoes ("fish") could be tracked by radar. It would be well to bear in mind the possibility that the journalists received their misinformation from Defense Department sources. One classified report in the files of Assistant Secretary of Defense John McNaughton describes how "*Maddox* detected one probable torpedo track on its radar screen."[102]

American newspapers in general did mention that North Vietnam had denied making any attack against the destroyers on August 4,[103] but none appeared to take seriously the possibility that the North Vietnamese denial might be honest. *Time* and *Newsweek* did not even mention the North Vietnamese denial. Some newspapers carried a UPI dispatch saying that North Vietnam had admitted the attack and had tried to justify it as self-defense.[104]

Press Coverage: North Vietnamese Motives

In considering the way the press accepted the government's claim that the United States had been doing nothing that might have provoked the North Vietnamese to attack U.S. Navy ships, there were some issues on which the press cannot be blamed, but others in regard to which it should have been more alert.

The press in general accepted the government's claim that the destroyers had been on a perfectly routine patrol. There was no quick or easy way the press could have learned otherwise.

The press for the most part gave the impression that the destroyers had remained at all times at least twelve miles from the North Vietnamese coast, respecting the twelve-mile limit claimed by most Communist countries.[105] There was no quick or easy way the press could have learned that the *Maddox* had in fact been going much closer to the Vietnamese coast than this. The *New York Times* eventually revealed that the *Maddox* had at some times gone within twelve miles of North Vietnamese territory, but gave the impression that the closest approach had been about nine miles.[106]

Many publications did mention that the North Vietnamese had claimed that their coast had recently been attacked from the sea, though *Newsweek* was a conspicuous exception. Only a few, however, notably *Time* magazine, the *New York Times*, and the *Arizona Republic*,[107] informed their readers that there was any truth behind the North Vietnamese charges.

This fits the general pattern of U.S. press behavior during this period of the war; reporters in Vietnam were much less willing to report on secret operations than they would become a few years later. Barry Zorthian, the man in charge of press relations for the U.S. Mission in Vietnam in 1964, later recalled: "Any knowledgeable correspondent in Vietnam in '64–'65 knew about black operations. They knew at least the broad outlines of Marops [operations by sea against North Vietnam], they knew things like the incipient Phoenix. And they didn't write about it. They knew about SOG but they didn't write very much about cross-border operations. They didn't write about LRRP teams. We talked about it and they wouldn't write. It was part of, to quote Dean Rusk, their being on the team."[108]

Information released from Hanoi did something to fill in the gaps left by the reticence of American reporters, but not much. The raids on the night of August 3–4, for example, were not announced in Hanoi until August 6. The delay was not extraordinary—it often took Hanoi a few days first to get detailed information about events in remote locations, and then to decide what to say about such events. When a U.S. government translation of the text became available on August 7, it was sufficiently inaccurate—the DRV announcement itself reflected a mistaken belief that the *Maddox* and *Turner Joy* had taken part in the raids, and the translator got the time of the raids wrong by ten hours—so that unraveling the truth behind the report would not have been easy.[109]

Journalists looking for explanations for North Vietnamese actions found a wide range of hypotheses. The *New York Times*, the only publication this author has checked that dealt at any length with the raids that were occurring against the North Vietnamese coast, was also the only publication whose reporters took seriously the idea that these raids might have been the reason North Vietnamese patrol boats had attacked an American destroyer they found near their coast. This explanation was in fact considered and rejected in *Time*.[110] It got into some newspapers other than the *New York Times* through syndicated columns by James Reston and Jack Anderson. Anderson's column in particular[111] contained by far the most accurate account of the first Tonkin Gulf incident published in 1964 by any magazine or newspaper this author has seen.

Even to the *New York Times*, however, this was only one of a range of possible explanations. Tom Wicker, one of the paper's top Washington correspondents, wrote, "The Chinese are believed here to be the instigators."[112] In the American press in general, Chinese instigation was the most popular explanation of North Vietnamese "aggression" against the U.S. Navy. (One rare variant suggested that the Russians, rather than the Chinese, might be responsible: "The deliberate effort to sink U.S. naval units on the high seas is obviously part of a larger pattern. Whether the script is being written in Peiping or Moscow is unimportant. The aggression against the United States is undoubtedly part of a long-term plan to destroy all American influence in Southeast Asia.")[113] More than a week after the incidents, the *Anderson Independent* published an editorial that simply assumed, as if there were no doubt about the matter, that the attacks on U.S. destroyers had been ordered by China.[114] A nationally syndicated column by David Lawrence stated: "The Red Chinese government has started a war with the United States. President Johnson, as commander in chief of the armed forces, has ordered military action in retaliation."[115] The *New York Daily News* twice suggested editorially that President Johnson launch airstrikes against China.[116] If this led to all-out war with China, that would be fine; a third *Daily News* editorial, commenting on reports that both the DRV and China were talking about revenge for the U.S. bombing of North Vietnam August 5, said: "In that event, it may be our heaven-sent good fortune to liquidate not only Ho Chi Minh but Mao Tze-tung's Red mob at Peking as well."[117]

Explanations of China's motives, in turn, included such possibilities as a desire to provoke a violent American reaction that would undermine the Soviet Union's policy of promoting "peaceful coexistence,"[118] or a Chinese plan to conquer all of Southeast Asia.

Aside from Chinese instigation, the explanations offered by the press for North Vietnamese actions included the following:

—The North Vietnamese were testing the United States, trying to find out how much they could do without provoking retaliation.[119]

—The North Vietnamese thought that if they could create an air of international crisis, then an international conference would be convened to deal with the problems of Southeast Asia, a conference that would lead to a settlement favoring the Communists.[120]

—The North Vietnamese "figured that by sinking an American destroyer in a successful strike they would embarrass the U.S." and create the impression "that the U.S. is a 'paper tiger.'"[121]

—The North Vietnamese had deliberately set out to provoke an American retaliatory strike against them, because they thought this would enable them to extract more foreign aid from China and the Soviet Union.[122]

—"The North Viet Red leaders are crazy."[123]

Press Coverage: Shades of John Wayne

There are elements in the American press coverage of Tonkin Gulf of a theme that would become very conspicuous in later thinking about the war: the idea that the United States, a peace-loving nation, was fighting in a very restrained and limited fashion.

The initial government announcements on the first Tonkin Gulf incident had given the impression that the North Vietnamese PT boats had gotten in the first shots—that until the PT boats opened fire, the *Maddox* either had not fired at all or had fired nothing but warning shots. The initial press accounts reflected this version of events. The Defense Department quickly released a more detailed chronology reflecting the reality that the destroyer had fired first.[124] Some publications, however, paid no notice to this chronology, and continued to print stories suggesting that the American ship had waited for the PT boats to fire before shooting back at them.[125] Even the *New York Times*, which published the text of the navy's chronology, went on to publish yet another story based on the idea that the PTs had fired first.[126]

Many published accounts suggested also that during the first incident the U.S. Navy had used minimal force to hold off the North Vietnamese attack, and made no effort to pursue and sink the PT boats after they broke off their attack. An editorial in the *Arizona Republic*, for example, said that the captain of the *Maddox* "obviously could have sunk the small boats had he so desired. But American policy discourages retaliation, and the destroyer's captain probably figured he had gone as far as Washington would permit in defending his own ship."[127]

A few publications eventually informed their readers that the U.S. forces had pursued the PT boats and attempted to sink them,[128] but others did not. The *New York Times* even repeated, well after it should have known better, the original version according to which there had been no pursuit.[129]

Aside from trying to make the United States look morally superior, much of the press, in its enthusiasm over a U.S. military victory, also showed some tendency to exaggerate the achievements of the airstrikes against North Vietnam on August 5. Little blame can be placed on newspapers that repeated exaggerated claims made by Secretary of Defense McNamara, according to which not only North Vietnamese naval vessels, but also the harbor facilities used by those vessels, had been heavily hit by the airstrikes of August 5. There should be blame, however, for the magazines that went far beyond even McNamara's claims, converting his statement that twenty-five North Vietnamese vessels had been destroyed *or damaged* into a statement that all twenty-five had been sunk.[130]

The press was, in fact, presenting a classic John Wayne image for American behavior: the quiet man who is not easily provoked, but whose wrath is devastating when he is pushed too far.

Press Coverage: Overall Attitudes and Patterns

These patterns did not result only from the patriotic reflex, still very strong in the press in 1964, which caused the press like the rest of American society to rally behind the president in a crisis. Press behavior was shaped also by the principles of "objective journalism," which meant in practice that the function of reporters was not to try to figure out what was going on and present their conclusions to the public, but simply to convey to the public the information they were given by what were supposed to be authoritative sources. Each reporter obtained information from his or her sources, in most cases government officials, and wrote stories based on those sources. Few made any effort to correlate their information with what other reporters were obtaining from other sources, and put together an overall picture.[131]

In more concrete terms, the press coverage of Tonkin Gulf seemed to follow two rules. The first was that the press should support our boys—support and praise the actions of the U.S. military. To this rule the author has been able to find no exceptions; nobody in the mainstream press appeared to have the slightest doubt about the competence or the moral correctness of any action the U.S. military had taken in the Gulf of Tonkin.

President Johnson and other top civilian officials were not so totally immune to criticism as the military was, but to the limited extent that they were attacked, it was mostly by people who charged them with hampering the actions of the U.S. military. Editorials in two newspapers, for example, forthrightly criticized the Johnson administration for not having permitted U.S. forces to retaliate against North Vietnamese PT boats on August 2.[132]

The press was very cautious in dealing with the way President Johnson imperiled the U.S. pilots making the airstrikes against North Vietnam on August 5, by going on nationwide television to announce those airstrikes well before the planes had reached their targets. No publication this author has seen directly criticized Johnson about this. Most covered the controversy that arose when Republican congressman Ed Foreman of Texas charged that President Johnson's broadcast had given advance warning to the North Vietnamese about the American airstrikes, but none directly said that Foreman's charges were valid, and only a few presented the facts in a way that might convey the impression that the charges were valid (which in fact they were). *Time* openly endorsed the Johnson administration defense against the charges.[133]

The second rule that the media seemed to follow in coverage of Tonkin Gulf was that the press should never accuse any U.S. government spokesman of making an incorrect statement, even if it noticed that he had made one. Neil Boggs was a correspondent for NBC News in Washington, covering the White House, the State Department, and to a small extent the Defense Department. He also had personal friends in the Defense Department, who sometimes gave him information that might not have come to him simply in his capacity as a correspondent. He comments that the press in this period said about Vietnam pretty much what the government wanted, in the way the government wanted it said. Correspondents in the field might sense inconsistencies in what the government was saying, but what was presented to the public did not reflect such suspicions.[134]

None of the press, not even the *New York Times*, showed any inclination to embarrass the government by pointing out errors or contradictions in government accounts of the events. If different sources provided flagrantly conflicting versions of events, both versions might be published, but neither news stories nor editorials pointed out the discrepancies.

For example, the Johnson administration had originally given the public the impression that the airstrikes on August 5 had already reached their targets by the time Johnson went on television to announce them. When this turned out not to be true, the administration shifted to a claim that the North Vietnamese had learned of the raid by radar detection of the approaching planes before President Johnson's announcement. The shift in stories should have provided a strong clue that Congressman Foreman's accusations were correct, but the press showed no inclination to remind readers of the first story, after the second had been substituted.

At least three reporters wrote articles for which they had consulted the authoritative reference work *Jane's Fighting Ships* to learn more about the North Vietnamese PT boat force. This work indicated (correctly) that the PT boats did not have the 37-mm cannon that the U.S. Navy was claiming those boats had fired at the *Maddox*. None of these reporters, however, pointed out the contradiction. They either gave only those facts from *Jane's* that did not contradict the navy's account,[135] or else gave the weapons data from *Jane's* without reminding readers of the exaggerated report from the navy.[136]

A number of U.S. reporters in Saigon had broken out of the usual patterns of American journalism by this time. The contradictions between what they heard from U.S. military officers in the field and what they heard from senior officials in Saigon had convinced them that what they heard from the senior officials was false, and the number of sources they had to use, collecting information from a large number of majors and colonels instead of getting it from a few top officials, was pushing them to synthesize to an unusual extent. The Saigon press corps, however, was not handling the Tonkin Gulf story. The journalists who did handle it would, for the most part, print what the government told them to print. The public was left in no doubt that on August 2 and 4 there had been totally unprovoked attacks on the U.S. Navy, and that the U.S. retaliation had been both thoroughly justified and splendidly successful.

The public descriptions of these incidents by the United States and the Democratic Republic of Vietnam were in many ways very similar. Each presented itself as a peace-loving government that had been forced into combat by the persistent aggression of the other.

Each also claimed that it had been the overwhelming victor in the combat forced upon it by the other's belligerence. Each significantly exaggerated the losses it had inflicted on the other. *Nhan Dan* editorialized that the sailors of the Vietnamese navy had taught the Americans that the Gulf of Tonkin was not their backyard pond.[137]

Soviet and Chinese Reactions

In the months preceding the August incidents, China had been making increasingly strong statements of support for the DRV. On July 24, Foreign Minister Chen I discussed the situation in Indochina with the Austrian journalist Hugo Portisch. He said: "We do not want to wage a war there. . . . We would feel threatened only if, perhaps, the United States would send up their 'special warfare' toward the North, if they attacked North Vietnam, that is, if the other side were to attack. This would directly endanger the stability of our border and of the neighboring Chinese provinces. In such a case we would intervene."[138]

If the Chinese were aware that some of the American pilots who provided air cover for the two destroyers on the night of August 4 overflew Chinese territory on their way back to their carrier, this would have made them feel even more directly involved in the situation in the Gulf of Tonkin. If the Chinese radar system were half as good as the United States claimed in other contexts, it would have had to pick up the planes that did this.

Within about twenty-four hours after the U.S. bombing raids of August 5, half a dozen MIG aircraft had been flown in from China to be stationed at Phuc Yen airfield near Hanoi. By August 7, the number was up to thirty-six. Seventy-five new anti-aircraft guns were set up around Phuc Yen at the same time;[139] these may also have been brought in from China. One PAVN officer has commented that this represented less support than China had promised—that the Chinese had said they would furnish pilots for the MIG fighters in such a situation, but when the crisis came they furnished only the planes and left the Vietnamese to fly them.[140] But if these planes really represented a reaction to the August 5 airstrikes, China's willingness to send them, in a very uncertain situation, represented a considerable degree of support.

U.S. records contain one fascinating hint that the decision to send these planes may already have been made before August 5. General Burchinal told Admiral Sharp, at 5:39 P.M. on August 4, that there was a report some aircraft might be about to move from China to North Vietnam.[141] On August 6, the Chinese government strongly suggested that China would defend North Vietnam against imperialist attack:

United States imperialism went over the "brink of war" and made the first step in extending the war in Indochina. . . .

Since the United States has acted this way, the Democratic Republic of Vietnam has gained the right of action to fight against aggression, and all the countries upholding the Geneva Agreements have gained the right of action to assist the Democratic Republic of Vietnam in its fight against aggression.

The Democratic Republic of Vietnam is a member of the Socialist camp, and no socialist country can sit idly by while it is being subjected to aggression. The Democratic Republic of Vietnam and China are neighbors closely related to each other like the lips and the teeth, and the Vietnamese people are intimate brothers of the Chinese people.

Aggression by the United States against the Democratic Republic of Vietnam means aggression against China. The Chinese people will absolutely not sit idly by without lending a helping hand. The debt of blood incurred by the United States to the Vietnamese people must be repaid.[142]

This attitude on the part of the Chinese may have strengthened the tendency, already noticeable in the U.S. government, to exaggerate the degree to which Beijing and Hanoi shared the same goals. When the Johnson administration briefed congressional leaders about the August 4 incident, approximately six hours after that incident ended, the administration is said to have interpreted it as a probing operation directed by China.[143] Henry Cabot Lodge, in Washington on August 10, told reporters that there were Chinese advisors with the Viet Cong in South Vietnam, that the North Vietnamese attacks on U.S. destroyers must have been cleared with the Chinese in advance, and that the DRV would be unable to end the war in South Vietnam without Chinese permission.[144]

The Soviet Union's reaction to the August events was very different from China's. When the United States announced the August 5 bombing of North Vietnam, Nikita Khrushchev quickly sent a message to President Johnson deploring the U.S. action. Khrushchev, however, took the tone of a distant and uninvolved observer of an unfortunate event. He did not suggest that the Soviet Union was aiding or might aid the DRV; he did not even suggest that there existed any friendship or ideological sympathy between the two countries. Indeed, from the way Khrushchev, three days after the incident of August 2, denied knowing anything about it beyond what the governments involved had told to the press, one would get the impression that the Soviet Union did not even have an embassy in Hanoi.[145] In fact, relations between the two countries had fallen to such a low ebb that Moscow had recalled its ambassador earlier in the year, without first choosing a successor. Il'ia Shcherbakov was finally chosen as the new ambassador on August 22, but he did not arrive in Hanoi until September 23. During the interim, Moscow depended for information on the Vietnam War more on its ambassador in Cambodia than on its embassy in Hanoi.[146]

Thomas Hughes, director of intelligence and research at the State Department, noticed almost immediately that Soviet comments had remained "devoid of the expressions of 'support and sympathy' for the North Vietnamese which have been standard themes in previous East-West crises."[147] Moscow did not seem to believe the DRV was telling the truth about the August 4 incident, though it is possible that Moscow simply did not understand the DRV's denial about attacking the two U.S. destroyers to mean that there had been no combat at all that night. In the United Nations Security Council on August 5, the Soviet representative used language suggesting that he accepted the reality of the incident of August 4.[148] He presumably knew about the DRV denial of the incident, which had been mentioned on the front page of the *New York Times* that morning. On August 6, the denial in Hanoi that DRV torpedo boats had attacked U.S. ships on the night of August 4 appeared in a small story on the front page of *Pravda*, but right beside it was a much more conspicuous announcement from TASS, the Soviet press agency, which said, "On August 4 American naval forces sank two torpedo boats," as an example of how aggressively the Americans were behaving in the Gulf of Tonkin.[149] A commentary broadcast by Radio Moscow on August 6 again said that the United States had sunk two vessels "belonging to the DRV."[150]

A long article titled "Aggression in the Gulf of Tonkin" published in *Pravda* August 7 seemed to take the DRV's denials of the incident more seriously, but even after this the Soviets may not really have understood that the DRV was telling the truth. Many years later, when the Soviet Union's Ministry of Foreign Affairs was assembling documents for a volume on Soviet-Vietnamese relations, it chose the TASS statement that *Pravda* had published August 6, accepting the August 4 incident as having actually occurred, to represent the Soviet view of the affair.[151]

The impression conveyed by the overall pattern of Soviet comments is that Khrushchev was worried that impetuous fools not only in Washington but also in Beijing and Hanoi might create a major armed conflict, and he was determined that the Soviet Union not be dragged into it. Soviet Foreign Minister Andrei Gromyko, in conversation August 8 with the Canadian ambassador to the USSR, "openly expressed the USSR's irritation at the uncomfortable position in which it had been placed by the Tonkin Gulf crisis."[152]

On August 7, when the crisis seemed at least for the moment to be cooling off, Khrushchev made a speech (published in *Izvestia* August 8) that almost said the Soviet Union would defend the DRV if it were the victim of aggression. Even then, however, he was careful of his phrasing. He said that the Soviet Union would fight if the United States launched an attack against the socialist countries (plural). The U.S. press mistakenly interpreted his statement as a clear commitment to defend the DRV, if war broke out simply between the United States and the DRV.[153]

Both Rusk and McNamara commented as early as August 6, in their Senate committee testimony, on the cautious attitude that the Soviet Union was show-ing.[154] By August 13, the CIA reported: "No significant Soviet military reaction to the crisis has been reported. The USSR's verbal attacks on the US in the present crisis have been so reserved that they have aroused Chinese criticism. . . . Soviet propaganda is, according to the US embassy in Moscow, 'now down to a trickle.' "[155]

The weakness of Soviet support shows in DRV publications of this period. Three compilations of statements by foreign governments and other organiza-tions were published in Hanoi, under titles such as "The Whole World Supports Us."[156] All three of them show a conspicuous contrast between statements from China suggesting that China will fight to defend Vietnam, and statements from the Soviet Union that denounce American actions but do not say the Soviet Union is even considering doing anything about the American actions other than denouncing them verbally. Two of these three collections convey the im-pression that the Soviet Union did not even believe the DRV was telling the truth about recent events; they include the TASS statement based on the as-sumption that the U.S. destroyers really had encountered torpedo boats on the night of August 4.

A published speech by Le Quang Dao, deputy head of the political directorate of the PAVN, said that in the battles of August 2 and 5, the DRV had not only defeated the Americans, but had also "struck a blow against revisionism," in other words against the doctrines that the Soviet Union was advocating in the Sino-Soviet dispute. Dao said that the revisionists claimed that weapons were the decisive factor in war, while the ability of the DRV Navy to defeat American forces with greatly superior weapons, on August 2 and 5, had proved that the spirit of the men using the weapons was the decisive factor.[157] Le Quang Dao's language was not quite so insulting to the Soviets as Song Hao's had been two months earlier, but the implication is the same; General Dao would not have been saying these things if the DRV had had much hope of persuading the Soviet Union to resume supplying the advanced weapons that the DRV so desperately needed. There was still a group of Soviet military experts in North Vietnam, holdovers from the days when relations had been better, but the DRV informed the Soviet Union that these men were no longer needed. By this time, however, the Soviet government had realized that it could not afford simply to turn its back on the Vietnamese situation. Before he was overthrown October 14, Khrushchev had begun the first steps toward what a few months later, under Leonid Brezhnev, would become a Soviet rapprochement with Hanoi.[158]

Vietnamese Actions: The American Interpretation

There is evidence that a number of senior American officials could provide no rational motive for the action they believed Hanoi had taken on the night of

August 4. They tended to read Hanoi's motives as a mirror of their own—based more on pride than on concrete national interest, and reacting to immediate changes in the short-term situation rather than to long-term goals.

William Bundy has stated: "The Administration simply had no clear theory at all, did not know what to make of the attacks, and in default of any coherent motive could only conclude that Hanoi wished to make a gesture of how strong and tough it was."[159]

There is some evidence that at least certain individuals saw the 34A raids against North Vietnam as the obvious explanation for North Vietnamese actions. McGeorge Bundy's handwritten notes of President Johnson's lunch meeting with his top advisors August 4 contains the lines:

What *is* 34-A role in all this?
Must be *cause*; no other is rational.
But not a sufficient cause?[160]

CIA Director McCone suggested a few hours later that the reason Hanoi was attacking vessels in the Gulf of Tonkin was that attacks had been made from the gulf against North Vietnamese territory.[161]

The State Department's Bureau of Intelligence and Research (INR), in a striking example of the American tendency to look at everything as public relations, suggested that even to the extent that OPLAN 34A was the North Vietnamese motive, this was for Hanoi a public relations issue: "The unescorted mission of the *Maddox*, close to North Vietnamese territory and coinciding with clandestine South Vietnamese activities along the coast provided an opportunity both to demonstrate Hanoi's determination to respond as well as to implicate the US publicly and directly in the 'South Vietnamese' raids." INR believed that Hanoi had expected to be able to attack the *Maddox* on August 2 without risking major retaliation. INR did not believe, however, that there could have been any such expectation on August 4; President Johnson had made the U.S. determination to retaliate for any second attack too clear. INR suggested that this was precisely the reason Hanoi decided to strike again on the evening of August 4.

If Hanoi could be deterred from its course of action in the Gulf of Tonkin by relatively low-cost aerial retaliation, how could it persuade its enemy it would stick to the present course in South Vietnam when greater costs were involved?

In short, having assured its people and the world that it would not compromise in the face of threatened escalation, Hanoi may have felt compelled to prove this point with the *Maddox*.[162]

Those interested in psychological explanations for political behavior might wish to consider the following speculation: If American policymakers had taken seriously the actual reason that PT boats had come out to fight an American destroyer in August 1964—that 34A attacks against North Vietnamese coastal facilities had made the coastal defense forces unwilling to tolerate the presence of hostile warships within gun range of those coastal facilities—it would have been hard to avoid noticing that the DRV coastal defense forces had achieved their goal. Washington kept U.S. Navy destroyers much farther from the coast after August 2 than before it—out of gun range, in fact. The fact that a few PT boats had succeeded in making the U.S. stay away from the coast of the DRV was not, however, one that any American official would have wished to notice consciously.

Hidden Doubts

The available documents show almost unanimous belief within the U.S. government in the reality of the August 4 incident. This picture is misleading; far more doubts existed than were ever committed to paper.

The skepticism that seems to have been widespread, among U.S. naval personnel in the Pacific, has been mentioned at several points in the preceding chapters. The dubiousness of the August 4 incident seems to have been understood at Pacific Headquarters in Hawaii, once there had been time to consider matters. As has already been mentioned, when the interrogators questioning the nineteen PT boat personnel captured in 1966 reported that they were trying to determine whether the prisoners knew anything about the August 4 incident, Pacific Headquarters ordered them not to ask the prisoners about this subject. (The nineteen men were kept segregated from other Communist prisoners, and they were all sent back to North Vietnam in 1967 and 1968, but this does not seem to have been a plot to conceal their knowledge of the spuriousness of the August 4 incident. Had there been such a plot, Tran Bao, the man who posed by far the greatest threat to the official version of the incident, would presumably have been included in the first group sent back to the North, in 1967. He was not, and J. Norvill Jones, a staff investigator for the Senate Foreign Relations Committee, was able to question him in Danang in January 1968. Bao strongly denied that the attack had occurred.)[163]

The inquiries that Washington sent out in the days following the incident did not encourage naval personnel to express their doubts. Alexander Haig, then an assistant to Secretary McNamara, has written, "Endless attempts were made [on August 4] . . . to verify that an attack had in fact taken place. But there were no devil's advocates on duty; the purpose of every inquiry was to verify the attack on the *Maddox* and the *Turner Joy*, not to question whether it had actually happened."[164]

Soon, however, the shakiness of the evidence began to disturb some officials in the Pentagon. Daniel Ellsberg has stated that Alvin Friedman, in his mission to the Pacific, "was not sent out there to find out whether or not there had been an attack" on the night of August 4. He was sent, rather, on "a desperate mission to shore up our case," to find information proving that there had been an attack. If what Friedman had actually found had been negative evidence, Ellsberg is confident that he would have brought it back; he would not have concealed it from his superiors or manufactured fake evidence—"but of course, such negative evidence would certainly not have been revealed to Congress or the public." When Friedman returned to Washington, "We all laughed at how thin the evidence was."[165] Not long after the incident, according to Alexander Haig, an investigation done within the Pentagon concluded that there had been no attack on the two destroyers on August 4.[166]

General Bruce Palmer, Jr., was at that time the U.S. Army's deputy chief of staff for military operations. Within twenty-four hours after the incident on the night of August 4, General Palmer had become convinced that the reported attack probably had not happened. It was a product of imagination in the minds of men who were expecting an attack, partly because the *Maddox* really had been attacked in the first incident, two days before: "The people who were reading the radar were overly anxious in looking for something."[167] "Briefings given the JCS indicated that *no* second attack ever occurred."[168] The conclusion that the August 4 attack probably had not happened was shared by most of the people in the Joint Staff environment, particularly those at General Palmer's level—the deputy chiefs of staff for military operations of the various services. This was true for all services, "even the Navy people."[169]

Many intelligence analysts also realized at a very early date that the evidence on the second incident was very weak. At the CIA, Deputy Director for Intelligence Ray Cline quickly developed doubts, which he took to the President's Foreign Intelligence Advisory Board as described above. A CIA officer specializing in the military aspects of Vietnam later told a fellow officer, Patrick McGarvey, that he had realized the evidence was weak, but had been told not to report his doubts. McGarvey quotes him: " 'We knew it was bum dope that we were getting from the Seventh Fleet, but we were told to give only the facts with no elaboration on the nature of the evidence.' The reason, in his words: 'Everyone knew how volatile LBJ was. He didn't like to deal in uncertainties.' "[170]

INR Director Thomas Hughes says that he, like other intelligence analysts, became skeptical of the reported attack on the *Maddox* and *Turner Joy* when the radio intercepts became available to the State Department; allowing for processing time, this would have been within forty-eight hours of the incident.[171]

Allen Whiting, head of the Far East Divison of INR, says that when he received the report of the August 4 attack, "I knew it couldn't have happened." The idea that the DRV could have done such a thing was "not to be taken seriously." Fred Greene, who had been acting head of the Far East Division while Whiting was out of town at the time the incident came up, was the one who looked at the intercepts (in sanitized form; they did not come to INR with full information about the exact time of intercept) and found them unconvincing.[172]

Whiting set himself to predicting how the DRV would react to having been bombed August 5 in retaliation for something the DRV had not done. He concluded that the DRV would feel compelled to demonstrate not being intimidated, that this would require an attack on a U.S. base, and that the bombers at Bien Hoa, in South Vietnam near Saigon, were the obvious target for such an attack. Accordingly, he recommended that the defenses of Bien Hoa be strengthened. The nonreality of the August 4 incident was explicitly included in his report, as part of the logic on which his prediction was based. Senior military officers in Washington refused his recommendation, saying it would not be appropriate to tell the base commander how to run his base.[173] When the Viet Cong in fact shelled Bien Hoa on November 1, four Americans were killed, many more were wounded, and several aircraft were destroyed.

On August 6, James Thomson of the NSC staff attended an interagency policy luncheon at the State Department. He was very startled to hear Walt Rostow at this luncheon say that it seemed unlikely that there had actually been an attack on the two U.S. destroyers on August 4. This was the first Thomson had heard that there was doubt about the reality of the incident. Rostow was openly gleeful about the fact that the U.S. armed forces had been turned loose to bomb North Vietnam in response to an attack that might not even have happened. When McGeorge Bundy heard of Rostow's remarks, he said that Rostow should be told to "button his lip."[174]

Toward Further Escalation

U.S. Planning Continues

Senior officials wasted no time in formulating plans for use of the resolution the Congress had passed. On the evening of August 7, about nine hours after the Senate vote, a message went out to Ambassador Taylor in Saigon: "We will be reviewing whole gamut operations against NVN with particular view to those most justifiable in terms of activity against South Viet-Nam. Would welcome any recommendation you have under this rough guideline." This message was marked as having been approved in substance by Dean Rusk, Robert McNamara, and McGeorge Bundy.[1] Taylor replied on August 9 with a variety of recommendations, the last of which was that the United States set a tentative target date of January 1, 1965, for the beginning of systematic U.S. bombing of North Vietnam.[2]

On August 14, all of the men who had approved the August 7 message, plus the Chairman of the Joint Chiefs of Staff, approved in substance a draft paper on U.S. courses of action in Southeast Asia. The draft was sent to Taylor and some others for comments. This draft accepted Taylor's proposal of January 1, 1965, as the tentative date for the beginning of systematic military action against the DRV. It stated, however, that this "contingency date for planning purposes" was to apply only in the absence of some major change in the situation, such as deterioration in the situation in South Vietnam or a great increase in the level of infiltration from the North, which might require action before 1965. The main motive for the proposed attacks on the North appeared to be maintenance of the morale of the RVN leadership.[3]

Ambassador Taylor soon laid out in more detail the considerations that would determine the schedule for escalation. If possible, bombing of the North should be postponed to January 1, to allow time for Premier Khanh to stabilize his government and improve his military position in South Vietnam. Given the likelihood that North Vietnam would respond to the bombing by greatly increasing the military pressure on the RVN, it seemed wisest to stabilize the situation in the South before escalating attacks on the North. Taylor recommended that the United States attempt to follow this course. On the other hand, he admitted, "It is far from clear at the present moment that the Khanh government can last until January 1, 1965." Taylor recommended that the United States be ready to initiate attacks on the North immediately if the situation in South Vietnam began to deteriorate dramatically.[4]

When advocating a delay in escalation, Taylor seemed to say that U.S. escalation should be conditional on an improvement in the Saigon government: "Since any of the courses of action considered in this cable carry a considerable measure of risk to the U.S., we should be slow to get too deeply involved in them until we have a better feel for the quality of our ally."[5] But in the event that the Saigon government began to collapse instead of stabilizing itself, he said the United States should attack the North immediately.

The Joint Chiefs of Staff disagreed with Taylor. It was too late to think of getting "a better feel for the quality of our ally" before committing the United States; "The United States is already deeply involved." And the Joint Chiefs did not have much hope that the situation in South Vietnam could be significantly improved before an escalation of U.S. action; they felt that rapid escalation was "essential to prevent a complete collapse of the U.S. position in Southeast Asia."[6]

There is a contradiction that shows very clearly in Taylor's statements, but also appears to some extent in those of other top officials, between the idea that the U.S. should not attack North Vietnam because Saigon was too weak to serve as a proper base for such attacks, and the idea that the U.S. would have to attack the North if Saigon weakened still further. Nobody seems really to have decided that the United States should bomb the North if the situation in the South improved, but not if the situation in the South continued to deteriorate. When top officials said that the United States should wait for the situation in the South to stabilize before starting to bomb the North, this seems to have meant one of three things:

1. They were not thinking clearly.
2. They wanted to attack the North after the 1964 election, regardless of developments in South Vietnam, but in the meantime they were hoping to motivate Saigon by saying that they would attack the North only if the situation stabilized in South Vietnam. This is the likeliest interpretation in the case of Ambassador Taylor.
3. They wanted an excuse for not attacking the North that would still allow them to appear "tough." Therefore they said they were waiting for the situation in the South to stabilize; but if the situation had in fact stabilized, they

would have changed their minds and said that attacks on the North were no longer necessary. This is the likeliest interpretation in the case of President Johnson himself, despite the way he told top officials in a meeting September 9 (according to McGeorge Bundy's summary of the meeting) that the reason for waiting to attack the North "must be simply that with a weak and wobbly situation it would be unwise to attack until we could stabilize our base."[7]

It is important to note that despite all the discussion of escalation, the overall pattern of U.S. government planning was still based on a hope that escalation could be handled cheaply; that Hanoi could be intimidated into giving up its goals, rather than having to be forced by a massive and costly military effort. Even while Washington was drawing up plans for escalation, it was allowing the actual size of the U.S. armed forces to shrink.

Washington remained determined also that escalation planning be kept primarily internal, a matter of contingency planning. On August 5, the Department of State informed the U.S. ambassador in Bangkok that the United States was considering putting ground troop units into Thailand. Officials in Washington wanted to get advance approval from the Thai government, in case such a move should turn out to be necessary, but they were not sure that the desirability of getting such approval outweighed the undesirability of discussing with the Thai government the uses to which such troops might be put. They asked the ambassador whether there was a serious risk that a request for the Thai government to approve the deployment of U.S. ground troop units in Thailand would lead to a "wide-ranging discussion" of their possible missions.[8]

The support of the American public for the August 5 "retaliatory" airstrikes had been very strong; policymakers who favored more U.S. bombing of the North naturally considered whether that, too, might take the form of retaliation for attacks on U.S. forces. One item on the agenda for a meeting on Vietnam August 8 was "Possible future US military moves." On McGeorge Bundy's copy, scribbled by hand next to this item, can be seen the words:

How to get it going
Reprisal?[9]

In early September, according to the *Pentagon Papers*, "the JCS urged that General Wheeler, their Chairman, propose a course of action involving air strikes against targets in North Vietnam. . . . What made this proposal particularly significant was that it called for deliberate attempts to provoke the DRV into taking action that could then be answered by a systematic U.S. air campaign."[10] It was apparently in response to this proposal from the Joint Chiefs that William Bundy drafted a position paper dated September 8, stating among other things that

U.S. naval patrols in the Gulf of Tonkin should be resumed very soon, initially beyond the twelve-mile limit and clearly dissociated from 34A maritime operations. . . .

The main further question is the extent to which we should add elements to the above actions that would tend to provoke a DRV reaction, and consequent retaliation by us. The main action to be considered would be running US naval patrols increasingly close to the North Vietnamese coast and/or associating them with 34A operations. Such extension might be undertaken if the initial US naval patrols had not aroused a reaction.[11]

That same day, Ambassador Taylor, Secretary Rusk, Secretary McNamara, and General Wheeler met, and approved Bundy's paper with some minor modifications, one of which was the suggestion that deliberate efforts to provoke a DRV attack on U.S. naval patrols might be recommended by early October; Bundy's draft had said not earlier than mid-October.[12]

After this meeting, Wheeler met with the other members of the Joint Chiefs, and on September 9 reported to Secretary McNamara their reactions to the paper Bundy had drafted. Wheeler said that all five members of the Joint Chiefs believed that military action against the DRV would be required for there to be "reasonable hope of eventual success" in South Vietnam. They disagreed only on the timing. The Air Force Chief of Staff and the Commandant of the Marine Corps argued that "time is against us" and that systematic bombing of the North should begin as soon as possible. They recognized the need for some "incident" to touch it off, but they considered the matter so urgent that they were willing to settle for the next battalion-size attack by Viet Cong forces against the ARVN as an adequate provocation. The other three members of the Joint Chiefs felt that the initiation of bombing could be postponed a bit longer; "we should not purposely embark on a program to create an incident immediately."[13]

U.S. Operations Continue

The OPLAN 34A raids were halted temporarily after the August incidents. All the PTs and Nasty boats were hurriedly moved south to Cam Ranh. The men of the Mobile Support Group in Danang got the impression that the reason for the move was fear of a possible Communist attack on Danang.[14] Not long afterward, the boats were brought back to Danang and raids on the North resumed. The United States also sent two destroyers, the *Morton* and the *Edwards*, into the Gulf of Tonkin in September on another DeSoto patrol. The plans for this patrol were much more cautious than those for the August patrol of the *Maddox*, more cautious than CINCPAC had wanted. The destroyers were not to go north of 19°50′ north latitude, and were to stay at least twenty miles from the Vietnamese mainland and at least twelve miles from islands.[15] The limit on approaches to land was followed by the caveat "except as authorized," but there is no available evidence that authorization for closer approaches was in fact expected. Admiral Sharp had suggested that a new DeSoto patrol be carried out out sooner than this, and on a less cautious plan, going slightly farther north, and approaching within eleven miles of the coast and four miles of islands.[16] The patrol commander later said that his superiors had never made clear to him just what this patrol was supposed to accomplish; he deduced that his primary mission was to show the American flag in the Gulf of Tonkin, and that any useful intelligence he gathered would be regarded as a bonus. In the section of his patrol report in which he made recommendations for the improvement of future patrols, the first suggestion on his list was that "the mission of the patrol be clearly stated in the basic patrol directive, so that the DESOTO Patrol Commander does not have to deduce his mission."[17]

This patrol led to another confusing incident, on the evening of September 18. From 1929H to 2212H, the radar of the destroyers showed what appeared to be a number of vessels in their vicinity, some of them moving at high speeds. The destroyers fired 342 rounds at these radar targets. According to Joseph Goulden, a court of inquiry held at Subic on September 21 and 22 decided that the destroyers had not, after all, been attacked by North Vietnamese patrol craft on that night.[18]

The evidence supporting the reality of the attack, as cited in contemporary reports, was very similar to the evidence cited in the reports on the August 4 incident. The two destroyers fired on radar targets they believed to be hostile vessels, and when some of the targets disappeared from the radar, this was interpreted as meaning that the hostile vessels had been sunk. The targets appeared and disappeared at comparatively close ranges. Thus the *Edwards* reported that skunk "G" had first been tracked at 4,400 yards (it was later decided that this radar target in fact represented the same enemy vessel as skunk "B," which had faded from the radar, apparently at an even closer range, shortly before). Skunk "I" was first tracked at 5,200 yards.[19] There were reports of sightings of wakes by pilots flying air cover overhead, though there are oddities in both of the available reports of pilot sightings. None of the pilots said they had seen actual vessels, only wakes.[20]

Sonar operators had reported hearing the screws of the enemy vessels. There were a few men who claimed they had glimpsed the gunfire of attacking vessels, or the attacking vessels themselves, from the destroyers; and there was a North Vietnamese radio intercept that was interpreted as indicating that DRV vessels were engaged in combat. The Joint Chiefs again recommended airstrikes against North Vietnamese targets, including petroleum storage facilities and airfields in the Hanoi-Haiphong area.[21]

The reports, however, contained more evidence against the idea of attack than had gotten into the reports on the August 4 incident. Messages from the destroyers after the incident showed more confidence in the reality of the targets on which they had fired than the message traffic from the *Maddox* had showed on August 5. They acknowledged, however, that the failure of their radar to track any target at ranges beyond 21,500 yards was an oddity (compare this with the way no report from the *Maddox* or *Turner Joy* had recognized any oddity in the failure of their radar to track targets at ranges between 10,000 and 20,000 yards). They also acknowledged clearly that all sonar reports had been spurious. Despite the fact that the destroyers had carried out a training exercise only the previous night, to give the sonarmen practice at recognizing the sounds their own vessels made during high-speed maneuvers, the excitement of first combat had taken hold and caused self-generated sounds to be mistakenly reported as enemy vessels. No radar use by the supposed enemy vessels had been detected, and it was quickly realized that there had been no radio intercepts containing genuine evidence of an attack.[22]

Where the reports of sailors who thought they had seen gunfire aimed at them on the night of August 4 had passed up the chain of command quickly, and indeed were being significantly exaggerated within hours of the incident, equivalent claims for the night of September 18 do not seem to have entered the reports for days.[23] When officials at high levels were considering the possibility of retaliation, they do not seem to have believed there was serious evidence that hostile vessels had actually fired on American ships. They believed that, at most, hostile vessels intending to attack the American destroyers had come close enough for the destroyers to fire on them with five-inch guns, but had never come close enough to be able to use their own weapons, which had a much shorter range.[24]

This time, the skimpiness of the eyewitness evidence, the failure of aerial reconnaissance to find any debris the following morning, and the dubiousness of the interpretation that was being placed on the intercepted North Vietnamese radio message were all discussed openly at top levels of the government. President Johnson was very doubtful about the supposed incident, despite the way Secretary Rusk "pressed on the President the importance of not seeming to doubt our naval officers on the spot."[25]

The Soviet public reaction was curious. A TASS International Service Russian-language broadcast, presumably directed mainly at audiences in Communist countries, ridiculed the U.S. claims that the destroyers had been attacked, and clearly suggested that the Americans had been shooting only at "ghosts" on their radar.[26] What TASS chose to broadcast in English, however, and what *Pravda* published on its front page September 22 (and what was selected years later by the Ministry of Foreign Affairs to represent the Soviet view of this incident in a collection of documents on Soviet-Vietnamese relations) was a statement that, while criticizing the United States for firing without just cause, did not express open doubts about whether there had been anything for the

Americans to fire at: "Two U.S. destroyers, which were in international waters, opened fire on ships they had not identified. A statement issued by Defense Secretary McNamara on 19 September admits that the 'unidentified' ships had taken no hostile actions whatever and the U.S. destroyers opened fire only conjecturing that the above-mentioned ships allegedly had hostile intentions. It was reported that five unidentified ships were allegedly fired at and that three of them were sunk."[27]

The Chinese government seemed much more certain that no combat had taken place, and ridiculed the Soviet Union for the comment about the three vessels having been sunk.

While the United States was trying to decide whether anything had really happened, there was a curious exchange between Washington and Saigon. General Wheeler asked Ambassador Taylor, in Saigon, about the appropriateness of American retaliation if it turned out that there had been genuine North Vietnamese vessels approaching the two American destroyers, but that the North Vietnamese vessels had been driven off by American fire without ever having fired on the American vessels themselves. Taylor replied that this would not be adequate provocation to justify American airstrikes against North Vietnam, but that the destroyers should be sent to resume their patrol, with the patrol track moved closer to shore (twelve miles from the coast instead of the previous twenty), and the United States should be ready to carry out immediate retaliatory airstrikes if the DRV provided "clearer provocation."[28] The Joint Chiefs had already decided to resume the patrol with the track modified to put the destroyers fifteen miles off the DRV coast; this is what was in fact done.[29] No "clearer provocation" followed.

The Consequences of Tonkin Gulf in Vietnam

In Saigon, ARVN officers and RVN civilian officials were highly enthusiastic about the airstrikes of August 5. A CIA analyst pointed out, however, that this enthusiasm was based on the assumption that these airstrikes were simply the first stage of a war between the United States and the DRV. The analyst warned that RVN officials might be seriously demoralized if the United States then returned to its former policy of trying to win the war within the borders of South Vietnam, instead of continuing attacks on the North.[30]

In Hanoi, meanwhile, DRV spokesmen claimed August 5 as a great victory, with exaggerated figures for the number of U.S. planes shot down. Collections of documents and articles were published under titles such as *The Warlike Conduct of the American Imperialists toward the Democratic Republic of Vietnam Was Appropriately Punished* and *The American Bandits Were Appropriately Punished*.[31]

Despite the claims of victory, the DRV also took August 5 as a warning. Premier Pham Van Dong said: "This criminal action was prepared in a planned fashion; it was the first step in carrying out the plot of 'carrying the war to the North.' "[32] The obvious interpretation of recent events was that the airstrikes represented the execution of long-prepared American plans,[33] and they had the appearance of preliminary stages. Ho Chi Minh warned that nobody should become complacent about the victory that had been won over the American aircraft on August 5; the Americans and their South Vietnamese lackeys would not be deterred from further actions; they would sooner die than abandon the course they had chosen.[34]

General Hoang Van Thai argued that one of the purposes for which the United States had staged the incidents was to set a precedent for future bombing of North Vietnam. He said the Americans were definitely planning to escalate the war, perhaps escalate it a great deal.[35]

Deputy Ambassador U. Alexis Johnson, in Saigon, had thought the DRV would want to take some dramatic retaliatory action to save face, though he seemed to doubt that the DRV would actually dare to do so.[36] Even CIA Director John McCone, who seemed to have a better sense of Communist behavior than most senior American policymakers, expected Hanoi to react to the American airstrikes of August 5 in a way that simply expressed anger, without serving any long-term purpose.[37] On September 9, President Johnson asked McCone why there had been no major reaction from the North Vietnamese after the Tonkin Gulf incidents. McCone replied that Hanoi was waiting and watching.[38] In fact Hanoi had reacted strongly, in ways not visible to the United States. In the early 1980s, officials in Hanoi told D. Gareth Porter: "A few days after the Tonkin Gulf reprisals the Vietnamese Communist leadership secretly convened a Central Committee plenum to consider the implications of the American move. Party leaders concluded that direct U.S. military intervention in the South and the bombing of the North were probable, and that the party and government had to prepare for a major war in the South. In September the first combat units of the Vietnam People's Army began to move down the Ho Chi Minh Trail."[39]

A knowledgeable former U.S. intelligence officer says the United States was not aware of the presence of any North Vietnamese units in the South at the time of the Tonkin Gulf incidents. His recollection, however, is that later evidence indicated that a couple of battalions had in fact entered Thua Thien province before Tonkin Gulf. Units of regimental size only started southward late in 1964.[40]

In June, the United States had used a Canadian diplomat, Blair Seaborn, to carry a message to Hanoi. On that occasion, Seaborn had been instructed to say that he was merely presenting to the DRV something that he was sure represented the American view. On August 8, however, the United States gave the Canadian government a message that Seaborn was to present to Hanoi, explicitly stating that it was a message from the U.S. government. The message started by expressing bafflement as to DRV motives in the Tonkin Gulf incidents; William Bundy has stated that Washington hoped that this would elicit from Hanoi some explanation of DRV motives in the incidents. The main point of the message, however, was a warning that "US public and official patience" was wearing thin, and that if the DRV persisted in its efforts to subvert and conquer South Vietnam and Laos, it could "expect to suffer the consequences."[41] Seaborn later described the reaction he received when he delivered this message to Premier Pham Van Dong in Hanoi: "Now he became visibly angry. For a moment or two I thought he was just going to get up and say 'That's the end of the interview, Seaborn. On your way!' "[42]

Pham Van Dong's anger seems natural if one considers the matter from his viewpoint. He knew that there had been no attack on U.S. ships on the night of August 4, and he would have assumed that the Americans knew the same. Given this assumption, the apparent meaning of the message Seaborn had brought was that the United States had decided to bomb North Vietnam in retaliation for the actions of Communist guerrillas in South Vietnam, while falsely claiming to be responding to actions of the North Vietnamese armed forces, and would do the same again if the guerrilla war did not end.

The logical conclusion would have been that it was pointless to avoid direct combat actions by North Vietnamese forces in an effort to avoid provoking the United States.[43] American actions only made sense on the assumption that the United States had decided on what later was called Rolling Thunder, the systematic bombing of North Vietnam. (If Hanoi had learned by this time about Ambassador Taylor's talk with Premier Khanh July 27 about planning for attacks on the North, this would have strengthened the conclusion.) Hanoi therefore reacted to the apparent American decision with a significant increase in the commitment of North Vietnamese resources to the war in the South (the first PAVN regiment started down the Ho Chi Minh Trail in September and October 1964, and the second in October),[44] a major upgrading of the Ho Chi Minh Trail to allow men and arms to move more easily from North to South, and an upgrading of the anti-aircraft defenses of North Vietnam, months before Lyndon Johnson actually committed himself to Rolling Thunder.

The People's Republic of China also took Tonkin Gulf as a dire warning. A number of American leaders had been making quite bellicose statements. Richard Nixon, for example, in a major article defining his policy on Vietnam for the 1964 presidential race, not only said that liberating North Vietnam from Communism should be made a goal of the Vietnam War, he said that the United States had made a mistake in the Korean War by not launching armed attacks across the Yalu River into Chinese territory.[45] Lyndon Johnson's public statements were more restrained, but the events of Tonkin Gulf would have suggested to Beijing as much as to Hanoi that in private the president was plotting a major escalation, and they took very seriously the danger that this would lead to war between the United States and China. Late in 1964 Beijing began what soon became a hugely expensive program of shifting Chinese industry away from coastal regions and into the mountains of western China, to make it less vulnerable to American bombing.[46] This was accompanied by a major expansion of the railroad network north of the Vietnamese border, greatly improving the ability of the DRV to obtain needed supplies overland if the port of Haiphong ever became unusable. The Chinese also began to build new military airfields north of the Vietnamese border. The Ningming field in particular, where work had begun by October, was in a location that made no sense as a base for air operations within Chinese airspace; the site had clearly been chosen with a view toward operations across the border, over North Vietnam.[47]

The overall result was that by the time the United States began major escalation of the American role in the war, in February and March of 1965, the Communist forces with which the Americans had to deal were stronger, better prepared, and better supplied than they would have been had the Tonkin Gulf incidents never occurred.

Consequences in the United States: The Phantom Streetcar

On February 7, 1965, Viet Cong guerrillas shelled a helicopter base at Pleiku, in the Central Highlands of South Vietnam. Several American servicemen were killed. The United States responded with airstrikes against the North, codenamed Flaming Dart. When McGeorge Bundy was asked why the United States had chosen to retaliate for the attack on Pleiku after taking no retaliation for other similar attacks in the recent past, he replied that such incidents were "like streetcars."[48] If you did not choose to climb aboard one, then another would come along soon, which would take you to the same place.

The extent to which the streetcars were interchangeable was illustrated by the origins of Flaming Dart. In January 1965 the United States decided to carry out another DeSoto patrol in the Gulf of Tonkin, to begin February 7. Not wishing to risk a repeat of the confusion and lack of coordination that had characterized the Pierce Arrow airstrikes of August 5, 1964, the relevant officers made careful preparations for the strikes, codenamed Flaming Dart, that would be conducted by both land-based and carrier-based aircraft if the DRV attacked this new DeSoto Patrol. The patrol was canceled at the last minute, on February 4, and two of the three aircraft carriers soon left their strike positions, but Flaming Dart was still basically ready to go—U.S. Air Force and VNAF aircraft ready in South Vietnam, one aircraft carrier in position and the other two not so far away that they could not get back to participate in the strike, targets selected, briefing materials available for pilots—when the attack on Pleiku came three days later.[49]

During the second half of 1964, four "streetcars" had come by—four incidents that Ambassador Taylor and others considered appropriate occasions for U.S. airstrikes against North Vietnam. The first, third, and fourth were genuine attacks on U.S. forces: the attack on the *Maddox* August 2, the attack on Bien Hoa air base November 1, and an attack on U.S. officers' quarters in Saigon December 24. The second streetcar, however, was a phantom: the imaginary attack on the *Maddox* and *Turner Joy*. President Johnson let all the real ones pass him by, and took his hugely important ride—not only carrying out the first airstrikes against the North but also obtaining the congressional resolution he had wanted—on the phantom streetcar of August 4.

It has sometimes been argued that Tonkin Gulf made no real difference in the course of history, because if there had been no August 4 incident, the United States would have done the same things not long after in response to some other incident. In a sense the logic is valid. The general drift of U.S. policy toward bombing the North shows very clearly in the files of the Johnson administration even before August 1964. It would be very difficult to argue that President Johnson, in the absence of Tonkin Gulf, would not have ordered reprisal bombing of the North after some other incident, and then proceeded onward to a campaign of systematic bombing—Rolling Thunder—at some time in the first half of 1965. In the absence of Tonkin Gulf, however, the circumstances surrounding Rolling Thunder would have been significantly different. The phantom streetcar had not taken President Johnson to quite the same destination as any of the real ones would have done.

In the short term the differences were all in the president's favor. When told that the North Vietnamese had gone fifty miles out to sea to make an unprovoked attack on U.S. ships, the American people, press, and Congress responded with a huge outpouring of support for their president and for his decision to retaliate. If President Johnson had had to make do with genuine incidents, none of which involved so brazen a challenge to the United States, public enthusiasm for retaliatory airstrikes would have been weaker, and he could not have gotten his resolution through Congress with so little debate or by so overwhelming a vote. Very probably he would not have been as successful as he was in defusing the Vietnam War as an issue in the 1964 presidential race, and the margin by which he defeated Goldwater might have been smaller. All of these things would have left him in a weaker position when the time came to initiate Rolling Thunder.

The phantom streetcar was a clean and shining vehicle, not stained with the mud of Southeast Asian jungles like most of the others on the line. There can be little wonder that President Johnson chose to climb aboard. The fact that it was a phantom, however, made it a very dangerous vehicle on which to travel. Senior officials seem to have been making an honest mistake when they launched the Pierce Arrow airstrikes in retaliation for an imaginary incident. Once committed, however, they had to conceal or obfuscate any evidence that turned up casting doubt on the reality of the August 4 attack.

This concealment could not be expected to work indefinitely; too many people knew too much. Neil Boggs, for example, a Washington correspondent for NBC in 1964, was aware that there were people in the Departments of State and Defense, including some at high levels, who had doubts that there had really been an attack against U.S. vessels in the August 4 incident. They felt that the White House had been so eager to take retaliatory action that not enough time had been spent making sure that there had really been something for which to retaliate. Some of these people shared their doubts with journalists, including Boggs. This was all totally off the record. None would allow his name to be given as a source in any story about such doubts. The journalists who had been given this information naturally came to share the doubts of their off-the-record sources, but this had hardly any influence on what was presented to the public, by either the broadcast or print media. "We didn't do too much with it because something like that obviously has to have a source pegged to it," said Boggs later.[50]

It was almost inevitable, however, that someone would someday go looking for more information, and would find enough to be able to present the story to the public. It was very likely that this would happen at a particularly bad time, when public disenchantment with the war had grown bad enough that the Johnson administration could not afford anything that would inspire further doubts. It was precisely when people lost faith in government policies that one should have expected them to begin asking probing questions about the origins of those policies. And those who unraveled what was unmistakably a cover-up can hardly be blamed if they wondered, from time to time, whether it really had begun with an honest mistake.

Not all Americans lost faith in the story their government had given them of the August 4 incident. Not all have lost faith even today. But those who did lose faith, before the end of the Johnson administration, included people whose trust the president needed very badly.

Notes

Abbreviations Used in the Notes

Bundy Memos	Lyndon B. Johnson Presidential Library, National Security Files, Memos to the President, McGeorge Bundy
Bundy MS	untitled draft memoir by William P. Bundy, in Lyndon B. Johnson Presidential Library, Papers of William P. Bundy, Box 1
CFL	Lyndon B. Johnson Presidential Library, National Security Files, Country File, Laos
CFV	Lyndon B. Johnson Presidential Library, National Security Files, Country File, Vietnam
"Command and Control"	"Command and Control of the Tonkin Gulf Incident, 4–5 August 1964"
DDRS	*Declassified Documents Reference System*
FBIS	U.S. Foreign Broadcast Information Service *Daily Report: Area Editions: Far East*
FOIA	Freedom of Information Act
FRUS-VN-64	*Foreign Relations of the United States, 1964–1968*, Vol. I, *Vietnam 1964*
GOT	*The Gulf of Tonkin, The 1964 Incidents*
GOTA	*Gulf of Tonkin Attacks*
Joint Chronology	"Chronology of Events, Gulf of Tonkin 4 August 1964" (COMDESDIV 192 [Herrick] to CTF 77, Ser: 002 of 13 August 1964)
Maddox action report	"Report of Tonkin Gulf, Action of 4 August 1964" (Ser: 004 of 25 August 1964)
Maddox Patrol Report	"July–August DESOTO Patrol conducted during the period 28 July–8 August 1964," Ogier to CNO, Ser: 002 of 24 August 1964
McNaughton Report	John McNaughton, "North Vietnam Attacks United States Naval Vessels in the Gulf of Tonkin—August 2–4, 1964," in McNTN VIII, #86a
McNTN VIII	Lyndon B. Johnson Presidential Library, Papers of Paul C. Warnke, Box 4, McNTN VIII
NHC	Naval Historical Center, Washington Navy Yard
NSC History	Lyndon B. Johnson Presidential Library, National Security Files, NSC Histories, Box 38
NSC Meetings File	Lyndon B. Johnson Presidential Library, National Security Files, NSC Meetings File
Pentagon Papers (Gravel)	*The Pentagon Papers* (Beacon Press)
Pentagon Papers (NYT)	Neil Sheehan et al., *The Pentagon Papers*
Public Papers	*Public Papers of the Presidents*

Special Subjects	*The Lyndon B. Johnson National Security Files: Vietnam, Special Subjects: National Security Files, 1963–1969*
Turner Joy action report	"Action Report for Gulf of Tonkin, 4 August 1964," Commanding Officer, USS *Turner Joy* [Barnhart] to Chief of Naval Operations, Ser: 004 of 11 September 1964
USVNR	*United States–Vietnam Relations, 1945–1967*
VNA	Vietnam News Agency
VNSF	*The Lyndon B. Johnson National Security Files: Vietnam: National Security Files, November 1963–June 1965*

Preface

1. Marolda and Fitzgerald, *From Military Assistance to Combat*, pp. 393–462.

2. Hoang Luu, "Vai thu nhan," p. 7.

Chapter One. Covert Operations

1. Ambassador Lodge to McGeorge Bundy, October 25, 1963, in *Pentagon Papers (NYT)*, p. 218.

2. McNamara, *In Retrospect*, p. 107; see also pp. 39–40, 101.

3. Colby, *Honorable Men*, pp. 170–71, 173; Nguyen Cao Ky, *How We Lost*, pp. 23–27; Tourison, *Secret Army*, pp. 19–20.

4. Colby, *Honorable Men*, p. 170.

5. Ibid.,. 173; Tourison, *Secret Army*, p. 44; *Chien Si Bien Phong*, p. 376.

6. Tourison, *Secret Army*, pp. 315–16; see also pp. 331–37.

7. Marolda and Fitzgerald, *From Military Assistance to Combat*, p. 148; *Chien Si Bien Phong*, p. 377.

8. CIA to State, July 7, 1964, in *VNSF* 4:910.

9. Ray S. Cline, Oral History 1, March 21, 1983 (LBJ Presidential Library), pp. 21–25.

10. VNA (English broadcast), June 3, 1964, in *FBIS*, June 4, 1964, JJJ5; Thomas L. Hughes, "Third Country Assistance to South Vietnam," Department of State Research Memorandum INR-33, August 28, 1964, in *VNSF*, reel 6, frame 205; *Chien Si Bien Phong*, pp. 397–406; CDR W. R. Quisenberry et al., "NVN PT Boat Exploitation Team Report," July 1966, IV-Q-2; *Lich su Hai quan*, 1985, p. 77.

11. Colby, *Honorable Men*, pp. 219–20.

12. *FRUS* January–August 1963, p. 91.

13. *USVNR*, Book 3, IV-C-2-a, p. 2.

14. Colby, *Honorable Men*, p. 220.

15. COMUSMACV OPLAN 34A-64, December 15, 1963, quoted in "MACSOG Operations Against North Vietnam" (Appendix C to MACSOG Documentation Study), C-7.

16. McNamara to Lodge, December 12, 1963, in *FRUS-VN-1961–1963*, vol. 4, p. 702.

17. COMUSMACV OPLAN 34A-64, December 15, 1963, quoted in "MACSOG Operations Against North Vietnam," C-5, C-7.

18. *USVNR*, Book 3, IV-C-2-a, p. 2.

19. "MACSOG Operations Against North Vietnam," C-12.

20. JCSM-426-64, May 19, 1964, in *FRUS-VN-64*, pp. 338–40.

21. Gittinger, *Johnson Years*, pp. 17, 179.

22. Informal conversation, General Nguyen Khanh, Austin, Tex., October 17, 1993.

23. "MACSOG Operations Against North Vietnam," C-7, C-10, C-11.

24. Ibid., C-12. Tourison, *Secret Army*, pp. 29, 212–13.

25. "Maritime Operations" (Annex D to Appendix C to MACSOG Documentation Study), C-d-20, C-d-21, C-d-10–11.

26. Ibid., C-d-11.

27. "Airborne Operations" (Annex B to Appendix C to MACSOG Documentation Study), July 10, 1970, C-b-90.

28. "Maritime Operations," C-d-26.

29. Interview with Cathal L. Flynn, Jr., August 1990.

30. Ibid.

31. Ibid.

32. *Chien Si Bien Phong*, pp. 384, 407.

33. Ibid., p. 291; Marolda and Fitzgerald, *From Military Assistance to Combat*, p. 341.

34. Interview with Cathal L. Flynn, Jr., August 1990.

35. *Chien Si Bien Phong*, pp. 413–14; Tourison, *Secret Army*, pp. 115–16, 335.

36. Interview with Cathal L. Flynn, Jr., August 1990.

37. Ibid.; "MACSOG Operations Against North Vietnam," C-38.

38. Adm. U. S. G. Sharp to Adm. Felt, "Subic-Danang-Saigon Trip Report," February 14, 1964, p. 1; Cmdr. Robert M. Laske, personal communications; interview with Lcdr. Burton L. Knight, March 16, 1989.

39. Lcdr. Burton L. Knight, personal communications.

40. Lcdr. Burton L. Knight, personal communications.

41. Marolda and Fitzgerald, *From Military Assistance to Combat*, pp. 338–39; Gibbons, *U.S. Government*, p. 284.

42. *Pentagon Papers* (Gravel), 3:118.

43. Personal communications, Burton L. Knight, Cathal L. Flynn, Jr., and Sven Öste, (a Swedish journalist who recently interviewed two of the Norwegians).

44. MAC SOG 4576, 041100Z June 1964, p. 6 (obtained under the Freedom of Information Act through the Office of the Assistant Secretary of Defense for Public Affairs). See also CINCPACFLT to CNO, 102342Z Oct. 1963; Adm. Sharp to Adm. Felt, "Subic-Danang-Saigon Trip Report," February 14, 1964, p. 1.

45. Lcdr. Burton L. Knight, personal communication, March 30, 1990.

46. Austin, *President's War*, p. 230.

47. "Maritime Operations," C-d-35–36; see also C-d-5, C-d-27.

48. "Logistics" (Appendix J to MACSOG Documentation Study), J-12–13.

49. Adm. Sharp to Adm. Felt, "Subic-Danang-Saigon Trip Report," February 14, 1964, p. 4; Interview with Lcdr. Burton L. Knight.

50. "Maritime Operations" C-d-32.

51. Lcdr. Burton L. Knight, interview, March 16, 1989.

52. Capt. Phil H. Bucklew, personal communications; Bucklew, *Reminiscences*, pp. 377–78. See also Windchy, *Tonkin Gulf*, p. 77.

53. Interview with Adm. Roy L. Johnson, August 10, 1988.

54. Robert M. Laske, Burton L. Knight, and Cathal L. Flynn, Jr., personal communications.

55. Interview with Lcdr. Burton L. Knight, March 16, 1989.

56. CINCPAC to JCS, 012205Z April 1964, pp. 4, 7.

57. Reported to the author by Sven Öste.

58. Valentine, *Phoenix Program*, p. 53. See also Wells, "Assault on Hon Me," p. 25.

59. Valentine *Phoenix Program*, p. 60; deck log, USS *Lawrence* (DDG-4); interview with the man in question.

60. Capt. Joseph B. Drachnik to Adm. Claude V. Ricketts, "Experience as Chief Navy Section MAAG, Vietnam, Dec 1961–Jan 1964," March 13, 1964, pp. 2–3.

61. CINCPACFLT to CNO, 102342Z Oct 1963; Marolda and Fitzgerald, *From Military Assistance to Combat*, pp. 208, 468.

62. COMUSMACV to CINCPAC, 292259Z May 1964, repeated as CINCPAC 010036Z Nov. 1964 (FOIA NHC); ADMINO CINCPAC, 021013Z October 1964 (FOIA NHC), citing CNO 152123Z Jan. 1964.

63. Dr. Ray S. Cline, personal communication, August 10, 1987.

64. McGeorge Bundy, "Air Drops in North Vietnam," July 24, 1964, *VNSF* 5:436.

65. Tourison, *Secret Army*, pp. 316, 335–37.

66. VNA (Vietnamese broadcasts), July 16 and July 21, 1964, both translated in *FBIS*, July 22, 1964, JJJ2–3; VNA (English), August 6, 1964, in *FBIS*, August 7, 1964, JJJ11; *Nhan Dan*, August 1, 1964, p. 4; *Chien Si Bien Phong*, pp. 414–15; CINCPAC to JCS, 012205Z April 1964 (FOIA NHC). See also Austin, *President's War*, p. 233.

67. *Nhan Dan*, August 1, 1964, p. 4; *Quan Doi Nhan Dan*, August 1, 1964, p. 1.

68. General Hoang Van Thai, "Bao cao," p. 5.

69. "MACSOG Operations Against North Vietnam," C-43; *Lich su Quan doi nhan dan*, p. 229.

70. Marolda and Fitzgerald, *From Military Assistance to Combat*, p. 343; "MACSOG Operations Against North Vietnam," C-43; *Chien Si Bien Phong*, p. 293; interview with Pham Van Chuyet, Hue, May 20, 1989.

71. General Hoang Van Thai, "Bao cao," p. 5.

72. Interview with Cathal L. Flynn, Jr.

73. General Hoang Van Thai, "Bao cao," p. 3.

74. MAC SOG, 031115Z June 1964 (FOIA); MAC SOG, 041100Z June 1964 (FOIA); Marolda and Fitzgerald, *From Military Assistance to Combat*, pp. 342–43; VNA (English), May 29, 1964, in *FBIS*, June 1, 1964, JJJ6.

75. General Hoang Van Thai, "Bao cao," p. 3.

76. Interview conducted at Nhat Le, May 1989.

77. COMUSMACV 301107Z July 1964 (FOIA).

78. Hovis, *Station Hospital Saigon*, pp. 146–47.

79. Officer interview.

80. Cmdr. Gerrell Moore, interviews.

Chapter Two. Thoughts of Escalation

1. McNamara, Memorandum for the President, "South Vietnam," March 16, 1964, in *Pentagon Papers* (Gravel), 3:500.

2. Robert McNamara, conversation with Randall Woods, July 12, 1990, used with permission of Robert McNamara and Randall Woods. See also McNamara, *In Retrospect*, p. 133.

3. Gittinger, *Johnson Years*, p. 17.

4. CINCPAC to JCS, 012205Z April 1964 (FOIA NHC).

5. Saigon 2412 to State, June 5, 1964, in *FRUS-VN-64*, p. 456.

6. M. V. Forrestal, Memorandum for the Record of a Meeting, White House, February 20, 1964, in *FRUS-VN-64*, p. 94.

7. JCSM-174-64, March 2, 1964, in *FRUS-VN-64*, p. 113.

8. Ibid., p. 116.

9. Memo, Michael Forrestal to McGeorge Bundy, March 18, 1964, in *FRUS-VN-64*, p. 174.

10. Futrell, *Advisory Years*, p. 201.

11. McNamara, *In Retrospect*, p. 114.

12. *Pentagon Papers* (Gravel), 3:503–4, 508–10.

13. "Command and Control," pp. 5–6, 83–87; Rear Adm. J. W. Davis, "Military Planning in Support of NSAM 288," DJSM 1069-64, June 25, 1964, *VNSF* 4:1003–20; *FRUS-VN-64*, pp. 171, 599n.

14. Robert McNamara, "Draft Scenarios for Recommendation 12 (NSAM 288)," April 23, 1964; Maxwell Taylor, "Draft Scenarios for Recommendation 12 (NSAM 288)," JCSM 422-64, May 16, 1964 (*DDRS* 1994: 1337, 1920).

15. *Newsweek*, March 9, 1964, p. 16; *Pentagon Papers* (Gravel), 2:96; Walt Rostow, Oral History, March 21, 1969 (LBJ Presidential Library), pp. 15–17.

16. *Chien Si Bien Phong*, p. 411.

17. Summary Record of the meeting on Southeast Asia, Situation Room, May 24, 1964, NSC History: Box 38, Vol. 1, item #10, pp. 5–6.

18. Ibid.

19. McGeorge Bundy to the President, May 25, 1964, in *FRUS-VN-64*, pp. 374–75; *Pentagon Papers* (Gravel), 3:169–70; Porter, "Coercive Diplomacy," p. 15.

20. Drawn up by a team headed by William Bundy; Austin, *President's War*, p. 235.

21. Text in *USVNR*, Book 3, IV-C-2-a, pp. 22–24.

22. Text in *FRUS-VN-64*, p. 364.

23. Text in *Pentagon Papers (NYT)*, pp. 286–88. This is probably a revised version, not Chayes's original.

24. CFV, Box 76.

25. SNIE 50-2-64, May 25, 1964, in *FRUS-VN-64*, p. 379.

26. *USVNR*, Book 3, IV-C-2-a, p. 22; *FRUS-VN-64*, pp. 366–67.

27. Westmoreland, *Soldier Reports*, pp. 105–6.

28. JCSM-471-64, June 2, 1964, in *FRUS-VN-64*, pp. 437–38.

29. Bundy MS, chapter 13, pp. 19, 21, 28.

30. *USVNR*, Book 3, IV-C-2-a, pp. 31–33.

31. W. H. Sullivan, "Memorandum on Situation in South Viet Nam," July 13, 1964, p. 5, *GOTA*, frame 84 (?).

32. McNamara, *In Retrospect*, pp. 128, 139–40.

33. Berman, *Fulbright*, p. 20; Woods, *Fulbright*, pp. 347–48.

34. Summary Record of a Meeting, White House, Washington, June 10, 1964, *FRUS-VN-64*, p. 492; see also pp. 490–91.

35. Quoted in Gittinger, *Johnson Years*, pp. 11, 44.

36. *Public Papers*, 1963, p. 33; 1963–1964, p. 183; 1965, p. 89.

37. *Public Papers*, 1963, p. 33; 1963–1964, p. 183; 1965, p. 89; 1966, p. 57; *Statistical Abstract of the United States, 1970*, pp. 246, 247, 338.

38. Taylor, *Swords and Plowshares*, pp. 304–14.

39. *Statistical Abstract of the United States, 1970*, p. 246.

40. Califano, *Triumph and Tragedy*, p. 32.

41. Westmoreland to Sharp, MAC 1975, 120612Z February 1968.

42. Krepinevich, *Army and Vietnam*, pp. 60, 63.

43. Rusk and McNamara to President Kennedy, November 11, 1961, in *Pentagon Papers (NYT)*, p. 151.

44. Survey taken October 29 to November 2, 1965, in *Gallup Poll*, pp. 1971–72.

45. McGeorge Bundy, Memorandum for the President, August 31, 1964 (Bundy Memos, Box 1).

46. Interview with Col. Bui Tin, Hanoi, May 4, 1989; Kahn, *On Escalation*.

47. Bundy MS, chapter 13, p. 23.

48. *Annual Report of the Director of Selective Service for the Fiscal Year 1967* (Washington, D.C.: Government Printing Office, 1968), p. 86.

49. *Public Papers*, 1963–64, vol. 1, p. 304; Geyelin, *Johnson and the World*, pp. 187–88.

50. *Foreign Operations Appropriations*, p. 418.

51. *New York Times*, April 17, 1964, p. 1.

52. Witcover, *Resurrection of Richard Nixon*, p. 77; *New York Times*, April 19, 1964, p. 82; *Washington Post*, April 19, 1964, p. 8.

53. *Washington Post*, April 19, 1964, p. 8.

54. Nixon, "Needed in Vietnam," pp. 41–42.

55. McNamara to Johnson, March 16 1964, in *FRUS-VN-64*, p. 159; cf. *USVNR*, book 4, iv-c-3, pp. 40–41.

56. "Summary Record of National Security Council Meeting No. 532," May 15, 1964 (NSC Meetings File, Box 1). See also McNamara to Johnson, March 16 1964, *FRUS-VN-64*, p. 165; McNamara, *In Retrospect*, p. 118.

57. Taylor to Rusk, July 25, 1964, *DDRS* 1979:91B.

58. Bundy MS, chapter 13, p. 17.

59. Bundy MS, chapter 14, p. 3.

60. Taylor to Rusk, July 25, 1964, *DDRS* 1979:91B.

61. *Chinh Luan* (Saigon), July 21, 1964, p. 4.

62. Quoted in Goulden, *Truth*, p. 32.

63. *Saigon Post*, July 23, 1964, p. 1; *Chinh Luan*, July 24, 1964, p. 1.

64. Taylor 235 to Secstate, 280843Z July 1964, *GOTA* frame 116.

65. Rusk 192 to Taylor, July 20, 1964, *DDRS* 1979:91A and also *GOTA* frames 88–89.

66. *New York Times*, August 2, 1964, p. 4; *Saigon Post*, August 3, 1964, p. 1.

67. *Southeast Asia Resolution*, p. 26.

68. CIA Intelligence Information Cable, July 31, 1964, in *CIA Research Reports: Vietnam and Southeast Asia, Supplement*, reel 2, frame 517.

69. Saigon 213 to State, July 25, 1964, *VNSF* 5:117–18. See also Saigon 214 to State, July 25, 1964.

70. State 253 to Saigon, July 25, 1964, *VNSF* 5:145–46.

71. Saigon 232 to State, July 27, 1964, CFV, Box 6, Vol. 14, item 33.

72. Saigon to State, August 3, 1964, in *FRUS-VN-1964*, p. 595.

73. Informal conversations, General Nguyen Khanh, Austin, Tex., October 17, 1993.

74. Wheeler to McNamara, JCSM-639-64, July 27, 1964, p. 1, NSC Meetings File, Box 1.

75. Ibid, p. 2.

76. Ibid.

77. McCone, Memorandum for the President, TS #185752-b, July 27, 1964, NSC Meetings File, Box 1.

78. William Bundy and Michael Forrestal to McGeorge Bundy, "Position Paper on Expanding US Action in South Vietnam to the North," July 31, 1964, text in Bundy MS, chapter 14, p. 13.

79. CINCPAC 022330Z Aug. 1964, as summarized in CINCPAC 050549Z Aug. 1964, NSC History, Box 38, *GOTA* Vol. 1, #178.

80. COMUSMACV, 020255Z Aug. 1964, MAC JOI 7253, *GOTA* frame 199.

81. This is the likeliest interpretation of a brief comment in Taylor 310 to Secstate, August 5, 1964, *GOTA* frame 135.

82. State 89 to Vientiane, July 26 1964, CFL: Box 268, Vol. 8, #24.

83. Vientiane 170 to State, July 27, 1964, CFL: Box 268, Vol. 8, #17.

84. Taylor 236 to State, July 27, 1964, FOIA State.

85. COMUSMACV to CINCPAC (MAC J31 7274), 021345Z August 1964 (LBJ Library), referring to JCS 7629 DTG 292104Z July 1964, CINCPAC 300528Z July 1964.

86. Summary Record of the Meeting on Southeast Asia, Cabinet Room, June 10, 1964 (Lyndon B. Johnson Presidential Library, National Security Files, Files of McGeorge Bundy, Meetings on Southeast Asia, vol. 1, Box 19, #14).

87. Bundy MS, chapter 14, pp. 10–11. The quote within the quote is from a memo of William Bundy to McGeorge Bundy, July 31, 1964 (*VNSF* 5:379).

88. Gittinger, *Johnson Years*, p. 40.

89. See Hallin, *"Uncensored War,"* pp. 75–76, for an analysis of conflicts between two of these messages.

90. William Sullivan, "Talking Paper for Canadians," May 22, 1964, in *FRUS-VN-64*, pp. 352–55. See also Porter, "Coercive Diplomacy," pp. 14–16.

91. Rusk 336 to Taylor, August 3, 1964, CFV, Box 7. See also Taylor 214 to Secstate, July 25, 1964, *GOTA* frame 108.

92. Ray S. Cline, Oral History 2, May 31, 1983 (LBJ Presidential Library), pp. 21–22. Gittinger, *Johnson Years*, pp. 24–25.

93. Summary of not-for-attribution press briefing by Gen. William Depuy, in COMUSMACV MAC OI 7523 to CINCPAC, 070719Z Aug. 1964, *GOTA* frame 173. See also *Time*, July 24, 1964, pp. 31–32.

94. *Newsweek*, July 27, 1964, p. 41; *Chinh Luan*, July 26–27, 1964, p. 1.

95. *The Situation in South Vietnam*, July 15, 1964, in *VNSF*, 4:937–39. See also Joseph Mendenhall, oral history (Washington: Foreign Affairs Oral History Program, 1991).

96. *Congressional Record*, May 9, 1968, p. 12620. See also Westmoreland, *Soldier Reports*, p. 105.

97. Saigon 279 to State, 020926Z August 1964, *VNSF* 5:558–59.

98. Drachnik to Ricketts, March 13, 1964, p. 9 (FOIA).

99. *Peking Review*, July 24, 1964, p. 6; see also *Nhan Dan*, August 3, 1964, p. 4.

100. Interview conducted in Hanoi, May 4, 1989.

101. CIA Report, "Communist Military and Economic Assistance to North Vietnam," n.d., *DDRS* 1993:1239, pp. 3, 13.

102. Interview with U.S. Naval officer.

103. Thomas L. Hughes, Director of Intelligence and Research, State Dept., "Khanh's Claims on Increased North Vietnamese Infiltration," July 17, 1964, *VNSF* 5:473.

104. General Hoang Van Thai, "Bao cao," p. 5.

105. *Situation in South Vietnam* (weekly publication, CIA), July 23–29, 1964, p. 18, in *VNSF* 5:504.

106. Radványi, *Delusion and Reality*, p. 37. See also Vientiane 437 to State, November 1, 1965, *DDRS* 1993:2802, pp. 1–2.

107. CIA Report, "Communist Military and Economic Assistance to North Vietnam," *DDRS* 1993:1239, pp. 3, 13.

108. Song Hao, "De cao," p. 2.

109. Ibid., p. 4.

110. Quoted in Amconsul Hong Kong 2193 to State, 240106Z June 1964, *VNSF* 4:488–90.

111. Bui Tin, *Following Ho Chi Minh*, pp. 54–55.

112. Ambassador Tovmasyan's name is also given as "Tovmasian," "Tovmasayan," or "Tovmassian" in various sources.

113. Maneli, *War of the Vanquished*, pp. 174–75, 180.

Chapter Three. The DeSoto Patrol

1. Rusk to Taylor, 1:41 P.M., August 2, 1964, *GOTA*, frame 124. CINCPAC 240124Z Jan. 1964, quoted in Marolda and Fitzgerald, *From Military Assistance to Combat*, p. 395; see also p. 396. Memorandum, Joint Reconnaissance Center, August 10, 1964, *GOTA*, frame 437. Galloway, *Gulf of Tonkin*, pp. 36–39.

2. Interview with Gerrell Moore.

3. Ibid.

4. "July–August DESOTO Patrol conducted during the period 28 July–8 August 1964" (Ogier to CNO, Ser: 002 of 24 August 1964), enclosure 13, p. 2 (in Naval Historical Center; referred to hereafter as DeSoto patrol report).

5. Interview with Capt. James Bartholomew, October 15, 1987.

6. Gerrell Moore, personal communication, May 12, 1992.

7. CINCPAC TO CINCPACFLT, 100342Z July 1964 (FOIA); Sharp, *Strategy for Defeat*, p. 39.

8. ADMINO CINCPAC, 152123Z Jul 64 (FOIA NHC).

9. Galloway, *Gulf of Tonkin*, pp. 38–39; Gibbons, *U.S. Government*, part 2, p. 283.

10. Interview with Gerrell Moore.

11. Futrell, *Advisory Years*, p. 228.

12. Interview with Gerrell Moore.

13. Ibid; *GOT*, part 2, p. 7.

14. Quisenberry et al., "NVN PT Boat Exploitation Team Report," pp. IV-G-10, IV-G-18.

15. Interview with Gerrell Moore.

16. Letter, Gerrell Moore, Sept. 18, 1982, shown to the author by Moore.

17. Interview with Gerrell Moore.

18. Ibid.

19. Ibid.

20. Probably JCS to CINCPAC, July 15, 1964; quoted in Goulden, p. 124.

21. *GOT*, pp. 25–26.

22. Interview with Gerrell Moore.

23. Ibid.

24. Cmdr. Robert M. Laske, personal communications.

25. Cmdr. Herbert Ogier, personal communication, June 29, 1987.

26. Interview with Gerrell Moore.

27. COMSEVENTHFLT, 260955Z July 1964 (FOIA).

28. Patrick Park and Ronald Stalsberg, personal communications. See also Goulden, *Truth*, p. 126.

29. Richard B. Corsette, personal communication, September 3, 1991. Radarman Andres Adamick also recalled cameras having been confiscated; Wise, "Remember the Maddox!," p. 123.

30. Gerrell Moore, personal communication.

31. Goulden, *Truth*, p. 127; some other authors have picked up this error from Goulden.

32. Marolda and Fitzgerald, *From Military Assistance to Combat*, p. 409. Sen. Wayne Morse, *Congressional Record*, February 29, 1968, p. 4963. Galloway, *Gulf of Tonkin*, p. 41.

33. Interview with Patrick J. McGarvey.

34. Prados, "Spooks in the Ether," pp. 19–20.

35. Interview with Cathal L. Flynn, Jr.

36. Lcdr. Burton L. Knight, personal communications.

37. CINCPAC, 012205Z April 1964 (FOIA). See also Tourison, *Secret Army*, pp. 120–21.

38. COMSEVENTHFLT, 260955Z July 1964 (FOIA).

39. Marolda and Fitzgerald, *From Military Assistance to Combat*, pp. 402–4.

40. Interview with Adm. Roy L. Johnson, August 11, 1988.

41. COMSEVENTHFLT, 260955Z July 1964 (FOIA).

42. CINCPAC to JCS (J3 for JRC), 290100Z Jan. 64 (FOIA NHC).

43. CINCPACFLT 190259Z May 1964, endorsed and expanded upon in CINCPAC 272258Z May 1964 (both FOIA NHC).

44. Dr. Ray S. Cline, letter to the author, August 8, 1987. See also transcript of *Vietnam: A Television History* (Boston: WGBH, 1983), episode 4, p. 6.

45. James Bartholomew, personal communications. See also Goulden, *Truth*, p. 127.

46. Army Museum, Hanoi. Tourison, *Secret Army*, pp. 146–48.

47. Unger to State, August 1, 1964, 011115Z, *DDRS* 1981-211C.

48. VNA (English), August 2, 1964, and VNA (Vietnamese), August 5, in *FBIS*, August 2, 1964, JJJ1, and August 6, 1964, JJJ6; *Nhan Dan*, August 3, 1964, p. 1, and August 6, 1964, p. 1. For the geography see U.S. Army Map Series L509, maps NE 48-2, 48-3, and 48-7.

49. Marshall Green, "Immediate Actions in the Period Prior to Decision," November 7, 1964, in *Pentagon Papers* (Gravel), 3:609. See also Austin, *President's War*, p. 25.

50. Saigon 2412 to State, June 5, 1964, in *FRUS-VN-64*, p. 456.

51. *Nhan Dan*, August 5, 1964, p. 4.

52. Maddox Note 003500, July 28, 1964 (Enclosure 13 to DeSoto patrol report).

53. *Nhan Dan*, August 5, 1964, p. 1. Also interview with naval officers, Ho Chi Minh City, May 1989.

54. DeSoto patrol report, p. 7.

55. JCS 7303 to CINCPAC, July 8, 1964, and CINCPAC to CINCPACFLT, 092122Z July 1964, in *VNSF* 4:797, 786.

56. Enclosure 6 to DeSoto patrol report.

57. Enclosure 5 to DeSoto patrol report.

58. "Command and Control," pp. 18, 19.

59. DeSoto patrol report: Narrative (enclosure 1), p. 5, and navigation log (enclosure 6).

60. *Nhan Dan*, August 4, 1964, p. 1, and August 7, 1964, p. 4; General Hoang Van Thai, "Bao cao," p. 3; Message from the DRV Foreign Minister to the Chair of the U.N. Security Council, August 19, 1964, in *Hanh dong chien tranh*, p. 41; Thuy, "Phan doi X doan Y," p. 37.

61. DeSoto patrol report, enclosure 1 (Narrative), p. 6.

62. Interview with Gerrell Moore.

63. Quoted in State 381 to Saigon, August 8, 1964, CFV, Box 7. See also Bundy MS, chapter 14, p. 16.

64. Quoted in McNamara, *In Retrospect*, p. 141.

65. *Pentagon Papers* (Gravel), 3:561, 562, 564.

66. Oral History, Earle G. Wheeler, August 21, 1969 (LBJ Presidential Library), pp. 21–22.

67. Marolda and Fitzgerald, *From Military Assistance to Combat*, p. 411; McNamara, *In Retrospect*, p. 130.

68. Interview with Gerrell Moore.

69. Ibid.

70. Gerrell Moore, personal communications.

71. Interviews with Gerrell Moore and one other officer.

72. Interview with Ronald Stalsberg, August 26, 1990.

73. " 'Phantom Battle,' " p. 59; *Maddox* CIC log (NHC).

74. Cmdr. Herbert Ogier, personal communication, September 16, 1986.

75. Patrick Park, personal communications; interview with Ronald Stalsberg.

76. Interview with Gerrell Moore.

77. One source says 40 mm; *Lich su Hai quan*, 1985, p. 56.

78. Quisenberry et al., "NVN PT Boat Exploitation Team Report," July 1966, pp. IV-E-1, IV-E-2, IV-I-2.

79. CINCPACFLT to CINCPAC, 051219Z Aug. 1964, CFV, Box 27: "Maddox Incident and Operation Pierce Arrow [1 of 3]," #40.

80. Quisenberry et al., "NVN PT Boat Exploitation Team Report," p. IV-I-1.

81. Discussion of People's Navy doctrine in the pages that follow is necessarily based on interrogation of the men captured in 1966, the only available source. The author is assuming that doctrine was approximately the same in 1964. It is not certain, however, that this assumption is correct.

82. Untitled, undated intelligence summary from NSC files, in *SS* reel 25, frame 82. *Jane's Fighting Ships, 1963–64*, pp. 53, 442; *1964–65*, pp. 53, 451.

83. *Lich su Hai quan*, 1985, pp. 93–94.

84. CTU 72.1.2 (relaying for CTG 72.1) to AIG 181, 020315Z Aug. 64 (FOIA NHC).

85. *Maddox* CIC log; CTG 72.1 to COMSEVENTHFLT, 020531Z Aug. 64 (FOIA NHC).

86. CTG 72.1, 050145Z August 1964 (FOIA NHC).

87. Shown to the author by officers of the People's Navy, May 27, 1989.

Chapter Four. The First Incident, August 2

1. An earlier hour, 1215G, is implied by Thuy, "Phan doi X doan Y," p. 37, but this seems unlikely.

2. Interview in Ho Chi Minh City, May 27, 1989. A very unclear passage in Bui Tin, p. 133, suggests an alternate scenario: that Minister of Defense Vo Nguyen Giap did not want an attack made, but that Party First Secretary Le Duan bypassed Giap and ordered the military to carry out the attack.

3. Thuy, "Phan doi X doan Y," p. 38; General Hoang Van Thai, "Bao cao," p. 3.

4. Marolda and Fitzgerald, *From Military Assistance to Combat*, p. 414; interviews with Gerrell Moore and one other officer.

5. Gerrell Moore, personal communication.

6. Goulden, *Truth*, p. 130.

7. Marolda and Fitzgerald, *From Military Assistance to Combat*, p. 415; McNaughton Report, p. 2, gives a time of 1357G.

8. CTG 72.1, 050145Z August 1964.

9. Cmdr. Herbert Ogier, September 16, 1986. Cmdr. Ogier's statement is supported by CTU 72.1.2 (relaying for CTG 72.1) to AIG 181, 021443Z Aug. 64 (FOIA NHC), which states, "Anticipating attack *Maddox* had opened Point Delta 15 miles to seaward prior to pursuit by P-4's."

10. Quisenberry et al., "NVN PT Boat Exploitation Team Report," p. IV-G-15.

11. Hong Thuy, "Thieu uy Nguyen van Gian," p. 25.

12. Sharp, *Strategy for Defeat*, p. 40.

13. Column published in many newspapers; see for example *Atlanta Journal*, August 16, 1964, p. 7-B.

14. William Bundy, personal communications.

15. Quisenberry et al., "NVN PT Boat Exploitation Team Report," p. IV-G-18.

16. Capt. John Herrick, October 13, 1986.

17. Cmdr. Herbert Ogier, personal communication, February 26, 1987. AP dispatch, published in *Arkansas Gazette*, July 16, 1967, reprinted in *Congressional Record*, February 28, 1968, p. 4581 (this is in fact one of the more important published accounts of the Tonkin Gulf incidents); also Windchy, *Tonkin Gulf*, p. 121; Wise, "Remember the Maddox!," p. 124; Richard B. Corsette, personal communications; Goulden, *Truth*, p. 132.

18. Marolda and Fitzgerald, *From Military Assistance to Combat*, p. 416; FOIA, Naval Sea Systems Command; CTG 72.1(?), 040229Z(?) Aug. 64 (FOIA NHC); Halpern, *West Pac '64*, p. 189.

19. Tourison, *Secret Army*, pp. 154–55, states that it was not Khoai but his chief of staff, Tran Bao, who led the attack; Tourison is the interrogator who questioned Tran Bao after Bao's capture by U.S. forces in 1966. This author, however, is more inclined to accept the statements from Marolda and Fitzgerald, *From Military Assistance to Combat*, p. 417 (probably based on communications intelligence), and from recent Vietnamese accounts, that it was Khoai. Tran Bao's personal participation in the attack appears for the first time in Tourison's 1995 book; it was not mentioned in the account of what Tran Bao said about the attack on the *Maddox* in Tourison's earlier book *Talking with Victor Charlie*, which Tourison says he actually wrote in 1967, less than eighteen months after the interrogation.

20. Quisenberry et al., "NVN PT Boat Exploitation Team Report," pp. IV-C-3, IV-E-2, IV-F-2.

21. USS *Cavalier* to Director of Naval Intelligence, 131115Z July 1966 (FOIA). See also CTU 72.1.2 (relaying for CTG 72.1) to AIG 181, 021443Z Aug. 64.

22. USS *Cavalier* to Director of Naval Intelligence, 131115Z July 1966 (FOIA).

23. Interview with Ronald Stalsberg.

24. The very first U.S. press release on the incident said that the PTs had and fired 37-mm guns; Goulden, *Truth*, p. 23.

25. General Hoang Van Thai, "Bao cao," p. 3.

26. Patrick Park, personal communication.

27. Ibid.

28. Ibid.

29. Interview with Ronald Stalsberg.

30. Richard B. Corsette and Ronald Stalsberg, personal communications; Halpern, *West Pac '64*, p. 189; Goulden, *Truth*, p. 133.

31. Interview with Ronald Stalsberg.

32. A message on which the identifying information is partially illegible, apparently CTG 72.1, 040229Z Aug. 1964, states that the firing time was fourteen minutes.

33. Interview with Ronald Stalsberg.

34. Richard B. Corsette, personal communication, September 3, 1991.

35. The CIC log is not fully legible, but appears to indicate the destroyer ceased firing at 1528G.

36. CTG 72.1, 020838Z Aug. 64 [1638H]; COMSEVENTHFLT to CTG 72.1, 020859Z [1659H].

37. The official report from the *Ticonderoga* says that T-339 was about five miles

behind the other two, but more detailed statements written informally by the pilots immediately after the action indicate that T-339 was only about one mile behind T-333 and T-336. CTG 77.5 to COMSEVENTHFLT, 021506Z Aug. 1964 (NHC); Stockdale and Stockdale, *In Love and War*, Appendix 1, p. 450.

38. Stockdale and Stockdale, *In Love and War*, Appendix 1, pp. 450–51.

39. Adm. James Stockdale, personal communication, June 7, 1995.

40. Friedman, *U.S. Naval Weapons*, p. 200.

41. CTG 77.5 to COMSEVENTHFLT, 021506Z Aug. 1964 (NHC).

42. Nguyen Thai Nguyen, "Qua tran chien dau," p. 14; Squadron 135 executive officer, cited in USS *Cavalier* to DNI, 131115Z July 1966 (FOIA); Stockdale and Stockdale, *In Love and War*, Appendix 1, pp. 451–52.

43. Squadron 135 executive officer, cited in USS *Cavalier* to DNI, 131115Z July 1966 (FOIA); *Quan Doi Nhan Dan*, August 11, 1964, p. 2; Quisenberry et al., "NVN PT Boat Exploitation Team Report," p. IV-H-5.

44. General Hoang Van Thai, "Bao cao," p. 6.

45. Adm. James B. Stockdale, Red Tie Luncheon, Admiral Kidd Club, San Diego, August 1, 1989.

46. Stockdale and Stockdale, *In Love and War*, pp. 6–9, 455; VNA (Vietnamese), August 12, 1964, trans. in *FBIS*, August 13, 1964, JJJ7.

47. *Maddox* CIC log, entries for 1808I and 1830I, August 2, 1964; interview with Adm. Roy L. Johnson, August 11, 1988; COMSEVENTHFLT to CTG 72.1, 020859Z August 1964 (FOIA NHC); CTG 77.5 021008Z August 1964 (FOIA NHC).

48. Interview with Vietnamese naval officers, Ho Chi Minh City, May 27, 1989; report of the interrogation of the executive officer of Squadron 135 in 1966, USS *Cavalier* to DNI, 131115Z Jul 1966; Sedgwick D. Tourison, Jr., personal communication, February 27, 1995; *Lich su hai quan*, 1985, p. 99.

49. CTG 77.5 to COMSEVENTHFLT, 021008Z, p. 2.

50. Cmdr. Donald Hegrat, personal communications.

51. Interview; source was not aboard the *Maddox* in 1964.

52. Marolda and Fitzgerald, *From Military Assistance to Combat*, p. 419.

53. *Southeast Asia Resolution*, p. 6.

54. Commander Seventh Fleet, FF/7/WRQ:rb, 3461, Ser N2-00114, 9 August 1966 (FOIA COMSEVENTHFLT). Quisenberry et al., "NVN PT Boat Exploitation Team Report," pp. IV-A-9, IV-B-1. USS *Cavalier* to CINCPACFLT, 131115Z July 1964 (NHC).

55. Robert McNamara, in *Executive Sessions*, p. 293. This passage was heavily censored in *Southeast Asia Resolution*, p. 14.

56. *Executive Sessions*, p. 294. This passage was entirely omitted from *Southeast Asia Resolution*, p. 16.

57. COMUSMACV to CINCPAC, 292259Z May 1964, repeated as CINCPAC 010036Z November 1964 (FOIA).

58. *Southeast Asia Resolution*, pp. 6, 7, 21, 32.

59. *Congressional Record*, August 6, 1964, p. 18404.

60. *Southeast Asia Resolution*, pp. 7, 21, 30, 32.

61. McNaughton Report; "Command and Control," pp. 100, 110–12. See also *USVNR*, book 4, IV-C-2-b, p. 5.

62. *GOT*, pp. 28, 31 (see also pp. 96–98).

63. McNamara, *In Retrospect*, p. 137.

64. Interviews with Thomas L. Hughes and Allen S. Whiting, September 19, 1994; Gittinger, *Johnson Years*, p. 24.

65. Windchy, *Tonkin Gulf*, p. 135; see also Goulden, *Truth*, p. 80.

66. *The Situation in South Vietnam*, July 30–August 5, 1964, p. 1, in *VNSF*, 5:744.

67. Saigon 282 to State, 030240Z Aug. 1964, FOIA State.

68. Notes of telephone call, McNamara-Ball, August 3, 1964, 9:55 A.M. Lyndon B. Johnson Presidential Library, Papers of George Ball, Vietnam 1, Box 7, #76.

69. Johnson, *Vantage Point*, p. 113.

70. DRV Ministry of Foreign Affairs, "Memorandum Regarding the U.S. War Acts against the Democratic Republic of Vietnam in the First Days of August 1964" (Hanoi: September 1964), quoted in Goulden, *Truth*, p. 80. See also message, DRV Foreign Minister to Chair, U.N. Security Council, August 19, 1964, in *Hanh dong chien tranh*, p. 41; *Nhan Dan* editorial, August 6, 1964, p. 1.

71. DRV Foreign Minister to Chair, U.N. Security Council; General Hoang Van Thai, "Bao cao," p. 3; *Quan Doi Nhan Dan* editorials, August 6, 1964, p. 1, and August 8, 1964, p. 1.

72. *Quan Doi Nhan Dan*, August 11, 1964, p. 2; Hong Thuy, "Thieu uy Nguyen van Gian," pp. 24–25.

73. *Hai Quan* no. 21 (November 1964), pp. 11–14.

74. *Quan Doi Nhan Dan*, August 11, 1964, p. 2.

75. *Hai Quan*, no. 21 (November 1964), p. 5.

76. Thuy, "Phan doi X doan Y," p. 38; Hong Thuy, "Thieu uy Nguyen van Gian," pp. 25–26.

77. Thuy, "Phan doi X doan Y," p. 38.

Chapter Five. The DeSoto Patrol Resumes

1. Interview with Adm. Roy L. Johnson.

2. COMSEVENTHFLT to CINCPACFLT, 031712Z Aug. 1964 (*GOTA*, frame 239).

3. Interview with Chad James, August 23, 1990.

4. JCS 7680, 021725Z Aug. 1964, text in *FRUS-VN-64*, p. 591. See also JCS 7700 (*GOTA*, frame 254), and CINCPAC to JCS, 032353Z Aug. 1964 (*GOTA*, frames 242–43).

5. Forrestal to Rusk, August 3, 1964, in *FRUS-VN-64*, p. 599.

6. Marolda and Fitzgerald, *From Military Assistance to Combat*, p. 421; see also p. 425.

7. Goulden, pp. 14, 137.

8. DeSoto patrol report, pp. 2, 7.

9. CTU 72.1.2 (relaying for CTG 72.1), 021443Z Aug. 64 (FOIA NHC).

10. CTG 72.1 to COMSEVENTHFLT, 040140Z August 1964.

11. Interview with Ronald Stalsberg.

12. Interview with Richard Bacino, April 8, 1990.

13. Interview with Chief Sonarman Joseph E. Schaperjahn, August 9, 1988.

14. Lcdr. Douglas G. Smith, "Personal Notes" furnished to the author.

15. Interview with John J. Barry.

16. Ibid.

17. COMUSMACV to Secretary of State, 040955Z Aug. 1964, *GOTA*, frame 190; see also following frame 433. Officer interview.

18. COMUSMACV to COMSEVENTHFLT, 031231Z; COMSEVENTHFLT to CINCPACFLT, 031712Z; JCS to CINCPAC, 032351Z Aug. 1964, in *GOTA*, frames 230, 239, 240–41 respectively.

19. COMUSMACV 301107Z July 1964 (FOIA NHC).

20. Karnow, *Vietnam*, p. 370. The suggestion may originally have come to Sharp from Adm. Moorer, Commander in Chief of the Pacific Fleet; see CPFLT 032259Z Aug. 64, cited in Marolda and Fitzgerald, *From Military Assistance to Combat*, p. 425.

21. CTG 72.1 to AIG 181, 031546Z Aug. 1964; CTG 72.1 to AIG 181, 040511Z Aug. 1964 (*GOTA*, frames 227, 248). See also letter of A. C. Lassiter, Jr. (Capt. Ogier's successor as commander of *Maddox*), Ser: 008 of September 16, 1964, modifying Capt. Ogier's DeSoto patrol report and attached to it.

22. Interview, Ho Chi Minh City, May 27, 1989.

23. General Hoang Van Thai, "Bao cao," p. 4.

24. Personal communications, Lcdr. Burton L. Knight. Cmdr. Robert Laske also says he has no recollection of a recoilless rifle larger than 57 mm having been used aboard the PTFs based in Danang.

25. Reske, *MACVSOG Command History*, p. 46.

26. Ibid., p. 45.

27. Interview with Cathal L. Flynn, Jr.

28. *Nhan Dan*, August 7, 1964, p. 4; message of the DRV Foreign Minister to the Chair of the U.N. Security Council, August 19, 1964, in *Hanh dong chien tranh*, p. 41; General Hoang Van Thai, "Bao cao," pp. 3–4.

29. Reske, *MACVSOG Command History*, p. 46 (the text has been sanitized, but the meaning is clear).

30. Interview with Ronald Stalsberg. See also Goulden, *Truth*, p. 139.

31. Charlton and Moncrieff, *Many Reasons Why*, p. 108. The interview was in late 1976 or early 1977.

32. *GOT*, p. 19.

33. Taylor to Secretary of State, August 3, 1964, *GOTA*, frames 615–16.

34. John McNaughton, "Plan of Action for South Vietnam," second draft, September 3, 1964, text in *Pentagon Papers* (Gravel), 3:558.

35. MAC SOG 7231, 031231Z August 1964.

36. *Unauthorized Bombing*, pp. 6–16, 22.

37. Cmdr. Robert M. Laske, personal communications.

38. Memo, CM-295-64, "OPLAN 34A—Maritime Operations," December 8, 1964, quoted in "Maritime Operations" (Annex D to Appendix C to MACSOG Documentation Study), page C-d-7. See also "MACSOG Operations Against North Vietnam," C-14, which states, "Clearance procedures were highly centralized throughout 1964."

39. Memo, Forrestal to Rusk, August 8, 1964, found by William Gibbons in Department of State Central File, Pol 27 Viet S, cited in Gibbons, *U.S. Government*, 3:10n. The author thanks Dr. Gibbons for supplying a photocopy of the original memo.

40. Memo, Forrestal to Rusk, August 3, 1964, in *FRUS-VN-64*, p. 598.

41. Bundy MS, chapter 14A, pp. 24–25.

42. Bundy MS, chapter 14A, pp. 24–25; also William Bundy, personal communications.

43. Text in *New York Times*, February 21, 1968, p. 12.

44. Summary Notes of 538th NSC Meeting, August 4, 1964, 6:15 to 6:40 P.M. (NSC Meetings File, Box 1). See also cable, Rusk to Ottawa and Saigon, August 8, 1964, CFV, Box 7; Goulden, *Truth*, pp. 14, 137; and Goulden's apparent source, *GOT*, p. 15.

45. Interview with Allen S. Whiting, September 19, 1994.

Chapter Six. The Second Incident, August 4

1. General Hoang Van Thai, "Bao cao," p. 4.

2. Interview with Chad James.

3. CTG 72.1 to AIG 181, 040635Z Aug. 1964, *GOTA* frame 253, corrected by NAVCOMMSTA PHIL 040830Z Aug. 1964, *GOTA* frame 266.

4. Personal communication, September 16, 1986.

5. Cmdr. George H. Edmondson, letter to the author, September 15, 1987.

6. Capt. James A Barber, Jr. (USN, Ret.), letter to the author, November 3, 1987.

7. Herbert Ogier, personal communications. Also Capt. Bryce. D. Inman, personal communications. Lcdr. Douglas D. Smith, however, considers this idea most unlikely.

8. Schratz, *Submarine Commander*, p. 122.

9. Capt. John Herrick and Cmdr. Herbert Ogier, personal communications.

10. Schreadley, *From the Rivers to the Sea*, pp. 68–69.

11. Capt. James A. Barber (Ret.), personal communications.

12. *Arkansas Gazette*, July 16, 1967, reprinted in *Congressional Record*, February 28, 1968, p. 4582.

13. Personal communications.

14. CIA Memorandum, "The North Vietnamese Crisis," August 6, 1964, in *CIA Research Reports*, 2:343. CTG 72.1 to CTF 77, 060830Z Aug. 1964 (FOIA NHC). CTF 77 to COMSEVENTHFLT, 071458Z Aug. 1964, *Special Subjects*, 24:786–87.

15. Lcdr. Douglas G. Smith, "Personal Notes."

16. Ibid.

17. The *Turner Joy*'s records on wave height are so unconvincing as to be useless; the twenty-four entries giving wave heights at hourly intervals for August 4, 1964, simply repeat the figure of two feet, twenty-four times. With winds shown in the same records as having varied from six to twenty-five knots, this record of absolutely uniform wave height cannot be taken seriously.

18. "Chronology of Events, Gulf of Tonkin 4 August 1964" (COMDESDIV 192 [Herrick] to CTF 77, Ser: 002 of 13 August 1964). Almost all of the joint chronology was incorporated with little or no change into two later reports from Ogier to the Chief of Naval Operations. The first of these, the DeSoto patrol report of August 24, 1964, added huge amounts of additional material. The second, "Report of Tonkin Gulf, Action of 4 August 1964," August 25, 1964, referred to hereafter as *Maddox* action report, contained only a few pages of material that had not been in the joint chronology.

19. "Action Report for Gulf of Tonkin, 4 August 1964," Commanding Officer, USS

Turner Joy [Barnhart] to Chief of Naval Operations, Ser: 004 of September 11, 1964 (NHC), p. I-1. Referred to hereafter as *Turner Joy* action report.

20. *Turner Joy* action report, pp. III-1, III-2.

21. Ibid., p. III-1; interview with John J. Barry.

22. *Turner Joy* action report, p. VI-1.

23. CINCPACFLT to CNO, letter FF1-1, 3000, Ser 31/0040, January 11, 1965.

24. Report released by NSA under FOIA.

25. "'Phantom Battle,'" p. 61; Robert McNamara, in *GOT*, pp. 10, 17, 92; CTU 72.1.2 to AIG 181, 042158Z Aug. 64 (two versions of this message have been consulted, one obtained from NHC, the other from the LBJ Library); Marolda and Fitzgerald, *From Military Assistance to Combat*, p. 426; "Chronology of Events: Tuesday, August 4 and Wednesday, August 5, 1964, Tonkin Gulf Strike," third draft, dated August 25, 1964, p. 3 (I thank the author of this report, Lawrence Levinson, for furnishing me with a copy).

26. Cmdr. Robert M. Laske, personal communications.

27. CTU 72.1.2 to AIG 181, 041240Z Aug. 64 (FOIA NHC).

28. Joint chronology, pp. 2–3; CIC log, *Maddox*; Surface Search Radar Contact Sheets, *Maddox*.

29. CTG 72.1 to CINCPACFLT, 062355Z Aug. 1964 (*GOTA*, frames 334–35).

30. Interview with Chad James.

31. Interview with John J. Barry.

32. Capt. Bryce D. Inman, personal communication, December 4, 1989.

33. Interview with Chad James; *Turner Joy* CIC log.

34. Primary Combat Information Net log, attached to *Turner Joy* action report.

35. Joint chronology, p. 4.

36. CTU 72.1 to AIG 181, 042158Z Aug. 64.

37. Joint chronology, p. 3.

38. Entry for 2105G, *Turner Joy* Primary Combat Information Net log, in *Turner Joy* action report, p. II-B-2. See also *Turner Joy* CIC log, August 4, entry for 2105G.

39. *Maddox* quartermaster log, 2039G; *Turner Joy* action report, September 11, 1964, pp. II-B-2, II-C-2; *Maddox* CIC log; *Maddox* track #23 (NHC); joint chronology, p. 4.

40. Quartermaster log, *Maddox*, 2059G; CTG 77.5 to COMSEVENTHFLT, 041408Z Aug. 1964, *Special Subjects* reel 24, frames 932–33.

41. *Turner Joy* CIC log.

42. CTU 72.1 to AIG 181, 042158Z Aug. 64.

43. Douglas G. Smith, "Personal Notes."

44. *Turner Joy* Primary Combat Information Net log.

45. Joint chronology, p. 1. The location of the square may have been specified in CINCPACFLT msg. 021104Z August 1964.

46. This passage appears in exactly the same words in joint chronology, p. 3; DeSoto patrol report, enclosure 12, p. 2; and *Maddox* action report, p. 4.

47. John Herrick, personal communication.

48. Quoted in Goulden, *Truth*, p. 40.

49. CIC logs, *Maddox* and *Turner Joy*; joint chronology, p. 4.

50. "NBC White Paper on Vietnam," April 27, 1985; Stockdale and Stockdale, *In Love and War*, pp. 13–19; Marolda and Fitzgerald, *From Military Assistance to Combat*, p. 431.

51. Interview with Adm. Wesley McDonald, February 3, 1987.

52. Joint chronology, p. 4.

53. *Turner Joy* action report, September 11, 1964, pp. II-A-1, II-C-3; Richard B. Corsette, personal communications; statements of Capt. Herrick and of Ltjg. F. M. Frick, in CTG 72.1 to COMSEVENTHFLT, 062355Z Aug. 1964 (*GOTA*, frames 335–36).

54. *Turner Joy* CIC log, 2132G; *Maddox* quartermaster log, 2131G; undated chronology, *Turner Joy*.

55. Statements of Capt. Herrick and of Ltjg. F. M. Frick, in CTG 72.1 to COMSEVENTHFLT, 062355Z Aug. 1964 (*GOTA*, frames 335–36).

56. Patrick Park, personal communications.

57. *Maddox* quartermaster log.

58. *Turner Joy* action report, pp. II-A-1, II-C-4.

59. The quartermaster log of the *Turner Joy* states that the ship commenced firing to port with five-inch guns at 2135G, and with three-inch guns at 2136G. There is no good explanation for the conflict between this and all the other records.

60. Interview with Chad James, August 23, 1990.

61. *Turner Joy* action report, pp. II-A-1, II-C-4; joint chronology, p. 4.

62. Telephone interviews with David Mallow, March 31 and April 5, 1993.

63. Austin, *President's War*, p. 283; see also Wise, "Remember the Maddox!," p. 126.

64. Statement of Capt. John Herrick, in CTG 72.1 to CINCPACFLT, 062355Z Aug. 1964, in *GOTA*, frames 334–35.

65. Capt. John Herrick, personal communications.

66. Interview with David Mallow.

67. Joint chronology, p. 4; DeSoto patrol report, enclosure 12, p. 3; *Maddox* action report, p. 5.

68. *Turner Joy* action report, p. II-C-4; joint chronology, p. 4.

69. *Maddox* action report, p. 11.

70. *Turner Joy* action report, p. I-2.

71. Marolda, "Tonkin Gulf," pp. 290–91.

72. Marolda and Fitzgerald, *From Military Assistance to Combat*, pp. 427–29.

73. Ibid., pp. 429–30.

74. Quoted in DuVall and Metzger, "Gulf of Tonkin Destroyer Retired," p. 17.

75. Sharp, *Strategy for Defeat*, p. 43.

76. CTG 72.1 to CINCPACFLT, 041442Z and 041452Z Aug. 1964 (FOIA).

77. Goulden, *Truth*, p. 146.

78. Patrick Park, personal communications.

79. Statement of Frederick Frick (see also statements of Richard B. Corsette, Kieth J. Bane, and John Herrick), in CTG 72.1 to COMSEVENTHFLT, 062355Z Aug. 1964 (*GOTA*, frames 334, 336).

80. Patrick Park, personal communications.

81. Interview with Lcdr. Douglas G. Smith, March 22, 1990.

82. *Turner Joy* quartermaster log.

83. *Turner Joy* action report, p. II-A-2; *Turner Joy* deck log.

84. *Turner Joy* action report, pp. II-A-2, II-C-5; *Turner Joy* deck log and CIC log; joint track chart.

85. *Turner Joy* action report, p. II-A-2; see also p. II-C-5, and CIC log.

86. *Turner Joy* action report, p. VII-2.

87. *Maddox* action report, p. 10.

88. Cmdr. Herbert Ogier, personal communication, September 16, 1986.

89. Interview with Joseph Schaperjahn.

90. Interview with Lcdr. Douglas G. Smith, March 22, 1990.

91. Cmdr. Herbert Ogier, personal communication, September 24, 1984.

92. Patrick Park, personal communications; see also Goulden, *Truth*, p. 12. Richard B. Corsette denies that the account of Park being ordered to fire on this occasion is accurate; personal communication.

93. " 'Phantom Battle,' " p. 62.

94. Stockdale and Stockdale, *In Love and War*, pp. 19–20.

95. Alvarez and Pitch, *Chained Eagle*, p. 8.

96. Ibid, p. 11.

97. Interviews with John J. Barry and Richard Bacino.

98. Levinson, *Alpha Strike*, p. 18.

Chapter Seven. The Evidence from the Destroyers

1. CTG 72.1, 041727Z August 1964 (FOIA NHC).

2. CTG 72.1 to AIG 181, 041754Z Aug. 1964. Text derived from comparison of three copies of this message, with minor variations and garbles. Two were obtained from NHC under FOIA; the third is in *GOTA*, frame 282.

3. Quoted in Scheer, "Tonkin," p. 20.

4. Interview with Capt. Bryce D. Inman.

5. *Turner Joy* to CINCPACFLT, 042310Z, lists sightings of a torpedo, of black smoke, and of the silhouette of a vessel, as well as radar tracking of targets.

6. Goulding, *Confirm or Deny*, p. 103.

7. Summary Notes of the 538th Meeting of the National Securiry Council, August 4, 1964, 6:15–6:40 P.M., in *FRUS-VN-64*, p. 611.

8. Memorandum of telephone conversation, August 6, 1964, in *FRUS-VN-64*, pp. 645–46.

9. JCS to CINCPAC (copies to *Ticonderoga*, *Maddox*, *Turner Joy*, etc.), 061642Z August 1964.

10. Personal communications.

11. Richard B. Corsette, personal communications, August 18 and 27, 1987.

12. Kerr, *Journey*, p. 178.

13. Ibid.

14. Joint chronology (COMDESDIV 192 to CTF 77, August 13, 1964).

15. Joint track chart, Naval Historical Center.

16. Interview with Joseph E. Schaperjahn, August 9, 1988.

17. [Presumably CTG 72.1] to AIG 181, 041754Z Aug. 1964, *GOTA* frame 282. See also COMSEVENTHFLT to CINCPACFLT, 042020Z Aug. 1964, *GOTA* frame 289. At an opposite extreme, about six hours after the action, the *Turner Joy* had much more

cautiously reported "confirm being attacked by 2 PT craft." *Turner Joy* to CINCPACFLT, 042310Z Aug. 1964, *Special Subjects* reel 24, frame 900.

18. *Turner Joy* action report, p. II-A-1.

19. Ibid., pp. II-A-1, II-C-3, II-C-4; *Maddox* action report, p. 5; Richard B. Corsette, personal communications.

20. Barber, "Tonkin Gulf: Comments," p. 324.

21. "Chronology," in *Turner Joy* action report, p. II-A-2.

22. "Chronology" and "Summary of Damage," in *Turner Joy* action report, pp. II-A-2 and IV-1.

23. Richard B. Corsette, personal communications.

24. Interview with Ronald Stalsberg; Friedman, *U.S. Naval Weapons*, pp. 238–39.

25. *Turner Joy* action report, esp. pp. III-1, III-2, VI-1, VII-1, VII-2.

26. FOIA Naval Sea Systems Command; *Turner Joy* action report, pp. III-2, VI-1.

27. Douglas Smith, personal communications.

28. Capt. John Herrick, personal communications. See also Goulden, *Truth*, p. 146, in which Herrick is quoted giving a vaguer and more impressive account of this incident.

29. Cmdr. George H. Edmondson, personal communication, September 15, 1987.

30. Lcdr. Douglas Smith says that he believes he had already become aware of the existence of radar phantoms in the Gulf of Tonkin. Personal communications.

31. Richard B. Corsette, personal communications.

32. Joint chronology, pp. 5, 7; *Maddox* action report, p. 11. The last detection of possible enemy radar recorded in the CIC log of the *Maddox* was between 1655G and 1716G.

33. Officer interview.

34. Marolda and Fitzgerald, *From Military Assistance to Combat*, p. 427, n. 79. The citation in Marolda and Fitzgerald's footnote is as follows: "See *Turner Joy*, action report, ser 004 of 11 Sep 1964, p. vi-2; DESDIV 192, Chronology, ser 002 of 13 Aug 1964, p. 2."

35. *Turner Joy* action report, p. VI-2. See also Goulden, *Truth*, p. 153.

36. A. C. Lassiter, Jr., letter, September 16, 1964, attached to and modifying DeSoto patrol report; Letter, Marolda to Moise, 5750, Ser CH/17073, November 18, 1987.

37. Patrick Park, personal communications.

38. Patrick N. Park, in "The Seeds of Conflict," an episode in the series "The Vietnam War with Walter Cronkite," CBS, 1987 (this interview came originally from a 1971 broadcast of "60 Minutes"). See also Goulden, *Truth*, p. 155.

39. Patrick Park, personal communications.

40. Interview with David Mallow.

41. CTG 72.1 to COMSEVENTHFLT, 062355Z Aug. 1964 (*GOTA*, frames 335–37).

42. *Maddox* action report, pp. 10, 11.

43. *Turner Joy* to COMSEVENTHFLT, 050511Z Aug. 1964, and *Turner Joy* to CINCPACFLT, 062331Z Aug. 1964.

44. *Turner Joy* to CINCPACFLT, "Proof of Attack," 062331Z Aug. 64, p. 1 (*GOTA* frame 330).

45. *Turner Joy* action report, p. III-4.

46. Joint chronology, pp. 4–5.

47. Interview with John J. Barry.

48. Statement of Ltjg. John J. Barry, August 7, 1964 (FOIA NHC).

49. Wise, "Remember the Maddox!," p. 126.

50. Interview with John J. Barry.

51. Statement of Ltjg. John J. Barry, August 7, 1964.

52. Joint chronology, p. 5.

53. Interview with Douglas Smith.

54. Interview with Joseph Schaperjahn.

55. Ibid. John Barry comments, "*This is not fact* but opinion and probability."

56. Interview with Lcdr. Douglas G. Smith, March 22, 1990.

57. Joint Chronology, p. 5.

58. Marolda and Fitzgerald, *From Military Assistance to Combat*, p. 429 n. 82, gives a misleading impression that the *Turner Joy* action report had said the *Turner Joy*'s sonar was of low quality.

59. Interview with John J. Barry.

60. *Turner Joy* action report, p. III-4.

61. Patrick Park, personal communications.

62. Interview with Joseph Schaperjahn.

63. See for example Turner Joy to COMSEVENTHFLT, 050511Z Aug. 1964; *Turner Joy* action report, p. VI-2.

64. Interview with Joseph Schaperjahn.

65. Interview with Capt. John Herrick, April 19, 1986. See also comments by Herrick in Goulden, *Truth*, p. 145, and by Herbert Ogier in Wise, "Remember the Maddox!," p. 126.

66. Scheer, "Tonkin," p. 22; also Herrick, personal communication, April 1986.

67. Statements of John J. Barry, Larry Litton, and Edwin Sentel, August 7, 1964 (FOIA NHC).

68. *Turner Joy* to COMSEVENTHFLT, 050511Z Aug. 1964. Note that in this report, "V" and "V-1" are treated as two separate contacts.

69. Interview with John J. Barry.

70. Windchy, *Tonkin Gulf*, pp. 271–74; see also Austin, *President's War*, pp. 280–81.

71. *Turner Joy* to *Maddox*, approximately 041635Z Aug. 64 (FOIA NHC). Other accounts referring to more than one torpedo having been seen by personnel on the *Turner Joy* include the following: CTU 72.1.2 (apprently relaying for CTG 72.1), 041848Z August 1964, NHC; Capt. Herrick, cited in Goulden, *Truth*, p. 145; *GOT*, pp. 58–59.

72. John J. Barry, personal communications.

73. Statement of Richard D. Nooks, August 8, 1964 (NHC).

74. Austin, *President's War*, p. 300.

75. Interview with Capt. John Herrick, April 19, 1986.

76. Statement of Richard Johnson, August 7, 1964; statements of Walter L. Shishim, Richard D. Nooks, and Gary D. Carroll, all dated August 8, 1964 (NHC).

77. *Turner Joy* action report, September 11, 1964, pp. II-A-2, p. II-C-5; Koplin's track chart.

78. Wise, "Remember the Maddox!," p. 127.

79. Statement of Richard M. Bacino, August 7, 1964 (NHC).

80. Richard M. Bacino, personal communications.

81. *Turner Joy* action report, pp. II-A-2, II-C-4, II-C-6.

82. Wise, "Remember the Maddox!," p. 126.

83. "Chronology," in *Turner Joy* action report, p. II-A-2.

84. Statements of Donald Sharkey, Kenneth Garrison, and Delner Jones, August 7, 1964; statements of Delner Jones and John Spanka, August 9, 1964 (NHC). *Turner Joy* to CINCPACFLT, 062331Z Aug. 1964 (*GOTA* frame 331); interview with Joseph Schaperjahn.

85. *Turner Joy* to CINCPACFLT, 062331Z Aug. 1964 (*GOTA* frame 331); statement of John B. Spanka, August 9, 1964.

86. Marolda, *By Sea, Air, and Land*, p. 51.

87. Press briefing given by Secretary of Defense Robert McNamara, August 5, 1964, starting at 12:02 A.M. EDT, transcript in *GOTA*, p. 3 of item starting on frame 691.

88. Summary Notes of the 538th NSC Meeting, August 4, 1964, NSC Meetings File, Box 1.

89. *Southeast Asia Resolution*, pp. 9, 16–17.

90. *Turner Joy* to COMSEVENTHFLT, 050511Z Aug. 1964; see also statements of SN Harvey Headley, SN Thomas Contreras, SN Donald Vance, and SN Anthony Rosenbaum, all dated August 8, 1964 (NHC).

91. Interview with Capt. John Herrick, April 19, 1986.

92. CTG 72.1 to AIG 181, 041754Z (FOIA NHC).

93. CTU 72.1.2 to AIG 181, 042158Z (FOIA NHC).

94. COMNAVBASE SUBIC to Chairman of the Joint Chiefs of Staff, 101155Z Aug. 1964, CFV, Box 227.

95. Capt. Bryce D. Inman, personal communications.

96. Wise, "Remember the Maddox!," p. 127.

97. Interviews with Gerrell Moore.

98. Patrick Park, personal communications.

99. Interview with Joseph Schaperjahn.

100. Interview with Richard M. Bacino, April 8, 1990.

101. Interview with John J. Barry.

Chapter Eight. Evidence from Other Sources

1. CTG 77.5, 041928Z August 1964 (FOIA NHC).

2. Cmdr. George H. Edmondson, personal communication, September 15, 1987.

3. Cmdr. George H. Edmondson, personal communications. See also Windchy, *Tonkin Gulf*, p. 204.

4. "NBC White Paper on Vietnam," April 27, 1985.

5. Cmdr. George H. Edmondson, personal communication, September 15, 1987.

6. "Desoto Ops—Afternoon 5 Aug [*sic*] 1964—Verification Proof of Attack," CTF 77 to CINCPACFLT, 070252Z Aug. 1964 (*GOTA*, frames 338–39). This report was also summarized by Secretary McNamara before the Senate Foreign Relations Committee in 1968; see *GOT*, p. 16.

7. Adm. James B. Stockdale, personal communication, March 1, 1985.

8. Cmdr. George H. Edmondson, personal communications.

9. Ibid., December 12, 1986; Windchy, *Tonkin Gulf*, p. 209.

10. Adm. James B. Stockdale, in Willenson, *Bad War*, p. 31.

11. Cmdr. George H. Edmondson, personal communication, September 15, 1987.

12. Adm. James B. Stockdale, personal communication, April 1, 1987.

13. Cmdr. Donald Hegrat, personal communications.

14. *Maddox* action report, p. 11.

15. Stockdale and Stockdale, *In Love and War*, p. 7.

16. Adm. James Stockdale, in "NBC White Paper on Vietnam," April 27, 1985.

17. Adm. James Stockdale, in Willenson, *Bad War*, p. 31.

18. CINCPACFLT 041708Z, *GOTA* frame 287.

19. Alvarez and Pitch, *Chained Eagle*, pp. 12–13.

20. COMSEVENTHFLT to CINCPACFLT, 041830Z Aug. 1964, *GOTA* frame 288.

21. This is confirmed by CTG 72.1 to AIG 181, 142158Z Aug. 1964, *SS* reel 24, frame 902, as well as by the pilots. The *Ticonderoga*'s aircraft were in the area continuously from about 2110G to 0050G, and the *Constellation*'s continuously from about 2315G to 0050G.

22. Chad James, interview and personal communication.

23. CTG 72.1 to CINCPACFLT, 041515Z Aug. 1964, FOIA NHC; Windchy, *Tonkin Gulf*, p. 192.

24. Wise, "Remember the Maddox!," pp. 126–27.

25. Marolda, "Tonkin Gulf," p. 297.

26. "*Tin-tuc to-chuc Hai-Quan Mien-Bac*" (information on the organization of the Navy of the North), report of the interrogation of prisoner #1623, Nguyen Van Hoa, August 15, 1967, pp. 14–17, 21, in National Archives, Suitland Reference Branch, Record Group 334, MACV CMIC Interrogation Reports, Box 45, CMIC #1623.

27. Ibid, p. 21.

28. Capt. Murphy (Naval Intelligence Command) to Capt. Kerr (Special Counsel to the Secretary of the Navy), May 6, 1968 (FOIA Naval Intelligence Command).

29. See Marolda and Fitzgerald, *From Military Assistance to Combat*, pp. 441–42.

30. Quisenberry et al., "NVN PT Boat Exploitation Team Report," esp. pp. IV-A-9, IV-B-1.

31. USS *Cavalier* to DNI, 131115Z July 1964; Tourison, *Talking with Victor Charlie*, p. 184.

32. Tran Bao.

33. Quoted in *GOT*, p. 75.

34. Tourison, *Talking with Victor Charlie*, pp. 183–85; idem, *Secret Army, Secret War*, pp. 155–57; and personal communications.

35. Personal communications.

36. Letter, U.S. Naval Institute *Proceedings*, July 1992, p. 26.

37. Cmdr. Robert Laske, personal communications.

38. Gittinger, *Johnson Years*, p. 29.

39. Personal communications. See also Ray S. Cline, Oral History 2, May 31, 1983 (LBJ Presidential Library), pp. 27–35.

40. Interview with Clark M. Clifford, April 3, 1992.

41. *Daily Diary*, reel 3.

42. Ball, *Past Has Another Pattern*, p. 379.

43. *GOT*, p. 92.

44. Report Number 12, furnished to the author by NSA; all deletions are by NSA.

45. *GOT*, p. 92.

46. Furnished to the author by NSA.

47. Memo, Carl Marcy to Senator William Fulbright, February 2, 1972.

48. Stockdale and Stockdale, *In Love and War*, pp. 453–55.

49. Memo, Carl Marcy to Senator William Fulbright, February 2, 1972.

50. Johnson, *Vantage Point*, p. 114. Johnson does not have to be referring to the specific intercept under discussion here; there was at least one other message intercepted either August 4 or 5 that referred to two "comrades" being sacrificed.

51. *GOT*, p. 18; Austin, *President's War*, pp. 339–40; transcript of telephone conversations, August 4–5, pp. 36–37 and perhaps also p. 15, in CFV, Box 228, "Gulf of Tonkin (misc) [2 of 3]," #26a; Marolda and Fitzgerald, *From Military Assistance to Combat*, p. 442.

52. Interview with Gerrell Moore.

53. CINCPACFLT to CINCPAC, 161407Z Aug. 1964, pp. 3–5, CFV, Box 228.

54. Interview with Capt. James Bartholomew, October 15, 1987.

55. Interview with John J. Barry; interview with Joseph Schaperjahn; CTG 72.1 to COMSEVENTHLFT, 050449Z Aug. 64 (FOIA NHC).

56. Press conference of August 5, 1964, reported in *Nhan Dan*, August 6, 1964, p. 1.

57. Pike, *PAVN*, pp. 108, 118–19 (pp. 110 and 122 in some printings of this volume). Several other authors have already published statements derived from Pike's.

58. *Vietnam: The Anti-U.S. Resistance War*, p. 61.

59. Ibid., p. 60.

60. Interview with John J. Barry.

61. Douglas Smith, personal communication, April 22, 1990.

62. Interview with Richard Bacino, April 8, 1990.

63. Lcdr. Douglas G. Smith, letter, April 22, 1990.

64. Adm. James B. Stockdale, personal communication, March 1986.

65. Transcript of *Vietnam: A Television History*, episode 4, p. 7.

66. Stockdale and Stockdale, *In Love and War*, pp. 35–36, 464n.

67. Capt. John J. Herrick, personal communication, April 7, 1986.

68. Personal communications.

Chapter Nine. Retaliation

1. CTG 72.1 to *Turner Joy*, 041720Z August 1964 (FOIA NHC).

2. Interview with Capt. Bryce D. Inman, October 19, 1989.

3. Gittinger, *Johnson Years*, p. 28.

4. Ibid., pp. 31–32.

5. Capt. James Bartholomew, personal communications; NAVCOMMSTA PHIL to COMSEVENTHFLT (relaying a message from CTG 72.1), 041642Z August 1964 (FOIA NHC).

6. Interview with Adm. Roy L. Johnson.

7. Transcript of telephone conversations, August 4–5, p.31, in CFV, Box 228, "Gulf of Tonkin (misc) [2 of 3]," #26a.

8. Telephone conversation between Secretary McNamara and Adm. Sharp, 4:08 P.M., CFV, Box 228, "Gulf of Tonkin (misc) [2 of 3]," #26b.

9. Prados, *Keepers*, p. 209.

10. Ball, *Past Has Another Pattern*, p. 379 (see also Goulden, *Truth*, p. 160, for a similar statement Johnson made—Goulden does not say to whom—in 1965).

11. *New York Times*, November 10, 1995, p. A3; Trewhitt, *McNamara*, p. 213; Henry L. Trewhitt, personal communication, December 1, 1994; Woods, *Fulbright*, p. 352.

12. McGeorge Bundy, Memo, "The Gulf of Tonkin Incident, September 18," Bundy Memos, vol. 5-8: Box 1.

13. Lawrence Levinson, "Chronology."

14. Haig, *Inner Circles*, p. 117.

15. "Command and Control," p. 8.

16. Scheer, "Tonkin," p. 18.

17. "Summary of Leadership Meeting, August 4, 1964" (Lyndon B. Johnson Presidential Library, Johnson: Meeting Notes File, Box 1).

18. CINCPACFLT to COMSEVENTHFLT, 041644Z Aug. 1964, *GOTA* frame 257.

19. "Chronology of Events of August 4–5, 1964: Tonkin Gulf Strike," *Special Subjects* reel 25, frame 353; handwritten notes, telephone call, Sharp to Burchinal, 11:18 A.M. EDT, in *Special Subjects*, reel 25, frame 332.

20. "Command and Control," p. 9; Levinson, "Chronology," pp. 6, 11–12, 14.

21. NPIC 080119Z August 1964, CFV, Box 227, Maddox Incident and Operation Pierce Arrow [1 of 3], #17.

22. "Command and Control," p. 13.

23. Burchinal to Sharp, telephone conversation, 10:59 A.M., telephone transcripts, p. 11.

24. "Command and Control," pp. 13–14.

25. CINCPAC to CINCPACFLT, 042035Z Aug. 1964, and CINCPACFLT to COMSEVENTHFLT, 042014Z Aug. 1964, CFV, Box 227, Maddox Incident and Operation Pierce Arrow, [2 of 3] #177 and [3 of 3] #175.

26. Telephone transcripts, p. 43.

27. Press Briefing by Robert McNamara, August 5, 1964, 9:00 A.M., transcript in *GOTA*, frame 709; Robert McNamara, interviewed by Peter Hackes, NBC television, 9:15 P.M., August 5, 1964, transcript in *GOTA*, frame 716.

28. *Southeast Asia Resolution*, p. 7.

29. Handwritten notes, telephone call, Sharp to Burchinal, 4:40 P.M., in *Special Subjects*, reel 25, frames 290, 336.

30. "Chronology of Events of August 4–5, 1964: Tonkin Gulf Strike"; Lawrence Levinson, "Chronology," gives somewhat earlier times.

31. Levinson, "Chronology," p. 26.

32. Transcript of telephone conversations, pp. 43. 46, 47, 48 (CFV, Box 228, Gulf of Tonkin (misc) [2 of 3], #26a.)

33. Ibid., p. 43.

34. Summary Notes of 538th NSC Meeting, August 4, 1964, 6:15 to 6:40 P.M. (NSC Meetings File, Box 1).

35. Transcript of telephone conversations, pp. 48–50. (CFV, Box 228, Gulf of Tonkin (misc) [2 of 3], #26a).

36. Ibid., p. 54.

37. Ibid., pp. 63–64.

38. *Daily Diary of President Johnson (1963–1969)*, reel 3.

39. CTG 77.5, 050414Z Aug. 1964, *Special Subjects* reel 24, frame 859.

40. Time chart and chronology, both apparently prepared by NSC staff, *Special Subjects* reel 25, frames 274, 361.

41. CTG 77.5 to CINCPAC, 050720Z Aug. 1964, *Special Subjects* reel 24, frame 864, says 1325H.

42. Time chart, apparently prepared by NSC staff, *Special Subjects* reel 25, frame 274.

43. Deck log, USS *Constellation*.

44. Goulden, *Truth*, p. 36.

45. *Special Subjects* reel 24, frame 757.

46. *GOT*, p. 23.

47. *Southeast Asia Resolution*, pp. 12–13. See also McNamara's statement to the press on this question, in Bromley Smith to the President, 081325Z Aug. 1964, CFV, Box 227, Maddox Incident [1 of 2], #21.

48. McGeorge Bundy, Memorandum for the President, September 4, 1964 (CFV, Box 77, Gulf of Tonkin, 8/64–9/64, #4).

49. CFV, Box 77, Gulf of Tonkin, 8/64–9/64, #4b (Top Secret Codeword).

50. CTG 77.6 to CTF 77, 050128Z Aug. 1964, *GOTA* frames 264–65.

51. "Chronology," *Special Subjects*, reel 25, frame 360.

52. Text in *Arizona Republic*, August 5, 1964 (Bulldog), p. 3. The text appears to have been included in a UPI despatch at 10:59 P.M. EDT: UPI A139N WA, in CFV, Box 228.

53. Stockdale and Stockdale, *In Love and War*, pp. 24, 27–29.

54. Stockdale and Stockdale, *In Love and War*, pp. 29–33; J. B. Stockdale, "First Strike on Vinh, August 5, 1964" (written approximately August 6, 1964; furnished to the author by Adm. Stockdale), p. 3.

55. Alvarez and Pitch, *Chained Eagle*, pp. 22–24; *Lich su hai quan*, 1985, p. 108.

56. CTG 77.6 to CINCPAC, 051430Z, CTF 77.6, 061010Z, and CTG 77.6 to CTF 77, 061729Z Aug. 1964, *Special Subjects* reel 24, frames 816–17, 789–91, 788.

57. *Southeast Asia Resolution*, p. 7.

58. Adm. James Stockdale, in Willenson, *Bad War*, p. 33.

59. Stockdale and Stockdale, *In Love and War*, p. 32.

60. *Nhan Dan*, August 6, 1964, p. 1; August 7, 1964, p. 1. *Quan Doi Nhan Dan*, August 8, 1964, p. 4, describes air attacks on villages in very vague terms.

61. *Quan Doi Nhan Dan*, August 8, 1964, p. 4.

62. CINCPACFLT to CNO, 051428Z Aug. 1964; CINCPAC to JCS, 052000Z Aug. 1964; CINCPAC to OSD, 060910Z Aug. 1964, *Special Subjects* reel 24, frames 820–21, 805–6, 1007–8. "Questions which May be Asked," August 16, 1964, in *Special Subjects*, reel 25, frame 267. See also CTG 77.5 to COMSEVENTHFLT, 051310Z Aug. 1964, and

NMCC OPSUM 103-64, Aug. 6, 1964, in *Special Subjects* reel 24, frames 826–27, 517–24; JCS 7762, 052303Z Aug. 1964, in *Special Subjects* reel 25, frames 41–43.

63. USS *Cavalier* to DNI, 131115Z July 1966, p. 2.

64. Nguyen Dinh Ty, "Vai kinh nghiem," pp. 15–16.

65. *Southeast Asia Resolution*, p. 18.

66. CINCPACFLT to CINCPAC, 161407Z Aug. 1964, pp. 6–7 (CFV, Box 228); words abbreviated in the original have been spelled out in full. See also Windchy, *Tonkin Gulf*, pp. 229–36.

67. *Phong khong khong quan*, pp. 73–74; see also General Hoang Van Thai, "Bao cao," p. 4.

68. *Phong khong khong quan*, p. 74.

69. Saigon 130 to State, July 17, 1964, *VNSF* 5:243–44.

70. Hoang Luu, "Vai thu nhan," p. 7.

71. CINCPACFLT to COMSEVENTHFLT, 050403Z Aug. 1964, *Special Subjects* reel 24, frame 890. CINCPACFLT to CINCPAC, 161407Z Aug. 1964, pp. 3–4 (CFV, Box 228).

72. *Lich su Quan doi nhan dan*, p. 232.

73. Marolda and Fitzgerald, *From Military Assistance to Combat*, pp. 381–87.

74. *Phong khong khong quan*, p. 76.

75. Vice Adm. James Stockdale, "A Talk to the Churchill Society of the Brigade of Midshipmen," U.S. Naval Academy, March 5, 1990, p. 2.

76. CTG 77.5 to COMSEVENTHFLT, 051310Z August 1964, CFV, Box 227, Maddox Incident and Operation Pierce Arrow [1 of 3], #38.

77. Alvarez and Pitch, *Chained Eagle*, p. 22.

78. JCS 7742 of 051553Z, referred to in CINCPAC to JCS, 062341Z Aug. 1964, NSC History, Box 38, GOTA Vol. I, #189.

79. Alvarez and Pitch, *Chained Eagle*, p. 17.

80. Levinson, *Alpha Strike*, pp. 23–24.

81. Hoang Luu, "Vai thu nhan," p. 7. See also the account of a reporter who witnessed the raid on Hon Gay, in *Quan Doi Nhan Dan*, August 8, 1964, p. 4.

82. Quisenberry et al., "NVN PT Boat Exploitation Team Report," p. IV-O-2.

83. Harris polls, in *Washington Post*, August 10, 1964, pp. A1, A4.

84. *Southeast Asia Resolution*, pp. 1–2.

85. "Special Message to the Congress on U.S. Policy in Southeast Asia," August 5, 1964, in *Public Papers*, 1963–64, vol. 2, pp. 931–32.

86. *Atlanta Constitution*, August 6, 1964, p. 1.

87. McGeorge Bundy memo to George Reedy, August 7, 1964, *GOTA* frame 418; Summary Notes of 538th NSC Meeting, August 4, 1964, NSC Meetings File.

88. Robert McNamara, conversation with Randall Woods, July 12, 1990, quoted by permission of Robert McNamara and Randall Woods.

89. "The Seeds of Conflict," episode of the CBS television series "The Vietnam War with Walter Cronkite."

90. *Congressional Record*, August 6, 1964, pp. 18402–403.

91. Ibid., p. 18539.

92. Memorandum for Discussion, June 10, 1964, *VNSF* 4:295.

93. Gruening and Beaser, *Vietnam Folly*, pp. 236–50.

94. Rusk 336 to Taylor, August 3, 1964, *VNSF* 5:560.

95. Telephone calls, August 3, 1964: McNamara-Ball 9:55 A.M., Bundy-Ball 10:15 A.M., Bundy-Ball 10:40 A.M., Lyndon B. Johnson Presidential Library: Papers of George W. Ball, Vietnam I, Box 7, #76, #80, #79.

96. McNaughton Report.

97. Department of State 439 to Saigon (representing the combined views of State, DOD, JCS, and the White House), August 14, 1964, *VNSF* 5:668.

98. See *Washington Post*, August 3, 1964, p. A-13: "American officials denied that there was any shelling of North Vietnamese islands in the Gulf of Tonkin."

Sen. George McGovern, however, on the Senate floor August 6, quoted an August 5 column by Murrey Marder in the *Washington Post*: "Despite some reports published yesterday, the State Department denial did not equally exculpate South Vietnam. It only denied American participation [in the July 30/31 raids]." Senator Fulbright said it was his understanding there had been raids. *Congressional Record*, August 6, 1964, p. 18402.

99. *New York Times*, August 6, 1964, p. 6; August 7, 1964, p. 6; State 381 to Saigon, August 8, 1964, CFV: Box 7.

100. Wise, "Aboard the Maddox," p. 21.

101. *Time*, August 14, 1964, p. 14.

102. "Tonkin Gulf Incidents" (no author, no date), McNTN VIII, #82.

103. *Anderson Independent*, August 6, 1964, p. 2; *Atlanta Constitution*, August 7, 1964, p. 6; *Atlanta Journal*, August 5, 1964, p. 12; *New York Times*, August 5, 1964, pp. 1, 3, and August 6, 1964, p. 6; *Arizona Republic*, August 5, 1964, p. 1. This story was phrased so unclearly in the *Seattle Times*, August 5, 1964, p. A, that few readers could have understood it.

104. *Atlanta Constitution*, August 6, 1964, p. 14; *Seattle Times*, August 5, 1964, p. A.

105. *Arizona Republic*, August 4, 1964, p. 4; *Anderson Independent*, August 16, 1964, p. 4; *Time*, August 14, 1964, p. 11.

106. *New York Times*, August 11, 1964, p. 15, and August 12, 1964. p. 10.

107. *Arizona Republic*, August 7, 1964, pp. 1, 7.

108. Willenson, *The Bad War*, p. 219.

109. Press briefing by Col. Ha Van Lau, spokesman for PAVN Headquarters, Hanoi, August 6, 1964, broadcast by Hanoi domestic service, 061430Z, trans. in *FBIS*, August 7, 1964, JJJ2.

110. *Time*, August 14, 1964, p. 13.

111. *Anderson Independent*, August 16, 1964, p. 4.

112. *New York Times*, August 5, 1964, p. 2. See also *Arizona Republic*, August 6, p. 10, August 9, p. 7, August 11, p. 2, and August 12, p. 7.

113. Editorial, *Arizona Republic*, August 6, 1964, p. 6.

114. *Anderson Independent*, August 13, 1964, p. 4.

115. David Lawrence, in *Arizona Republic*, August 8, 1964, p. 6; *Atlanta Journal*, August 7, 1964, p. 22.

116. *New York Daily News* editorials, August 4, 1964, p. 23, and August 13, 1964, p. 41.

117. *New York Daily News* editorial, August 6, 1964, p. 37.

118. Editorial, *Anderson Independent*, August 13, 1964, p. 4.

119. Column by Drew Pearson, claiming to represent President Johnson's opinion, *Anderson Independent*, August 8, 1964, p. 4; James Reston, *New York Times*, August 6, 1964, p. 8; *New York Daily News*, August 5, 1964, p. 18; *Time*, August 14, 1964, p. 11.

120. *Atlanta Constitution*, August 10, 1964, p. 4; *New York Daily News*, August 6, 1964, p. 4; *Time*, August 14, 1964, p. 11.

121. *Time*, August 14, 1964, p. 11, described this as the "most plausible" explanation.

122. Column by Drew Pearson, claiming to represent President Johnson's opinion, *Anderson Independent*, August 8, 1964, p. 4; *New York Times*, August 6, 1964, p. 9; *Time*, August 14, 1964, p. 11.

123. *New York Daily News*, editorial, August 7, 1964, p. 29.

124. Publications that took proper account of this chronology include *Arizona Republic*, August 4, 1964, p. 1; *Time*, August 14, 1964, p. 12.

125. *Anderson Independent*, August 7, 1964, p. 4; *Newsweek*, August 17, 1964, p. 19.

126. *New York Times*, August 4, 1964, p. 2, and August 5, p. 3.

127. Editorial, *Arizona Republic*, August 4, 1964, p. 6. See also *Atlanta Constitution*, August 3, 1964, p. 3; *New York Times*, August 3, 1964, pp. 6, 7, and August 4, 1964, p. 1.

128. *New York Daily News*, August 4, 1964, p. 2; *Time*, August 14, 1964, p. 12.

129. *New York Times*, August 9, 1964, section 4 (The Week in Review), p. 1.

130. *Newsweek*, August 17, 1964, p. 18; *Time*, August 14, 1964, p. 15.

131. On the question of "objective journalism," see Hallin's excellent book *The "Uncensored War."*

132. Editorials, *Seattle Times*, August 4, 1964, p. 8; *Arizona Republic*, August 4, 1964, p. 6.

133. *Time*, August 14, 1964, p. 15.

134. Interview with Neil Boggs, September 6, 1990.

135. *New York Times*, August 3, 1964, p. 6; UPI, in *Atlanta Constitution*, August 3, 1964, p. 7; *New York Daily News*, August 3, 1964, p. 12.

136. *New York Times*, August 5, 1964, p. 3.

137. *Nhan Dan* editorial, August 7, 1964, p. 1.

138. *Der Kurier* (Vienna), August 1, 1964, trans. in *New York Times*, August 7, 1964, p. 7; Rogers, "Sino-American Relations," p. 296.

139. *The Situation in South Vietnam*, August 7–13, 1964, *VNSF* 5:783.

140. Interview with Colonel Bui Tin, Hanoi, May 4, 1989.

141. Transcript of telephone conversations, August 4–5, 1964, pp. 41–42, CFV, Box 228, Gulf of Tonkin (misc) [2 of 3], #26a.

142. Statement issued in English by Xinhua News Agency, August 6, text in *New York Times*, August 7, 1964, p. 7.

143. Windchy, *Tonkin Gulf*, p. 10.

144. Ibid., p. 28.

145. Khrushchev to Johnson, August 5, 1964, in *GOTA*, frames 649–52.

146. Gaiduk, "Vietnam and the Transition," p. 11, supplemented by personal communications; "The Situation in South Vietnam," September 24–30, 1964, p. 11, *VNSF* reel 7, frame 671.

147. "Soviet Reactions to Tonkin Gulf Crisis," Dept. of State INR Intelligence Note, August 7, 1964, *Special Subjects* reel 24, frame 512.

148. *New York Times*, August 6, 1964, p. 9.

149. *Pravda*, August 6, 1964, p. 1.

150. Quoted in U.S. Foreign Broadcast Information Service *Daily Report: Supplement: World Reaction Series*, 1964 no. 2, August 6, 1964, p. 3, in *Special Subjects* reel 24, frame 535.

151. *Pravda*, August 7, 1964, p. 3; *Sovietskii Soyuz–V'etnam*, pp. 80–81.

152. CIA weekly report, *The Situation in South Vietnam*, August 7–13, 1964, *VNSF* 5:783.

153. *New York Times*, August 9, 1964, pp. 1, 36, 37.

154. *Executive Sessions*, pp. 292, 296 (these passages were censored from their testimony in *Southeast Asia Resolution*, pp. 12, 18).

155. *The Situation in South Vietnam*, August 7–13, 1964, p. 16, in *VNSF*, 5:783.

156. *Nhan Dan*, August 7, 1964, pp. 1–2; *Quan Doi Nhan Dan*, August 8, 1964, p. 4; *Hanh dong chien tranh*, pp. 123–51.

157. Le Quang Dao, "Phat huy manh me uu diem," p. 3.

158. Gaiduk, "Turnabout?"

159. Bundy MS, chapter 14A, pp. 27–28. See also cable, Rusk to Ottawa and Saigon (approved in draft by McNamara and McGeorge Bundy), August 8, 1964, CFV, Box 7.

160. Handwritten notes, Lunch, August 4, 1964, Lyndon B. Johnson Presidential Library: Papers of McGeorge Bundy.

161. Summary Notes of 538th NSC Meeting, Aug. 4, 1964, NSC Meetings File, Box 1.

162. "Peiping and Hanoi: Motivations and Probable Reactions to Gulf of Tonkin Crisis," INR Research Memorandum RFE-56, August 6, 1964, *Special Subjects* reel 24, frames 526, 528.

163. Personal communications, J. Norvill Jones; *New York Times*, March 30, 1968, p. 11, and October 22, 1968, pp. 1, 4.

164. Haig, *Inner Circles*, p. 124.

165. Dr. Daniel Ellsberg, personal communications.

166. Haig, *Inner Circles*, pp. 122–23.

167. Interview with General Bruce Palmer, Jr., September 21, 1994.

168. General Bruce Palmer, Jr., in Gittinger, *Johnson Years*, p. 159.

169. Interview with General Bruce Palmer, Jr., September 21, 1994.

170. McGarvey, *CIA*, p. 17.

171. Thomas L. Hughes, personal communications.

172. Interview with Allen S. Whiting, September 19, 1994.

173. Ibid.

174. Interview with James C. Thomson, Jr., September 19, 1995.

Chapter Ten. Toward Further Escalation

1. State 379 to Saigon, 10:30 P.M., August 7, 1964, *VNSF* 5:588.

2. Saigon 364 to Secretary of State, August 9, 1964, *VNSF* 5:632–33.

3. State 439, "eyes only" to Ambassador Taylor, Ambassador Unger, and Adm. Sharp, August 14, 1964, *VNSF* 5:670.

4. Saigon to State, August 18, 1964, text in *Pentagon Papers (NYT)*, pp. 349–52.

5. Ibid., p. 349.

6. JCS to Secretary McNamara, August 26, 1964, in *Pentagon Papers (NYT)*, p. 354.

7. Memorandum for the Record, September 14, 1964, Bundy Memos, Box 1.

8. State 178 to Bangkok, August 5, 1964, *Special Subjects* 24, frame 616.

9. William P. Bundy, "Suggested Agenda for Saturday Meeting" (copy addressed to McGeorge Bundy), August 7, 1964, *Special Subjects*, reel 24, frames 514–516.

10. *Pentagon Papers* (Gravel), 3:193. See also 3:110.

11. Ibid., 3:561.

12. Ibid., 3:562.

13. Gen. Earle G. Wheeler, "Courses of Action for South Vietnam," September 9, 1964, CM-124-64, in ibid., 3:564.

14. Interview with Lcdr. Burton L. Knight.

15. CINCPACFLT to COMSEVETHFLT, 120203Z Sep. 1964, *Special Subjects* reel 25, frames 249–50.

16. CINCPAC to JCS, 080155Z Aug. 1964, *Special Subjects* reel 24, frames 1001–2.

17. E. E. Hollyfield, Jr., DeSoto patrol report, September 24, 1964, pp. 1, 7, and also p. 1 of Enclosure 12.

18. Goulden, *Truth*, p. 159.

19. CTU 77.6.6 to CINCPACFLT, 191406Z Sep. 1964, *Special Subjects* reel 25, frames 143–45; DeSoto patrol report, September 24, 1964, chronology, p. 3, entries for 182044H, 182048H.

20. CTG 77.6, 182110Z Sep. 1964, CTG 77.7, 181722Z Sep. 1964, and CTU 77.6.6, 191406Z Sep. 1964, in *Special Subjects* reel 25, frames 193, 208, 143–45.

21. McGeorge Bundy, memo dated September 20, 1964, "The Gulf of Tonkin Incident, September 18," Bundy Memos, vol. 5-8: Box 1. CTU 77.6.6 to AIG 181, 181542Z Sep. 1964, McNTN VIII.

22. CTU 77.6.6 to AIG 181, 171215Z Sep. 1964; CTU 77.6.6 to COMSEVENTHFLT, 181824Z Sep. 1964; CTU 77.6.6 to CNO, 190138Z Sep. 1964; CINCPAC to JCS, 190706Z Sep. 1964; in *Special Subjects* reel 25, frames 154, 203, 175, 104–6.

23. See DeSoto patrol report, September 24, 1964, "Summary of Visual Sightings."

24. CINCPAC to JCS, 190706Z Sep. 1964, *Special Subjects* reel 25, frame 106, stated "no gun fire from any of these unidentified craft was detected." See also CTU 77.6.6 to AIG 181, 181542Z Sep. 1964, MCNTN VIII.

25. McGeorge Bundy, memo dated September 20, 1964, "The Gulf of Tonkin Incident, September 18," Bundy Memos, vol. 5-8: Box 1. CTU 77.6/6 to AIG 181, 181542Z Sep. 1964, McNTN VIII. CINCPAC to JCS, 190706Z Sep. 1964, *Special Subjects* reel 25, frames 104–6.

26. Tass International Service, 2208 GMT, September 19, 1964, trans. in *FBIS Area Editions: USSR and Eastern Europe*, September 21, 1964, BB 11.

27. Tass International Service (English), 1357 GMT, September 21, 1964, in *FBIS Area Editions: USSR and Eastern Europe*, September 21, 1964, BB 10 (see also Tass (English), 1451 GMT, September 21, 1964, in ibid., September 22, BB 22); *Pravda*, September 22, 1964, p. 1; *Sovietskii Soyuz–V'etnam*, pp. 82–83.

28. Wheeler JCS 4588-64 to Taylor, 182042Z Sep. 1964, and Taylor MAC 5107 to Wheeler, 190040Z Sep. 64, in *Special Subjects* reel 25, frame 137.

29. DeSoto patrol report, September 24, 1964, enclosure 1, p. 11.

30. CIA Intelligence Information Cable, Saigon, August 6, 1964, in *CIA Research Reports*, Reel 4, frames 1–3.

31. *Hanh dong chien tranh; Ke cuop My*.

32. Speech of September 2, 1964, in *Hanh dong chien tranh*, p. 7.

33. *Nhan Dan*, August 6, 1964, p. 4.

34. *Lach truong anh dung*.

35. Hoang Van Thai, "Bao cao," pp. 9–10, 13–14.

36. Saigon 330 to Secstate, 061244Z Aug. 1964, *GOTA* frame 151.

37. Summary Notes of 538th NSC Meeting, Aug. 4, 1964, NSC Meetings File, Box 1.

38. McGeorge Bundy, Memorandum for the Record, September 14, 1964, Bundy Memos, Box 1.

39. Gareth Porter, "Lessons of the Tonkin Gulf Crisis," *The Christian Science Monitor*, August 9, 1984, p. 15. See also Porter, "Coercive Diplomacy," p. 20.

40. George Allen, personal communications.

41. Bundy MS, chapter 14, pp. 47–48.

42. Blair Seaborn, in "Days of Decision," episode of *The Ten Thousand Day War* (International Television Productions Ltd. and Cinequity Funding, 1980).

43. See Porter, "Coercive Diplomacy," pp. 19–21.

44. U.S. intelligence summary in *Congressional Record*, May 9, 1968, p. 12620.

45. Nixon, "Needed in Vietnam," pp. 41–42.

46. Naughton, "Third Front," pp. 351–86; Zhai, "Beijing," pp. 237–38, 243–44.

47. Whiting, *Chinese Calculus*, p. 176; Zhai, "Beijing," pp. 235–36.

48. Halberstam, *Best and the Brightest*, p. 533.

49. *Pentagon Papers* (Gravel), 3:298–302; Marolda and Fitzgerald, *From Military Assistance to Combat*, pp. 495–96.

50. Interview with Neil Boggs, September 6, 1990.

Bibliography

Comments on Archives

The main repository for documents on the actual events in the Gulf of Tonkin in August 1964 is the Naval Historical Center, in the Washington Navy Yard in Washington, D.C. For the overall context of U.S. policy toward Vietnam in 1964, the Lyndon B. Johnson Presidential Library, in Austin, Texas, is best.

The deck logs of U.S. naval vessels are held by the National Archives in the National Records Center, Suitland, Maryland.

The CIC logs and quartermaster logs of U.S. naval vessels are not routinely preserved. Some pages from these logs from the destroyers involved in the Tonkin Gulf incidents, however, are in the Naval Historical Center.

A few key documents relating to Tonkin Gulf were not in the LBJ Presidential Library, so I donated photocopies I had obtained from the Navy and the Pentagon. These include the logs of the destroyers, portions of the major after-action reports, and a sanitized version of "Command and Control of the Tonkin Gulf Incidents." I was startled to find soon afterward that the LBJ Library had established a formal collection for these documents: the "Edwin E. Moïse Papers."

Serials

Anderson Independent (Anderson, S.C.)
Arizona Republic
Atlanta Constitution
Atlanta Journal
Charlotte Observer
Chinh Luan (Saigon)
Daily News (New York)
Hai Quan (Haiphong?)
Life
New York Times
Newsweek
Nhan Dan (Hanoi)
Peking Review
Quan Doi Nhan Dan (Hanoi)
Saigon Post
Seattle Times
Time
The Times (London)
U.S. Foreign Broadcast Information Service *Daily Report: Far East*
U.S. News & World Report
Veteran
Washington Post

Microfilmed Document Collections

CIA Research Reports: Vietnam and Southeast Asia, Supplement. Frederick, Md.: University Publications of America, 1986.
Daily Diary of President Johnson (1963–1969). Frederick, Md.: University Publications of America, 1980.
Declassified Documents Reference System. Woodbridge, Conn.: Research Publications.
Gulf of Tonkin Attacks. Reel 1 of *Vietnam: National Security Council Histories* (also published as *The War in Vietnam: Classified Histories by the National Security Council*). 8 reels. Frederick, Md.: University Publications of America, 1981.
The Lyndon B. Johnson National Security Files. Vietnam: National Security Files, November 1963–June 1965. 17 reels. Frederick, Md.: University Publications of America, 1987.
The Lyndon B. Johnson National Security Files. Vietnam, Special Subjects: National Security Files, 1963–1969. 36 reels. Frederick, Md.: University Publications of America, 1987.

Books and Pamphlets

Alvarez, Everett Jr., and Anthony S. Pitch. *Chained Eagle.* New York: Fine, 1989.
Austin, Anthony. *The President's War.* New York: Lippincott, 1971.
Ball, George. *The Past Has Another Pattern.* New York: Norton, 1982.
Bucklew, Phil H. *Reminiscences of Captain Phil H. Bucklew, USN (Ret.).* Annapolis, Md.: U.S. Naval Institute, 1982.
Bui Tin. *Following Ho Chi Minh: The Memoirs of a North Vietnamese Colonel.* Honolulu: University of Hawaii Press, 1995.
Califano, Joseph A. Jr. *The Triumph and Tragedy of Lyndon Johnson.* New York: Simon and Schuster, 1991.
Charlton, Michael, and Anthony Moncrieff. *Many Reasons Why: The American Involvement in Vietnam.* 2d ed. New York: Hill and Wang, 1989.
Chien Si Bien Phong (The Border Guards). Vol. 1. Hanoi: Bo tu lenh Bo doi Bien phong, 1984.
Colby, William. *Lost Victory.* Chicago: Contemporary Books, 1989.
Colby, William, and Peter Forbath. *Honorable Men.* New York: Simon and Schuster, 1978.
Cuoc khang chien chong My cuu nouc vi dai. Vol. 2, *1961–1964.* Hanoi: Su That, 1974.
Executive Sessions of the Senate Foreign Relations Committee together with Joint Sessions with the Senate Armed Services Committee. Vol. 16. Washington, D.C.: Government Printing Office, 1988.
Foreign Operations Appropriations for 1965. Part 2. Hearings before the Subcommittee on Foreign Operations Appropriations, House Appropriations Committee. Washington, D.C.: Government Printing Office, 1964.
Foreign Relations of the United States, 1964–1968. Vol. 1, *Vietnam 1964.* Washington, D.C.: Government Printing Office, 1992.
Friedman, Norman. *U.S. Naval Weapons.* London: Conway Maritime Press, 1983.

Futrell, Robert F. *The United States Air Force in Southeast Asia: The Advisory Years to 1965*. Washington, D.C.: Office of Air Force History and Government Printing Office, 1981.

Gallagher, Hugh G. *Advise and Obstruct: The Role of the United States Senate in Foreign Policy Decisions*. New York: Delacorte, 1969.

Galloway, John. *The Gulf of Tonkin Resolution*. Rutherford, N.J.: Farleigh Dickinson University Press, 1970.

The Gallup Poll: Public Opinion 1935–1971. Vol. 3, *1959–1971*. New York: Random House, 1972.

Gardner, Lloyd C., ed. *The Great Nixon Turnaround*. New York: New Viewpoints, 1973.

Generous, Kevin M. *Vietnam: The Secret War*. New York: Gallery, 1985.

Geyelin, Philip. *Lyndon B. Johnson and the World*. New York: Praeger, 1966.

Gibbons, William C. *The U.S. Government and the Vietnam War: Executive and Legislative Roles and Relationships*. Part 2, *1961–1964*. Washington, D.C.: Government Printing Office, 1984.

Gittinger, Ted, ed. *The Johnson Years: A Vietnam Roundtable*. Austin: Lyndon Baines Johnson Library, 1993.

Goldwater, Barry M., with Jack Casserly. *Goldwater*. New York: Doubleday, 1988.

Goulden, Joseph. *Truth is the First Casualty*. Chicago: Rand McNally, 1969.

Goulding, Phil G. *Confirm or Deny: Informing the People on National Security*. New York: Harper and Row, 1970.

Gruening, Ernest, and Herbert W. Beaser. *Vietnam Folly*. Washington, D.C.: The National Press, 1968.

The Gulf of Tonkin, The 1964 Incidents. Hearing before the Senate Foreign Relations Committee, February 20, 1968. Washington, D.C.: Government Printing Office, 1968.

Haig, Alexander. *Inner Circles*. New York: Warner, 1992.

Halberstam, David. *The Best and the Brightest*. New York: Random House, 1969.

Hallin, Daniel. *The "Uncensored War": The Media and Vietnam*. New York: Oxford University Press, 1986.

Halpern, Samuel. *West Pac '64*. Boston: Branden Press, 1975.

Hanh dong chien tranh cua de quoc My doi voi nuoc Viet-nam dan chu cong hoa da bi trung tri dich dang (The warlike actions of the American imperialists toward the Democratic Republic of Vietnam were appropriately punished). Hanoi: Nha xuat ban Su that, 1964.

Havens, Thomas R. H. *Fire Across the Sea: The Vietnam War and Japan, 1965–1975*. Princeton: Princeton University Press, 1987.

Hovis, Bobbi. *Station Hospital Saigon*. Annapolis: Naval Institute Press, 1991.

Jane's Fighting Ships. London: B.P.C. Publishing, 1963–65.

Johnson, Lyndon B. *The Vantage Point: Perspectives of the Presidency, 1963–1969*. New York: Holt, Rinehart and Winston, 1971.

Kahn, Herman. *On Escalation*. New York: Praeger, 1965.

Karnow, Stanley. *Vietnam: A History*. New York: Viking, 1983.

Ke cuop My bi trung tri dich dang [The American bandits were appropriately punished]. Hanoi: Nha xuat ban Quan doi nhan dan, 1964.

Kerr, Andy. *A Journey Amongst the Good and the Great*. Annapolis: Naval Institute Press, 1987.

Krepinevich, Andrew F. Jr. *The Army and Vietnam*. Baltimore: Johns Hopkins University Press, 1986.

Lach truong anh dung: 5-8 [Heroic Lach truong: August 5]. Thanh Hoa: Ty van hoa—thong tin Thanh-hoa xuat ban, 1964.

Levinson, Jeffrey L. *Alpha Strike Vietnam: The Navy's Air War, 1964 to 1973*. New York: Pocket Books, 1990.

Lich su Hai quan nhan dan Viet nam [History of the People's Navy of Vietnam]. [Haiphong?]: Bo tu lenh Hai quan, 1980.

Lich su Hai quan nhan dan Viet nam [History of the People's Navy of Vietnam]. Hanoi: Nha xuat ban Quan doi nhan dan, 1985.

Lich su Quan doi nhan dan Viet nam [History of the People's Army of Vietnam]. Tap 2, quyen mot. Hanoi: Nha xuat ban Quan doi nhan dan, 1988.

McGarvey, Patrick. *CIA: The Myth and the Madness*. New York: Saturday Review Press, 1972.

McNamara, Robert S., with Brian VanDeMark. *In Retrospect: The Tragedy and Lessons of Vietnam*. New York: Times Books, 1995.

Maneli, Mieczyslaw. *War of the Vanquished*. New York: Harper and Row, 1971.

Marolda, Edward J. *By Sea, Air and Land: An Illustrated History of the U.S. Navy and the War in Southeast Asia*. Washington, D.C.: Naval Historical Center, 1994.

Marolda, Edward, and Oscar Fitzgerald. *The United States Navy and the Vietnam Conflict*. Vol. 2: *From Military Assistance to Combat, 1959–1965*. Washington, D.C.: Naval Historical Center, 1986.

Miller, Merle E. *Lyndon: An Oral Biography*. New York: Putnam, 1980.

Nguyen Cao Ky. *How We Lost the Vietnam War*. New York: Stein and Day, 1984.

The Pentagon Papers: The Defense Department History of United States Decisionmaking on Vietnam. 4 vols. Boston: Beacon Press, 1971.

Phong khong khong quan [Air defense and air forces]. Vol. 1. Hanoi: Nhan xuat ban Quan doi nhan dan, 1978.

Pike, Douglas. *PAVN: People's Army of Vietnam*. Novato, Calif.: Presidio Press, 1986.

Prados, John. *The Hidden History of the Vietnam War*. Chicago: Ivan R. Dee, 1995.

———. *Keepers of the Keys: A History of the National Security Council from Truman to Bush*. New York: Morrow, 1991.

Public Papers of the Presidents. Washington, D.C.: Government Printing Office, various dates.

Radványi, Janos. *Delusion and Reality: Gambits, Hoaxes, and Diplomatic One-Upmanship in Vietnam*. South Bend, Ind.: Gateway, 1978.

Reske, Charles F., ed. *MACVSOG Command History: Annexes A, N and M (1964–1966)*. Sharon Center, Oh.: Alpha Publications, 1992.

Rusk, Dean, as told to Richard Rusk. *As I Saw It*. New York: Norton, 1990.

Schratz, Captain Paul R. *Submarine Commander: A Story of World War II and Korea*. Lexington: The University Press of Kentucky, 1988.

Schreadley, Commander R. L. *From the Rivers to the Sea: The United States Navy in Vietnam*. Annapolis: Naval Institute Press, 1992.

Shapley, Deborah. *Promise and Power: The Life and Times of Robert McNamara*. Boston: Little, Brown, 1993.

Sharp, Admiral U. S. Grant. *Strategy for Defeat: Vietnam in Retrospect*. San Rafael, Calif.: Presidio Press, 1978.

Sheehan, Neil, Hedrick Smith, E. W. Kenworthy, and Fox Butterfield. *The Pentagon Papers as Published by The New York Times*. New York: Bantam, 1971.

Singlaub, John K. *Hazardous Duty*. New York: Summit, 1991.

Solis, Lt. Commander Gary D. *Marines and Military Law: Trial by Fire*. Washington, D.C.: History and Museums Division, Headquarter, U.S. Marine Corps, 1989.

Southeast Asia Resolution. [Censored] transcript of a joint hearing before the Committee on Foreign Relations and the Committee on Armed Services, U.S. Senate, August 6, 1964. Washington, D.C.: Government Printing Office, 1966.

Sovietskii Soyuz–V'etnam, 30 let otnoshenii, 1950–1980: dokumenty i materialy [Soviet Union–Vietnam, thirty years of relations, 1950–1980: documents and materials]. Moscow: Izdatelstvo Politicheskoi Literaturi, 1982.

Statistical Abstract of the United States, 1970. Washington, D.C.: Government Printing Office, 1970.

Stockdale, Jim, and Sybil Stockdale. *In Love and War: The Story of a Family's Ordeal and Sacrifice during the Vietnam Years*. New York: Harper and Row, 1984.

Taylor, Maxwell. *Swords and Plowshares*. New York: Norton, 1972.

Tourison, Sedgwick D. *Secret Army, Secret War*. Annapolis: Naval Institute Press, 1995.

——. *Talking with Victor Charlie: An Interrogator's Story*. New York: Ivy Books, 1991.

Unauthorized Bombing of Military Targets in North Vietnam. Hearing before the Armed Services Investigating Subcommittee of the House Armed Services Committee, June 12, 1972. Washington, D.C.: Government Printing Office, 1972.

United States–Vietnam Relations, 1945–1967. 12 vols. Washington, D.C.: Government Printing Office, 1971.

U.S. War Crimes in Vietnam. Hanoi: Juridical Sciences Institute, State Commission of Social Sciences, n.d.

Valentine, Douglas. *The Phoenix Program*. New York: William Morrow, 1990.

Vietnam: The Anti-U.S. Resistance War for National Salvation 1954–1975: Military Events. U.S. government translation JPRS 80963. Distributed by National Technical Information Service, 1982. (in Vietnamese) Hanoi: Nha xuat ban Quan doi nhan dan, 1980.

Vietnam: A Television History [transcript of television documentary]. Boston: WGBH, 1983.

Westmoreland, General William C. *A Soldier Reports*. New York: Doubleday, 1976.

Whiting, Allen S. *The Chinese Calculus of Deterrence: India and Indochina*. Ann Arbor: University of Michigan Press, 1975.

Willenson, Kim et al. *The Bad War: An Oral History of the Vietnam War*. New York: NAL, 1987.

Windchy, Eugene. *Tonkin Gulf*. Garden City, N.Y.: Doubleday, 1971.

Wise, David. *The Politics of Lying*. New York: Random House, 1973.

Witcover, Jules. *The Resurrection of Richard Nixon*. New York: Putnam, 1970.

Woods, Randall B. *Fulbright: A Biography*. New York: Cambridge University Press, 1995.

Articles

Barber, James A. Jr. "Tonkin Gulf: Comments." In *New Interpretations in Naval History*, edited by William Cogar, pp. 323–28. Annapolis: Naval Institute Press, 1989.

Duvall, Donna, and John Metzger. "Bulletin Board: Gulf of Tonkin Destroyer Retired." *Soldier of Fortune*, May 1983, p. 17.

Gaiduk, Ilya V. "Turnabout? The Soviet Policy Dilemma in the Vietnamese Conflict." In *On the Edge: JFK, LBJ, and Vietnam*, edited by Lloyd Gardner, with Ted Gittinger. Austin: University of Texas Press, forthcoming.

———. "Vietnam and the Transition from Khrushchev to Brezhnev, 1964." Paper presented at a conference, "Vietnam: The Early Decisions, 1961–1964," Austin, Texas, October 17, 1993.

Hoang Luu. "Vai thu nhan qua tran chien dau voi may bay My o Song Gianh" [Experiences acquired during the battle with American aircraft at the Gianh River]. *Hai Quan* no. 21 (November 1964): 7–10.

Hong Thuy. "Thieu uy Nguyen van Gian" [Ensign Nguyen Van Gian]. *Hai Quan*, no. 20 (October 1964): 24–26.

Le Quang Dao. "Phat huy manh me uu diem, tich cuc rut kinh nghiem, nghiem khac voi khuyet diem, de cao canh giac, san sang chien dau bao ve vung bien, vung troi mien bac, gop phan nhat to quoc." *Hai Quan* no. 20 (October 1964): 2–5.

Marolda, Edward. "Tonkin Gulf: Fact and Fiction." In *New Interpretations in Naval History*, edited by William Cogar, pp. 281–303. Annapolis: Naval Institute Press, 1989.

Naughton, Barry. "The Third Front: Defense Industrialization in the Chinese Interior." *China Quarterly*, no. 115 (September 1988): 351–86.

Nguyen Dam. "May kinh nghiem ve tran chong dich tap kich vung bien Quang-binh (1 thang 7 nam 1964)" [Lessons of the battle against the enemy attack on the coast of Quang-binh (July 1 1964)]. *Tap chi Quan doi nhan dan*, no. 94 (August 1964): 31–33.

Nguyen Dinh Ty. "Vai kinh nghiem ve sua chua hu hong ham tau trong chien dau" [Some lessons about the repair of damage to vessels in battle]. *Hai Quan* no. 21 (November 1964): 14–16.

Nguyen Thai Nguyen. "Qua tran chien dau voi khu truc ham my" [Experience of the battle with the American destroyer]. *Hai Quan*, no. 21 (November 1964): 11–14.

Nixon, Richard M. "Needed in Vietnam: The Will to Win." *Reader's Digest*, August 1964, pp. 37–43.

"The 'Phantom Battle' that Led to War." *U.S. News & World Report*, July 23, 1984, pp. 56–67.

Porter, Gareth. "Coercive Diplomacy in Vietnam: The Tonkin Gulf Crisis Reconsidered." In *The American War in Vietnam*, edited by Jayne Werner and David Hunt, pp. 9–22. Ithaca: Cornell University Southeast Asia Program, 1993.

———. "Lessons of the Tonkin Gulf Crisis." *Christian Science Monitor*, August 9, 1984, p. 15.

Prados, John. "Spooks in the Ether: The War of the Radio Waves." *Veteran* 15, 5 (May 1995): 19–20.

Rogers, Frank E. "Sino-American Relations and the Vietnam War, 1964–66." *China Quarterly*, June 1976, pp. 293–314.

Scheer, Robert. "Tonkin—Dubious Premise for a War." *Los Angeles Times*, April 29, 1985. Reprinted in *Vietnam: A Decade Later*. Los Angeles: The Los Angeles Times Co., 1985.

Song Hao. "De cao canh giac san sang chien dau chong huu khuynh, hoa binh chu nghia" [Heighten vigilance, prepare to struggle against rightism and pacifism]. *Tap chi Quan doi nhan dan*, no. 94 (August 1964): 1–10.

Thuy. "Phan doi X doan Y da anh dung danh duoi khu truc ham Ma-doc My ra khoi vung bien mien Bac" [Section X of squadron Y heroically drove the American destroyer *Maddox* away from the coast of North Vietnam]. *Hai Quan*, no. 19 (August 1964): 37–38.

Wells, Tim. "The Assault on Hon Me." *Veteran* 11, 7 (July 1991): 25.

White, John. "The Gulf of Tonkin Investigation." *Veteran* 9, 8 (August 1989): 15, 34–36.

Wise, Bill ("with the help of U.S. Navy Intelligence and the Department of Defense"). "Aboard the Maddox." *Life* 57, 7 (August 14, 1964), p. 21.

Wise, David. "Remember the Maddox!" *Esquire*, April 1968, pp. 56–62, 123–27.

Zhai, Qiang. "Beijing and the Vietnam Conflict, 1964–1965: New Chinese Evidence." Cold War International History Project *Bulletin*, nos. 6–7 (Winter 1995–96): 233–50.

Unpublished Documents

"Action Report for Gulf of Tonkin, 4 August 1964." Commanding Officer, USS *Turner Joy* [Barnhart] to Chief of Naval Operations, Ser: 004 of September 11, 1964 (NHC).

Bundy, William P. Untitled draft memoir, in Lyndon B. Johnson Presidential Library, Papers of William P. Bundy, Box 1.

"Chronology of Events, Gulf of Tonkin 4 August 1964." COMDESDIV 192 [Herrick] to CTF 77, Ser: 002 of August 13, 1964 (NHC).

"Command and Control of the Tonkin Gulf Incident, 4–5 August 1964." Office of the Director of Defense Research and Engineering, Weapons Systems Evaluation Group, Critical Incident Report No. 7, February 26, 1965 (FOIA ASD).

General Hoang Van Thai. "Bao cao ve cac tran chien dau tu ngay 2-8 den 5-8-1964" [Report on the battles from August 2 to 5, 1964]. Hanoi: Tong cuc chinh tri, 1964.

"July–August DESOTO Patrol conducted during the period 28 July–8 August 1964." Commanding Officer, USS *Maddox* [Ogier] to CNO, Ser: 002 of August 24, 1964 (NHC).

Levinson, Lawrence. "Chronology of Events: Tuesday, August 4 and Wednesday, August 5, 1964, Tonkin Gulf Strike." Third draft, dated August 25, 1964.

McNaughton, John. "North Vietnam Attacks United States Naval Vessels in the Gulf of Tonkin—August 2–4, 1964." Undated, unsigned preliminary draft. Lyndon B. Johnson Presidential Library, Papers of Paul C. Warnke, McNTN VIII, #86a.

MACSOG Documentation Study, July 10, 1970. In papers of the Senate Select Committee on POW/MIA Affairs (Sedgwick Tourison papers), Record Group 46, National Archives. Components of this study have been cited separately as follows: "MACSOG Operations Against North Vietnam" (Appendix C); "Airborne Operations" (Annex B to Appendix C); "Maritime Operations" (Annex D to Appendix C); "Logistics" (Appendix J).

Quisenberry, Commander W. R. et al.. "NVN PT Boat Exploitation Team Report." July 1966. In NHC.

"Report of Tonkin Gulf, Action of 4 August 1964." Commanding Officer, USS *Maddox* [Ogier] to Chief of Naval Operations, Ser: 004 of August 25, 1964 (NHC).

Stockdale, James B. "First Strike on Vinh, August 5, 1964." Written approximately August 6, 1964.

Wright, Marshall, and Sven F. Kraemer, Vietnam Information Group. "Presidential Decisions: The Gulf of Tonkin Attacks of August 1964." November 1, 1968 (NSC History).

Index